LOIS HOROWITZ

KNOWING WHERE TO LOOK

THE

ULTIMATE GUIDE TO RESEARCH

Writer's Digest Books

CINCINNATI, OHIO

To my father

First edition.
Second printing, 1985
Third printing, 1986

Library of Congress Cataloging in Publication Data

Horowitz, Lois, 1940-
    Knowing where to look.
        1. Libraries and readers—Handbooks, manuals etc. 2. Library resources—Handbooks, manuals, etc. 3. Research—Methodology—Handbooks, manuals, etc. 4. Reference books—Handbooks, manuals, etc. 5. Libraries—Handbooks, manuals, etc. I. Title.
Z710.H67   1984   025.5′67   84-20876
ISBN 0-89879-159-6

PERMISSION ACKNOWLEDGMENTS

Grateful acknowledgment is made for permission to reprint excerpts from the following:

American Statistics Index, 1979 issue, published by Congressional Information Service, Inc.

Applied Science & Technology Index, 1977 issue, published by The H.W. Wilson Co.

Art Index, Vol. 24 (November 1975-October 1976), Vol. 29 (November 1980 to October 1981) and Vol. 30 (November 1981-October 1982), published by the H.W. Wilson Co.

Business Periodicals Index, 1983 issue, published by The H.W. Wilson Co.

CIS/Index and Abstracts to Publications of the U.S. Congress, 1980 issue, published by Congressional Information Service, Inc.

CIS U.S. Congressional Committee Hearings Index, 1969 issue, published by Congressional Information Service, Inc.

CIS U.S. Congressional Committee Prints Index, published by Congressional Information Service, Inc.

CIS U.S. Serial Set Index, 1857-79 issue, published by Congressional Information Service, Inc.

Cumulative Subject Index to the Monthly Catalog of United States Government Publications, 1900-71, published by Carrollton Press.

Cumulative Title Index to United States Public Documents, 1789-1976, published by United States Historical Documents Institute.

Index to Legal Periodicals, Vol. 17 (September 1973-August 1976), published by The H.W. Wilson Co.

Index to U.S. Government Periodicals, 1980-81 issues, published by Infordata International, Inc.

Magazine Index, 1979-84 microfilm edition, published by Information Access Corp.

Public Affairs Information Service Bulletin, 1980 issue, published by Public Affairs Information Service, Inc.

The San Diego Union, Reference Librarian columns published between 1979 and 1984.

Statistical Reference Index, 1981 issue, published by Congressional Information Service, Inc.

Subject Guide to Books in Print, 1978/79, 1982/83 issues, published by R.R. Bowker & Co.

Transdex Index, 1980-81 issues, published by Bell & Howell Co., Micro Photo Division.

Writings on American History, 1935 issue, published by the American Historical Association.

ACKNOWLEDGMENTS

No one acquires skill in research without the cooperation and presence of many people and organizations. I want to express my sincere appreciation to:

Bernadine Clark and the staff of Writer's Digest Books for their guidance and suggestions for a better book.

Jerry Warren, Al JaCoby, Karin Winner, and J.D. Alexander of the *San Diego Union* who gave me valuable newspaper space and a free hand to write "The Reference Librarian" column.

The *San Diego Union* readers, who asked me excellent questions, many of which are reprinted in this book, and literally forced me to stretch my skills.

Phil Smith, Paul Zarins, Sue Galloway, Ulla Sweedler, Cynthia Prescott, George Soete, Karen Lindvall, Edie Fisher, Bob Westermann, and Anita Schiller of the reference department of the University of California—San Diego for being so supportive when I needed them. Special thanks to Penny Abell, Karin Welsh, and several other UCSD Library staffers who encouraged me to start writing.

My writing friends from the San Diego Writer/Editors Guild, who offered good friendship, good ideas, and understanding.

The countless reference book publishers who issue incredible research tools. Without their publishing efforts, our research efforts would be unproductive.

The people of California for supporting some of the best libraries in the country.

And special thanks to my husband, Al, our children, Karin and Mark, and our two cats who uncomplainingly (sometimes) fended for themselves while I wrote this book.

CONTENTS

PART ONE

RESEARCH OVERVIEW

Why Research and Why This Book
INTRODUCTION

It is better to light one candle than to curse the darkness.
—Chinese proverb

I recall reading the story of how the *Guinness Book of Records* was born. It was born in a bar. The concept, that is.

As a librarian, I can relate to that. Librarians all over the country routinely answer questions by phone over the roar of background laughter and the din of clinking glasses. People everywhere seem to wile away their spare moments looking for answers—and making bets. This particular group of people settled theirs by calling the library.

This book is about winning your *own* bets and finding your *own* answers—at the library, with a computer, or in an out-of-print book. What's the secret? Research. Knowing how to do it and not being afraid of it. Research is important because not all questions are as frivolous as those dreamed up in a bar. And the information you're after is the answer to the problem you're trying to solve.

I recall an anecdote I used once to begin an article about the importance of book indexes.

> Dr. Watson reached for the book wedged between two dusty tomes on the shelf. "The antidote, what was the antidote?"
> "Hurry, Watson," Holmes urged. "Marston can't last more than a minute."
> Dr. Watson's fingers flew frantically over the pages until he reached the back of the book.
> "Ach," he exclaimed. "No index!"

Exaggerated though it may be, the story proves a point. Not having the information you need, *when* you need it, leaves you wanting. Not knowing where to look for that information leaves you powerless. In a society where information is king, none of us can afford that.

The idea for this research guide came from my observations as a reference librarian in both public and academic libraries. Day after day for ten years, I watched consumers, parents, business people, students and teachers, writers, reporters, and others come to me for the information they needed to do their jobs and handle their problems. I also saw professional researchers—historians and biographers—seeking dates, names, and places from the past.

Not only was it obvious to me that *every* kind of library user had information needs, it was equally clear that among the countless nonlibrary users, there had to be questions that weren't being answered at all. I was both amazed and saddened that our library systems invest so much money in resources that reach so few people. The answers to many problems and questions are clearly there and free for the asking.

WHO NEEDS INFORMATION

No matter who you are, you need information.

If you're a consumer, you know that many of life's frustrations could be eliminated or controlled with the right piece of information. It may be the address of a particular company to complain to about a faulty sink or to write to for reliable instructions on hand cleaning an expensive silk blouse. Perhaps someone has offered you a price for your heirloom doll, and you want to determine its actual value before selling it. Or, you need reliable, up-to-date guides to plan your houseboating vacation.

If you're a parent, your information needs revolve around satisfying a child's latest "what if" question. In search of answers, you confront encyclopedias, dictionaries, and experts who have been through the adventure that is parenting. You have to know why the earth is round, who invented bubblegum, and what it means to be divorced.

If you're a business person, you know that information allows you to compete and thrive. Whether it's market research to determine shifting populations by income in a particular state, or statistics on the percentage of teenagers who buy books, you need it yesterday. Depending on your particular field, you may need to know experts in the poultry business, the market share of each low-sodium food item, the states without an income tax, the number of podiatrists in the country. Finding the answers quickly (or at all) could mean the difference between profit and loss.

Small businesses have information needs, too. As a prospective retailer, you'll have to know the start-up costs of a business, city and state licensing requirements, how and where to get merchandise, the dates and locations of trade shows, etc. One woman recently asked me for information on how to buy wholesale Italian gold jewelry for her newly formed business. I consulted the *Directory of Conventions* and referred her to a list of jewelry trade shows that are held all over the country to bring together jewelry makers and importers with customers and retailers like herself. I also suggested she check the library for jewelry trade directories and the Yellow Pages of large cities such as New York and Los Angeles for names of other wholesalers. Not having this information was holding her back!

If you intend to stay in business, your need for information does not stop. Studies show that 90 percent of all small businesses fail in the first year. Poor management and ignorance, or, put another way, lack of information, is often the reason.

If you're a student or teacher, your information needs are usually geared toward a subject, class, or project. You probably know *something* about libraries—you may recall, for example, a brief library tour. But do you know where to find specific information about surrogate mothers, the history of OPEC, or state-by-state presidential election results?

If you're a writer, the information you want must be accurate and up-to-date. You must constantly check and double-check facts; you can't afford to waste time on cumbersome and directionless research techniques because, for a writer, time is money.

As you may have already discovered, some projects take more time to research than to write. Ernest Hemingway once said that he always had seven-eighths beneath the surface for every eighth that showed. For a writer, that seven-eighths is information, and he reaches it through research.

Knowing where to look benefits the advanced as well as the beginning writer. Whether you need a little or a lot of information, research is an integral part of your craft. Screenwriter Lawrence Kasdan (*Raiders of the Lost Ark, The Empire Strikes Back*) says that being a writer is like having homework the rest of your life.

If you're a reporter, it's often homework due tomorrow morning. Information you get from interviewees—names, addresses, spellings, dates—must be verified. Memories are not always exact, and your readers count on accuracy. And because you frequently cover a variety of subjects or beats, you have to know where to look for answers in a number of unrelated topical areas.

I learned this by observing my colleagues at *The San Diego Union*, where I write a column entitled, "The Reference Librarian." (In the column, I respond to readers' reference questions and focus on how I find my answers.) Even though reporters at the *Union* normally write in one area (the arts, food, etc.), an emergency may require that they substitute (with little or no notice) for other writers. When our newspaper's music critic changed jobs, music events still had to be covered, and other reporters stepped in to carry the ball. Reporters don't know something about everything, but they can't afford to be ignorant about where to find out.

If you're a genealogist, historian, or scholar, you're probably familiar with ships' passenger lists and little-known manuscript collections. But think of the time you've spent in roundabout searches for a middle name. Genealogy requires some of the most sophisticated forms of research; yet, because it is known as a hobby, most people underestimate the research know-how required to reconstruct a family tree. Professional genealogists tell me that many family histories are riddled with errors, omissions, and inaccuracies. Armed with a basic knowledge of research techniques, yours needn't be thus flawed.

No one has a personal knowledge of everything he needs to know. Few of us have the unlimited means to call or travel freely to get information firsthand or to hire an expert to get the answer for us. And I don't know anyone yet who has conquered time travel so as to gather information about the past or the future.

DEBUNKING THE MYTHS ABOUT RESEARCH

Since information is a universal need, knowing where to get it is crucial. And knowing where to look for it is the key. NOT KNOWING translates to lost time, effort, and enthusiasm. Research makes the difference.

I recently met a woman who had sold a historical novel. She told me she was already "researching" her next book. Always ready to hear about a fact-finding venture, I asked about her techniques. In this case, my curiosity did me in. Listening to her research methods (or lack thereof) was painful. She had no clear idea of how to start except to visit bookstores. Not once had she stepped foot inside a decent-sized library; therefore, it took her months of random hunting to get a few books, many of them not the ones she originally wanted. I told her I could have done it all for her in a few days at a local university library.

Her response was, "Oh, the university library is too far away." (20 miles). I was sure she just didn't believe me. To her, using an academic library was just as risky as her own haphazard methods.

She's not alone. Many people are skeptical about doing research and pursuing information on their own. They hold fast to some age-old myths about the research process. Let's take a critical look at some of the qualms people have about doing research and getting information. And then let's dispose of them accordingly.

―――――――――― MYTH 1 ――――――――――
Research Is Dull

Research has a bad reputation. People think it's boring. Who wants to listen (yawn) to someone explain how to interpret a periodical index? That's enough to turn anyone off, and it does—especially if it's their first and only encounter with a periodical index.

Contrary to popular belief, research is exciting detective work. I recall one woman who was doing her family history. She asked me to verify the location of our local post office in the late 1890s, when her mother worked there. Imagine her elation when I actually found her mother's name in an article in an 1890's issue of the newspaper. What about the man who wanted information on a nationally reported incident involving him and an Air Force colleague in the 1950s? I found him an article mentioning both their names in a 30-year-old issue of *The New York Times* on microfilm. And then there's the woman who wanted to get rid of some old camera magazines, until I discovered her set was valued at several thousand dollars. (She sold them on consignment through a photo gallery, and made a killing.)

These are not unique stories; this kind of research goes on everywhere. Looking for information is often one surprise after another. Genealogists, historians, and professional researchers already know what others are just discovering.

───────────── MYTH 2 ─────────────
Research Is Tedious and Hard

Yes, some research requires diligence and hard work, and it may appear tedious. But other research tasks such as finding addresses, facts and figures, names and biographical information are quick and easy when you know where to look. If you think of research as genealogists and scholars do, the potential excitement of the find will more than compensate for some apparent tedium. A seasoned researcher, by habit, often asks himself, "What single piece of information will I find in this hunt that will pull all the loose ends of the mystery together?" Nothing is more exhilarating than leafing through a stack of papers in search of that elusive fact . . . and finally finding it.

───────────── MYTH 3 ─────────────
Research Is Only for Students

I hope we've already begun to shatter this myth. Since information is a lifelong need, it makes sense that research is a skill worth cultivating. But many people erroneously consider research to be an invention of the educational system, a device designed to keep students busy while they are in school.

Several years ago, a study of public library use in New England (conducted by Ching-chih Chen and Peter Hernon[1]) reported that the various research needs named by respondents involved their daily concerns: jobs, education and schooling, health, household and maintenance, child care, personal relations, energy, money matters, hobbies, and consumer issues. Indeed, these needs go far beyond term papers and science experiments.

[1] Reported in *Information Seeking*, by Chen and Hernon. Neal-Schuman Publishers, Inc. 1982.

Some professionals even use their research skills daily. Lawyers and doctors can't practice without access to current developments in their fields, for example. A surgeon may consult with his colleagues and always bones up on the latest research in medical journals before a complicated operation. A lawyer checks legal codes, precedents, and procedures before every case.

Because education is so highly valued in this country, libraries are funded on their strength to provide learning tools for *students*. Ironically, students are just one small group of those who do research. Or need to.

The rest of us need research skills, too, to get the information necessary to perform the tasks of everyday living—borrowing money, making simple household repairs, determining our eligibility for various social security benefits, choosing the best life insurance plan.

_____ MYTH 4 _____
Libraries Don't Have Information—Just Books

Books provide information, and libraries provide books. People who need information sometimes don't realize that libraries are information centers as well as book lenders. In the New England survey mentioned earlier, libraries were ninth in a long list of information-seeking patterns (among those who bothered with libraries at all). Prior to contacting a library, people sought information by (1) drawing from their own experience; (2) asking a friend, neighbor, or relative; (3) checking a newspaper, magazine, or book; (4) calling a store, company, or business; (5) asking a coworker; (6) contacting a professional such as a lawyer or doctor; (7) checking with a government agency; (8) hearing the information on radio or TV.

Furthermore, various library-user studies periodically reported in professional library journals show that between 10 and 20 percent of all adults account for 90 to 95 percent of all books borrowed from U.S. libraries. And only three of ten adults use libraries at all. Library information services, as underused as they are, not only offer a wealth of resources in traditional print material (books and magazines), they hold even greater promise for the future through computers and microfilm.

Libraries are changing. What has happened, especially since the 1970s, is nothing short of science fiction—yet few people know about it. One estimate says that over half the printed materials ever produced have appeared since 1900. Another says the number of articles published annually doubled between 1966 and 1974. The task involved in collecting and organizing these materials and making them accessible to the public is boggling. The problem is not too little information, but too much.

More books, pamphlets, and newspapers than ever before are being copied onto microfilm. This format allows libraries and other interested organizations to buy more information and store it in less space. (An average microfiche, a 4x6-inch card of microfilm, accommodates approximately 100 pages.)

Libraries are actually buying other libraries on film. Instead of traveling hundreds of miles to use special or original material existing in only one archive in the country, it's now as close as your nearest microfilm reader.

Libraries have come a long way since the days when books were chained to the shelves and caretakers posted warnings to discourage book use. ("Steal not this book, mine honest friend, For fear the gallows be thine end.")[2] We are now an enlightened society encouraged to pursue education. That means open access to books and information in all its forms and media. Libraries do indeed have information. Lots of it. (See Chapter 2 for an overview of the kinds of libraries and information centers at your disposal; Chapter 6 for a look at the library as a research tool.)

———————————————— MYTH 5 ————————————————
The Best Way to Do Research Is to Call Your Librarian

If that were true, there'd be no need for this book. "Information needs" as a major human characteristic would be nonexistent. Unfortunately, calling a reference librarian doesn't always work.

Librarians in large libraries are limited to one department: history, science, art and music, literature, etc. They do not have easy access to the entire library collection. And you are not the only client they must serve.

I have researched and fully answered over 2,000 questions for my column, "The Reference Librarian." To do that, I've used the entire collections (not just the reference sections) of three local libraries. Unencumbered by time, geography, or politics, I've also made countless phone calls to experts. This kind of research exceeds the normal service librarians can give, because they are usually bound to a single subject department with a time limit (perhaps 10 minutes or less) in which to handle most reference queries.

Some information seekers pride themselves on having a librarian spend an hour or an afternoon researching a question for them. For all the times I was able to do that for someone, I had to turn down 49 others.

All researchers, regardless of their task, need some measure of independence. Librarians are not always there when you need them, nor are they equally skilled in all research topics.

To be independent, one of the things you must do is become aware of the volume of information available to you. Incredible new publications and new formats for information come out regularly—17th- and 18th-century American newspapers on microfilm, Gallup Polls in monthly maga-

———

[2]Anonymous. Found written in a book per item in *Notes and Queries*, series 9, vol. 1, May 7, 1898, page 366. I should mention, too, that pre-20th century librarians often had to pay for lost books.

zine formats, the text of translated foreign broadcasts on microfilm, an English translation of the Soviet encyclopedia. Expecting a librarian to do all the work is not only unrealistic, it also cheats you out of the excitement of finding answers for yourself and discovering tidbits only you would recognize as being relevant to your information search.

WHY THIS BOOK

Knowing Where to Look is different from other books on research. It doesn't merely list books and leave you wondering what to do with them. I don't believe lists by themselves are effective. So throughout the book, I give you tips on how, when, and why to use the books I recommend. I share information directly from them to demonstrate what they do and don't do. I show you how to apply their information to your unique needs and interests. I introduce you to new materials, both print and nonprint, and show you new ways to use already-familiar reference sources. Where to get answers and information—as quickly and efficiently as possible—is the focus of this book.

In these ways, I've modeled this book after the library research courses I taught at the University of California—San Diego for five years. As you read, you'll be amazed at the incredible amount of information that exists and the equally vast amount that's available to you if you know where to look.

The first part of the book is a research overview. You'll learn about libraries and other organizations that collect information. You'll be introduced to two strategies for doing research: The first helps you establish a reference frame of mind and enables you to answer quick research questions; the second offers you a nine-point plan for attacking in-depth research projects. (Both of these approaches have evolved from my years of answering questions.) Next you'll get some clues on why libraries and other information centers do things as they do, to minimize your frustration at apparently senseless rules and policies. Besides learning how to avoid research traps, you'll gather some tips (again learned from experience) applicable to any research venture.

The second part of the book covers the basic tools of research: resources such as the library itself, in- and out-of-print books, select reference works, almanacs and dictionaries, magazines, newspapers, and government publications. The discussion of some of these apparently "standard" research tools includes showing you how to use them in ways and formats (microfilm and in computers) you may not have tried before. The chapters on using computers and microform in your research suggest that these two media are here to stay.

Part three of *Knowing Where to Look* deals with where to look for special kinds of information: biographical data, addresses, statistics, original materials (such as manuscript collections), quotes, pictures, legal references, and the input only experts can give.

Part four is the final chapter of the book. It shows you how using the research tools and techniques in combination leads you to specific resources that have the answers you need. This chapter dissects five sample information searches; it gives you a step-by-step look at what you might find by following the nine-point plan for solving a research problem.

Other things to notice about the book are the chapter summaries highlighting the major points discussed in each chapter. Should you want to review the key points for locating biographical information, for example, you would simply flip to the summary at the end of Chapter 15 and refresh your memory. Page numbers in the outline will direct you to the specific place in the chapter where a certain discussion begins.

Throughout the book, you'll find questions and answers (Q&As) illustrating particular points of research I have covered since 1979 in my newspaper column, "The Reference Librarian." (If any of them should resolve a nagging question you've had, be sure to update the answer by checking recent sources.) The purpose of my column is not to be just another question/answer medium, but rather to tell readers how and where I find their answers. By including the Q&As in this book, I'm sharing the information with you as well. I hope that you will marvel, as I do, at the myriad of information sources available to us—and some as obvious, and as taken for granted, as the Yellow Pages.

This book would not have been possible without the opportunity to fully research and answer those thousands of varied questions. The experience has helped my own research skills soar. (Reference librarians don't answer *all* the questions we're asked. We must often refer the information seeker to possible sources where he has to do his own digging.)

EMBARKING ON THE RESEARCH PROCESS

You may choose to start your own digging on a small scale. As the saying goes, the only way to eat an elephant is one bite at a time. When you've skimmed this book, you'll know which sections will be of immediate use to you. You'll probably want to read those chapters first, but you'll delve back into the book constantly (be sure to use the index for locations) for research tips and reference-book reminders.

As with learning any new skill, the first steps of the research process may seem difficult. But once you're familiar with even the basic information-finding resources, you'll realize that the initial time spent was an investment in the benefits you'll reap later. I compare it with learning to use my word processor. In the beginning, I was ready to toss it out the window in sheer frustration. Now, for all the time and labor it saves me, I wouldn't trade it for the world.

This book on research is designed to make your life—and your search for information—easier. It will suggest tried-and-true routes and easier ways to get the information you need right now. And beyond that, it will give you confidence to find for yourself the information you'll need next month or next year . . . because after reading it, you'll know where to look.

2

INFORMATION IS EVERYWHERE

*Knowledge is of two kinds. We know a subject ourselves
or we know where we can find information upon it.*
—Dr. Samuel Johnson, 1775

Information is a loaded word. It is facts and knowledge, insight and answers. It comes not only from encyclopedias, books, and magazines, but also from reading a stack of correspondence or a newspaper clipping; from talking to a specialist or listening to a recording; from watching a film or scanning a food label; from catching a glimpse of a footnote or overhearing a conversation. (One of my recent questions was answered from a report I heard on the evening news.)

The resources which provide information are housed in libraries, records centers, city offices, museums, public corporations, private organizations, and personal files—to name a few places. As you read this book, you'll become more aware that information in its varied shapes and forms is all around you.

LIBRARIES HOLD THE KEY

Libraries have always been with us—ever since man first scratched messages in clay. The medium of print is powerful, as demonstrated by the dictator who burns books and the average person who supports libraries financially even in the hardest of times. Indeed, libraries as dispensers of books are essential to the perpetuation of culture and knowledge.

To draw from this wealth, one of the most important things to realize about libraries (after you recognize them as information centers) is that no two are alike.

Several years ago, a reporter for *The San Diego Union* bemoaned what he considered to be the extravagance of duplicate libraries in our community at a time when library budgets were squeezed. He proposed that the San Diego Public Library, in a crowded downtown area, maintain its present size and the University of California—San Diego (UCSD) library, surrounded by spacious canyons in another part of town, serve as a regional library to which all community residents could come. Building expansion could easily be done adjacent to the site, he claimed.

This writer labored under the common misconception that libraries are all alike and that large libraries just have more of whatever small libraries already have. This is a gross oversimplification; and needless to say, it prompted one of the longest "letters to the editor" the newspaper had probably ever received. It came from the university librarian who had not even been interviewed for the article.

The prime contributor to the misunderstanding about the homogeneity of libraries is the almost incomprehensible number of books which have been and are presently being published. This includes juvenile books, reprints, vocational school texts, biographies, novels, etc. *Books in Print*, the annual compilation of all in-print and forthcoming titles from more than 15,200 publishers, lists about half a million books in print for the current year; 35,000 to 40,000 of those are new books published annually. Of that group, public libraries generally do not and cannot acquire every new book issued (nor do they need to). Many books give the same or similar information, and libraries must, for financial reasons, draw the line somewhere.

Not only do libraries not buy every book published, they don't all buy the same ones. Academic libraries do not collect the same *kinds* of books as public libraries. From my informal observation and use of both facilities, I suspect the duplication between the UCSD and the San Diego Public Library, while no official study has been taken, is probably less than one-third. UCSD is far from a duplicate facility, because its users and the public library's users have different needs.

So it is with other libraries which build their collections with their specific users' needs in mind. You wouldn't expect to find much material on doll collecting, for example, in a college of engineering library. As a researcher, you will want to learn the special strengths of all the libraries in your area. (To identify specific libraries and research organizations by name, location, or subject, consult the directories listed on pp. 20-22.)

PUBLIC LIBRARIES

Public libraries come in all sizes and offer varying services to researchers. Most neighborhood branches of a large library system usually have the *Reader's Guide to Periodical Literature* and perhaps one or more other indexes to magazines. They maintain small, though useful, collections of reference books like encyclopedias, dictionaries, quotation books, *Subject Guide to Books in Print*, etc. They may also offer research opportunities not available at the main library branch—allowing back-issue magazines to circulate, for example. (Small libraries don't keep magazines permanently beyond a few years, so they're more likely to lend them.)

The branch may also function as an intermediary between you and other libraries. Through it, you may be able to order, pick up, and drop off reserve books and interlibrary loan materials. Since many libraries are now connected by computer and microfilm catalogs, it's easy to see what different libraries in your area own without visiting or calling each one.

Some branch libraries are informal and have giveaway or exchange racks of free materials donated by patrons. One freelance writer I know finds new markets for her articles this way. From her library's giveaway rack, she finds and studies trade, professional, hobby, and organization magazines she's never seen before.

In addition, small libraries often have more fundraising book sales of duplicate or dated titles than their larger counterparts which have neither the time nor the volunteer staff to coordinate the sales. A book sale may be the perfect place to pick up useful material at bargain prices. I recently found an old Bartlett's *Familiar Quotations* for $1. It's not uncommon for paperbacks to go for 25¢ at these sales.

However convenient and helpful they may be, public libraries, either the main or a smaller branch, are not necessarily equipped for every type of research project. They simply don't have everything you'll ever need.

Q. I'm writing an article and need the history of Fernando de Noronha, a small archipelago about 400 kilometers northeast of Brazil. I find almost no references except for a few sentences in Morrison's *Voyages.*

I can read Portuguese, and I expect the best books will be in that language. Can you advise?

A. Certain kinds of questions cannot be researched successfully at many public libraries, and this is one of them. An academic library is more likely to have the specialized materials you need.

I find references to many books and articles in Portuguese and some in English in several bibliographies of Brazil and Latin America such as *A Guide to the History of Brazil, 1500-1822.* Check these and others at an academic library near you under the headings BRAZIL—BIBLIOGRAPHY and LATIN AMERICA—BIBLIOGRAPHY and request the things you need through the public library's interlibrary loan service. Though the Portuguese references will not likely be available at your own library, the English language materials may be available there.

Some of the wealth public libraries do own is hidden in basements, offices, and files, because many libraries are overcrowded, or eventually will be. As libraries continue to add books, microfilm materials, magazines, records, maps, videocassettes, and handmade files, they wage a constant struggle for storage and display space. Much of the information they collect is harder to display than books; therefore, it's harder to see and consequently, to know about and use. For example, the following list shows some files individually created by librarians at the San Diego Public Library:

■ Monthly art bulletins from major California art galleries and museums;

■ A list of tutors and translators in the community;

■ An autograph file of famous autographs on letters, books, and other manuscripts in the rare book room;

■ A card file listing individual biographies found in collective works in the library's collection but which are not covered in published indexes;

■ A card index of all songs in the library's collection of songbooks, many of which are not included in published indexes.

Many libraries focus on regional files covering events, history, and services unique to their area. For example, in addition to those mentioned above, the San Diego Public Library also has a local author file and a California pamphlet file (clippings and reports as well as pamphlets that have anything to do with California topics: agriculture, tourism, universities, etc.).

The Los Angeles Public Library has an intriguing crime file containing over 18,000 items from the *Los Angeles Times* and books on true crimes. It covers local crimes (Hillside Strangler, the Slasher, etc.), police and government corruption, and gang activity such as the Mexican Mafia. The file, started in 1930, is especially valuable to movie studio researchers and writers.

While libraries everywhere create homegrown files (often called vertical files because they're kept in vertical file drawers), these minicollections are quite individual, and the types vary from library to library. They are almost always created, however, because of a demand for that kind of information by library users.

When a librarian seems to pull an answer from the air, ask her where she got it. Often, she'll tell you the library has a special in-house file that contains the information. She may even come up with a complete list of files for your future reference.

Besides files and books, libraries also collect a variety of unconventional materials:

■ Postcards and pictures (photographs, clippings from magazines, etc.);

■ Street maps for U.S. and major foreign cities;

■ U.S. and foreign college catalogs (print or microfilm);

■ Out-of-town telephone books (print or microfilm copies);

■ Local telephone books and city directories going back several decades.

The list may even extend to menus, board games, posters, and other items.

ACADEMIC LIBRARIES

The thought of setting foot inside a college or university library jars
many novice researchers. Don't let the high ceilings and volumes of
books intimidate you. Many of these libraries not only permit unrestrict-
ed use of their facilities, but they may also sell fee cards which allow you
to check out books. In the San Diego area, the cost for different categories
of users (senior citizens, students of other colleges, Friend of the Library
members, etc.) ranges from $10 to $50 per year. Private schools may
charge more—well over $100 a year, in some cases, if they offer fee cards
at all. (Interlibrary loan is one way to get around libraries with restricted
lending policies. See Chapter 6.)

Academic libraries hold special attraction for researchers. Unlike public libraries that largely buy new books to serve recreational and informa-
tional needs of the general public, academic libraries cater to a different
audience. Their mission—to serve the research needs of scholars, students, and researchers—means that they buy books (out-of-print, as well
as in-print) in many fields, at a scholarly or professional level, in several
languages, and from all over the world. Overlap between the holdings of
a public and an academic library is unintentional and in most cases, small.

Academic libraries also have subject materials many public libraries
lack. In doing historical research, for example, you'll find an academic library to have a larger and more complete collection of history journals
than a public library. The library at the University of California—San
Diego owns the *Pennsylvania Magazine of History and Biography* from 1906
to the present and the *Jewish Quarterly Review*, published in London from
1888 to 1908; the San Diego Public Library does not.

A university's medical school library contains material too specialized
and technical for a public library to collect. But if that's what you're after,
you would have access to *Index Medicus*, a medical index on computer.
You could gather information on a personal health problem or find reliable, firsthand research to include in your book, article, or paper. Private
laboratories and small businesses in the medical field find such libraries
perfect for using important materials they can't afford to buy. In fact,
many companies with only minimal funds for elaborate libraries purchase
corporate library cards for local university libraries.

Check the major courses of study offered by local colleges to determine the subject strengths of their libraries and bookstores. (There's usually a copy of the school catalog at the public library as well as at the institution itself.) For example, the University of Illinois at Urbana is known
for its majors in communications and geology; the University of Missouri
in Columbia offers special programs in journalism and veterinary medicine; majors in theater and film-making are featured at the University of
California at Los Angeles; Columbia University is known for its School of

Social Work. Each of these universities has exceptional library collections in those fields.

As a rule, you should use the largest library you can find for your research project. Very often, it will be the academic library, not the public library, in your community. Besides having a larger selection of research materials (recent and back-issue magazines, for example), it generally has the finding tools (subject indexes, bibliographies, etc.) that identify other important items for your search.

COMMUNITY COLLEGE LIBRARIES

Much of the curriculum of every community college is devoted to teaching the trades and other vocational pursuits. Therefore, its library and bookstore are heavily endowed with texts in fields such as police and fire science, cosmetology, real estate, travel agency management, electrical wiring, drywall construction, carpentry, and bookkeeping. As with traditional academic libraries, these institutions may offer fee cards and free, in-house use of their collections.

One attractive feature of using both academic and community college libraries is that they're usually open on weekends and very late at night; this is a great help to researchers who work at other jobs during the day. Remember though, that hours frequently change according to seasons, semesters, and final exam schedules. Always call first.

HISTORICAL SOCIETY LIBRARIES

Historical societies vary in organization from being a loosely knit group of historically minded citizens with little research experience but plenty of volunteer time to staff the library collection, to a well-funded facility with at least one skilled archivist, historian, or librarian on the staff. Whatever the conditions of their operation, their collections focus on the history of their region. They may own documents and original materials available nowhere else—Civil War diaries kept by local veterans, company account books and ledgers, photos, newspaper clippings, archaeological records of the area, defunct society minutes and membership roll books, local family histories, artifacts, and more.

Q. I recently acquired a candy-kneading table with a finished-marble top. The base bears a metal plate saying Grunwald & Co., 138 Miller St., North Tonawanda, NY. Is there a way to find out about this company and its years of operation?

A. Back issues of the *Thomas Register of American Manufacturers* or other manufacturers' directories are good to check in tracing large manufacturers. (The *Thomas Register* from 1905 on is on microfilm but not available in every large library.)

Historical societies and local libraries are often best equipped to answer questions about their own communities, since they usually keep their old telephone books and city and other local directories. Two addresses to write to from the *Directory of Historical Societies and Agencies in the U.S. and Canada* are the Historical Society of the Tonawandas, 113 Main St., Tonawanda, NY 14150 and Buffalo-Erie County Public Library, One Broadway, Buffalo, NY 14203 (North Tonawanda is a suburb of Buffalo).

Old records and documents are often donated to area historical societies when companies, groups, and schools disband or go out of business. Other material may come from community residents.

As you can see, historical societies own a great deal of nonbook material, much of which is rare and fragile. Since their cataloging systems may also be unique, staff members will be instrumental in providing guidance.

Historical societies sometimes keep erratic hours, so call ahead. Some may charge a library user's fee for nonsociety members. If you're anticipating a long-term project that will require extended use of a historical society's library, consider joining for a year. Annual fees are usually reasonable—many are less than $50. Members may get free library privileges as well as other benefits: discounts at the society's bookstore, a subscription to the historical magazine or newsletter, free or reduced admission to lectures, workshops, or trips, and invitations to social or fundraising events.

MUSEUM LIBRARIES

Museum libraries are usually subject-oriented according to the focus of the museum itself, be it general science or guns. Museum curators are often specialists in their fields, and museums, especially the large ones, keep special libraries to support their research. (For more than 40 years, Margaret Mead was a curator at the American Museum of Natural History in New York City where she did much of her research.)

Museum libraries may be open only for staff research and/or membership use, depending on their size, staffing, and budget. But those that are closed to the public often handle mail or phone queries from legitimate researchers. Rules of operation and use vary; check museums in your area and write or call out-of-town museums. The larger the museum, its library, and budget, the better its collection and service to the public.

Q. I recently saw a newspaper copy of Frederic Remington's painting, *Mexican Cavalry Moving*. I have queried some western art galleries as to the location of the original and whether one can get a reproduction, but letters come back saying, "We don't know." Can you help?

A. Remington was a prolific artist, and one book, *Frederic Remington: Artist of the Old West*, by Harold McCracken, includes a checklist of more than 2,700 of his drawings and paintings. But *Mexican Cavalry Moving* is not on it. Check a library devoted to collecting Remingtoniana. The largest is the Amon Carter Museum Library, 3501 Camp Bowie Blvd., Fort Worth, TX 76101. Others are listed in Lee Ash's *Subject Collections*, available in large libraries.

COMPANY LIBRARIES

Large companies such as the Automobile Club of Southern California, Twentieth Century-Fox Motion Picture Studio, Hallmark Cards, Inc., and Pillsbury Co., have extensive libraries, generally to help their employees perform their duties more efficiently. Since they exist to carry out the work of the firm, many companies do not fill requests for information from the public. Other companies, however, perform unique research and, like museum libraries, may gladly fill mail and phone requests (related to their operations) from legitimate researchers.

If a company has one of the few libraries that specialize in the topic you're researching (rubber research or moped design, for example), don't hesitate to write or call them for information, advice, or leads. They may provide you with information for the publicity value it brings them when they're mentioned in your book or article. They may put you in touch with one of the key experts in the field who, as it turns out, works for their company. Or, they may provide you with precise references to the periodicals and books in which their research was reported and save you the time and possible expense of digging it out yourself.

Information about a company and its product or service is usually readily available through its public relations office. Sometimes this office works with the company's library in providing you with the information you're after.

SPECIAL COLLECTIONS AND SPECIAL LIBRARIES

Public and academic libraries usually have separate rooms to house rare and unique materials which they buy or receive as gifts. These special collections may include first editions, letters, incunabula (the first books printed between the invention of the printing press in the mid-15th century and the end of the century), dime novels, original manuscripts; even odd items such as china, artifacts, clay tablets, jewel-embedded book bindings, tapestries, paintings, and records. These special rooms in libraries house the hard-to-handle items, many of them valuable, that the library cannot accommodate in its regular collection. Rare-book rooms may contain items focusing on one subject or a dozen—but in most cases, the items are irreplaceable.

Special libraries, as contrasted with special collections, often collect in a particular *subject* area, whether the materials are rare or easy to get. (Often, there's a mix; but the emphasis is on the subject, not the rarity of the items in the collection.) A medical or education library, and a department library within a university are examples of special libraries.

Q. As a child in the 1940s, my son appeared as an extra in *Here Comes the Bride* with Bing Crosby. How can I get a copy of the photograph (called a "still") of the orphan scene in which he appeared?

A. Most major film studios no longer have the complete archives they maintained until the 1950s. Instead, they supply certain libraries with materials for preservation. According to Lee Ash's *Subject Collections,* the UCLA Theater Arts Library owns more than 170,000 stills of films from 1905 to the present. Unless they can readily identify the picture, you'd have to go to UCLA yourself. They can make picture copies for under $10.

Some special libraries focus even more narrowly than medicine, education, or another subject discipline. In Atlanta, for example, the Center for Disease Control has a 15,000-plus-item collection on mosquitoes. Such thorough coverage of a narrow topic means that the collection and its staff should be able to answer any question on that subject.

Subject collections are invaluable in many ways. For example, Alfred Whital Stern's collection of Lincolniana, owned by the Library of Congress, brings together a variety of items: rare and recent books on Lincoln and his time, pamphlets, broadsides (posters), ephemera, photographs, postage stamps, even campaign bandanas and other memorabilia. With such varied material housed in one place, you could easily note relationships and patterns in Lincoln's life that you might otherwise have missed by using separate collections. In fact, with so many resources in one place, you could do much of your work on Lincoln quickly and inexpensively. You wouldn't have to travel to distant collections.

Be sure to call before visiting a special or subject collection, especially if it's part of a larger organization. It may keep hours different from the main library or institution which houses it.

NEWSPAPER LIBRARIES

Many large newspaper libraries have a reference book and magazine collection for the staff to use in verifying information. Their most valuable asset, however, is their own newspaper. Most newspaper staffs clip the articles from each issue and batch them into subject files. Reporters use the category files for quick access to previously written articles when updating an old story or tackling a new one.

Community members and outside researchers find the clipping files extremely useful, too. Unfortunately, they are discovering that an increasing number of newspaper libraries are closing their doors to the public, or, they're providing limited service because of the high cost. Such limited service may include opening the library to telephone queries for a few hours a day or selling news photographs taken by staff photographers.

Many newspapers refer the public to local libraries which subscribe to the newspaper and its index. The information from the newspaper is therefore still available, though not in the unique clipping file arrangement. (See Chapter 11 for more information on newspaper libraries.)

LOCATING LIBRARIES AND SPECIAL COLLECTIONS

Now that we've run through the various kinds of libraries at your disposal, it would be helpful to find out where they are.

The following directories identify libraries of every imaginable kind from zoo libraries to church libraries all over the United States and Canada. Some directories include a geographical breakdown so you can tell which libraries exist in your area (along with their policies, collection strengths, etc.). Some directories provide a breakdown by library department and have a subject index. Many of the directories overlap to some extent and may provide different information on the same library. As with any research situation, you'll often find it useful to check more than one directory. All of the following are available in large libraries.

1. *American Library Directory.* Jaques Cattell Press/R.R. Bowker Co. Annual with supplement.

This is an alphabetical-by-state list of approximately 30,000 U.S. and Canadian libraries: public, academic, company, museum, newspaper, special subject, private, historical society, hospital, church, bank, military, government, law, association, and more.

ALD has no subject index. Its primary use is to find addresses and other information, such as budget size and subject strength for a library whose name you already know. It's also a good tool for identifying libraries in a particular city.

2. *Directory of Special Libraries and Information Centers.* Five volumes. Gale Research Co. Issued every two years with supplements.

This directory gives the same information as the *American Library Directory* for the same scope of libraries. The arrangement, however, is alphabetical by library regardless of its location in the country. (There is an accompanying geographical volume.) Contrary to what the title suggests, public and academic libraries *are* included. Each subject department of those libraries is listed separately rather than the library as a whole. The subject index will direct you to appropriate special collections.

Q. I have a letter written in 1940 that mentions one of my ancestors. The letter, which had no return address, said that some research material was in the Mc-Clung Historical Collection of the Lawson McGhee Library. Can you tell me where this library is located?

A. The *Directory of Special Libraries and Information Centers* gives the address of the Lawson McGhee Library (part of the Knoxville-Knox County Public Library), as 500 W. Church Ave., Knoxville, TN 37902. The McClung Historical Collection consists of the history and genealogy of Knoxville and the Southeastern states.

---

3. *Research Centers Directory*. Gale Research Co. Published every three to four years with supplements. (Also available in microform.)

RCD lists in-house research centers, herbariums, observatories, laboratories, and other research groups affiliated with universities, government agencies, companies, foundations, associations, and other organizations which have substantial libraries and respond to public inquiries. Research in all subject areas—from science to the humanities—is covered. The directory is arranged by broad subject categories. Check the indexes in the back by subject, geographical location, or research center name.

4. *Directory of Historical Societies and Agencies in the United States and Canada*. American Association for State and Local History. Issued every three years.

This is a geographical list of historical and genealogical societies with addresses. (Historical societies are also listed in the first two directories mentioned above.)

Q. I am doing a family search and have reached an impasse on some information on my grandfather. He was a Civil War vet and afterwards belonged to Heinzleman Post #33 of the Grand Army of the Republic in San Diego. I cannot locate any records of this post as the GAR vets are now gone. Where would their records be?

A. Records of local organizations and businesses often wind up in the area's historical societies. I called the San Diego Historical Society. They have membership and burial records of Post #33 of the GAR for certain years.

---

5. *Subject Collections*, by Lee Ash. R.R. Bowker Co. Published approximately every five to seven years.

This directory is arranged by subject only. It identifies the subject collections in 7,000 academic, public, museum, and historical society libraries nationwide.

6. *Writer's Resource Guide*, edited by Bernadine Clark. Writer's Digest Books. Updated and expanded edition. 1983.

WRG lists some 1,600 foundations, associations, government agencies, companies, museums, historical societies, and special collections in 30 subject categories with information on the specific services they provide, how to contact them, and other research tips. The subject index and the title (organization) index direct you to specific collections.

WHERE ELSE TO LOOK FOR INFORMATION

Libraries are information meccas. But they're not the only places to find answers to your research questions.

For some searches, you may have to go directly to the source of the information: the company, agency, or organization that knows the ins-and-outs of your particular subject. Many public agencies and private corporations are willing to help a researcher with a genuine concern or question. You can find them in the Yellow Pages or through various directories (*Garment Manufacturers Index, Horse Industry Directory*, etc.) identified in *Directory of Directories*. (Chapter 9)

One way to make initial contact with any organization is through the public relations office (also known as community relations, press, or public information office). In writing an article about decorative knot tying using seamen's knots, I once called the local Navy public affairs office in San Diego. They found local instructors for me to contact. (If you've ever tried to figure out which Navy office you need by scanning the endless listings in the San Diego phone book, you can appreciate just how difficult a task this is.)

Always keep in mind, though, that the goal of any public relations office is to present the organization it serves in the best possible light and to get favorable media coverage. It's your responsibility to penetrate their bias when getting information from them.

HOSPITALS AND CLINICS

Medical establishments can provide a lot more than health care—especially if you're a researcher. They may conduct research, for example, and offer a variety of innovative programs. Select hospitals have unique and costly equipment necessary for the performance of certain medical procedures available only in a particular state or region. A hospital burn unit, for example, has special equipment and procedures for operating it. Employees in the unit may be able to tell you about the day-to-day use of the equipment, its advantages and disadvantages; and they'll be able to tell you about the functioning of the center itself.

You may hear about the equipment through newspaper, magazine, or

TV coverage. The hospital's community relations office can give you further details. Freelance writer Thelma White discovered a ballet-for-athletes clinic sponsored by a San Diego hospital. When she called their community relations office, they arranged for her to interview the instructor.

FEDERAL AND STATE GOVERNMENT AGENCIES

Local branches of government offices such as the Internal Revenue Service often provide free oral or printed information to taxpayers. The office of the Small Business Administration (SBA) dispenses free and low-cost advice to business people. They may also arrange seminars and distribute government-published literature answering questions most frequently asked by prospective entrepreneurs.

In an agricultural area, state, federal, and county agricultural agencies disseminate information about crops, pests, and related subjects.

Q. I hear that in this country, including California, oranges are injected with a chemical to keep them fresh all year round. Is this true? If so, what chemical is it, and is it harmful to our health?

A. The San Diego County Farm and Home Advisor for citrus fruits says that, to his knowledge, oranges in this country are not injected with any chemicals.

Once the oranges are picked, they are sent to a packing house where they are graded. Scarred and diseased oranges are removed, then the oranges are washed in hot water and detergent. They are dried and coated with a food-grade wax. They are graded again and sorted by size. After a two-to-seven-day storage period, they are shipped.

The only chemical they may come in contact with is the biphenyl lining in the shipping boxes, and this touches only the outer oranges. All such substances are screened by the FDA.

Your voice in Congress is another potential information resource. National and state legislators with local offices serve as a pipeline to state issues and will send their constituents and other interested citizens information on request.

Q. A recent newspaper item said that a state-funded corporation to help aspiring inventors would be created under a bill approved by the state assembly. The bill is sponsored by Assemblyman Larry Kapiloff, D-San Diego. How can I get more information about it?

A. The bill has not yet been made into law. According to Kapiloff's office (in the San Diego phone book under Kapiloff's name), the bill has just passed one of several hurdles to come. It must also be approved by the state senate. To keep informed on the bill's progress, contact Kapiloff's office.

As you'll see in the chapter on government resources, federal lawmakers, enforcers, and interpreters are prolific information generators. Check the Yellow Pages for branch offices of federal government agencies. Or consult the *U.S. Government Manual* (the official handbook of the federal government which covers all agencies of the executive, legislative, and judicial branches, as well as other government-related commissions and organizations). You'll find regional addresses for everything from FDA consumer affairs offices to field organizations for the National Oceanic and Atmospheric Administration.

CONSULATES AND EMBASSIES

Foreign consular offices provide much information about their countries, some of which is hard to find in standard reference books. Commercial liaisons offer lists of wholesalers and manufacturers and give tips on how to deal with them. Travel information is also available. Consult the State Department's *Foreign Consular Offices in the United States* (annual) for consulate addresses.

Embassies represent their home government in a foreign country. The information they provide covers such diverse areas as education, culture and art, history and politics. Names of ambassadors and embassy addresses are found in the *Diplomatic List*, a quarterly State Department publication, available in large libraries. Many embassies respond to written requests for information; some make their libraries available for on-site research.

If not accessible in a large library, both of these publications are available from government bookstores or directly from the Superintendent of Government Documents.

CHAMBERS OF COMMERCE

There are some 7,000 chambers of commerce in American cities and towns, and dozens of chambers representing foreign countries such as the Netherlands Chamber of Commerce in the United States located in New York City. They exist to attract income and investment to their area. Because they appeal largely to businesses and tourists, they provide statistics, photographs, economic reports, surveys, and other data concerning taxation, local manufacturers and products, hotel rates and convention facilities, import and export tariffs, and other related information.

Area libraries often own copies of directories and reports issued by the local chamber of commerce. You can find addresses for chambers of commerce in Johnson's *World Wide Chamber of Commerce Directory*.

TRADE, PROFESSIONAL, AND HOBBY ASSOCIATIONS

Most of the organizations listed in *Encyclopedia of Associations, Writer's Resource Guide*, and other references issue information about themselves via brochures, newsletters, and magazines. Whether they're groups of barbed-wire collectors, left-handers, chemical engineers, cattle ranchers, teachers of English as a second language, or people who share the name Jim Smith, they'll tell you about their purpose, their activities, and their publications. They may also have relevant statistics, reports, and studies to share with the public. (See Chapter 16 for more information on how to contact these resources.)

DON'T STOP WITH THESE

The list of information sources is endless; you're limited only by your imagination. Any person, place, or thing that has information you need is a potential resource. In addition to those mentioned in this chapter, don't forget banks, zoos, churches, radio and TV stations, and businesses in your area. They're as close as your telephone.

Q. Can you give me any information on a local man who converted distilled water into power to operate a car? The story was covered on Channel 10 here in San Diego some months ago.

A. According to the newsroom at Channel 10, TV stations are required by law to keep copies of their local news broadcasts for five years. They say that although theirs are arranged by date, there's a subject approach, too. They found the story about an Encinitas man who created his own steam car. His name and address are enclosed.

Don't limit yourself in your quest for answers. Assume that the information you need is *somewhere*, because it is. People, whether acting alone or on behalf of a society, have the genetic urge to document, classify, and collect. Information truly IS everywhere.

——————————— *CHAPTER SUMMARY* ———————————

I. Information comes in many forms and from many places.
II. The library is the manager of a wealth of information; yet no two libraries are exactly alike. (page 12)
   A. Public libraries serve the general public in a variety of ways with books, vertical files, reference assistance, etc. However, they do not have the resources or the space to handle every research problem. (page 12)
   B. Academic libraries are especially geared to research; they often have the subject materials and resources that public libraries lack. (page 15)
   C. Community college libraries have resources that reflect the trade and vocational pursuits of their curricula. (page 16)
   D. Historical society libraries focus on the history of their region and own much original as well as published material. (page 16)
   E. Museum libraries are usually subject oriented and reflect the focus of the museum collection. (page 17)
   F. Company libraries are set up to serve the employees of the firm. They sometimes offer expert assistance to researchers interested in their company's products or services. (page 18)
   G. Special collections usually contain rare or valuable items housed apart from a library's regular collection. Special libraries collect material in a particular subject area. (page 18)
   H. Newspaper libraries serve the newspaper staff. Some of them offer limited reference service to the public. (page 19)
   I. Various library directories exist to help you find the particular library for your research needs. (page 20)
III. Beyond the library, there are hundreds of other information centers at your disposal.
   A. Hospitals, government agencies, the military, consulates and embassies, chambers of commerce, trade and professional associations, etc., are often eager to handle information requests from the public. (page 22)
   B. Assume the information you need is *somewhere*, because it probably is.

3

STRATEGIES FOR FINDING INFORMATION

Plan: A method devised for . . . achieving an end.
—Webster's Dictionary

Learning how to do research takes time. But you'll find it IS a worthwhile investment, because ignorance can be costly. The investor who lacks current information on food crops could risk his savings in the commodities market. The songwriter who neglects getting information on copyrighting his work may lose his right to profit from it. The handyman who doesn't verify the proper techniques or city laws for adding a patio to his home may find himself having to tear it down later. Lack of information carries a price.

Inefficient research methods also exact a toll. Stumbling aimlessly in search of information is frustrating and takes longer than having a plan of attack. (You recall the historical novelist who took three months to find books, many of which were not the ones she originally wanted.) It's expensive, too, even though the public library and other information agencies may be free. Their information is not, at least in terms of your time.

Consider the task of an executive secretary who must get a company's address for the boss or inquire about various hotel rates in another city. The search process could take half an hour or more. And the price of the information is more than the cost of a few phone calls. It's also the cost of the secretary's wages and benefits. Not knowing the best way to get that information or the best place to look for it means more time spent and more costs incurred. (At a wage of $10 an hour plus company benefits equal to the hourly wage, a half-hour effort for the information could cost the company $10.)

No matter what the task, we learn by doing. Once you become familiar with a handful of basic reference publications and organizations and their services, you can channel all your energy into getting correct answers quickly and efficiently instead of leaving the information search to a random effort at best. By following a few simple research techniques described in this book, your quest for information will yield positive results—quickly.

TWO KINDS OF RESEARCH

In 10 years of helping people find answers, I've found that most research can be divided into two types: quick-answer research and in-depth research.

Questions that call for a pat or quick answer may take a few minutes to an hour to research. These kinds of questions usually result in a fact, statistic, address, a quantity, even a short why or how-to response. Some quick-answer questions would be the following: What is the address of NBC? How much salary does the Queen of England receive? Where was Henry Kissinger born? What are the symptoms of angina pectoris? Questions like these usually have definite, straightforward responses. And most of their answers are found in a library's reference section.

Questions that require in-depth probing, on the other hand, may result in a history, analysis or interpretation, discussion, or other detailed report. Some likely candidates for an in-depth search would be these: What is the history of kokeshi dolls? What kind of affliction is night blindness? How should herpes be treated? How can I trace my family tree? Doing in-depth research usually takes several steps, various resources, and many hours, days, or weeks of your time. When I'm researching a complex project, I use an in-depth approach to finding information. And I use the entire library, as well as sources outside the library, as my resources.

QUICK-AND-DIRTY RESEARCH

For either type of research question, the key to success is having a plan. Questions that call for quick-and-dirty research are usually answered with a three-step strategy.

Step 1. Use directories, almanacs, encyclopedias, dictionaries, general reference books, and computerized data bases.

The path to finding quick answers often begins with directories. Their diversity and number are astounding, and the best selection is usually in large libraries. (Small neighborhood branches usually have only a few of the more general varieties, but there are exceptions, depending on the definition of "small" and "large" in your area.)

Whatever the size or endowment of your library, it should have some directories available for ready reference. The topics they cover run the gamut of human experience. If you want to know what happened to a magazine no longer on the newsstands, you'd check *New Serial Titles*. To find out the ratings of college engineering programs throughout the country, you'd check *The Gourman Report*. To rent stock music for your student-made film, you'd look up firms in *Audiovisual Market Place* or the Yellow Pages of large city phone books. The reference tool I find most useful for identifying directories is the *Directory of Directories* (see Chapter 9).

There are directories for practically any subject. A woman once asked me if I knew of a directory of eligible bachelors. My instincts told me it was an impossible question, especially since this particular woman had a reputation for asking *that* kind of question. But, I kept my thoughts to myself, checked the *Reader's Guide to Periodical Literature*, and referred her to some magazine articles on small groups of eligible bachelors. I told her that so far as I knew, there was no such directory.

That was one of my favorite stories about impossible questions—until a year later when this kind of directory began popping up all over the country.

Besides directories, the prime resources for tackling quick-answer questions are almanacs, encyclopedias, and specialized dictionaries.

Q. Which state has the longer coastline, Florida or California?

A. Florida's Gulf and Atlantic coastlines total 1,350 miles, second to Alaska's 6,640-mile coastline, according to the *Hammond Almanac*. California is third with a coastline of 1,264 miles.

All of these ready-reference publications are arranged in formats that encourage consultation rather than cover-to-cover reading, and they comprise the major portion of any library's reference section. They are arranged in alphabetical or categorical order; they have one or more easy-to-use indexes and ample cross references. (See Chapters 4 and 5 for more tips on using them.)

Q. What is meant by the Dow-Jones Averages?

A. The *Encyclopedia Americana* says the D-J Averages are nothing more than a statistical indicator of stock market movements determined by averaging the end-of-the-day prices of 65 representative stocks: 30 of the most commonly quoted industrial stocks, 20 transportation stocks, and 15 utility stocks. It was devised by Charles Dow in 1884. (Dow was the first editor of *The Wall Street Journal*.)

Another measure of stock market activity is the New York Index which averages every stock traded on the New York Stock Exchange.

In addition to print resources, it makes sense that the computer would be involved with giving quick answers. Indeed, computerized research services are becoming available to more and more people as reference books go on-line. Their texts are entered into computers, and as more libraries subscribe to them, the information they contain will be easy to get. (Most of the chapters in this book include a section on use of the computer in conjunction with various resources, e.g., newspapers, encyclopedias, etc.)

Step 2. Use the subject approach.

If, in your preliminary search, you don't find a directory or encyclopedia that will be a likely resource, zero in on the subject of your search. When I don't know which particular reference book to check, for example, I go to the reference shelf where books on my specific subject are grouped. Invariably, one of the books there has the answer or a lead.

Someone once asked me for the address of a particular paralegal organization which, she did not hesitate to say, had already been unsuccessfully searched for by several other libraries in town.

Even though she told me the *Encyclopedia of Associations* had already been checked, I rechecked it as I usually do, in case the answer or a clue had been overlooked.

When I didn't find the organization listed there, I went to the law section of the reference shelves and skimmed through a variety of books. I noticed a dictionary of legal terms entitled *Paralegal's Encyclopedic Dictionary*. I found the organization's address in an appendix.

Step 3. Think in categories.

Yet another way to approach finding an answer to a quick question is to categorize everything capable of being categorized. (Skilled researchers subconsciously do this to get their search started.) For example, if a teenager asks me for the addresses of organizations that will help him find a pen pal, I would think "association" and then check the *Encyclopedia of Associations*. (The category, *association*, is used in the broad sense. The National Safety Council, the American Medical Association, Girl Scouts of America, and the Model T Ford Club of America are all "associations" and are listed in this incredible resource.)

For a list of past winners of the Pulitzer Prize, I would think of the category, award or prize winners. A search through a library catalog or the *Directory of Directories* under scholarships, prizes, etc., would name an appropriate reference. And since prize winners constitute a "list," I would also try *The Book of Lists* or an almanac which includes many lists.

NO GUARANTEED ROUTES

As you can see, it's possible to get an answer from more than one reference book. Consider the task of finding the address of a particular medical school in Bethesda, Maryland. Sources you might check are a directory of colleges, a directory of medical schools, and the Bethesda Yellow Pages.

Sometimes the category (and subsequent references you pursue) is not the shortest route to an answer. In fact, if a supposedly "quick" question is not resolved with the three-step approach, you may have to try the in-depth plan to find your information. Perhaps your "easy" question is more involved than you realized.

I recall my experience in trying to find the address of the Intrepid Museum Foundation. To start the search I categorized the topic and subsequently tried directories of museums and foundations. No luck. The researcher then added that the *Intrepid* was a Navy-ship-turned-museum and was to be berthed in New York Harbor. (A valuable clue.) I categorized again, this time checking the index to *The New York Times* in case it had been covered in the newspaper. I found several items on the Intrepid Museum. But before suggesting to the researcher that he try a time-consuming search through microfilmed articles for the foundation's address or another clue to it, I took a chance and categorized once more—this time by city. I checked the Manhattan telephone book. The foundation was listed.

When you categorize questions, you must consider the possibility that you're categorizing differently than the particular reference books you are using. In one search, I had to locate special U.S. collections with extensive material on Alexander Graham Bell. Lee Ash's *Subject Collections* had no resources listed under the inventor's name, and this surprised me. Then I tried the term TELEPHONE and found a gold mine. Part of knowing where to look is knowing what to look under.

Q. I cannot locate a specific directory of dog- and cat-food producers in the United States. I need the names of officers and financial data for the food producers. Do you know of a reference book that would supply this information?

A. There aren't enough pet-food producers to fill a directory of substantial size. Look in a general directory of manufacturers such as *Standard & Poor's Register of Corporations, Directors and Executives,* available in large public libraries. One volume of this directory identifies company products by their Standard Industrial Classification (SIC) numbers. The SIC number for pet-food manufacturers is 2047. Under this number in an appendix is a list of about three dozen companies that make pet food. Check *Standard & Poor's Corporation Records* for detailed financial data.

By now you're probably thinking, "That's fine for experienced researchers who already know about these directories. But what about me?" In fact, even the most seasoned researchers still find publications they haven't used before. Don't despair. The way to approach quick-and-dirty research is to make what may seem like a rash generalization.

Assume there are publications covering just about every subject. Actually, that's close to the truth. In general, people ask the same questions all over the country. And there's an excellent chance that someone somewhere has already gathered and published the information that answers many of your questions. Your task, then, is to identify the publications that give those answers. (Many "quick" research questions are answered in the Q&A features throughout this book.)

FINDING BOOKS BY SUBJECT

Finding the ready-reference books that hold your "quick" answers is not hard with the help of some useful tools. *Subject Guide to Books in Print (SGBIP)* is the source I use most to identify *any* books on *any* subject. Covered in more detail in Chapter 7, the multivolume *SGBIP* offers you a panorama of what's available on your particular topic. If you want to make colonial furniture, you look under FURNITURE MAKING; if you need a reference for determining the authenticity of carved whale teeth, check *SGBIP* under SCRIMSHAW.

There are also some guides (available in large libraries) that specialize in identifying reference books that will answer your quick question. The guides are arranged alphabetically by subject: CITIZEN'S BAND RADIO, CITY PLANNING, CIVIL RIGHTS, CIVIL SERVICE, etc. If you're looking for reference books that list associations, you would look up the term ASSOCIATIONS in one of the guides below. To get the name of a directory of camps, you would look under CAMPS.

None of the guides to reference books included here lists *every* possible source, but they're excellent places for new and even experienced researchers to begin. Even if the library doesn't own a reference book they recommend, the librarian may suggest another, or you can order it through interlibrary loan.

1. *Concise Guide to Library Research*, by Grant W. Morse. Fleet Academic Editions, Inc. 2nd ed. 1975

2. *How to Do Library Research*, by Robert Downs and Clara Keller. University of Illinois Press. 1975.

3. *Where to Find What: A Handbook to Reference Service*, by James M. Hillard. Scarecrow Press, Inc. 1975. Rev. Ed. 1984.

4. *Where to Find More: A Handbook to Reference Service*, by James M. Hillard. Scarecrow Press, Inc. 1977.

5. *Finding the Source*, by Benjamin Shearer and Barbara Smith Shearer. Greenwood Press. 1981.

(The familiar Winchell's (Sheehey's) *Guide to Reference Books* is a broader, more comprehensive tool than you'd need for quick research. It's used more for in-depth research and may be too overwhelming to use for easy-to-answer questions.)

DOING IN-DEPTH RESEARCH

Sooner or later, you will need information that is not neatly summarized in an almanac chart or an encyclopedia entry. In-depth research of a subject, trend, idea, or phenomenon is not usually a one-step experience.

In my years of answering questions, I eventually fell into a pattern of steps that repeated again and again no matter what the question was.

Most of the chapters in this book discuss various components of the in-depth research plan. The strategy consists of checking the following sources:

1. Periodical articles;
2. Books;
3. Encyclopedias;
4. Reference books (directories, bibliographies, etc.);
5. Government documents;
6. On-line data bases;
7. Microform;
8. Original sources (private papers, public records, etc.);
9. Experts and organizations.

It's not necessary to adhere rigidly to this particular sequence of resources, nor will you have to check every one of the nine kinds of items. (Chapter 23 shows you how these resources are used together to gather information for five different research projects.)

The more you use the various resources (the steps in the strategy), the more familiar you will become with using them in combination. You'll also recognize that this in-depth approach to finding information incorporates the steps involved in the "quick-and-dirty" plan. After all, you may still have to check the quick-answer sources (directories, almanacs, etc.) in your in-depth search. The difference is that a complex search doesn't stop there.

Keep in mind that the nine-step pattern is simply a guideline to be adapted to suit whatever your research task. You'll find that some of the nine steps will uncover useful material for your search; others will not. You should, however, consider all or most of the steps since you can't tell what you will find until you try them. You will usually identify far more books and articles than you need.

At that point, your job will become one of careful screening to weed out the duplicate and irrelevant items. Of course, there may be other searches where you will have to settle for *anything* you can find, because there won't be much.

As you check out each of the nine kinds of resources, you will gather a checklist of references. Check first to see if your own library has the publications you want. Consider borrowing those not in your library through interlibrary loan (Chapter 6). You may occasionally want to buy some of the books you've identified in your search; these titles can be found in bookstores or ordered directly from the publisher. Be wary of entries for books in *SGBIP* or elsewhere that don't list page count. Price is no indication of a book's size. Even at $15, a title could still be a pamphlet.

Once you find the resources on your list and begin examining them further, you will discover that some are less appropriate (or sometimes more appropriate) than you thought they would be. This is a routine and normal part of in-depth research. (This bears out the you-can't-tell-a-book-by-its-title tip discussed on page 51.)

In addition, you'll discover that many of the books and articles will pop up repeatedly in different sources. It's better to find items mentioned more than once than not to find them at all. Sometimes, you will locate a reference late in your search that you wish you'd encountered earlier. Things don't always show up when and where you want them to. And sometimes you miss them even when they *are* there. Researchers involved in in-depth information searches recognize these "facts of life" as common research situations.

WHATEVER THE TASK, HAVE A PLAN

Neither the three-part strategy for plugging into quick-and-dirty research nor the nine-step, in-depth research pattern is set in stone. These are guidelines—starting points for any information search. The more research you do, of course, the better equipped you will be to follow your own instincts. You'll quickly discover that research often involves trial and error with a variety of subject terms in a number of different publications. No two research ventures are exactly alike—but that's half the adventure.

The important thing I've learned about research is that it's easier than it appears. With at least a starting point, a direction, a library suited to your purposes, and familiarity with the *Subject Guide to Books in Print*, you'll uncover answers with less effort than you imagined. And with some additional perseverance, you will successfully conduct in-depth research projects, too. Research is not as complicated as it appears if you know where to look for information.

_____ *CHAPTER SUMMARY* _____

I. Most research problems fall into one of two broad categories— quick to answer or in depth. To solve either kind you need a plan.

II. To find ready facts and answers to quick questions, take a three-step approach. (page 28)
  A. Check directories, almanacs, encyclopedias, dictionaries, general reference books, and computerized data bases. Various guides help you identify these appropriate resources.
  B. Check by subject. Look for relevant books on the reference shelves in the subject of your question. The *Subject Guide to Books in Print* is one invaluable resource.
  C. Think in general or specific categories. A quest for a list of baseball greats should lead to a who's who in baseball; the name of a pen pal should lead to a directory of associations or perhaps a youth magazine with classified ads.

III. In-depth research generally requires several steps. It means tapping a number of different kinds of resources to get background information on your subject. (See Chapter 23 for sample information searches.) Consult the following for in-depth research questions:
  A. Periodical articles
  B. Books
  C. Encyclopedias
  D. Reference books (directories, bibliographies, etc.)
  E. Government documents
  F. On-line data bases
  G. Microform
  H. Original material (private papers, public records, etc.)
  I. Experts and organizations

IV. Both the quick and in-depth research plans are guidelines for solving research problems. They should be adapted to fit your particular research needs.

4

Things No One Ever Tells You:
HOW TO AVOID
RESEARCH TRAPS

There is no useful rule without an exception.
—Thomas Fuller, M.D.

Information seekers are no different from other people. They're reasonable (usually), intelligent people with reasonable, intelligent questions. But especially for the uninitiated researcher, getting answers to those questions can be fraught with frustration. And one of the most frequent remarks I hear from researchers who've had an exasperating, fruitless search is, "I've tried everything."

It takes a tactful librarian not to offend a patron by suggesting that he "take another look" when he swears he has thoroughly checked his resources. In most of my experiences, however, I've found the answer where a researcher has already looked.

The problem is usually not the researcher's carelessness. His frustration is often the result of falling into one of countless research traps, which are really library rules and policies of which he knows little or nothing. Avoiding the traps and learning the rules come with experience—and forewarning.

All organizations create rules and policies to operate efficiently. But unless you know what they are, they may appear senseless and arbitrary. As an information seeker, the rules are the things you're supposed to know to make your job easier—and they're the things no one ever tells you.

Q. There seems to be a policy in libraries that some books other than those categorized as reference may not be checked out. Is there a cost restriction whereby expensive titles do not circulate?

A. For several reasons, most libraries have restricted loan policies for certain kinds of materials. For example, magazines and rare books aren't loaned because, if lost, they can't be replaced easily, if at all. (Libraries that do lend magazines usually do so because they don't keep them permanently.)

Other books that may be restricted are art and photography books whose color plates are frequently torn out. Books with records, maps, or loose parts, that could easily get lost or stolen, also must be monitored. Each library establishes its policies based on its own experiences, but many such restrictions are common to all libraries and research establishments.

Most of these potential research traps fall into two broad categories: the first deals with classification, spelling, and filing systems; the second has to do with access both to the library itself and to the materials in it. Once you know about these apparent obstacles and how to use or circumvent them, your research will be considerably simplified and your headaches reduced.

SUBJECT CLASSIFICATION SYSTEMS

It helps to be at least broadly familiar with the two most commonly used subject classification systems: Library of Congress (LC), used in large libraries, and Dewey Decimal, used in small libraries. Knowing their basic setups can help you avoid some problems and guide you in the right direction when tracking a resource.

For example, a journal called *Personal Injury Magazine* sounds like a law journal. But its broad LC call number is P which indicates it's a literature title. (If you charged over to a law library's magazine stacks looking for *Personal Injury Magazine*, you would be wasting your time looking for something that wasn't there.) On the other hand, *Personal Injury Commentator*, starting with the call number K, *is* a law journal.

A broad version of the LC subject classification looks like this: (The complete version occupies several volumes.)

A	–	General Works
B	–	Philosophy, Psychology, Religion
C	–	Auxiliary Sciences of History (Archaeology, Genealogy, etc.)
D	–	History: General and Old World
E, F	–	History: America
G	–	Geography, Anthropology, Recreation
H	–	Social Science
K	–	Law
L	–	Education
M	–	Music and Books on Music
N	–	Fine Arts
P	–	Language and Literature
Q	–	Science
R	–	Medicine
S	–	Agriculture
T	–	Technology
U	–	Military Science
V	–	Naval Science
Z	–	Bibliography, Library Science

The Dewey Decimal system is fairly uncomplicated and is preferred by small libraries. The more books a library owns, the more flexible and expandable the subject classification system must be—and the more limited the DD system becomes. Nevertheless, if your public library uses this method, knowing the DD number (or at least the general category) assigned to a book can steer you in the right direction.

Let's say you're looking for an exercise book. If all other exercise books you've used are in the 700s (in the DD system, sports and exercise fall in the same subject area as fine arts), a book entitled *Forever Fit* with a 300 (social science) call number would *not* be an exercise book (regardless of its title). When you use a library often, you become familiar with the subjects that are grouped in the same broad classification area. Law, business, and education books, for instance, are in the 300 (social science) classification.

DEWEY DECIMAL SYSTEM

000–	General Works	500–	Natural Science
100–	Philosophy	600–	Useful Arts
200–	Religion	700–	Fine Arts
300–	Social Science	800–	Literature
400–	Language	900–	History, Biography

The Library of Congress receives copies of all books submitted to the Copyright Office, and LC catalogers are the first to assign LC and Dewey Decimal numbers to all books. One way this information is shared with other libraries nationwide is through the cards individual libraries buy from the Library of Congress and also via the computerized cataloging system shared by thousands of libraries nationwide. Sometimes libraries must alter the Library of Congress's assigned call number, usually when it's too long for their purposes, or if it has already been given to another book.

For example, the Library of Congress has assigned to Todd Gitlin's book (on television), *Inside Prime Time*, the LC number PN 1992.3 U5 G57 and the Dewey number 384.55'4'0973. Libraries using the LC system might make a minor change in one or two of the last two numbers (57) if those numbers were already assigned to another book. Most small libraries would use only the first four or five numbers of the Dewey number. In any event, call numbers in libraries nationwide are the same or similar.

SPELLING AND TERMINOLOGY TRAPS

Be aware that a library's catalog, whether it's card, computer, or microfilm, can deter you in many ways from finding what you want. Though the catalog tells you every book the library owns and where you can find it, finding it is not always the easiest part. Spelling variants, inconsistent terms, awkwardly worded subjects, and misfilings can challenge even the most determined researcher.

Computer catalogs resolve most of such problems inherent in fixed card files, but the computer is not a cure-all. It still stores errors that people feed into it. If you assume the computer is The Perfect Machine, you might accept everything it says without question.

Nevertheless, computers will solve most card catalog problems dealing with inconsistencies of language. So why discuss card catalogs when they're on the endangered species list? For a very good reason. The rules of spelling and terminology that apply to card catalogs are the same rules that apply to other printed documents: books, directories, indexes, and dictionary catalogs (card catalogs which have been published in book form. See G.K. Hall catalogs in Chapter 7.) No matter what the plight of the traditional card catalog, these reference books will remain with us for a long time.

Q. Can you find the address of an East Coast company called Robert Shaw Co.? No one can locate it for me; yet I know it exists.

A. By chance, I looked under the first name and found a firm called Robertshaw Controls Co. with main offices at 1701 Byrd, Richmond, VA 23261. Other divisions in other parts of the country are listed in *Thomas Register of American Manufacturers* under R.

Both card and dictionary catalogs actually become sociological records of our language, because they record book titles with the exact spellings and terms popular at the time the books were published. But, times change. For example, GIPSIES is now spelled GYPSIES; THE EUROPEAN WAR is now known as WORLD WAR I. Then there are terms, such as LASER, ASTRONAUT, INTERFERON, BATTERED WIVES, that simply didn't exist years ago.

These catalogs also include unusual, archaic, and foreign words, because library cataloging rules dictate that titles be recorded exactly as they appear on the book. *The Compleat Clown*, therefore, does not appear near *The Complete Clod* in a printed list. Titles starting with the word MEDIEAVAL and MEDIEVAL are widely separated in a card file or printed bibliography by titles starting with the word MEDICAL. This simple spelling variation can cause researchers to miss one or the other batch of titles.

BOOK TITLES
The Mediaeval Mind
Medical Problems in China
Medical Questions for the Layman
The Medical Wonder
Medieval History

Names can also create confusion for the information seeker. They are potential traps not only in their spelling, but in the possible detours that can result from following up on the wrong person.

> Attwater, Donald
> Attwell, Henry
> Attwood, Charles
> Atwater, Donald

In a computer catalog, the spelling difference or change in terminology can easily be integrated, or a user alerted to the variation. But in a printed bibliography or traditional card catalog, you get the information—warts and all. You may receive no tip-off to a spelling variant, or worse yet, never see the notation telling you about it.

Traditionally, large libraries have had difficulty keeping their card catalogs up to date not only because they buy books faster than they can catalog them, but because of routine housekeeping chores. Imagine the task of manually updating the files for the huge number of books in the New York Public Library (one of the five largest in the country) when the term EUROPEAN WAR was changed to WORLD WAR I. The prospect of erasing and retyping the new heading on hundreds of catalog cards, or producing completely new cards, is prohibitive for library staffs in terms of time and labor. That's why such changes are seldom made in large libraries. A Band-Aid solution such as a cross reference is often applied instead: WORLD WAR I see EUROPEAN WAR, 1914-1918.

Unfortunately, "See" references don't satisfactorily solve the problem of changing terminology. Eventually, computers will make that change not only possible, but effortless. For now, though, be alert to cross-reference notations that allow you to find *all* the resources on your subject.

UNUSUALLY WORDED SUBJECTS

Another problem you may encounter in your research is that of awkwardly worded subjects—LIBERTY OF SPEECH, instead of freedom of speech, INTERNATIONAL BUSINESS ENTERPRISES instead of multinational corporations.

Q. I'd like to get information on a plant we call a "burn" plant. I don't know the botanical name for it, but we have many growing in our garden, and we use them to soothe damaged skin.

A. The chapter on burns in *Plant Medicine and Folklore*, by Mildred Fielder, names several: aloe, scarlet globe or prairie mallow, thimbleweed, hound's tooth, and many others.

Subject Guide to Books in Print lists many books on this subject under the term BOTANY, MEDICINAL. Check these texts for illustrations to identify your plant.

Not every topic is worded as simply as HUMMINGBIRDS or CALEN-DAR. Some are more obtuse and complicated. Your task is to figure out the term and, often, the arrangement of words that is used in the particular reference book or library catalog you are using. It's not always easy—trial and error (and perseverance) work best.

Books on the Securities and Exchange Commission, for example, appear in many printed sources under UNITED STATES—SECURITIES AND EXCHANGE COMMISSION. Books on measurement file under MENSURATION. As mentioned earlier, be alert to cross references and other clues that will lead you to the proper term and the appropriate resource.

Q. I'm ready to sell a business which has grown considerably, but I want to sell it myself without a broker. Are there any books giving advice on this subject?

A. *Accountants Index* uses the term BUYING AND SELLING A BUSINESS. *Business Periodicals Index* uses BUSINESS, SALE OF. Each leads to articles on the sale of specific enterprises such as radio stations or auto dealerships. General articles talk about things like how to evaluate good will.

Books on the subject in *Subject Guide to Books in Print* are grouped under a broad heading, BUSINESS ENTERPRISES, which means you must scan the entire list to find the few books on selling a business. One book I found is *Guide to Selling a Business*, by Stanley Rubel.

Most reference books and card catalogs use terms provided by a standard list so each library uses similar terminology. Unfortunately, two major sets of standards exist. Small libraries use the *Sears List of Subject Headings* and large libraries use the *Library of Congress Subject Headings*.

The reason for the two standards is that large libraries have different needs from small libraries. Large libraries have more books on more subjects and therefore have a definite need to finely subdivide book topics. A small library, on the other hand, may have so few books on Italy that it simply files them all under ITALY. A large library with more books on the subject will prefer more precise subdivisions such as ITALY—EDUCATION, ITALY—HISTORY, etc.

Special libraries also have needs different from general libraries. Medical libraries use specific medical terms for subject headings, those suited to the kind of books they buy and which are not prevalent in public libraries.

Despite good intentions and attempts to standardize subject headings, finding a resource you need can be a major effort. Someone will still do things his own way, and as a result, nailing down the term that leads you to an answer may test your ingenuity.

When you're struggling with the proper subject term to search, or you decide the search is just taking too long, try this shortcut. Check the copyright page of a book you already know on that subject. A copy of the catalog information (called Library of Congress Cataloging in Publication Data) is printed on it.[1]

At the bottom of the entry is a list of subject terms. It tells you what subjects the book is about and also how the subject headings are worded. The same information is found on a printed catalog card. (See item *10* in catalog card format below.)

This is the standard format of a printed catalog card. The format of computer and microfilm catalogs varies slightly, but all the following information is provided.

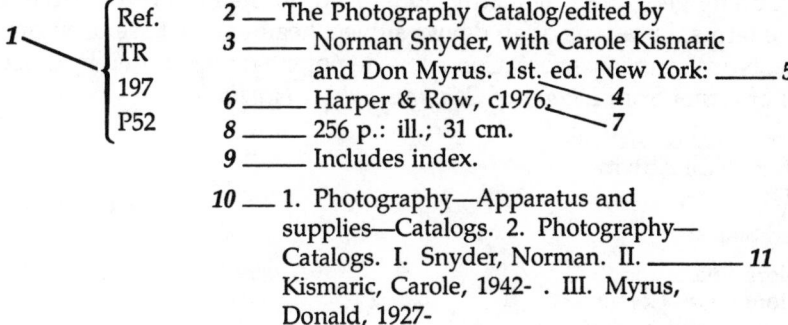

1 – Call number
2 – Title
3 – Author, editor, or compiler
4 – Edition
5 – Place of publication
6 – Publisher
7 – Copyright date
8 – Collation (number of pages, illustrations, charts, tables, etc., width of the book in centimeters. The physical description helps distinguish among editions.)
9 – Notes
10 – Subject tracings (those with Arabic numbers; they're selected by the book's cataloger from a standard list).
11 – Added entries (those with Roman numbers; these most often record a coauthor's name).

Some subjects are really spin-offs of others, or they're contained within them. This is a problem when you limit your search to one very specific phrase. Maybe the term you're using is not valid or standard.

---

[1]This applies only to the books of publishers who participate in this cataloging program which began in 1971. There are currently about 1,800 publishers cooperating in this venture; this means that about 75 percent of trade books published in the United States are covered by the program.

Q. Where can I find information on a breed of dog called the pit bull?
A. There is no information under that term. The dictionary explains that pit bull is another name for bull terrier under which there is a great deal of information. *Subject Guide to Books in Print* has several books under DOGS-BREEDS-BULL TERRIERS. One of them is *This is the American Pit Bull Terrier*, by Richard Stratton.

Other problems with subject terminology involve the use of apparently ambiguous phrases, constructions that seem incongruous, and overlapping geographical subdivisions. And, in their effort to precisely define terms, librarians often devise subject headings that seem synonymous. No system is perfect. Consider the potential traps posed by these pairs of terms from *Library of Congress Subject Headings:*

Students-Political Activity
Youth-Political Activity

America
United States

Folk-lore-Charleston, S.C.
Folk-lore-South Carolina
Folk-lore-Southern States

IN DEFENSE OF SUBJECT HEADINGS

Several years ago I read a magazine article by Ralph Nader criticizing the then Ma Bell for creating too many Yellow Page headings to force businesses to buy more advertising. He asserted that appliance or bedding dealers, with a separate category under which to advertise, might be forced to consider additional advertising under a general category like FURNITURE.

I saw this problem differently. To a librarian, it points out the difficulties inherent in creating "The Perfect Subject Heading" and assigning books, or in this case, businesses, to their proper category. After all, what would furniture dealers do if they had no general category under which to advertise? Should the existence of the FURNITURE heading be interpreted as coercion against bedding or appliance dealers who might then be faced with another choice?

In libraries, extra points of entry—additional subject headings and authors—are made to cover other options. Even so, oversights or disagreements of judgment in selecting the appropriate subject terms and call numbers still occur. There's a story that points out the difficulties book catalogers have in assigning some books to the "proper" subject classification.

It is said that not only will two catalogers disagree with one another on how/where a book should be classified, but the same cataloger may disagree with *herself* a few days later. (Is a book on educational psychology better shelved with books on education or psychology? Should a book on religious hymns be shelved with books on religion or music?)

A law student once asked me why the library didn't supply another copy of a book on each subject shelf where it would logically fit. He wanted to know why you couldn't put one copy of an ancient Israeli art book on the art shelves and another on the archaeology shelves. It sounds reasonable, but with an average of two to three subjects a book could reasonably accommodate, a library could swell to double or triple its present size.

Filing Rules

Alphabetizing titles or other terms is not as simple as it seems. Contrary to everything you've ever learned, B does not always follow A. Two different filing systems, resulting in different arrangements of terms, coexist in printed catalogs, indexes, and reference books. These filing systems are called WORD-BY-WORD and LETTER-BY-LETTER.

The WORD-BY-WORD filing arrangement observes spaces between words and punctuation marks. (Most large libraries also use a "form" subarrangement of person/place/thing which is very confusing unless you happen to know the rules it follows.) The WORD-BY-WORD system yields the arrangement below.

> Economics-History
> Economics-History-Bibliography
> Economics-History-Congresses
> Economics-History-To 1800
> Economics-History-19th C.
> Economics-History-20th C.
> Economics-History-Argentine Republic
> Economics-History-Europe
> Economics-History-France
> Economics-History-U.S.
> Economics-France-History

The rule here (there are other rules in other kinds of examples), if you're into that sort of thing, goes like this: After the first dash (ECONOMICS-. . .) the terms follow the sequence "what, when, where." Therefore, you would have something like this:

> ECONOMICS-HISTORY   [what]*
> ECONOMICS-1965-   [when]
> ECONOMICS-FRANCE   [where]

The rule after the *second* dash also follows "what, when, and where."

---

*Brackets, in library language, means the information did not appear in the book cited but instead was determined from other sources.

See? No alphabetical order because ECONOMICS-HISTORY [what] comes before ECONOMICS-FRANCE [where]. These rules make sense provided you know them. But they're not self-explanatory. (And the "rules" are even harder to see when the subject headings are aligned as they are in a card catalog.)

I've always maintained that if a library staff needs a 100-page manual and weeks of instruction to learn the complicated WORD-BY-WORD filing rules, then how can libraries turn the public loose on the catalog with no help at all?

The LETTER-BY-LETTER system considers each letter in the order in which it appears and ignores all punctuation, spaces, references to chronology, etc., as in the Economics-History example. Despite a certain lack of logic attributed to it by detractors, the LETTER-BY-LETTER system is still the one researchers automatically follow, and, therefore, the one they usually prefer. Unfortunately, not all printed resources oblige. Compare the alphabetical arrangement of the same list of books below according to the two filing systems.

TITLE WORD-BY-WORD:	TITLE LETTER-BY-LETTER:
Three Paths Along a River	*The Threefold State*
Three Philosophers	*Three Paths Along a River*
3,000 Futures	*Threepenny Opera*
3 Years Among the Comanches	*Three Philosophers*
The Threefold State	*3,000 Futures*
Threepenny Opera	*3 Years among the Comanches*

ACCESS

Now that you've been forewarned about the potential research pitfalls arising from less-than-standard spelling, terminology, and filing system rules, it's time to consider the obstacles to accessing the particular resources you need.

MAGAZINES AT THE BINDERY

A chronic annoyance to researchers is the sending of magazines or newsletters to the bindery. Having loose issues bound together like a book is convenient, except when they've been sent out just when you happen to need one of them.

If you must have an article from the bindery-bound magazines, request it through interlibrary loan (Chapter 6). That's your Plan B. Although the article may arrive simultaneously or even after the return of the bindery issues, it's a chance you have to take.

Magazine and newsletter subscriptions on microfilm will greatly reduce this problem in the future, but not every publication is currently available in that format.

SPACE PROBLEMS

Space is a problem in any company or organization that collects things. For libraries, space conservation is a fact of life. Many libraries shelve very large books (also called oversized or folio books) in a section separate from where they belong categorically simply because they don't fit on the regular shelf. This arrangement may cause a researcher to miss an important title.

When you're shelf browsing, remember to check the oversized or folio section for other titles on your subject. Since many people forget, are unaware of its existence, ignore the notation identifying an oversized book in the catalog, or don't know what folio means, you could possibly find an untouched bonanza in oversized books.

Another space concern results when one subject produces more books than others, causing uneven and erratic growth on book shelves. I recall the time I decided to be a good samaritan and return a book to the library reference shelves. When I got to the space where the book belonged, the shelves were packed so tightly that I couldn't squeeze it in. I gave it to a student shelver, knowing she'd have to spend half an hour shifting rows of books to create an opening.

General crowding in libraries often forces the staff to shift some materials to locked rooms or basements. This creates a dependence on an often inadequate catalog or a librarian's memory for information. More significantly, it removes the materials from your view.

CLOSED STACKS

Related to the problem of out-of-view materials is the issue of closed stacks, a situation many libraries must adopt because of a high book-loss rate and chronically messy stacks. Closed stacks mean that books must be paged by a clerk. The book retrieval procedure takes twice as long as doing it yourself, and you can't browse the shelves in hopes of finding something intriguing by accident.

If you're doing an in-depth project where you'll need several books at one time, it's worth asking the head librarian for a stack pass. Exceptions to the closed-stack rule are often made for serious researchers.

One way to partly get around the closed stacks situation is to use the library's shelf list. This is a special file on cards, microfilm, or computer, usually kept in an employee work area. The file entries are arranged in the same order as the books appear on the shelf, that is, by their subject classification or call number. Getting permission to use this file is usually no problem. It's the next-best thing to browsing the actual shelves.

Besides providing another approach to finding books, a shelf list is an inventory record of every book a library owns. Books may be off the shelf (checked out, misshelved, missing, or sitting on a table), but the shelf list shows what would be there if all the books were in place.

SEPARATING BOOKS ON THE SAME SUBJECT

One oddity often seen on book shelves (and reflected in the shelf list) is regular-sized books on the same subject shelved in two different places. How does this happen? As knowledge expands, trends develop, and people's interests change, books follow suit.

Decades ago, books on sewing and the technical aspects of needlework were shelved with books on home economics, a sub-subdivision of home "industry." When interest in needlecrafts exploded and books on its artistic side proliferated, they were shelved with arts and crafts in a different section. To needleworkers, there was no need to split hairs and shelve books on minor aspects of the same field in different sections, but it happened then—and it still does. Unfortunately, this situation makes shelf browsing only partially successful.

Telling patrons about these changes or quirks in the arrangement of library resources is not often done because of the time involved. And if you tried to keep patrons abreast of routine changes via signs, the library walls would resemble the graffiti in the New York subway. From a variety of experiences and experiments, many librarians believe that too many signs confuse patrons more than enlighten them.

How about using the wooden "dummy block" signposts on the shelves to alert browsers to another place where related material is stored? Many librarians limit the use of these "cross references," because they take up precious book space.

One footnote to all this book shifting. While books on the same subject are being separated on the shelf, books on unlikely subjects can wind up sitting next to each other. (Consider that in the Dewey Decimal system, a book on repairing china and a Beatles songbook would both be cataloged under the 700s, Fine Arts.) This situation is very common in small libraries for a different reason—there aren't enough books in the collection to show the logical flow of related subjects. Take a number of books off a library shelf, push the remaining books together, and you'll have the same effect.

Recataloging books to keep them together in some logical fashion is a nice thought. But it's inefficient, because it is a costly, never-ending process. As a serious researcher, you'll simply have to catch the separation of subject matter on the shelf by searching and finding the books you need through the library catalog.

LIBRARY HOURS AND PARKING

Dealing with the accessibility (or lack thereof) of the books you need is one kind of research frustration. But trying to access the library, within the hours you can get there, can be a challenge unto itself.

Library hours are sometimes a real trap for the unseasoned researcher.

To maintain your equilibrium, always call a library or research establishment before you visit. Public libraries may change their hours in the summer or close on holidays that are different from banks or schools.

College libraries change hours during semester breaks and vacations. Some close early on Fridays, extend hours during finals, or remain open to midnight on weekends. Nothing is more frustrating than traipsing out to a college library at 8 a.m. only to discover it doesn't open that day until noon, or going to the library's special collections department only to be told it keeps hours different from the rest of the library.

Branch or department libraries at a university may also have operating schedules different from the main library. Telephone listings for the college as a whole don't always give all library locations on a campus. The absence of a listing in the phone book may not necessarily mean the absence of another library. Check one of the libraries listed by phone to determine where you should be going and during what hours.

Museum libraries may be closed on Mondays. Historical society libraries, too, have unique schedules. By calling first, you'll not only avoid a problem with hours, but the librarian may be able to tell you where to find material even more relevant to your search *before* you make the trip and THEN make that discovery.

Finally, parking is a potential problem at some libraries. Sometimes it is free (At UCSD, for example, on-campus parking is free at night and on weekends); other times you may have to feed the meter or buy a parking sticker. Public libraries may have limited parking space—getting there early or late may be your best bet. Call first and ask about visitor passes, fees, or special hours when parking is free.

Part of the mystique people attribute to research has to do with the "unknowns" described in this chapter. Now you *know* the research traps to avoid and the procedures to follow to get the most out of any information center. That gives you a head start—before you even begin your information search.

CHAPTER SUMMARY

I. Avoid many potential research frustrations by learning the rules and policies of the libraries you use. (page 37)
II. Learn about classification, spelling, and filing rules.
  A. Knowing the basics of the Library of Congress and Dewey Decimal systems will save you steps. (page 38)
  B. Beware of spelling and terminology inconsistencies in library catalogs and printed directories—Aeroplane instead of Airplane, Pugilism instead of Boxing. (page 39)

C. Watch for unusually worded subjects—Railroads, Underground instead of Subway. (page 41)
D. B does not always follow A. Know the word-by-word and the letter-by-letter filing systems. (page 45)

III. Learn to track down a book or magazine in spite of problems with accessibility.

A. When magazines are at the bindery, borrow your material through interlibrary loan. (page 46)
B. Libraries have space problems; don't forget to check the oversize or folio section in addition to the regular shelves. (page 46)
C. Some libraries have closed stacks; ask for a stack pass or use the library's shelf list. (page 47)
D. Not all books on the same subject are shelved together. Use the library's catalog to locate a particular book. (page 47)
E. Check library hours and parking facilities in advance. (page 48)

5

Before You Begin:
RESEARCH TIPS
LEARNED ALONG THE WAY

You are not born for fame if you don't know the value of time.
—Luc de Clapiers,
Marquis de Vauvenargues, 1715-1747

Whether your research project calls for a quick, straightforward approach or becomes a detailed, in-depth information search, you don't have all the time in the world to locate the material you need. As I discussed in the previous chapters, determining your research strategy and knowing the potential pitfalls in your path are crucial to an efficient search. But time and effort must be considered, too. I know few people who have unlimited amounts of either.

Therefore, before you begin any information search, you should take along some tested advice. This is usually the insight someone else has discovered *the hard way*. Here then, is my bag of tricks—a handful of tips that will save you time and toil. They're the same reminders I give myself whenever I'm looking for answers.

Don't Judge a Book by Its Cover (or Title)

Reference books—even the standard ones—can be tricky. Their titles don't always reflect the whole scope of their contents. In fact, they may include much more information than their titles or tables of contents suggest. For example, *Play Index* is used primarily to locate plays in anthologies, but it also has an appendix giving the number of male and female characters in each play. (This extra information might be of particular interest to a researcher working on a project in women's studies.)

Another example of getting more than you bargained for in a reference book is *Newspapers in Microform: United States, 1948-1972*. This resource actually includes newspapers published since the 18th century. Likewise, the reference book, *-Ologies and -Isms*, doesn't limit its coverage to words ending in these two suffixes. It also lists words ending in -graphy, -metry,

-philia, -mancy, and about two dozen other suffixes.

If a particular reference book is on the broad subject you're research·ing, check it anyway. You may be surprised at the bonus information you find.

Similarly, you may find that books written on the same subject can vary widely. Sound-alike titles don't guarantee the same contents. One book may be short and skimpy; another long and comprehensive. Some books are highly readable; others are not. One book may focus on a tiny aspect of an issue; other books will emphasize global trends resulting from it. *Cook's & Diner's Dictionary*, compiled by editors at Funk & Wagnalls, and *A Dictionary of Cooking*, written by Ralph and Dorothy De Sola, have the same library subject classification number and are approximately the same size; yet each contains terms the other does not.

Remember that the question you are researching is not necessarily tricky or unanswerable. The hang-up could be that you're using the wrong book. It's best to check several titles on the same subject. Otherwise, you haven't really tagged all the bases in search of your answer.

Q. I am looking for the name of the ship on which playwrights Gilbert and Sullivan sailed to America in 1883 or 1884. I also need the dates of arrival and departure and a copy of the passenger list. I've looked through all the books I could find on these men, but none seemed to have the information.

A. I checked through several books on Gilbert and Sullivan at a large library and finally found the information. *The Story of Gilbert and Sullivan*, by Isaac Goldberg, says they arrived in New York City from England on the Cunard steamship *Bothnea* early on November 5, 1879.

The National Archives has most existing American passenger lists covering 1820-1902. They are arranged first by year, then by shipping line. To borrow passenger lists in microform, request forms from a library or from the National Archives, Washington DC 20408.

Know How the Reference Book Is Arranged

Not only do reference books often include more information than their titles imply, they usually must be used in certain ways, or you'll miss the answers to your questions. Many directories must be used, for instance, from back to front. *Ulrich's International Periodicals Directory* and the *Encyclopedia of Associations* are both arranged by topic rather than alphabetically. The ONLY way to find an entry in them is to check the index first.

Other directories are arranged geographically or chronologically. If you don't catch this when you open the book, you might start looking for the right thing in the wrong section. For example, the *Modern Language Association Bibliography* (which lists literary criticism articles) incorporates several arrangements simultaneously. First, it's arranged by country (e.g., United States); then chronologically (twentieth century); then alphabetically by author (John Updike, Kurt Vonnegut).

One Japanese dictionary (*The Modern Reader's Japanese-English Charac-ter Dictionary*, by Andrew Nelson), unlike other Japanese-English diction-aries, is arranged by the number of strokes in the character. It cannot be used by just anyone—unless one knows the special rules used in writing Japanese characters.

Become familiar with any reference book's physical arrangement *be-fore* you use it.

Be Wary of Book Indexes

Just because a book includes an index doesn't mean it will lead you to your answers. Not all indexes are created equal; therefore, not all of them are equally useful. But using an index is often an essential and integral part of finding information. (Imagine trying to find a product in a Sears catalog without one.) And in most cases, researchers would choose an-other book altogether, rather than struggle with one that lacks an index.

Librarians, educators, and other book buyers often use a book's index (and whether it has one at all) as one of the criteria for selecting or reject-ing the title. Indexes vary in quality. Some are too detailed and refer you to scores of terms for which there is little information in the text; others are too cursory and cover only the major points of the book. Indeed, a book's index can determine the book's worth for you. If the book has the infor-mation you need, but the index doesn't reflect it, the book is only margin-ally useful to you.

I recall researching the origin of the Alcoholics Anonymous motto, called the Serenity Prayer. I checked several histories of the organization, but none of the books I consulted had the term "Serenity Prayer" or "mot-to" in their indexes. I assumed the information wasn't there.

Normally, this might have ended my search. I didn't have the time to examine closely any of the books to see if the motto was buried in the pag-es. When, however, in one very detailed book, I scanned the chapter notes (footnotes are sometimes compiled into a list of "notes" at the end of each chapter or at the end of the book itself), as I often do when I'm stuck, I did find a note with a page reference to another book that men-tioned the prayer and its reputed origin. After spinning around for 15 more minutes, I wound up back where I started with the book I first checked. The information was in it all along, but it wasn't mentioned in the index.

(A researcher who eventually writes his own book should take pains to avoid the very things he finds inadequate in other indexes.)

Don't Sabotage Your Search by Thinking
Only One Particular Book Will Do

When people encounter an interesting book, they often want to refer to it again—weeks, months, or even years later. (Usually they no longer recall the exact title or author.) Rather than canvassing the earth for one particular title, you can save a lot of time by realizing that there is frequently more than one route to the information you seek and more than one book that has the answer.

A man once asked me to find a book on the history of currency which he recalled was titled, *Money.* He had last read it some 30 years earlier. I told him there were dozens of histories of currency and several by that title published since then. I suggested that unless he needed that particular book for a reason, he'd easily get the information he wanted from another. I referred him to the library catalog and *Subject Guide to Books in Print* for probable titles.

Follow Leads and Hunches

As I've already pointed out, not all research follows a direct path or takes a single step such as looking up an item in an encyclopedia. You may have to take a series of preliminary steps or do some creative thinking to find the information you need. For example, what if you need the address of a manufacturer, but the only clue you have is a trade name. That brand name should lead you to the *Trade Names Dictionary* in order to identify the manufacturer. Then you'd have to double check the address given there against a recent phone book for the city in which it is located, since the *Trade Names Dictionary* is not issued annually, and some addresses in it are likely out of date.

Finding an answer via a circuitous route is not uncommon. I remember a woman who wanted to know how to twist balloons into animal shapes. We checked several party books. But we finally found directions for how to do it in a chapter of a book on clowns. Don't hesitate to follow up on odd clues, hunches, or loosely related subjects.

Q. I am interested in sewing from my own dress designs, and I'm looking for information on the art of figure draping. Can you offer any suggestions?

A. I discovered that books on figure draping are buried within the larger topic of dressmaking. Under the latter term in *Subject Guide to Books in Print,* you'll find some relevant books in the group of several dozen listed. One is *Design Through Draping,* by M. Gene Shelden.

Know When and How to Ask for Help

After you've researched a question as far as you can on your own and you're still minus the answer, consult a librarian or some expert on the subject. But take care how you do it. There's a way to ask a question—and a way not to. (Incorrectly phrased questions are often responsible for inadequate or incomplete answers.)

The formula for asking questions effectively has three parts: state your problem clearly; tell why you need the information; give all the information you have.

Let's say you want to know whether the Dreadful department store existed in your area in the early 1960s. You might approach the librarian with the question "Do you have the city directories covering the 1960s?" In this case, her answer will be a flat yes or no. If it's no, you're stuck.

But if you had stated your problem differently, you could have avoided a dead end. Consider this approach: "I want to know if the Dreadful department store was operating in this area in the early 1960s on Broadway near Fifth Avenue." Now the librarian knows what you want and can provide a variety of alternatives: old telephone books, old newspaper articles, or a file kept in the local history room on the Dreadful clan who owned the store.

Besides a statement of your research problem, it's helpful for the librarian to know why you need the information. Do you want background on a Sacramento-based company because you're interested in applying for a job with them, or buying their stock? Each problem requires a different research approach. One path might lead you to the *National Job Finding Guide* or the *Los Angeles Times Roster of California's Leading Companies*, while the other might take you to *Standard & Poor's Corporation Records* or *Walker's Manual of Western Corporations*.

What if you're researching the Dreadful family for a local history magazine article, or out of plain curiosity because you knew their daughter? In either case the years during which their store operated may be only part of a larger question. Be sure and mention that to the librarian.

Maybe your real point is to determine whether the family lost its fortune at about that time. This could lead the librarian down a still different research path. If the library has a special newspaper clipping file of city philanthropists, you might be able to find information on the financial activities of the Dreadfuls and the details of their monetary fall from grace.

In my experience as a reference librarian, I have frequently suspected that people ask for a particular reference book without stating their true question. Too often, because of lack of time or a deluge of patrons, I haven't been free to pursue the question further. (It's hard to respond, "What do you need that book for?" without sounding impertinent or crazy.) When there was time to discuss a research problem further, I could usually get the information the person needed, because I explored just why he needed it.

Give the librarian or your expert resource all the information you have no matter how insignificant, incomplete, or meaningless it seems to you. That disjointed phrase or casual remark might be just the comment that helps her most.

Even though it's not always possible or necessary, when you're working on an in-depth project, you may want to cultivate the friendship of one librarian whose service seems thorough and dependable. Over time, she may develop an interest in your project and enrich it with further suggestions and resources you wouldn't have thought of yourself.

Another tip for asking questions of any resource person is to avoid expressing your problem in broad terms: "Give me all the information you have on the Dreadfuls." Granted, a librarian will eventually get you to narrow it down. But if you're making the request by mail, this kind of statement is the kiss of death for an answer. Your letter would probably be tossed out, because libraries are not staffed to handle through the mail those requests that are not clearly presented and easily focused.

Whenever Possible, Do Your Own Research

If you must enlist someone's help, don't expect as much as you'd be able to get yourself. If you've ever sent someone on a "simple" errand only to have him come back with the wrong thing, you know what I mean.

If a librarian asks your surrogate researcher even one clarifying question about the information *you* need, he may not know the answer. The result? He'll be stuck, and you probably won't get exactly what you need.

Not only is it more efficient to do your own fact-finding, it's also more rewarding. You often pick up along the way glorious tidbits that would be unrecognizable to anyone else. It's frequently these accidental finds that provide the best information for your project. (See the section on luck at the end of this chapter.)

Select the Amount and Kind of Information You Need According to the Size and Scope of Your Project

If you need just a little information on the Americas Cup for a short paper, report, or article, check such sources as magazine or encyclopedia articles that provide summaries or brief accounts. Don't try to wade through a thick book when a journal article offers the amount and kind of material you need.

On the other hand, if you're tracing the evolution of an art style, you should be prepared to consult several reference books and subject books that discuss the emergence.

Though finding little or no information on a topic is a potential research frustration, there's a different problem in finding too much information. For an example of having too much information on a subject, check the President's name in a periodical index. How do you select and reject from the volume of material you may find?

Don't worry about using every book or article on a subject for which you need only cursory information. If you're checking a magazine index for articles on employment and you see 25 references listed, you can certainly read all of them if you wish—but you probably don't have the time. Examine the titles closely. You may be able to eliminate many, because they treat a very specific aspect of the topic.

For example, if you're researching the employment patterns of only chief executive officers of large corporations, you can skip the articles on part-time jobs and jobs for teens. Select a few that seem appropriate from the remaining articles and forget the rest. Information eventually begins to repeat itself, so it's not necessary to read everything published on a subject.

Once you've completed your project you may still wind up with a great deal of leftover material. It's not possible to know in advance what you will and will not use, but a certain amount of judgment comes with experience. The more you research, the better prepared you'll be to pick and choose from the resources at your disposal.

Don't Believe *Everything* You Read

It's an old maxim, but for researchers it's a caveat worth heeding. It's easy to become enamored with the wonder of books and the sheer amount of information available. Remember, though, that all the information is set in reality. Not only does it come in a variety of shapes (books, pamphlets, microfilm reels) and sizes (quotations, articles, multivolume encyclopedias), it also comes in a variety of writing styles, tones, persuasions, and accuracies. Any research tool is ultimately only as valuable as the skill of its user. Information, in whatever form, should be gathered and interpreted with care and scrutiny.

I recall a former teacher who told this story about the power of the printed word. A young librarian was applying for her first job, and the crusty head librarian handed her a book. "Tear it up," she commanded. The young librarian stared in amazement and hesitated. "I can't," she said.

We were told the young librarian didn't get the job. The point my instructor tried to make concerned book selection and rejection (not censorship). But there's a message for researchers here, too.

Indeed, it's difficult for some people to part with *any* book, because it's hard to doubt or question what they see in print. But questioning, verifying, and thinking about the information you find is part of the research process. Just as judgment is involved in knowing how much material you need for your project, so is judgment necessary in deciding what to do with and how to interpret the information you find.

Know When to Stop

Eventually you'll reach a point of diminishing returns. At this stage, all the obvious or available sources have been checked. Maybe you have all you need; maybe you don't. But continued checking uncovers little or nothing. (If you're finding suspiciously little information or nothing at all, especially when you think information *does* exist, recheck your facts. Something may be incorrectly copied: a date, a spelling, or perhaps a misplaced word.)

After you've double-checked your facts and contacted every even *mildly* recommended source, it's probably time to call a halt to your search. Another reason to end it is that the information you're finding is no longer new—you already have it. These are both indications that you've exhausted your available resources, and for the time being, at least, there's nothing more to find.

ORGANIZATION IS A MUST

Besides saving you time and effort, the above tips suggest one more very important component of any successful research venture—that is, the need to be organized. Even if you're not organized by nature, you will soon develop good research habits out of self-defense. The most complete set of notes doesn't mean a thing if you can't decipher them. And nothing is more life-threatening than the tension resulting from your loss of an important note, page number, or reference. Not being organized is hazardous to the health of your research project.

So how do you get organized?

Write clearly. Whether you use shorthand, longhand, or your own cryptic system of hieroglyphics, you'll be glad you wrote neatly and clearly when the time comes to consult your scribbles. "Did I mean 'mind' or 'mine'?" In some cases, two words may actually fit the context of a sentence but will provide opposite meanings—raise and raze, for example.

Write on one side of the page, even if you're desperate for paper. You've surely heard the horror stories of people turning their homes or offices upside down looking for that missing page, only to find it days later on the back of another piece of paper. It's also easier to spread out pages and see your work at a glance when it's all on one side.

Use large margins and wide spacing between lines. This will give you enough room to add information and revise without having to constantly retype or rewrite the page to understand it.

Copy the source from which you got that precious tidbit. Include the page number, author, title, and even the call number and library from which you borrowed the book. Don't trust your memory. Copy everything that will make it easy to find the publication again if you need it. Take an extra 10 seconds now to save yourself 10 minutes, or more, later.

Q. I would like a copy of the front page of a Saturday morning edition of *The San Diego Union* from March 1979. I don't recall the exact date, but the article I need appeared on the front page and concerned a young South African woman and her son, Andre, who had a close encounter with a spaceship and six dark-skinned aliens.

A. For this question, I didn't use the index to the *Union*, because it covers only

Southern California news. My eyes are still spinning from checking the front page of *every* March 1979 edition on microfilm—and I don't find this article. The search will be impossible to continue without more concrete clues. (Perhaps it was another newspaper?)

Query a UFO group like the UFO Information Retrieval Center, Box 57, Riderwood MD 21139 or other UFO groups listed in the *Encyclopedia of Associations*. They may know of the event, because they collect, analyze, publish, and distribute information and reports on unidentified flying objects.

I recall another question where having specific, accurate information would have saved me countless steps. It was a question about the theme music from the film, *The Lion,* starring Burt Lancaster and Claudia Cardinale. *The New York Times Film Reviews* revealed that *The Lion* starred William Holden and Capucine. A cross-check in *The Motion Picture Almanac* did not show a film with "lion" in the title as a credit for either Lancaster or Cardinale. An unfortunate dead end. Later, I received letters from many readers telling me that the correct title of the film was *The Leopard*.

Watch people's names. Copy their first and middle initials carefully. Smith, Jones, Johnson, Cohen, Peterson, Garcia, and Anderson are not the world's only common names. Even when paired up with first names, you'll discover three or four clones: Robert C. Garcia, Robert L. Garcia, Robert R. Garcia. Which one is yours?

Genealogical researchers find that in searching through records one or two centuries old, many people have the same first, middle, AND last name. (This is one way errors creep into family histories. Genealogical researchers have told me they have two sets of parents for the same person. The reason is usually that they are dealing with two different people bearing the same name.) It's with good reason that in requests for copies of birth certificates, you're asked to include the person's full name, sex, race, the names of both parents (plus the mother's maiden name), and hospital or birth address.

It's hard enough to track down people whose same-sounding surnames are spelled differently (Kaufman, Kauffman, Kaufmann, Coffman). Don't create additional problems by being careless in recording the specifics of their first and middle names.

Jot down all sources you've tried, even when you've found nothing. When you resume the search some other time, this precaution will keep you from repeating those steps. Also, if you turn the search over to someone else, they'll want to know what you've already checked.

Don't use abbreviations unless you're absolutely certain you know what they stand for. Did that "econ." stand for economy, economics, economic, economical, or WHAT? I still abbreviate when taking notes, but I add the suffix to remind myself of the actual word.

Some books contribute to this problem by shortening names or periodical titles without a key to interpret them. Note the initials and abbreviations in the following:

> Hewitt, J., and Goldman, M. (1974). Self-esteem, need for approval and reactions to personal evaluations. *J. Exp. Soc. Psychol,* 10, 201-210.

> Hunt, M.M. *The Natural History of Love.* Alfred A. Knopf, N.Y. (1959).

It is sometimes possible to guess a journal abbreviation, but not always. I've seen examples where the abbreviation "Psych." was used to stand for psychiatry in one instance and psychology in another.

In the second example above, looking for "Hunt" without knowing what M.M. stands for would be time-consuming. "Hunt" is a fairly common name, and you'd have to go through every "Hunt" in an entry that has a first name starting with M. That drags out the search, and you may have to backtrack to get the information before resuming.

(When doing your own research project, don't follow as models those books that use confusing shortcuts.)

Spell it out. Transmitting information orally without spelling certain words or distinguishing among letters (was it "m" or "n"?) can be troublesome. Following up on what you think you heard is not enough. Over the telephone "b" and "p" sound alike, as do "s" and "f" and other letter pairs.

I once interviewed a woman about her trip to New Zealand. During the interview she told the name of an author there whose works are distributed in this country. "His name is Norris Shadbolt," she said. (At least that's what it sounded like to me.) Since I often follow my own advice, I asked her to spell his first name even though I knew what I heard. She replied, "M-O-R-R-I-S, I guess." Those last two words were the tip-off. I called the library to confirm it. In fact, his name was Maurice.

Q. Can you help me locate the words to a song, popular during World War II? The title is "Mares Eat Oats and Does Eat Oats." I remember the tune but cannot recall the words and have had no success in locating them. Any help will be appreciated.

A. I remember this infectious song, too, but I could not find it until I stumbled across the reason: Reference books spell it "Mairzy Doats."

Popular Music: An Annotated Index (the 1940-1949 volume) says this nonsense rhyme song, written in 1943, became a bestselling record in 1944, recorded for Decca by the Merry Macs. *Popular Song Index* indicates that the full words and music (mares eat oats and does eat oats and little lambs eat ivy, a kid'll eat ivy too, wouldn't you, etc.) appear in the *Big Band Songbook* (1975) by George T. Simon. You can get it at the library or through the interlibrary loan service.

With all your precautions and attempts to be completely organized in your research, mistakes still happen. In a recent edition of a San Diego newspaper there appeared an apology for a previous error concerning Colonel Grey's Chutney. The item explained that the error occurred because a copy editor had called his wife to double-check their cupboard to be sure Grey was spelled with an E. "Yes," his wife replied. "It's G-R-E-Y." Unfortunately, that wasn't the only thing the copy editor should have checked. The product turned out to be *Major,* not *Colonel* Grey's Chutney.

LUCK WILL REWARD YOU

Armed with your bag of research tips and the incentive to maintain an organized information search, you will likely resolve some of the problems you've encountered with past research projects and avoid making the same mistakes in future efforts. As a result, you may even experience some lucky finds. In fact, it's quite common in research.

In 1977, Max Gunther wrote a book called *The Luck Factor* in which he speculated on why some people were luckier than others. In analyzing personality types, Gunther discovered that those who were lucky more often than other people cast their nets farther and more frequently than those who were not—thus increasing their chances of success. In other words, the more times you cast your line in the water, the better your chances of catching a fish.

The same thing can be said for research. Information seekers who seldom visit a library or contact an expert will seldom find answers. In researching questions for my newspaper column, I frequently find answers to other questions (ones I haven't yet started researching) because of the very fact that I use large libraries.

For example, I recall two obviously unrelated questions I once researched. One was a question concerning small claims court. The other dealt with the early history of North Island, part of San Diego County.

In my search through *Subject Guide to Books in Print,* I identified a book on small claims court called *Sue the B*st*rds.*[1] I checked the library's catalog for this title, and in doing so, I noticed a card in front of it by E. Sudsbury (SUD, SUE). It was entitled *Jackrabbits to Jets: The History of North Island* and was written and published locally. It was the very book I needed to answer my question on the early history of North Island. By pure chance— luck, you might say—I had found my resource for the question I hadn't yet begun researching.

---

[1]Remember, there is usually more than one route to take in getting information. In the small claims court question, I'd usually check the library's catalog first. When there's a choice of tools to try, the one you select often depends on two things: your personal preference for certain reference sources and nothing more scientific than using the resource you're standing closest to at the time.

There is no reason why your research projects can't yield similar pleasant surprises. Armed with your own bag of tricks and a basic understanding of the research process, you're ready to learn about the countless resources that will help you corral the information explosion and enable you to ferret out the right answers. The second part of *Knowing Where to Look* introduces you to, or perhaps refreshes your memory about, the tools and equipment of the research trade.

CHAPTER SUMMARY

I. This chapter includes a list of tested hints to make your information search easier.
   A. Don't judge a book by its cover or title; books usually contain more than their titles suggest. (page 51)
   B. Many reference books have unique arrangements. Study their physical layouts so you don't miss any information. (page 52)
   C. Be wary of book indexes; their usefulness and completeness vary. (page 53)
   D. Don't inhibit your search by thinking just *one* book will have the answer you need. (page 53)
   E. Much research consists of several steps, not just one. Accidental leads and tips are an important part of the process. (page 54)
   F. Know when and how to ask for help. (page 54)
   G. Do your own research. Don't send someone else to do it for you. You can't expect a stand-in to answer questions about *your* project. (page 56)
   H. How much and what kind of information you need depends on the size and depth of your project. (page 56)
   I. Don't believe everything you read. (page 57)
   J. Part of any successful research project is knowing when to stop. (page 57)
II. Being organized (copying names exactly, checking spellings, recording resources used, etc.) is the mark of a serious and frequently successful researcher. (page 58)
III. Don't rule out luck as a factor in research. (page 61)

PART TWO

RESEARCH TOOLS FOR EVERYONE

6

Age-Old Resource with New-Age Services:
THE LIBRARY

How people love an old saying!
They are always quoting there is nothing new under the sun,
yet there is something new every day.
—E.W. Howe

It's appropriate that we begin our discussion of research tools with perhaps the most all-encompassing tool of all: the library. Most of the specific reference materials in this book are available in one kind of library or another. For years, this institution has been completing homework assignments, verifying hunches, providing directions, settling arguments, and answering every research question under the sun.

The library of today is a far cry from the earliest collections of clay tablets that served as "libraries" for researchers in the Mideast. Today's library is a mixture of tradition and technology; its collections and services are expanding daily to meet the needs of a demanding public. And this is just the beginning.

To give you an idea of what you can expect from your library in the future, let's propose a scenario. Suppose you want a copy of that old best-seller, *The Godfather*, by Mario Puzo.

You visit your neighborhood library. Although it's small, this library carries 30 times as many books as the branch libraries of the 1980s—ALL of the 750,000 books by now in print.

The books are not on the shelf, however. The clerk searches a file cabinet for a tiny piece of film, inserts it into a copier/printer, and pushes a button. Magic happens. Pages shoot out at the rate of five per second. Within a few minutes, the clerk hands you a quick-bound copy of *The Godfather*. When you're finished reading it, you don't have to return it.

Maybe you'd prefer your book in the less popular microfiche version. (*The Godfather* is reproduced on five microfiche cards, each one accommodating up to 100 pages.) You'll be able to read the "book" on your portable lap-model microfiche reader at home. And you won't have to return the microfiche.

Both scenarios are technologically possible now. When problems with new copyright issues, bookkeeping, and social acceptance of microforms are resolved, we may borrow some of our future library books in just this way.

Although these advances seem completely futuristic and beyond our present discussion, they're really not. We're already reaping the benefits of technology; the result is the streamlining of current library services. There are more options now for getting a book you need and more opportunities for finding the answers you want.

Let's first look at where and how to get a book when for one reason or another it's not available at your library.

INTERLIBRARY LOAN

"Getting a book" is, in fact, the goal of many library patrons. In most cases, you can't borrow books from a library without a borrower's card. At first glance, it would seem then that your library use would be restricted to the library for which you have a card. Not so.

If you have no card for a particular library system, or if you live too far from a library that has the materials you need, there is a way to get your home library to penetrate these political and geographical barriers for you. The answer is interlibrary loan (ILL).

Q. I read an article about a woman who has a successful business designing the interiors of log homes. I am sure she has written a book about it. The local bookstores say they cannot help without the author and title of the book. If you don't know of this book, can you refer me to another on the subject?

A. *Subject Guide to Books in Print* (SGBIP) uses a broad heading, INTERIOR DECORATION, under which I found some relevant books. One is *The You-Do-It Book of Early American Decorating*, by Rose Gilbert and Patricia McMillan. Under LOG CABINS in *SGBIP*, there is one pertinent book, *How To Build and Furnish a Log Cabin*, by W. Ben Hunt.

In *Reader's Guide to Periodical Literature* under HOUSE DECORATION, there's a mixture of articles on all kinds of decorating. One relevant article is "Do It Your Way: Country Decorating." It ran in the April 1979 issue of *Good Housekeeping*.

Back-issue magazines are in the library. Check interlibrary loan if your library doesn't own the books or articles listed above.

Most libraries participate in this reciprocal program to borrow books, articles, and microfilmed material on behalf of their patrons. (Some special libraries don't participate in ILL because little or nothing in their collections circulates.)

Participating libraries will not lend *everything* through ILL. There are some restrictions. For example, most libraries won't lend genealogies, current reference books, the latest fiction and nonfiction releases, very old and valuable books, and magazines. (In the case of magazines, most libraries will photocopy articles for you. More on this to come.)

Q. Where can I find skits by Carol Burnett or other entertainers?
A. Television scripts are unpublished, so they are not available commercially. Scripts *are* collected by the Theater Arts Library at UCLA (405 Hilgard Ave., Los Angeles CA 90024). Although their published library catalog doesn't list any for the Burnett Show, call or write anyway, since the catalog is a few years old. Even so, they are not available for loan or use outside the library. According to the library, the copyright law also prohibits photocopying them. But you can use the materials there.

General humorous plays can be found through *Play Index* under the term COMEDY and other suggested terms given such as DOMESTIC COMEDY. These plays are in published anthologies such as *Four Short Plays* compiled by Edward Thompson, and are easy to get in libraries.

HOW ILL WORKS

Most interlibrary loan requests for books, articles, or microfilm items are sent on their way by computer from your neighborhood or main branch library. (You don't want to know how it used to be done. But picture your request on the end of a dart aimed at a target labeled with library names; now you have an idea of how it was in pre-computer days.)

Today, a librarian may sit in front of a computer terminal that resembles a typewriter keyboard attached to a television screen. Since computers are now commonly used in libraries to jointly catalog and identify the materials they own, you don't have to know ahead of time which library owns the book you need. If the book is unique in some way—if it's issued in few editions or if it's regional, for example—the librarian may ask if you know who has it to speed up the process. (Many of these special books may take years before they're entered into library computers, and as a result of not being listed now, they're harder to find.)

She types into the computer the author and title of the book you've requested. Seconds later, a full bibliographic description of the book (number of pages, publisher, date of publication, edition) appears, then a coded list of libraries nationwide that own copies of the book.

Almost 3,000 U.S. libraries, both public and academic, participate in a joint computer cataloging system called OCLC (On-line Computer Library Center, Inc.).[1] Since all these libraries share the same data bank

---

[1]OCLC first stood for Ohio College Library Center. It was originally created to merge the library holdings of Ohio college libraries. The Ohio system proved adaptable to library needs nationwide and soon expanded to include them. Although OCLC's first function was to jointly catalog books, it's now used for interlibrary loan, too.

showing their holdings in a sort of giant all-in-one nationwide catalog, it's easy to see what other libraries own. Interlibrary loan requests are also processed through this cataloging system.

Before you actually make your request, ask about possible fees. On occasion, a public library may charge for making photocopies (sometimes up to $1 per page), and/or the borrowing library may charge a handling fee of 50¢ or more. The librarian should tell you about any surprise costs and allow you the option of canceling your request.

Shop around. If you live in a large city where library cards cover both the county and city library systems as they do in my area, one library system may charge a handling fee while the other may not. Such are the vagaries of regulations among neighboring library systems. Naturally, if you have a choice of libraries to visit, you'll want to initiate your request at the one that doesn't charge.

Once you determine that you want to get a particular book through interlibrary loan, the librarian chooses the nearest possible library from which to borrow the requested item. (The closer the library, the shorter the wait to receive it, since it is shipped via fourth class mail to the borrowing library.) The librarian pushes a button that places the request at the other library. When the order is filled and the item arrives at the borrowing library, you'll get a call to pick it up. (You will return the item to the borrowing library, and they'll mail it back for you.)

With some variations, this is how ILL currently works. If the lending library's copy of the book is checked out, it will inform the borrowing library by computer so it can quickly send the request elsewhere. In smaller libraries which do not yet use computers, the service may still be done the old way, by mail. In time, though, the old system will be phased out.

With the help of the computer, ILL is no longer the hit-and-miss affair it once was when the borrowing institution requested the book from the library "most likely to have it" and then hoped that it did. When the entire process (including placing the request with as many libraries as necessary) was handled by mail, the procedure could take a month or more. Now it has been reduced to one to two weeks.

Things can still go wrong, of course. As in any organization, requests get lost and librarians take vacations or get sick. Ask the librarian for your library's normal turnaround time. If you don't hear anything within that time, follow up on your request.

NEW MATERIALS THROUGH INTERLIBRARY LOAN

Researchers have been so accustomed to long waits for material borrowed on interlibrary loan that many still avoid the system whenever possible. But things have changed. Not only has the waiting period been shortened dramatically, but because of the greater number of materials now on microfilm, previously off-limits items can now be borrowed. The Boston newspaper headlining the Boston Tea Party is one example. No library would have parted with the original. But now, with the availability of microfilm copies and in some cases paper reprints, libraries will risk lending such an item, because they can easily replace lost or damaged copies.

In the past, fragile items were not only unavailable for loan, they often couldn't even be used if you traveled to the library that housed them. Now, because of microform, you can look forward to borrowing such historical items as *Plain Concise Practical Remarks on the Treatment of Wounds and Fractures*, by John Jones, M.D. (published in 1775); *The Method of Instructing Children Rationally in the Arts of Writing and Reading*, by Joseph Neef (published in 1813); a year's worth of *Godey's Lady's Book*; the Perth Amboy (N.J.) *Evening News* of 1941; and original Civil War pamphlets denouncing slavery.

Now, more than at any other time, you should be looking to interlibrary loan as an unparalleled, bottomless pit of research wealth. This is not the time to abandon it.

RESERVING A BOOK

What about getting books that your own library owns? The most frequent complaint researchers make is that books are seldom on the library shelf when they need them. This is one of the problems that will easily be solved in the future with new technology like that described in the beginning of this chapter.

If a book isn't on the shelf when you need it today, should you give up even without the availability of these futuristic systems? No. You have other options. In addition to the new, streamlined interlibrary loan service, there's also the reserve or notify system.

Through the reserve system, your public library may call you or send you a postcard when the previous borrower returns the book you want. The library will then hold the book for you for a limited time.

If you own a borrower's card at an academic library, books can often be reserved for you even if you're not a student or faculty member. Although the privileges are usually less liberal than those for students and faculty, check those that come with a fee card.

You may be able to initiate a reserve request by phone either at the main library or at a branch, depending on local rules. Some library systems prefer to take reserves in person, because they collect fees (often the cost of the postcard, sometimes with an additional nominal fee) and/or require identification. Other libraries may not offer the service at all. But with the advent of computers and automated circulation systems, a reserve setup becomes an automatic by-product.

If you're an independent researcher, the reserve system in an academic library doesn't always work in your favor. It's common for an instructor at the university to assign certain library books for class reading. He may put these on "class reserve" for all or part of the term. This essentially means that students may read them only in the library for an hour or two at a time. These restrictions allow an entire class to complete recommended reading assignments. But the books are monopolized and completely unavailable for borrowing by anyone else during that time. If you need a book that's on class reserve at an academic library, try ILL or your own large public library.

You may have to persevere to make that first reserve or interlibrary loan request. Some library services are little publicized and infrequently used. Others are so new to a library that some library staff members may not be familiar with them. It's up to you to inquire about how to get books not currently available.

RECALLING A BOOK

A recall system is more common in academic than in public libraries. Under this system if you need a book that is currently checked out, the borrower who has it will be notified to return it *if* he has had it for a reasonable time (usually about two or three weeks). This system is especially geared to academic libraries for two reasons: First, faculty and graduate students may have an unlimited or longer-than-normal borrowing period. As a result, they sometimes forget to return books they are no longer using. Second, student demand for certain books is extremely high. Some titles are often needed simultaneously by several people to fulfill course requirements.

Q. I have a library card at a local college library and cannot decide which system for getting unavailable books is fastest: the recall system or borrowing the book through interlibrary loan.

A. The recall system, common in academic libraries, depends on the cooperation of the person who has the book. It may take a few days or a few weeks for the book to be returned. If the borrower happens to be a professor who is on sabbatical, he might not even see the notice. After two or three weeks of waiting, I'd try another way to get the book.

With the help of computers, the interlibrary loan system is faster than ever these days. But if the book is already checked out at the library from which it is being requested, then the request will have to go elsewhere. The more times it has to travel, the longer it takes for you to get your book.

I don't usually like to recommend initiating two requests simultaneously, but if you desperately need a book in a hurry, place requests through the recall method and interlibrary loan at the same time, in hopes one of them will work quickly. When you get the book through one system, don't forget to cancel the other request. It will be appreciated.

WHAT'S A REFERENCE BOOK?

Generally, librarians select as "reference" those books that provide quick answers and are not assumed to be needed by library patrons for extended use. They are books not usually read from cover to cover. (These are the reference books—almanacs, directories, dictionaries—that you will use for much of the "quick-and-dirty" research described in Chapter 3.)

If a library provides a reference service whereby a librarian answers questions for people who come in or call, it needs a certain basic collection of reference books that give ready answers.

For example, one of the most frequently asked questions in libraries concerns addresses. People want to know how to contact rock star Michael Jackson, an art gallery handling Eskimo art, the French Embassy in Washington, DC, or a group of first-day-cover collectors. For this reason, dozens of directories with names, addresses, facts, and figures are kept in reference collections: directories like the *Handbook of Private Schools, International Film & TV Yearbook, Graduate Study in Psychology, National Directory of College Athletics, National Roster of Black Elected Officials, Yearbook of International Organizations,* ad infinitum.

Designating certain books as "reference" is not an exact science. Reference departments create guidelines to follow, but some of them are subject to interpretation. Some librarians, for example, choose books of essays for their reference sections, because they contain lengthy bibliographies, even though they also include lengthy essays which can't be read quickly.

All reference books don't fit a neat definition of "reference." Librarians select publications that consist primarily of facts and figures, addresses, tables, statistics, and other lists of frequently requested information. Even with that guideline, *People's Almanac* (which I believe fits the definition) is marked as reference in one library I use, but not in another.

BORROWING REFERENCE BOOKS

This lack of agreement and scientific definition can work to your advantage and allow you to borrow "reference" books from some libraries. It certainly can't hurt to ask for something if you need it. Most people assume a book marked "reference" can't be checked out. But there are ways.

It's true that if a librarian allows a patron to check out a reference directory, it conflicts with her ability to provide reference service. And librarians must have access to the most current directories and reference books, because these publications provide the most answers for the greatest number of people during library hours—but what about after hours? Librarians may sometimes agree to lend a reference book overnight, provided you get it back first thing in the morning. They can do it, because it doesn't conflict with the reference service they offer during the hours the library is open.

In addition, they understand that some quick-reference books can be used for lengthy, time-consuming projects. A travel writer might need the *Ayer Directory of Publications* to check all newspapers of more than 100,000 circulation that carry a travel page. This could take an hour, and the writer might prefer taking the directory home to work with it there. Entrepreneurs might want to use the *California Manufacturers Register* to check all California firms dealing in solar energy products; a student might want to check the *American Art Directory* for programs, entrance requirements, and scholarships at art schools and colleges; an investor might want to spend some time with *Moody's Industrial News Report* in researching various companies.

If a book marked "reference" can't be checked out (even with papal dispensation or your very explicit reasons for needing it), ask if the library owns duplicate copies or earlier editions of the current reference book. Old editions usually circulate. They can be helpful when time is short, if you observe their main limitation, datedness.

Q. I've been writing for months to a hardware store, the chamber of commerce, and a department store in New Orleans about a bread box called the Brisker. So far, I have received no answers. Is there a book listing brand names and their manufacturers so I can write directly to the manufacturer?

A. The *Trade Names Dictionary*, published by Gale Research Co., shows that the Brisker is made by Brisker Products. Besides indicating the maker of a certain product, this directory also gives the company's address, but that's in a separate listing. (In this case, Brisker's address is easy to find, since the company and the trade name are the same, and the entries are right next to each other. This actually means that you can also use this directory just to get the addresses of manufacturers in case another directory is not handy.) The address of Brisker is 2339 Gilbert Ave., Cincinnati OH 45206.

After you've examined the back-edition of the reference book and selected the information you need, use the library's current edition to verify and update it.

Normally, encyclopedias are considered reference books too, but you may be able to check out individual volumes, as many libraries buy a set just to circulate. Some articles are quite long and can't be read quickly. The article on libraries in the *Encyclopedia Americana* is a history from the early libraries of ancient civilizations to the present. It runs over 50 pages.

Many large public and academic libraries keep old encyclopedias in the stacks, and individual volumes can usually be checked out. Subjects, like NINTH CENTURY and NIRVANA, and certain biographical and geographical entries don't change from one edition to another within a 10- or 20-year period. So, older editions can be both convenient and useful. (See Chapter 8 for more tips on using old encyclopedias in research.)

COMPUTER CATALOGS

If you're not sure what reference book or specific title will satisfy your research needs, approach the library catalog. If it's a computer catalog, you're in for a genuine treat.

For years, researchers have gotten less than full benefit from many libraries because of manual record keeping. It was not uncommon for a library's card catalog to show fewer books and materials than it actually owned. When I was a librarian at UCSD I once searched, unsuccessfully, everything I could find for information on a specific island in the Azores group off the coast of Portugal. Finally, I decided to identify special collections on the Azores at other libraries in the country and have the researcher contact them directly. Lee Ash's *Subject Collections* listed only one special collection on the Azores in the entire country. It was in my own library, UCSD.

The reason I didn't find it is that most of that particular department's materials were not yet recorded in the library's general catalog which I happened to check.

Because computers are fast, versatile, and take up little space, libraries and information centers are improving their record keeping immensely. Unrecorded materials and backlogs are now diminishing, and it may seem as if library collections are growing faster than normal. Some will be growing rapidly as more libraries buy out-of-print books now issued in microform. But much of what appears to be new material in library catalogs is not new at all. These entries are simply the hidden materials that, because of lack of time, libraries and research organizations had not previously cataloged.

Computer catalogs are indeed ringing the death knell of the old familiar card catalog. Libraries that have already installed them enter all their book records into a data bank by author, title, and often by subject or key word. You then look for the books which that library owns, on a TV screen rather than in their card catalog. For circulation purposes, zebra labels, like those on grocery items, are affixed to the books and to your library card. A scanner automatically enters transactions into the computer's memory, matching book with borrower.

If you use a word processor, you're already aware of the multiple talents of computers. Sentences and paragraphs as well as words can be inserted or moved or deleted at a simple command. In the computer catalog, thanks to electronics, the rigidity of printed or typed card files is no longer a problem. Lists of authors and titles can easily be expanded, changed, and retrieved. Storage space is also greatly reduced. Finally, automation speeds up the actual process of looking for a book by confining all your checking to a terminal in a single location. Running from drawer to drawer is no longer necessary. (See Chapter 13 for more information on automation and computers in research.)

Some bonus services have emerged as a result of automation. For example, a computer catalog can list borrowed books by subject to show topics most in demand in that library. Book buying can reflect these precise statistics on reader preferences. Another plus if a printer is available is that you or the library staff might easily compile a bibliography on a certain subject. The computer would do the leg work and "gather" appropriate titles from the collection.

Finally, different libraries (public and academic) within a county or state can link up so they share a single catalog of books. Local interlibrary lending then becomes automatic and routine rather than a special procedure you have to initiate. With book delivery by van among regional libraries, you have access to more titles than ever.

MICROFILM CATALOGS

Some libraries use microfilm instead of card or computer catalogs. They're called COMCATS (Computer Output Microfilm CATalogS), and through them you look up the books you want. One of the benefits of this system is the same as that for computer catalogs: You can see which books other area libraries own.

Recently I wanted to find books on investing in gems. My branch library owned two books, but they were both checked out. Since my library has no system to notify patrons when books return, I checked the COMCAT and discovered that the main branch of my library system owned about half a dozen. (I was also able to tell which of the other library branches owned copies of these books.)

Before my library system started using COMCATS, library patrons had to call the central library, ask them to check their catalog (in this instance, it would have been by subject), and read off the titles of books they owned. (We had to call a separate department to check the branch holdings, and few patrons did it.) The system discouraged patrons, because there was little they could do independently. Therefore, they seldom carried a search that far, opting to do without the books instead.

Had I done this search through a computer catalog, I would have had more flexibility. The microfilm catalog is actually a reproduction of catalog card entries, and looking up a book this way is subject to the same restrictions as using anything on microfilm. You have to go through the reel until you get to the part of the alphabet you need. Its subject headings, like those in a card catalog, are rigid and not always consistent. But the COM-CAT does offer more information than a traditional card catalog; it gives you the holdings of more libraries.

A computer catalog is still the best. You need only key in the title (or key words) of your book, and a list of books appears on the screen. In time, most, if not all, libraries will have computer catalogs.

Even though your library has automated catalogs, you may notice that the card catalog has not yet disappeared. Many libraries nationwide have not added any new cards to their card catalogs for several years, but they keep them as a back-up system. They won't be removed until automated catalogs are fail-safe. After all, if the system goes down, how will you look up a book?

RESEARCH CENTER NETWORKS

When a librarian discovers that your research question will take more than a routine five or ten minutes to answer, she'll probably show you the appropriate references to use and let you proceed on your own. Occasionally you'll be that one lucky person out of 50 to whom she decides to give an hour for reasons known only to her. She may ask for your phone number and promise to call when she finds the answer. What happens next may be one of two things. Either she'll tackle your question later, or she'll pass it on to a research center that services some or all libraries in your area.

Most research centers are headquartered in a large public library with auxiliary staff stationed in neighboring public and/or academic libraries. The centers exist to handle the toughest or most time-consuming questions, queries judged and screened by a reference librarian. Therefore, the questions referred to a research center originate with a librarian rather than with you.

Librarians at research centers have a slightly different modus operandi from librarians stationed at reference desks in their home libraries. Because the research center librarian is more mobile, she can check an entire library, not just the reference section, in search of an answer. She may also make calls within the community or out of state. She may have access to electronic data bases, a service not necessarily offered at other reference stations. And, in general, she can spend more time on questions. She is, in a sense, the librarian's librarian.

Research centers usually communicate with their auxiliaries and the referring librarian by telephone or other electronic means such as telex. Either the research center librarian or your original contact will call you when they complete the search.

If you want to be sure the nagging question you've taken to the limit of your researching ability will get this extra attention, let the librarian know you're not ready to give up. Perhaps the question can best be researched in another local library with more pertinent materials.

Since research centers are more or less invisible, the librarian may forget to refer a question there. If you don't bring this to her attention, the matter may be closed. Ask tactfully whether your library system has a research center and whether your question can be referred.

TELEPHONE REFERENCE SERVICE

Most large public libraries provide reference service by phone. There are limits on a librarian's time, so she can't always answer lengthy questions, especially while you're hanging on. Nevertheless, a great many questions can be answered this way. (Don't worry about trying to distinguish between quick and time-consuming questions; the librarian will let you know which is which. Don't hesitate to pose any research problem. Often, she can't predict which is which until she starts looking for the answer.)

Try calling local academic libraries, too. They often handle telephone reference questions and usually don't ask your affiliation before handling your query. In surveys of their patrons conducted at the UCLA and UCSD libraries during the late 1970s, the reference staffs discovered, with surprise, that approximately 50 percent of their phone reference questions were asked by community members rather than by their students and faculty. (I should mention that the University of California is a tax-supported university, and its policies may be more liberal than those of private schools.)

No matter which library you call, be prepared for busy signals. You may have more luck during off-hours such as dinnertime. Plan to bring a book or some other work to the phone with you to avoid wasting time. Librarians normally give preferential service to the person who has walked into the library over the person who calls. Therefore, even if you connect, you may still spend some time "on hold."

Be patient. If you're sure the library is open when you're calling (even though the phone has rung 15 times), hang on. Librarians who are helping walk-in clients get tied up and can't always get to the phone quickly.

WHAT TO EXPECT FROM A LIBRARIAN

Reference librarians and library personnel are busy people. They maintain files, go to meetings, buy books, plan exhibits, give tours, and perform a variety of other duties in addition to helping researchers at a reference desk. And just as we mentioned in Chapter 2 that no two libraries are alike, we should also realize that every librarian is unique.

Librarians have different work experiences, backgrounds, interests, and styles. They don't have the same professional strengths; some are simply more thorough than others. The same research question can be handled quite differently and successfully by any number of librarians.

Q. In researching artists of the 1940s, I have been unable to find any information on the life of George Petty or the lovely calendars he painted. Petty originated the centerfold in *Esquire* magazine in the 1940s.

A. The film librarian at UCSD recalls the Petty Girls and a film of that name made in 1939 starring Robert Cummings and Joan Caulfield, but biographical information on Petty is sparse. The Author Index to *Esquire, 1933-73*, lists all issues in which Petty's art appeared as well as one article in the January 1939 issue which he wrote on his elephant hunt in Africa.

Librarians at a large public or academic library may work primarily in one subject department. That means that while they may be whizzes in their own domain, they are probably less familiar with other collections in the library. As a result, they may be unable to make accurate referrals to other material and departments. And because they seldom carry a search beyond their own walls, few librarians make referrals to agencies outside the library.

Librarians who are experts in specific subject areas usually refrain from giving personal advice or interpretations, especially in fields like medicine or law. Instead, they'll refer you to experts. They won't refuse to show you material to use as you see fit, but their real role is to refer, not to advise. (Giving factual answers like addresses should not be confused with interpreting information, however.)

A librarian's experience, or lack of it, affects her service, too. Perhaps she's new at the job, or new to this particular library, and fails to tell you that. How will her command of the collection affect your search?

Maybe the person you approach for help is a well-meaning student, volunteer, or temporary employee. There's a great temptation for inexperienced personnel to deal answers off the top of their heads rather than look them up. RESEARCHER: "I'd like to find out the cost of a copy of a death certificate from Iowa." INEXPERIENCED VOLUNTEER: "They cost about $2." This is unscientific and unprofessional, of course, but it still happens. Every fact should be verified no matter how obvious the answer seems.

When librarians work in pairs, personalities may come into play. One may be sensitive about being interrupted or corrected in public. This could make it awkward for the other to intervene and offer suggestions. Many seasoned researchers routinely ask more than one librarian for advice, because they've experienced a wide range of responses. (They're tactful about it, of course, often doing so by telephone or returning another time.)

You should know that a librarian cannot always come up with answers on the spot. And she doesn't know every title the library owns. New acquisitions and new formats are continually being added to the collection. Sometimes, she may think of something 15 minutes or two days after you've gone and have no way to contact you. (I can't tell you how many times I've stumbled over answers I couldn't find earlier in the day or week, only to have no one to give them to.) It's a good practice to leave your name and phone number with her in case the flash of inspiration strikes after you've gone home.

Despite some of the near-miracle finds librarians manage on some days, they are still human. If a librarian is rushed or tired as you approach the desk, you could even get a wrong answer. I once phoned for the mailing address of King's Canyon National Park, and a very irritable librarian gave me the address for Sequoia National Park. The incorrect answer would have appeared in the newspaper had I not double-checked.

If a librarian is busy when you approach, she may simply point to a book or a section of the library and let you take it from there. Without knowing it, you may miss out on added information you would otherwise have gotten if she weren't busy. After you've followed up on her suggestion, if you see that the reference desk is clear, you may want to approach her again for other leads.

Finally, don't expect a librarian to do extensive research for you. She'll answer brief questions routinely, but in most instances, she'll refer you to a particular reference book or other resource for in-depth investigation. You'll benefit anyway from gathering your own data and likely pick up additional information you hadn't counted on.

Q. I think only five of San Diego's charity balls which began in 1909 were held outside the Hotel Del Coronado in Coronado. Please give me a list of those which were held (where and when) in the city of San Diego.

A. The years 1851-1975 are covered by the microfilm copy of the index to *The San Diego Union* with a gap in the indexing for 1903-1929. The index after 1975 is not yet on film, but it is maintained by the San Diego Public Library on cards.

By checking the term CHARITY BALL, you'll find hundreds of entries to newspaper articles. This particular function is held in February, so that should help narrow your hunt.

A shorter route might be to check with the sponsoring group to see if they maintain scrapbooks and files.

Libraries and librarians are a big part of the research arena. And as the world of information grows, so, too, do the capabilities of its resource centers and their personnel to access, organize, and retrieve information. A library's real potential and a librarian's special expertise are truly known only to those researchers who use them—and use them often.

—————————————— *CHAPTER SUMMARY* ——————————————

I. Library services are expanding daily to meet the needs of a public hungry for information. Changes in size and accessibility of collections, and the broadening of the kinds of services libraries offer, make research easier for everyone. (page 65)

II. There are several ways to get the book(s) you need.
   A. Interlibrary loan lets you borrow books, articles, and microform materials from distant libraries. (page 66)
   B. If a book you need isn't on the shelf, some library systems will notify you through their reserve system when the book has been returned. (page 69)
   C. In academic libraries, ask about getting a book through the recall system. (page 70)
   D. Reference books sometimes circulate. Ask about overnight borrowing privileges or last year's edition of a book. (page 71)
   E. Computer catalogs break down barriers imposed by the rigid language of words and terms used in card files. Both computer and microfilm catalogs tell what is owned by other libraries in an area. (page 73)

III. Library services provide assistance both for in-depth and quick research.
   A. Research center networks are the librarians' librarians. Many libraries have a special staff to handle difficult or time-consuming questions. (page 75)
   B. Most large public and academic libraries offer reference help by phone. When asking your question, be sure to state your problem and why you need the information. (page 76)
   C. Librarians answer questions, suggest resources, and offer guidelines for finding research material. The quality of service may vary depending on whom you ask. (page 76)

7

Research Tools That Stretch Your Mind:
BOOKS

*The real purpose of books is to trap the mind
into doing its own thinking.*
—Christopher Morley in
Reader's Digest, July 1958

$\mathbf{B}$ooks are like people. They can move you to tears, anger, laughter, action—or they can bore you to death. Books *are* people. They're authors talking to us through the medium of print. There's no better way to get expert advice without hiring an array of expensive professionals than by first checking a book. There you will find answers, questions, and ideas that breed better ideas. Books can help you complete a research project, and they can change your life.

Since I began writing my "Reference Librarian" column, my life has changed slightly. My friends now ask me lots of questions they never asked me before. I don't have the answers in my head, of course, but I know where to look for them. Often, I can look while they wait, because I own a set of *Subject Guide to Books in Print* (*SGBIP*), my personal favorite reference book.

My friend, Dave Toman, for example, asked me if there was any information on problems people encounter when working a swing shift. His department was soon to begin working from midnight to 8 a.m. for nine months, and as their supervisor, he wanted to anticipate any problems (especially with motivation) he and the group might expect.

I had never researched the subject before, but I approached the finding of information on the broad subject in the same way I usually do. I looked for books on the subject in my current *SGBIP*, and I finally found the subject heading used—SHIFT SYSTEMS. Two of the books listed were *Living with Shift Work & Enjoying It*, by Michael Venditti, and *The Human Aspects of Shiftwork*, by James Walker.

Another question came from my friend, Lisa Renz. She was enjoying a series on public TV about a British spy who lived during World War I. She became fascinated with his exploits and wanted to know more about him.

She couldn't find him in her encyclopedia and could only give me his last name, Riley. How could she find something to read about him? I checked my *SGBIP* under Riley and found nothing. Then I looked under SPIES and among the three dozen books listed, I found Reilly, Sidney. *Britain's Master Spy: The Adventures of Sidney Reilly.* It was a reprint of a book first published in 1933.

WHERE AND HOW TO LOOK FOR BOOKS

This process of identifying books is an interesting one: It's easy to do but hard to think of. When we do find relevant books on a subject, it's just as we often find articles: by accident. Many of the books we use for information are the ones we happen to stumble across in bookstores and libraries.

There's nothing wrong with using books that catch your eye. I do it all the time. The one thing that we don't do often enough, though, is deliberately look for books when we have a question or research challenge as in the examples above. (That means going beyond checking a library catalog or asking a bookstore clerk if they carry a certain book.) Too often, we let the books find us.

The following example shows how one researcher hunted for books on a subject. I don't recommend her procedure, because life is too short. Unfortunately, this is the way most people do research. This particular researcher is the novelist I mentioned in Chapter 1 (I'll call her Jean). As you may recall, she was gathering material for her Civil War romance novel set in the West.

When I first asked Jean how she found the books she needed, she couldn't recall specifics, because her system progressed from one accidental step to another. She spent three months in a random hunt for books, with two results. First, she didn't get much of what she originally sought. Second, the process of identifying and finding a few books took far longer than she had hoped to spend. After I tell you her search method, I'll tell you how I would have done it.

Jean's first problem was in identifying appropriate books. First she checked the library (hers is a small-town library) for histories of the period. She checked the bibliographies of those books and copied the titles of other books that appealed to her. As I already mentioned, this research plan is typical. It's the spin-off method that many students and researchers fall into—one book mentions another, and that book mentions something else. Pretty soon, you have a growing list of books (but not the books themselves).

One thing Jean found "somewhere in print" was a reference to some government-published materials on the Civil War. She sent away to "the government" for information. (She couldn't recall the name of the department or agency.) They sent her a bibliography of titles.

Then she randomly visited used bookstores in our area and checked the bibliographies of more books. She added the titles she found to her list.

A book dealer she spoke with suggested she contact the Arizona State Historical Society. They sent her, yes, another list of books.

During one part of Jean's hunt, she saw some mention of the University of Nebraska Press. When she contacted them, they sent her their publications catalog. It showed two reprinted diaries that appeared on her growing list, and she bought them.

Because the old diaries gave personal glimpses into the lives of people of that period, Jean decided she wanted to find more. During another accidental hunt, she saw one in a secondhand bookstore. It wasn't on her list, but it was a diary. Since she'd been having so much trouble getting the books she needed, she bought it.

Armed with a long list of books, Jean still didn't have any idea how she was going to get the ones she lacked. (When she explained this to me, she never mentioned trying interlibrary loan.)

GIVING A SEARCH DIRECTION

What would I have done differently? I would have started a planned search through *Subject Guide to Books in Print*. It's an excellent bibliography that lists many reprints as well as current histories. You can find a ton of relevant material quickly without a directionless hunt through the bibliographies of scattered history books which, themselves, can be troublesome to find. (Most libraries, regardless of their size, own a set of *SGBIP* even if they don't have many of the books it lists. You can always get the books through interlibrary loan.) As an example, Jean could have checked these subject headings in *SGBIP*: FOOD—HISTORY; TRANSPORTATION—HISTORY; AMERICAN DIARIES.

I would also have checked *Writings on American History*, the index to history magazines covered in Chapter 10. (For more information on researching a historical novel, check the sample search in Chapter 23.)

Then I would have checked a large library nearby to see if it owned any of the books or articles I wanted. I'd have borrowed the rest through ILL.

Had Jean checked with a knowledgeable librarian (many people use the library and never ask librarians for help), she might have discovered that even though most of the books on her list were published over 50 years ago, many have since been reprinted. She could easily have borrowed them through interlibrary loan. If she had checked the local university libraries, she would likely have found some of them on the shelves.

Many writers and researchers already use the largest libraries they can find, because they've discovered the enormous wealth of printed material that exists there—something Jean will eventually find out, too.

As with reference books on the subject you're researching, assume there are books on just about any topic, and that they're available somewhere. All you need to do is to identify them.

KNOWING WHAT'S AVAILABLE

There are between 35,000 and 40,000 new books published every year. (That's over 100 new books a day!) These new titles are part of the 500,000 books in print each year. With those figures, you wouldn't think you'd have problems finding books.

But let's take a closer look. In truth, there's a vast difference between the number of books in print and the number we actually see in bookstores and libraries. A large chain bookstore, for example, carries about 30,000 books, and they're usually the newest releases and the fastest selling of fairly current books. Although large public and academic libraries may have collections of one million books or more, they've often been developing these collections for 50 years or longer.

The table below allows you to compare the differences between books in print, new books, and books available in libraries and bookstores.

Books in a large university library system	2,000,000
Books in an average large city library	1,000,000
Number of books in print every year	500,000
New books published every year	40,000
Average number of books in a chain bookstore	30,000
Books in an average neighborhood branch library	20,000

The greatest danger with having access to only a portion of what's available is that you may assume that books on certain topics don't exist. This misconception is confirmed daily by novice nonfiction writers who, when they propose a book idea to a publisher, say that theirs is the only book on that subject. Yet, when editors in publishing houses check *SGBIP,* they may find several, even dozens, of books on the same topic.

Prospective writers must know what's already been published on their subject. If they complete their books and try to sell them to a publisher *before* they know what else is on the market, they risk wasting time and effort working on something for which there is no need. (The cardinal rule for writers, as well as entrepreneurs, is to find a need and fill it.)

Q. Is there a source that lists the addresses of the bureaus of corrections in every state? I'm writing a book on capital punishment and plan to include a comprehensive list of all people executed in every state since each attained statehood.

A. I hate to rain on your parade, but such a book already exists. A monumental list occupies over half of William Bowers' *Executions in America*, published in 1974 by Lexington Books. If you still need the addresses of the bureaus of corrections, they're in the *National Directory of State Agencies* complete with phone, zip code, and director's name.

Graduate students, scientists, historians, and other researchers embarking on long, in-depth projects can also waste precious time and effort if they can't determine what has already been done. We've all heard the stories of inventors who, after years of work and frustration, without any knowledge of each other's work, apply for their individual patents just days apart. UCSD professor Dick Friedman reflected the fear most researchers have: "It would be terrible to do years of work only to find that someone has already done it."

One way to find out what research other people are doing is to contact someone in the field. Bernice Kert, a Los Angeles writer preparing to embark on an ambitious project about the women in Ernest Hemingway's life (*The Hemingway Women*. Norton, 1983), started by asking her agent if such a book could be sold to a publisher. Her agent thought that it could. Bernice then contacted a prominent Hemingway biographer whose book she had just read, to ask if he knew of any others working on or planning such a project. Considering the extent of the undertaking (researching and writing the book finally took six years), her precautions were wise.

Genealogists should do likewise. They often spend decades gathering the material they eventually incorporate into their family histories. Before you start yours, contact other family members. One of them may already have done much of the same work you're contemplating.

Q. How do you get a Library of Congress number? I am writing a family history and will have it privately printed.

A. The Library of Congress number is a chronological number assigned by the Library of Congress to books they catalog. It corresponds to the number in the lower right-hand corner of their catalog cards.

Write to the Chief of the Card Division, Library of Congress, Washington DC 20540. If you have the book copyrighted, however, you needn't contact the Card Division, as the steps towards cataloging and affixing the number automatically follow. Commercial publishers take care of this step for their authors, but for privately printed books, the author must do it himself.

When your book is cataloged, it will be mentioned in the next supplement of the bibliography, *Genealogies in the Library of Congress*. This is one of the first places a family-history researcher checks to see if a lineage has already been done.

Sometimes it isn't easy to find out what other researchers are presently doing, especially if they're located in other parts of the world, which is often the case in scientific research. It's easy, however, to find out what's already been done. There's an incredible research tool that will tell you.

BOOKS IN PRINT

Books in Print (*BIP*), published by R. R. Bowker Co., is an annual set of books that tells what's in print and for sale this year. It comes in three multivolume subsets—Author, Title, Subject—and is found behind the counter of most bookstores and in the reference section of most libraries of all sizes.

Bookstores and libraries use *BIP* mainly for ordering books. But there are other uses for it, too. San Diego school teacher Dina Naiman recently checked the Title volume of *BIP* for a book on oil drilling. Her husband owned the first volume of a two-volume set. He looked all over town for the second volume but couldn't find a copy. He wanted to buy it, but he was hesitant because he had never seen it. Dina identified it through *BIP*, and borrowed it on interlibrary loan to look at it. It turned out to be too technical.

Dina also used *BIP* to verify a book by Stephen King, *The Dark Tower: The Gunslinger* that was unfamiliar to her. She saw it mentioned in another of his books, and being a fan, wanted to buy it. None of the local bookstores she checked owned it. In the Author volume of *BIP* under King's name, she found the publisher's name and ordered a copy.

Subject Guide to Books in Print (*SGBIP*) is the subset of *BIP* used to identify the existence of books on a particular subject in print during a given year. Months ago, I checked *SGBIP* to be sure *this* book hadn't already been written. Even though I hadn't seen a book done in quite the way I was planning to do it, I knew it was best to check.

I began my search with the term RESEARCH. This rather broad term yielded a list of more than 125 titles. On closer examination, I discovered that most of the titles under the heading dealt with scientific research or writing a research paper. A few, however, intrigued me, and I jotted them down.

Other terms I checked started with the word *library* (LIBRARY SKILLS, LIBRARIES—HANDBOOK, MANUALS, ETC., and others). I found several more titles under these.

I found most of the books on my list at the library and studied their content. I joyfully discovered that none bore any resemblance to my proposed book—except for one thing. One of them had already taken *my* title.

My search in *SGBIP* was worthwhile for two reasons: It allowed me to check my competition to make sure I wouldn't duplicate something already in print, and it prevented me from choosing a title already in use. (Duplicating a title does not violate copyright laws except if it's well known like *Catch-22*, but it can confuse researchers and the book-buying public.)

How to Interpret Entries in *Books in Print*

Books in Print, like other reference works, relies heavily on abbreviations and symbols for repetitive terms. If reference books didn't use abbreviations, the volumes would be bulky, oversized, and hard to handle. Abbreviations save space, but often perplex the user of the book. This sample entry from *SGBIP* will explain some of the abbreviations commonly used in that resource.

1   2
Hudson-Evans, Richard. *The Handbook of Motorcycle Sport.*
3   4   5   6   7   8
LC 78-2771. (Illus.) 1978. 11.95. (ISBN 0-668-04629-5, 4629). Arco.

1 — Author.
2 — Title.
3 — Library of Congress number. (This is a chronological number assigned to books when they are cataloged by the Library of Congress.)
4 — Abbreviation for illustrations.
5 — Date of publication.
6 — Price.
7 — International Standard Book Number. (The ISBN is like a fingerprint. It's a unique number assigned to every book. Each edition of a book has a separate ISBN. It helps in more precise ordering and processing.)
8 — Publisher. (Even if you're not familiar with a publisher's name, you will be able to find it in the listing, because it always appears as the last item in the entry. A complete list of publishers and their addresses is included in the last volume of the Title subset of *BIP* and also at the end of *SGBIP*.)

Other abbreviations, which are not listed in this particular entry, are easy to figure out. Pap., for example, stands for paper copy; ed. stands for edition; vols. stands for volumes. All abbreviations are interpreted in a key in the front of the first volume of *BIP*.

A final note about reading the *BIP* listings. You may notice that most of the entries listed don't include the number of pages in the book. Before buying any book mentioned, ask a librarian to check other reference sources for you (the library's on-line catalog, for example) in search of the page count. You might think twice about buying a $9.95 book that has only 80 pages in it.

USING *SGBIP* IN RESEARCH

The real value of *SGBIP* is similar to that of a periodical index. Both research tools help you identify printed material on a subject. One helps you identify magazine articles, the other books.

Since there are about 500,000 books available for sale each year, and since that's over 16 times the number of books carried by the average chain bookstore, it's well worth a careful look.

Checking *SGBIP* is like using the catalog of an enormous library. The only difference is that many of the books listed may not be in your local library. If a book mentioned in *SGBIP* isn't owned locally or is otherwise unavailable (lost, checked out, etc.), at least you'll know what to borrow through interlibrary loan.

FROM AZALEAS TO ZEBRAS

My back copy of *SGBIP* helps me answer specific questions by telling me if there's any book on my subject. (For certain topics, books published several years ago are just as useful as newly published books. Sometimes they're *more* useful.) I've often used *SGBIP* to answer questions for my "Reference Librarian" column: "How should I take care of guppies?"; "How can I find out if my 100-year-old family Bible has any value?"; "What information is there on careers in the fashion modeling business?"

I found books on all these topics under their appropriate subject headings: GUPPIES, BOOK COLLECTING, AND MODELS/FASHION.

Q. Can you find out how long it took to go by horseback from Pittsburgh to Philadelphia in the 1760s? Also, what types of transportation were available then?

A. There are many books which describe life in different eras. One series contains titles that begin with the words Everyday Life. . . . Check these in the Title volume of *BIP*. A book I used was called *Home Life in Colonial Days*. Books on the history of transportation are also helpful. One is *The History of Travel in America*, by Seymour Dunbar. Subject headings to check in library catalogs and *SGBIP* are TRANSPORTATION—HISTORY, PENNSYLVANIA—HISTORY—COLONIAL PERIOD, CA. 1600-1775, even PHILADELPHIA—HISTORY.

The books say that depending on the terrain, the horse, and the load carried, it could average 26 hours to travel 80 miles. (Pittsburgh and Philadelphia are about 300 miles apart.)

Inland travel before the turn of the 19th century was crude. The horse alone or in teams pulling wagons (or sleighs in snowy weather) was the prime means of transportation. Canals and waterways were not improved until after 1800, although small craft and flat boats were in use. Ferries were still unsophisticated, slow, and dangerous during the flood season.

FINDING TEXTBOOKS

A novelist needn't visit Paris to describe vividly and realistically the Champs-Elysees. Certainly a historian can't go back to the Paris of 1940 to describe it as it was then. Similarly, good detective fiction need not be written only by a criminologist, nor medical fiction only by a doctor. Imagination, drive, writing skills, and research are the main ingredients of a convincing story.

Let's say you're *not* an expert in criminology, but you want either to write a detective novel or to find out more about your legal rights. How can you learn the techniques of police interrogation, the tricks used in questioning to get the truth, the things a police officer can and cannot legally do, the procedure for a polygraph test, or the components of a written report? Spending time with a police department representative might be one way to find out. But what happens if you doubt the objectivity of his information? Must you visit the local police station for many weeks and take copious notes on police routines? That's another possibility—*if* you have weeks to spend.

You don't have to abandon your research, or, as a novelist, avoid certain episodes at the expense of realism. You might try textbooks. Check *SGBIP* where you'll find an inventory of police officers' textbooks. (Text editions are often indicated with the abbreviation, *text ed.*; at other times you can tell by a book's title that it is probably used as a textbook.) Officers attend the police academy, just as doctors attend medical school and plumbers attend trade school. Everyone, including truck drivers and hairdressers, uses textbooks to learn the skills of his profession or trade. My search for information on the police topics above yielded a text called *Criminal Investigation* written by John Horgan, an instructor at San Bernardino County Community College in California.

If you plan to proceed with that detective novel, you may need a Houdini-like knowledge of locks. *SGBIP* lists a text for locksmiths called *Introduction to Locks and Locksmithing*. Further information on bugging devices and the law appears in *The Big Brother Game*. I found all of these books in *SGBIP* under their appropriate subject headings.

Test *SGBIP* yourself. Look under the term POLICE. (Also note the subheadings under that term.) You'll be astounded at what's available.

The selection below comes from a back copy of *SGBIP*. (Entries omit ordering information and spell out abbreviated publishers' names. See page 87 for a complete entry and its components.)

POLICE
>Baldwin, Roger. *Inside a Cop: The Tensions in the Public and Private Lives of the Police*. 1977. Boxwood.
>Berger, Melvin. *Police Lab*. 1976. Harper-Row.
>Flynt, Josiah. *Notes of an Itinerant Policeman*. 1972.
>Reprint of the 1900 edition. Arno.

POLICE—EQUIPMENT AND SUPPLIES
>Hansen, David, & Kolbmann, John. *Closed Circuit Television for Police*. 1970. C.C. Thomas.
>Robinson, Roger. *The Police Shotgun Manual*. 1973. C.C. Thomas.

POLICE—HANDBOOKS, MANUALS, ETC.
>Cappel, Robert. *S.W.A.T. Team Manual*. 1979. Paladin Enterprises.
>Doane, Gerald. *Hostage Negotiator's Manual*. 1977. Police Press.
>Moyer, Frank A. *Police Guide to Bomb Search Techniques*. 1980. Paladin Enterprises.

POLICE QUESTIONING
>Van Meter, C. *Principles of Police Interrogation*. 1973. C.C.Thomas.

Using *SGBIP* is one of the easiest ways to identify books that give inside information about a topic you're researching. Many of the books under the POLICE headings above are typical of those offered by publishers whose books aren't usually found in public libraries or bookstores. These books are most likely found in the libraries and bookstores of the community colleges or trade schools that teach police courses. You can also borrow the books via interlibrary loan or purchase them directly from the publishers listed in *SGBIP*.

FINDING THE HISTORY OF SHOES AND OTHER THINGS

Everyone, everyplace, everything has a history. It's safe to assume that whatever the subject you're researching, it has a past—it may be 10 years or 10,000, but it's still a history. What's more, there's probably been a book written about it. Look for the history of something; you may come up with a real find. Here are some "histories" from *SGBIP* with the term under which each was found:

BOOTS AND SHOES
    Wright, Thomas. *Romance of the Shoe.* 1968.
      Reprint of the 1922 edition. Gale.
BRIDGES—HISTORY
    Boyer, Marjorie N. *Medieval French Bridges.* 1975. Mediaeval
      Academy of America.
    Reier, Sharon. *The Bridges of New York.* 1978. Quadrant Press.
BRITISH BROADCASTING CORP.
    Goldie, Grace. *Facing the Nation: Television and Politics,*
      1936-1976. 1977. Humanities.
CIVIL RIGHTS
    Palumbo, Michael. *Human Rights: Meaning and History.*
      Snyder, Louis, ed. 1981. Robert E. Krieger Publishing Co.

In using *SGBIP*, you'll discover that placing books in a precise subject category is not an exact science—or even consistently followed. You'll have to skim the titles themselves to determine whether any histories on a subject are included. As you can see from the above list, they aren't always in a subdivided category called HISTORY—but they're definitely there.

FINDING CENTURY-OLD BOOKS

Some books, such as the works of Shakespeare, Twain, and Poe, are constantly reprinted. These classics will always be with us. Other books, many of them nonfiction and out of print (e.g., *The Legal Rights, Liabilities & Duties of Women,* by Edward Mansfield, published in 1845), are selected for reprinting by reprint publishers. They're listed in *SGBIP* as new copies currently for sale. (Reprint publishers often create series which they sell to academic libraries—a series on women in history, for example. They develop a series by scanning old bibliographies for out-of-print books like the Mansfield title above; they then request permission to reprint them. Permission isn't needed, of course, if the copyright has expired and the book is already in the public domain.)

Reprints are useful in doing original research. They give perspectives of past times that aren't always seen in current books on the same subjects. For example, a book written on voting rights for women in the 1920s may project a different mood from a book recently written on the subject. Furthermore, many old books aren't loaned through interlibrary loan. If old books were not reprinted, we'd be cut off from many useful resources.

A sampling of reprints on fascinating topics that I found while scanning the Ss in *SGBIP* includes:

SATANISM
> Lodge, Thomas. *Wits Miserie & the Worlds Madnesse.* 1969.
> Reprint of the 1596 ed. Walter J. Johnson.

SCHOOL DISCIPLINE
> Campbell, Nellie M. *The Elementary School Teacher's Treatment of Classroom Behavior Problems.* 1970.
> Reprint of the 1935 ed. AMS Press.

SERMONS
> Annesley, Samuel. *Puritan Sermons,* 1659-1689. 6 vols.
> Nichols, James, ed. 1981. Reprint of the 1845 ed. Labyrinth Press.

SEX CUSTOMS
> Fowler, Orson S. *Amativeness.* 1978. Reprint of the 1935 ed.
> AMS Press.

Whether or not you do a lot of research, it's extremely handy to own a set of *SGBIP*. You needn't buy a new set (currently selling for about $100). It's not hard to find a secondhand, earlier edition in a bookstore for $10 or less. Better yet, get a discard from a branch library that keeps only the most recent edition. Naturally, you won't use an old copy for current information, but there are still many uses for *SGBIP,* especially if you can't get to a large library as often as you'd like.

BIP SPIN-OFFS

Books, especially novels, often spin off into movies. Sometimes books spin off into other books.

R.R. Bowker Co., the publisher of *BIP,* regularly issues several specialized *BIP* takeoffs appealing to different research audiences. Like *BIP,* they are published every year. For the most part, they duplicate the main *BIP* set, but in some cases they include additional subject headings unique to that field, magazines (serials) in the field, and pamphlets. Subject *BIP*s should be available in libraries that specialize in each particular subject.

1. *Business and Economics Books and Serials in Print.*
2. *Children's Books in Print.*
3. *El-Hi Textbooks in Print.*
4. *Medical Books and Serials in Print.*
5. *Religious Books and Serials in Print.*
6. *Scientific and Technical Books and Serials in Print.*
Law Books in Print is published by Glanville, Inc.

When I began teaching research classes to high school students several years ago, I wondered if there were any booklets in print on the topic of library research for teens, as I wanted to use one as a supplementary text. I checked *SGBIP* and didn't find anything satisfactory. (There were a few books, but they were too long for my purposes.) I was quite surprised, however, to find more than a dozen booklets through *El-Hi Textbooks in Print.* Almost none of these were mentioned in *SGBIP.*

In addition to the subject-focused books-in-print directories, there are other cumulations issued by R.R. Bowker Co.:

1. *Forthcoming Books in Print.* (This is used to project the books that will be published within the next six months. On occasion, titles listed here are different from the final version. In some instances, too, a book may be canceled and not come out even though it has been announced.)

2. *Large Type Books in Print.* (This *BIP* lists books currently in print in large type for people with vision problems.)

3. *Paperbound Books in Print.* (Although *BIP* does list books with paper covers, *PBIP* includes all trade paperbacks and paper-cover text editions published in the United States.)

These Bowker cumulations come in handy. Greg Joseph, a reporter at the *San Diego Tribune*, recalls an instance in which *Forthcoming BIP* came to his rescue. He was to interview an author, but to his dismay, found that he had lost the author's book and the time of their appointment. Furthermore, he couldn't recall the book's title, the author's name, or the publisher. He did, however, remember the book's subject, and he said he would recognize the author's name if he heard it. I called the library and asked the librarian to check *Forthcoming BIP* under the subject. The librarian found the book. Along with it came the publisher. From there we got the publisher's phone number to find out when the interview was scheduled to take place.

All the *BIP* sets are unquestionably valuable. But they only tell you about books that are in print. A great deal of research is also done from books which are no longer in print. The way to find out about such books is to look for them in a bibliography.

BOOKS TO FIND BOOKS: BIBLIOGRAPHIES

"Bibliography" is a word with many meanings. Its most familiar definition is "a list of publications: books, articles, newspapers, documents, reports, etc." Bibliographies often appear at the ends of research papers, books, encyclopedia or magazine articles, reports, dissertations, or other works. They indicate which publications were consulted in preparing the material. Sometimes they suggest readings for further study.

A bibliography can also be a book that consists entirely of suggested readings, such as *John F. Kennedy: A Comprehensive Historical and Legal Bibliography, 1963-1979*, the 442-page document on the assassination of President Kennedy. This incredible collection of materials includes references to articles in American and foreign newspapers and magazines, books, government documents, and unpublished reports (with information on where to find them). From the perspective of a researcher considering a reexamination of the assassination, this access to a comprehensive list of previous writings compiled in a single volume is an incomparable time- and labor-saving device.

Bibliographies can focus on any subject. Some profile the life and work of a famous person. Let's say you're researching the definitive work on Benjamin Franklin, and you want to read material published in the 18th century when he lived. Though you don't want to copy information from secondary or recent sources, you don't know how to identify old articles and books. What should you do?

Use a bibliography. *SGBIP* lists *Franklin Bibliography: A List of Books Written by or Relating to Benjamin Franklin*, compiled by Paul L. Ford. It's a reprint of an 1889 publication and lists books (and articles, despite the title) written by and about Franklin dating back to the 18th century.[1]

Another type of bibliography may chronicle an era or focus entirely on a single subject, like costume for instance. Margaret Mitchell eloquently describes the fashions worn by Scarlett O'Hara and her contemporaries in *Gone With the Wind*. Her descriptions of the fluttering ribbons on their bonnets and the lace trim on their pantaloons reflect her careful research. Mitchell may have visited museums or researched books depicting the era. A researcher today can just as easily locate appropriate books and articles by checking a bibliography on costume.

Bibliography of Costume, by Hilaire Hiler, identifies so much material on various aspects of costume that it's hard to believe it exists. There are separate sections on footwear, church vestments, weaponry, gloves—every kind of body covering imaginable by type, place, and time. This bibliography is listed in *SGBIP* under COSTUME—BIBLIOGRAPHY.

The idea of a subject bibliography is to save you the time and trouble of culling your reading material from a variety of periodical indexes, old *SGBIPs*, and other reference books. (Imagine how many sources the compiler checked for the Kennedy assassination bibliography above.) Before you begin your research, try to find a subject bibliography. It will reduce

---

[1]Since a bibliography covers materials as far back as the compiler decides to go, you may have to check more than one bibliography on that subject. The limits of what to include and exclude in each bibliography are a personal decision the compiler makes.

or eliminate a search through individual periodical indexes and reference books, because much of the material in a bibliography will duplicate it.

Q. I'd like to locate a book I recall reading as a child. It was on the history of Wilkes-Barre, Pa. I don't have the title or the author.

A. A four-volume set called *United States Local Histories in the Library of Congress: A Bibliography* is a reliable source for naming such histories. It shows over a dozen of them published in the past century about Wilkes-Barre. Many are pamphlets with less than 60 pages. The largest publication is Oscar Jewell Harvey's six-volume set published between 1909 and 1930 called *History of Wilkes-Barre*. Some volumes in this set are biographical sketches of prominent citizens and genealogical material.

The above bibliography will save you the trouble of checking the individual volumes of a reference set called *Cumulative Book Index*. In addition, *CBI* misses many of the pamphlets the bibliography lists. The book you're referring to is likely one of those mentioned in *United States Local Histories in the Library of Congress*.

FINDING BIBLIOGRAPHIES

Once you recognize the research potential of a good subject bibliography, you'll want to know whether any exist for the subject you're researching.

A reliable way to identify a bibliography is to check a library catalog or recent or back copies of *SGBIP*.

The following bibliographies are listed in *SGBIP* under the subject headings shown here:

DEATH—BIBLIOGRAPHY
>Fulton, Robert. *Death, Grief and Bereavement:*
>*A Bibliography, 1845-1975.* 1976. Arno.

PRISONERS
>Bowker, Lee H. *Prisons and Prisoners: A Bibliographic Guide.*
>1978. R&E Research Associates.

PROPAGANDA-BIBLIOGRAPHY
>Lasswell, Harold D., et al., eds. *Propaganda and Promotional Activities:*
>*An Annotated Bibliography.*
>1969. Reprint of the 1935 edition. University of Chicago Press.

As with the earlier example using history books, the subject categories are not consistently subdivided using BIBLIOGRAPHY. If you skim the book titles listed under the major subject heading, and there *is* a bibliography in print on that subject, you'll find it.

When you verify that a bibliography for your research topic exists, the next step is to find a library that owns it. Since small branch libraries are not research-oriented, they usually don't own subject bibliographies. The larger the library, the greater the chance they'll have some. Bibliographies that cover broad topics—religion or English literature, for example—are often kept in the library's reference section and can't be checked out. Others dealing with specific people such as Emily Dickinson or specific subjects such as wind power usually circulate. If the bibliography you need is not available in a library near you, try to borrow it through interlibrary loan.

PUBLISHED CARD CATALOGS

Another useful resource to consult in your search for books is the card catalog of a special library. Many such catalogs are available in book form. More than 350 card-catalog compilations are published by G.K. Hall & Co. of Boston, and many are available in large libraries. (Each page of a G.K. Hall catalog consists of a reproduction of as many as 40 catalog cards which have been laid out flat and photographed.)

Since many special libraries catalog articles as well as books, and because special libraries collect so extensively in a particular field or subject, G.K. Hall catalogs serve as effective subject bibliographies, especially on topics where existing bibliographies and indexes are incomplete or inadequate.

Q. Who are some of the authors or anthropologists who have written on or studied the pueblo of Tesuque, New Mexico?

A. Tesuque, a village of less than 500 people according to *Webster's New Geographical Dictionary,* is located in the Sangre de Cristo Mountains, seven miles north of Santa Fe. It is known for its pottery making and painting.

The best anthropology "index" is the multivolume *Subject Catalogue of the Peabody Museum of Archaeology and Ethnology of Harvard University,* published by G.K. Hall of Boston. It lists both articles and books dealing with life in Tesuque. Check this catalog in a large library.

G.K. Hall catalogs come in a variety of subjects and set sizes. If you're working on a World War II project, for example, you might check G.K. Hall's three-volume *Subject Catalog of the World War II Collection of the New York Public Library.* If you want to research an anthropology topic, try the 50-plus volume set, entitled *Author and Subject Catalogues of the Library of the Peabody Museum of Archaeology and Ethnology of Harvard University.* (This G.K. Hall resource lists more articles in the field than any anthropology index I have ever used.)

The small sample of G.K. Hall catalogs below shows the variety of disciplines for which there are special "subject bibliographies."[2]

1. *Automotive History Collection of the Detroit Public Library.* Two volumes. 1966.

2. *Catalog of Periodical Literature in the Social and Behavioral Sciences Section, Library of the Institute for Sex Research, Indiana University.* Four volumes. 1975.

3. *Catalog of the Foreign Relations Library, Council on Foreign Relations, Inc. New York.* Nine volumes. 1969.

4. *Catalog of the Naval Observatory Library, Washington, D.C.* Six volumes. 1976.

5. *Manuscripts of the American Revolution in the Boston Public Library.* One volume. 1968.

6. *Woods Hole Oceanographic Index, Woods Hole, Mass.* Fifteen volumes. 1946-73.

Despite their publication dates, many of the G.K. Hall catalogs are still in print, and they're listed in *SGBIP* under the appropriate subject term. G.K. Hall also issues an annual publisher's catalog showing all titles the firm has published. (Some libraries keep it in their reference section.) Hall catalogs are further mentioned along with other publishers' directories of holdings at the end of a library's listing in Lee Ash's *Subject Collections.* Therefore, if you're looking for a special oceanography collection in the country, you will find a listing in Ash's *Subject Collections* for the Scripps Institution of Oceanography in La Jolla, California. You'll also notice that at the bottom of Scripps's entry, there's a reference to G.K. Hall's *Catalogs of the Scripps Institution of Oceanography Library.* If a large library near you owns that set, you'll be able to see what Scripps owns as well as use it as a subject bibliography for oceanography and marine sciences.

BUYING OUT-OF-PRINT BOOKS

If you're involved in a long research project, you might consider buying instead of borrowing some of the books you've identified. If the books are out of print (OP), you might assume you can't get them, except accidentally by finding them in bookstores. (An OP book is one which the publisher no longer has in stock. The publisher may no longer be in business, either.) There is, however, a specific approach to take for finding out-of-print books you can buy.

Ask a secondhand book dealer to find them for you. Most secondhand book dealers offer a search service to do this. Through their channels of communication with other dealers, they'll try to locate any out-of-print book you request.

The system works well. A dealer advertises his "wants" in a magazine called *AB Bookman's Weekly.* A second dealer who owns the wanted book

[2]Only base sets are listed here. Periodic supplements are issued to bring them up to date.

offers it to the first dealer for a certain price. When the two dealers agree on their price, the first dealer will quote his charge to you. Since second-hand books are often inexpensive to begin with, even the markups to cover profit and costs keep most OP books reasonably priced. There's no obligation to buy, however, since Dealer Number One has not yet purchased the book from Dealer Number Two. You may cancel the order, or perhaps negotiate for a lower price, if the quoted price seems too high.

One way to possibly bypass this mill is to consult a specialty dealer on your own. If you want a specific out-of-print book on Aubrey Beardsley's drawings, for example, chances are high that an art book specialist may have it right in stock.

Q. Where can I write for these out-of-print books: *The Story of an Irish Sept*, by N. McNamara (London, 1896); *The Pedigrees of MacConmara of County Clare* (1908)? I have no idea who published them. I checked the local library with no results.

A. If you borrow them through the library's interlibrary loan service, provided a library will lend them, you needn't know the publisher, since the library's computer can give that information. To buy them, check with a secondhand bookstore. Most offer out-of-print search services to locate old books. Or, try Goodspeed's Book Shop, 7 Beacon St., Boston, MA 02108, a specialist in genealogy books.

Specialty book dealers are listed in several directories normally shelved next to one another at the library. Updates are frequently issued so use the most recent ones in print. The two directories below should be available in large libraries:

1. *Directory of American Book Specialists: Sources for Antiquarian and Out-of-Print Titles*, edited by R.H. Patterson, 1981. 4th ed. Continental Publishing Co. 1981.

2. *Directory of Specialized American Bookdealers, 1981-1982*, by the Staff of American Book Collector. Arco Publishing, Inc. 1981.

Another tip for locating book dealers is to try the Yellow Pages of regional telephone books available in the library. Dealers in Western Americana should be concentrated most heavily in Western cities; dealers in Spanish language books will mostly be found in the South and the West; most dealers in Amish books would likely be found in Pennsylvania Dutch country.

Q. Can you help me find Ayn Rand's *Atlas Shrugged* in Spanish? I did get *The Fountainhead* in Mexico City several years ago but haven't had any luck with *Atlas*.

A. I checked *Libros en Venta*, the Spanish *Books in Print* and *Atlas Shrugged* has been issued in Spanish. A large dealer in Spanish-language books, according to *American Book Trade Directory*, is the Spanish Bookstore, 2326 Westwood Blvd.,

Los Angeles, CA 90064. Others are located in the Southwest and other cities with large Spanish-speaking populations. They can be found through their ads in the Yellow Pages of their phone books available in a large library.

The Manhattan *Yellow Pages* also shows numerous secondhand book dealers with their specialties mentioned right in the ads. New York has a reputation for having just about everything, and the Manhattan phone book is a reference source by itself. Copies should be available in large libraries.

BOOKS IN MICROFORM

Interlibrary loan is not the only way to get OP books your library doesn't own. A substantial number of OP books have been around for decades in microform sets, but they were hard to find in libraries, because the individual books within the microform sets were not individually cataloged. Therefore, they didn't show up in library catalogs.

Library access is not an easy task, because the purchase of a single microform set of books may mean adding thousands of new books to a library's collection. Now that on-line catalogs are becoming common, the books in those microform sets will soon be listed there. (See Microform Chapter) As more and more microform books appear in on-line catalogs, with the names of the microform collections they are part of and the libraries that own them, they'll be easy to find and borrow through interlibrary loan.

Many book and magazine collections in microform are based on publications which are old and narrowly focused. As these publications become scarcer in their print versions, they are the first to be preserved on microform. Because of this medium's low cost and its space appeal, libraries are buying thousands of old books in microform, books they would otherwise not be able to get.

Publishers are following suit and issuing microform book collections according to category—time period (18th or 19th century books); region (books of the South or the West); or subject (fiction, genealogy, architecture).

I've listed some general and subject book collections to give you an idea of what's currently available. These are also likely to be the ones many large libraries own. (The sets covering very narrow subjects will likely be of interest only to special libraries. For example, *Early American Medical Imprints, 1668-1820*, is something a medical, rather than a large, general library would buy.)

The ones I've chosen represent nearly a fourth of those in print, but more microform sets of books continue to be issued every year. Eventually, all print materials will likely have a microform counterpart. (See Chapter 14 for information on how to find particular books in microform.)

■ *American Prose Fiction, 1774-1900.* Lost Cause Press. (Microfiche). Research Publications. (Microfilm).

The books microfilmed for this collection are listed in a three-volume, printed bibliography called *American Fiction, 1774-1900,* by Lyle Wright (Huntington Library, 1957-1969). The combined microform sets contain up to 11,000 titles, the complete work of EVERY major and minor American novelist published in America between 1774 and 1900. Many of these works, the "junk" literature of their time, were never reviewed and are no longer available in the original.

Beyond its potential for literary research, *American Prose Fiction* is valuable for its historical, religious, social, and philosophical views of the period.

■ *Early American Imprints* (Series 1 and 2), 1639-1819. Readex Microprint.[3]

This two-part set includes books and pamphlets listed in the 14-volume bibliography called *American Bibliography, 1639-1800,* by Charles Evans (American Antiquarian Society, 1949-59; reprinted by Scarecrow Press, 1967) and the 22-volume supplement called *American Bibliography, 1801-19,* by Ralph Shaw and Richard Shoemaker (Scarecrow Press, 1958-66). The collection numbers about 90,000 items plus over 12,000 additional, never-listed titles that the publisher found after the microfilming project began in the mid-1950s.

This comprehensive set purports to include everything published in America between 1639 and 1819. (Magazines, city directories, and newspapers mentioned in the printed bibliographies above are reproduced in separately filmed collections and are covered in other chapters.)

Since the *EAI* set claims to include most of America's published output prior to 1820, the pre-1820 books in other microform sets of out-of-print American books such as *Western Americana* and *American Fiction, 1774-1900* should duplicate it. So far, no title-by-title comparison has been made, but numerous duplications have been easily spotted, and more will become apparent as the books in microform sets are cataloged and start appearing in computer catalogs. This will give you even more chances to find useful OP books for your research.

■ *Early English Books,* Series 1 (1475-1640) and Series 2, (1641-1700). University Microfilms International.

This set is based on the books and pamphlets of the late 15th through the 17th century listed in Alfred Pollard and Gilbert Redgrave's three-vol-

---

[3]Microprint is opaque microfilm and is read on a special microprint reader.

ume bibliography entitled *A Short-Title Catalogue of Books Printed in England, Scotland and Ireland and of English Books Printed Abroad, 1475-1640* (2d ed., rev. & enl. London: Bibliographical Society. 1976-) and Donald Wing's three-volume supplement by the same title covering 1641-1700 (2d ed., rev. & enl., New York: Modern Language Association, 1972-).

A printed reel guide covers Series 1. This guide directs you to a book's precise location on a particular reel of microfilm. This guidance is necessary, because books are not arranged in a logical order (alphabetical by author, for example) on the microfilm reel. (They're arranged in the order in which they were found by the publisher and subsequently filmed.) Unfortunately, no printed author/title/subject guide for Series 1 currently exists.

Series 2, however, is covered by a very useful printed guide providing author/title/subject approaches. It's entitled *Accessing Early English Books, 1641-1700*. (University Microfilms International, 1981.)

Some of the subjects of the 17th and 18th Century books and pamphlets in Series 2 as shown in its printed guide include:

DISTILLATION
>*The art of Distillation; or, A treatise of the choicest spagyrical preparations, experiments, and curiosities, performed by way of distillation. Together with . . . the anatomy of gold and silver . . . by John French. 250 pages. London. 1664.*

DIVORCE
>*An answer to a book, intituled, The doctrine and discipline of divorce, or, A plea for ladies and gentlewomen, and all other maried women against divorce. 44 pages. London. 1644.*

DOMESTIC ECONOMY
>*Five hundred points of good husbandry, by Thomas Tusser. 161 pages. London. 1663.*

DRAKE, FRANCIS, SIR, 1540?-1596
>*The life and death of the valiant and renowned Sir Frances Drake, by Samuel Clarke. 71 pages. London. 1671.*

DREAMS
>*The interpretation of dreams, by Artemidorus Daldianus. 4th ed. 175 pages. London. 1644.*

DRINKING CUSTOMS
>*The great evil of health-drinking; or, A discourse where in the original evil, and mischief of drinking of healths are discovered and detected, and the practice opposed, by Charles Morton. 128 pages. London. 1684.*

■ *Library of American Civilization*. Library Resources, Inc.

LAC is a collection of 20,000 selected books, book chapters, articles, pamphlets, documents, biographies, fiction, etc. that portray the social, political, and economic growth of America from the 18th century to World War II. Much of the collection's contents are duplicated in other microform sets, but its published subject index makes items in the collection very easy to identify. For that reason, I recommend *LAC* highly.

LAC's printed companion guide is the four-volume *Microbook Library of*

American Civilization. (Library Resources, 1971-72). In addition to the subject index, the volume called *BiblioGuide Index* is also useful. It constitutes a bibliography by broad subject.

To use the *BiblioGuide*, first check the table of contents. If you're researching daily life in the 19th century, for example, you'll notice Category 29 (Daily Life). Beneath that are subcategories ranging from "Home Furnishings; interior decorating" (29.4) to "Sports and games; gambling" (29.8). The titles of books and articles microfilmed in *LAC* on these subjects are listed within the *BiblioGuide Index*. Three books in Category 29.2 (Domestic and Family Life) are *Mothers Who Must Earn*, by K.S. Anthony; *Traps for the Young*, by A. Comstock; and *The Young Man's Guide*, by W.A. Alcott.

Bibliographical information (publication date, magazines in which the articles ran, etc.) is not given in the *BiblioGuide*. These vital pieces of information appear in the *Microbook's* title or author volumes. (Whenever a piece of information such as a book's publication date is not in one volume of a set, it's usually in another. These are the common shortcuts publishers use to save space; unfortunately, they also confuse researchers.)

■ *Western Americana: Frontier History of the Trans-Mississippi West, 1550-1900.* Research Publications.

This collection of some 7,000 titles is based primarily on Wright Howes' *U.S.iana, 1650-1950: A Selective Bibliography in which are Described 11,620 Uncommon and Significant Books Relating to the Continental Portion of the United States.* (Rev. & enl. Bowker, for the Newberry Library. 1962.) The microform collection features an assortment of federal and state documents; directories; guidebooks; state and regional histories; memoirs, reminiscences; travel accounts; and primary and secondary histories, many by the ordinary people (sodbusters, livery stable keepers, homemakers, etc.) who settled and built the West. Subjects covered include Indian/White contact, the fur trade, urban development, women, conservation, Mormonism, westward expansion, early industry, and the railroads.

Books are not only a primary ingredient of the research process, they are a stimulus for growth. It's humbling to think that none of us will ever tap the resources of every book; nor will we ever fully grasp how much information is contained in their pages. But there is value in being aware of their seemingly endless numbers. For a researcher, that translates into believing that at least one (or two or three) of them will have that elusive bit of information.

—————————— *CHAPTER SUMMARY* ——————————

    I. Though books are the foundation of many research projects, libraries and bookstores carry only a fraction of the total number of books in print for the year. Don't assume that what you see is all there is. (page 84)

   II. *Books in Print (BIP)* is the information seeker's invisible library. The valuable set comes in author, title, and subject subsets; it allows you to see what books are for sale this year. (page 84)

      A. *Subject Guide to Books in Print (SGBIP)* lists 500,000 books on all topics. It includes textbooks, histories, and reprints of out-of-print books. (page 87)

      B. Several subject-focused *BIP* spin-offs (children's books, medical books, etc.) are published to help you focus your search. Others identify paperbacks, books to be published in coming months, and large-type books. (page 92)

 III. Bibliographies are books that help you find other publications in and out of print. (page 93)

      A. Locate bibliographies by checking your library catalog and *SGBIP.* Also try a G. K. Hall catalog on your subject. (page 95)

      B. To buy an out-of-print book, contact a secondhand book dealer. Also check the Manhattan Yellow Pages or directories of book specialists. (page 96)

 IV. Many out-of-print books are issued in microform. They exist as part of subject collections. Printed subject bibliographies help you identify them, since microform sets are usually based on previously published bibliographies. (page 98)

8

The Old Regulars:

ENCYCLOPEDIAS, ALMANACS, DICTIONARIES, CHRONOLOGIES, AND YEARBOOKS

*As sheer casual reading matter, I still find
the English dictionary the most interesting book in our language.*
—Albert Jay Nock,
Memoirs of a Superfluous Man

The term "reference book" conjures up an image of a book or set of books crammed with information. Actually, this is a fairly accurate picture. And for this reason, books fitting this description—encyclopedias, almanacs, dictionaries, chronologies, and yearbooks—abound in a library's reference section.

But we do these resources an injustice when we lump them together as "standard" reference books. Indeed, they have distinct personalities, different strengths, and a variety of research uses.

ENCYCLOPEDIA HISTORY

Encyclopedias are not new concepts. Man has always had a penchant for organizing information as soon as there was enough information in a subject to organize. The first known encyclopedias date back to ancient Greece. These were created by the learned men of that time to summarize and transmit man's general knowledge to succeeding generations. The word *encyclopedia* comes from the Greek, and in fact means general (enkyklios) education (paideia).

Encyclopedias have survived for thousands of years, and they show little sign of abating. But times have changed. Our knowledge and our world have expanded far beyond the narrow vistas of ancient times. Now there's too much information to fit comfortably in a set of 20 or 30 books. As you will see later in this chapter, we now have scores of single- and multivolume encyclopedias—each devoted to one subject exclusively!

The one thing we *can* say about encyclopedias, however, is that they are obvious. Generally straightforward and almost always available, they are used by students and their parents alike—often when they don't know where else to look. It would be foolish, however, to entrust all research problems to this one resource. Encyclopedias can't do everything. But the things they can do, they do very well.

GENERAL ENCYCLOPEDIAS OFFER VARIETY

General encyclopedias provide information on well-known subjects in major fields of study: the arts, history, geography, science, etc. But general encyclopedias are like flowers. There are roses, and there are roses.

So that you can use the set best suited to your information search, it's important to recognize their individuality. Some encyclopedias, like the *World Book*, aim at a young adult audience; others, like the *Encyclopedia Americana*, offer more in-depth coverage. Compare entries in any two apparently similar encyclopedias, and you'll immediately detect differences. Some sets prefer short articles over long ones. An article in one encyclopedia may emphasize one significant point, while an article on the same topic in another set may focus on a different aspect of the topic. And all general encyclopedias don't necessarily cover the same ground. Compare these subjects covered by two encyclopedias.

ENCYCLOPEDIA AMERICANA	WORLD BOOK
Navajo (3 pages)	Navajo Indians (¼ page)
Navajo Mountain (2 short paragraphs)	No entry
Navajo National Monument (¼ page)	Navajo National Monument (6 lines)
Navajo Sandstone (¼ page)	No entry
Naval Academy, U.S. See United States Naval Academy (1 page)	Naval Academy, U.S. See United States Naval Academy (1 page)
No entry	Naval Architect. See Ship (Designing and constructing a ship) (¼ page, part of a 19-page article on SHIP)
No entry	Naval Attache. See Attache. (¼ page)
Naval Conferences (½ page)	No entry
Naval Observatory (¼ page)	Naval Observatory, U.S. (1 paragraph)

Editorial boards decide on an encyclopedia's objectives. They hire experts in various fields to write most of the articles. As they do with books and magazine articles, the editors decide what to include and what to omit. An encyclopedia's eventual character is therefore molded by the people who contribute to it.

Another thing you should notice about encyclopedias is the presence of subtle biases and viewpoints. These are most evident in an encyclopedia like the *Great Soviet Encyclopedia*, an English translation of a Russian encyclopedia. In the *GSE*, for example, "Vietnam War" is entered under "A"—AMERICAN AGGRESSION IN VIETNAM. Of course, biases are less obvious in most encyclopedias. But when you are sorting through and studying the information, you should know they exist.

In view of these variances, especially among apparently similar encyclopedias, it pays to check more than one in your information search.

Q. Why is the day divided into 24 parts?

A. The most interesting thing about encyclopedias is that they're all so different. I checked four including the *Great Soviet Encyclopedia* under DAY, and while all acknowledge that the earth rotates on its axis in 24 hours, none except the *World Book* tells why. The 24-hour division is believed to have come from ancient Babylonian astronomers who arbitrarily divided the periods of daylight and darkness into 12 parts each. This division was also based on their mathematical calculations of the earth's movements.

Consulting an encyclopedia often yields more than just an answer to an individual question. In addition to the facts, encyclopedias often provide general overviews of a subject and often recommend further reading.

Q. Please give information and/or references regarding the Canadian railway accident in 1886 involving Jumbo, the circus elephant. Apparently, the circus elephants were walking on the tracks in Ontario, Canada, when a train approached from the rear.

A. You've already provided the facts, so I'll contribute some references. In the article entitled CIRCUS in Canada's *Encyclopedia Canadiana*, there's a picture of the late Jumbo propped up against an embankment. The Barnum and Bailey company had just finished a one-night stand in September 1885 in St. Thomas, Ontario, when the accident occurred. The bibliography also mentions an article in the November 12, 1955 issue of Canada's biweekly magazine, *Maclean's*, which you can borrow from a large library or through their interlibrary loan service. It's entitled, "The Tragical Death of the Great Jumbo."

Encyclopedia articles may be over 50 pages long—or less than two paragraphs. And they cover a multitude of unexpected subjects.

Q. I am interested in becoming a chiropractor. Where are the schools, what are the qualifications, and how long does it take?

A. The reference book, *Patterson's American Education*, lists 16 chiropractic colleges in the United States.

A one-page overview in the *Encyclopedia Americana* says that admission to most chiropractic colleges requires a high school diploma or its equivalent. The four-year curriculum consists of three basic science courses (anatomy, chemistry, and pathology) and chiropractic subjects such as spinal analysis and palpitation.

More details are covered in *Your Future as a Chiropractor*, by G. Howard Poteet, available in a library or bookstore.

Q. I would like to know the history of the Passion Play, the story of Christ and the Crucifixion. Where might I find this information?

A. I found this information under PASSION PLAY in the *Encyclopedia Americana*. (Entries for it also appear in others, such as the *Encyclopedia Britannica* and *Collier's Encyclopedia*.)

Beginning with the church service as a dramatic representation of the suffering and death of Christ, the Passion Play reached its highest popularity during the Middle Ages (14th-16th centuries) and is still performed today. The most famous performance is the one which began in the Bavarian village of Oberammergau in 1633. It is performed every 10 years (with some exceptions) and attracts thousands of tourists. The tradition started when the villagers vowed to repeat it regularly in gratitude for their escaping the bubonic plague of the 14th century.

Besides answering questions, providing insights and overviews, and suggesting additional resources, encyclopedias are good mind joggers. If you experience "researcher's block" (not knowing where to start, or coming to a dead end), they may suggest leads to break the impasse. A woman once asked me if there was a name for the fear of writing or signing one's name in front of others. She also wanted a referral to an organization that could help her overcome her problem.

Since I had no clear idea exactly where to begin, I "categorized" her broad subject (PHOBIAS) and checked that term in the *Encyclopedia Americana* for some general background. (I had no preconceptions of whether the encyclopedia would help or what I would find. Frequently you won't find the answer, but you will find clues.) The article came through with the perfect lead and my next step. It said there are about 350 phobias named in a good medical dictionary. I then checked the term PHOBIA in several large medical dictionaries, and the closest I could find was graphophobia, the fear of writing. I referred the woman to books and articles on phobias and gave her a community directory of health care specialists and clinics for further information.

As mentioned earlier, general encyclopedias are geared to various audiences. And it is not necessarily the biggest or most detailed set that best suits your research needs. There are children's encyclopedias, for example, which can be especially helpful when you're looking up something you know nothing about. Volumes such as the *Britannica Junior* or the *New Book of Knowledge* explain complex subjects—nuclear energy, the stock market, or the Supreme Court—in a simple way. Children's encyclopedias (and books, too) focus mostly on a topic's highlights. Maybe that's all you need to clear up a misconception or get your project started.

NEED FOR SUBJECT ENCYCLOPEDIAS

The information explosion has demanded that we rethink the old definition of encyclopedias as "general" reference tools. Today, we have single- and multivolume subject encyclopedias devoted to one topic or discipline (art or American history, for example). These are often more useful for a serious researcher, because they provide in-depth coverage—something not always possible when the whole world is your subject matter. For example, the article on Picasso in the *Encyclopedia of World Art* is longer and more detailed (but still shorter than a book) than the comparable entry in the *Encyclopedia Americana.*

Subject encyclopedias *do* cover general topics, but their focus is specialized. For example, the *Encyclopedia of World Art* and the *Encyclopaedia Judaica* both include entries for specific countries, but the information focuses on the art and Jewish history of those countries respectively, rather than on general data.

Compared with general encyclopedias, subject encyclopedias are less current, as they are revised less often. Some have not been updated for decades; yet, despite their age, they remain the standard in their field. The *Encyclopedia of Religion and Ethics* and the *Encyclopedia of World Art* are two such "standards." Depending on your particular information needs, consider the date an encyclopedia was published when you use it.

Notice, too, that some subject encyclopedias are "general" subject-oriented (art), and others are very specific (photography). Some are technical (*Encyclopedia of Practical Photography*) or geared to a particular profession (*Encyclopedia of Library and Information Science*). Some subjects (animals and wildlife) are covered in more than one subject encyclopedia, and others not at all.

I've selected a list of subject encyclopedias to show you the variety of topics they address. In the interest of space, I've omitted those covering specific fields (library science and photography, for example). I've also omitted the many encyclopedias of less than 10 volumes. (These are usually on library shelves right next to the larger sets or in their proper subject section, so you'll find them easily.)

Subject encyclopedias generally contain more elaborate bibliographies of recommended reading than do general encyclopedias. Also, they include biographies of people prominent in the field or subject of the encyclopedia—John Dewey in the *Encyclopedia of Education* and Edgar Cayce in *Man, Myth and Magic*, for example.

1. *Afro American Encyclopedia*. 10 volumes. Editorial Book Publishers. 1974. (This encyclopedia has a young adult slant and covers black life, history, politics, culture, education, etc., in Africa, the United States, West Indies, Canada, and Latin America.)

Sample Entries: Folami, Raj; Folk Dances, Music and Lore; Forten Sisters; Fort Sumter; Franklin, Aretha; Freedmen's Bureau; Freedom's Journal; Free Negro: Virginia; Fugitive Slave Act of 1850; Garvey, Marcus; Georgia: Black Elected Officials, 1971-72.

2. *Encyclopedia Canadiana*. 10 volumes. Grolier of Canada. 1977. (Covers Canadian culture, life, politics, history, geography, people, and other aspects of Canadian life.)

Sample Entries: Boundaries, International; Bourget, Ignace; Bowfin, Bowling, Lawn; Bowmanville; Bow River; Boy Scouts; Brewing Industry; Bridges.

3. *Encyclopaedia Judaica*. 16 volumes. Macmillan. 1972. (Covers all areas of Jewish history, religion, philosophy, culture, education, literature, etc.)

Sample Entries: Jacob, Blessing of; Jacob Ben Asher; Jacoby, Oswald; Jamaica; Japan; Javits, Jacob Koppel; Jealousy; Jefferson, Thomas; Jeremiah; Jericho; Jewish Socialist Workers' Party.

4. *Encyclopedia of Education*. 10 volumes. Macmillan. 1971. (Covers the history, theory, and philosophy of education. Includes numerous entries for educational organizations; fields of study; and countries, with overviews of their educational systems.)

Sample Entries: Textbooks; Thailand; Theater, Children's; Trade and Industrial Education; Transformational Grammar; Transportation and School Busing; Tunisia.

5. *Encyclopaedia of Religion and Ethics*. Scribner's Sons. 1913-27. (Covers all religions, ethical systems, customs, philosophies, and related subjects in anthropology, folklore, biology, psychology, economics, sociology, and other fields.)

Sample Entries: Austerities; Baghdad; Berkeley, George; Burial; Confessions; Fiction; Hymns.

6. *Encyclopedia of World Art*. 15 volumes. McGraw-Hill. 1959-68. (Covers architecture, painting, sculpture, and other art techniques of all countries and periods.)

Sample Entries: Greek Art: Guinean Cultures; Gupta; Historiography; Household Objects; Human Figure; Humanism; Hungary; Images and Iconography.

7. *Grzimek's Animal Life Encyclopedia.* 13 volumes. Van Nostrand Reinhold. 1972. (Each volume covers a different category of animal: Insects, Mammals, Birds, Mollusks, and Echinoderms, etc. Material is also arranged in chapters rather than in alphabetical order.)

Sample Entries (from volume on Mammals arranged not alphabetically, but in animal kingdom categories): Gibbons; Anthropoid apes; Orangutan; Gorilla.

8. *Illustrated Encyclopedia of Mankind.* 20 volumes. Marshall Cavendish. 1978. (Covers the technology, social structures, art and music, laws, beliefs, and general life-style and customs of racial and ethnic cultures of the 20th century.)

Sample Entries: Kubu (Sumatra); KuKuKuKu (Papua, New Guinea); Kurds (Middle East); Labrador Eskimos (Canada); Lacandon (Mexico); Lao (Indo-China).

9. *International Encyclopedia of Higher Education.* 10 volumes. Jossey Bass. 1977. (Its 282 articles cover an international perspective of the administrative, political, economic, social, scientific, historical, and contemporary concerns of higher education.)

Sample Entries: Philippines, Republic of the; Philosophies of Higher Education, Historical and Contemporary; Philosophy (Field of Study); Photography and Cinematography (Field of Study); Presses, College and University; Prisoners, Postsecondary Education Programs for.

10. *International Encyclopedia of Psychiatry, Psychology, Psychoanalysis, Neurology.* 12 volumes. Van Nostrand Reinhold. 1977. (Covers human personality growth and development from the perspective of psychiatry, psychology, neurology, psychosomatic medicine, biochemistry, ergonomics, and related disciplines.)

Sample Entries: Individual Psychology; Industrial and Organizational Psychiatry and Psychology; Infancy; Infrahuman Language; Ingratiation; Instinctive Behavior; Intelligence.

11. *International Encyclopedia of the Social Sciences.* 18 volumes. Macmillan. 1968-79. (Covers the concepts, theories, and methods of anthropology, psychology, geography, economics, statistics, political science, history, etc.)

Sample Entries: Psychosomatic Illness; Public Administration; Public Expenditures; Punishment; Putnam, Frederic Ward; Quality Control; Queues; Race Relations.

12. *Jewish Encyclopedia.* 12 volumes. Funk & Wagnalls. 1903-06. An early encyclopedia covering Jewish history, culture, literature, etc., up to the time of its publication. It's interesting to note the number of historical subjects treated by this encyclopedia that do not overlap with *Encyclopaedia Judaica.*

Sample Entries: Columbus, Christopher, and the Jews; Cologne (Germany); Commandments, The 613; Commerce; Conrad (Cuntze) of Winterthur; Converts to Christianity, Modern; Cooking Utensils; Costa, Da, Pedigree.

13. *McGraw-Hill Encyclopedia of Science and Technology.* 15 volumes. 5th edition. McGraw-Hill, 1982. (Covers all branches of the hard sciences and technology: astronomy, biochemistry, geology, mathematics, physics, etc.)

Sample Entries: Spiral; Statistics; Steam, Stauromedusae; Steel Manufacture; Storm Surge; Sun; Supernova; Superplasticity; Swamp, Marsh, and Bog.

14. *Man, Myth and Magic.* 24 volumes. Marshall Cavendish. 1970. (Covers folklore, mythology, religions, the occult, astrology, etc.)

Sample Entries: Tantrism; Taoism; Tara; Tarot; Tattooing; Taurus; Taylor, Thomas; Tea-Leaf Reading; Teresa of Avila; Theosophy; Thor.

15. *Modern Encyclopedia of Russian and Soviet History.* (Completed to 37 volumes), Academic Press International. 1976-8 . (Covers people, places, and theories dominant in Soviet history. The set is heavily biographical.)

Sample Entries: Saint Petersburg Treaty of Alliance of 1812; Saint Petersburg Union of Struggle and Emancipation of the Working Class; Sakhalin Island; Saltovo-Maiatskoe Culture; Samoed Peoples; San Francisco, Conference of 1945.

16. *New Catholic Encyclopedia.* 15 volumes, with supplements. Publisher's Guild in cooperation with McGraw-Hill. 1967-79. (Covers the structure, history, philosophy, doctrine, and discipline of the Catholic church.)

Sample Entries: Magnanimity; Magnericus of Trier, St.; Magnificence; Maimonides (Moses ben Maimone); Maine; Mainz; Majoristic Controversy; Malines Conversions; Malmesbury, Abbey of.

17. *New Grove Dictionary of Music and Musicians.* 20 volumes. Macmillan. 1980. (Covers the aesthetics, analysis, history, performing practice, sociology, and theory of music.)

Sample Entries: Olsen, Ole; Opera; Opus; Orchestra; Organ; Paganini, Niccolò; Pandero; Panpipes; Paso Doble.

18. *New International Wildlife Encyclopedia.* 21 volumes. Purnell Reference Books. 1980. (Covers the habits, habitat, life history, breeding, behavior, and distribution of animals and insects.)

Sample Entries: Marmot; Marsupial Frog; Minnow; Mite; Moorhen; Mosquito; Peafowl; Periwinkle.

19. *Standard Encyclopaedia of Southern Africa.* 12 volumes. Nasou, Ltd. 1970-76. (Covers the natural history, history, geography, politics, business, culture, and anthropology of the area.)

Sample Entries: Ishango; Islamic Architecture - East Africa; Itala, Italeni, Battle of; Italians; Jacaranda; Jackals and Foxes; Jade; Jameson Raid; Jamestown; Jesuit Mission, Old; Jews.

In addition to the multivolume encyclopedias described above, there are other smaller reference books of one or two volumes with "encyclopedia" in their titles. They usually include brief, dictionary-like definitions. They are not encyclopedias in the traditional sense, but they use the word encyclopedia in their titles to indicate that they offer a compendium of information on a topic. If you scan the shelves in a large library, you'll find many one- or two-volume encyclopedias like the *Concise Encyclopedia of Living Faiths* or the *Encyclopedia of Psychoanalysis*.

Whether or not these are really encyclopedias would involve an academic discussion of interest to few of us. Most researchers don't care, as long as they get the information they need. If a brief answer or description is what you want, a one-volume encyclopedia covering your subject may just give it to you. You can identify both single- and multivolume encyclopedias through Sheehy's *Guide to Reference Books* available in large libraries.

Q. My wife and I disagree as to whether avocados are fruits or vegetables. Our Webster's dictionary says the avocado is the edible fruit of various tropical American trees, but we're uncertain whether that expression means it's a fruit. Can you help?

A. According to *The World Encyclopedia of Food*, the avocado, native to Central and South America, was first planted commercially in California at the turn of the century. Part of the description reads, "For a fruit, the avocado is unusually nutritious."

ENCYCLOPEDIA REVISIONS

Even though most general encyclopedias are revised every two or three years, it's difficult to determine the actual amount of revision they undergo unless you compare articles. The copyright date of the set is not alone an accurate clue to the recency of the material within. (A publisher needs less than 10 percent textual change to apply for a new copyright.) In truth, most publishers revise only a portion of their encyclopedias because of the high cost of a complete overhaul in the short time between editions.

Entries for static subjects in the arts and humanities—Michelangelo or Charles Dickens, for example—may change little if at all through several editions over 10, 20, or more years. The same article may actually appear in successive editions until a new contributor rewrites it, in which case the emphases, but not necessarily the content, may shift. On the other hand, rapid advances occurring in scientific fields like medicine and astronomy require that the articles for these subjects be updated more often.

Large libraries recognize the research value of old encyclopedias and keep back copies for borrowers to check out. They are handy to use if you keep their date limitations in mind. In addition, branch libraries often buy extra sets of current encyclopedias to circulate for the convenience of reading long articles at home.

NEW USES FOR OLD ENCYCLOPEDIAS

Very old encyclopedias (50 years or older) take on a new meaning in research. Many of the subjects they covered have changed dramatically from the day the volumes were published. Instead of becoming useless with age, however, these encyclopedias reflect the flavor of their time. Much like old newspapers, magazines, and books, they are wonderful for historical research.

Published in 1813, *Pantologia; A New Cyclopaedia . . .* (12 volumes. London, G. Kearsley) offers this charming entry on Alexandretta:

> Alexandretta is the port of Aleppo, from which it is now distant 28 or 30 leagues. It is now little else but a heap of ruined houses chiefly inhabited by Greeks who keep tippling houses for sailors. The air is very unwholesome, and therefore the better sort of inhabitants, during the hot weather, live at a village called Bayland on a mountain about 10 miles off, where there is wholesome water and excellent food. What surprises strangers most, when they arrive at this place, are the pigeons that carry letters to Aleppo, which they reach in about three hours. These pigeons are of a singular kind, and are very much celebrated throughout the east. Lat. 36.34 N., Long. 36.20 E.

Consider the wealth of information you could glean from reading the articles on these subjects included in an 1813 encyclopedia: ANATOMY, ARCHITECTURE, UNIVERSITIES, WINE, PRINTING, PROJECTILES, and ELECTRICITY. In the entry for California, for example, *Pantologia* describes the "divers Nations"[1] in a way that reflects the knowledge and thinking of the day. *Pantologia* also gives a great many statistics and mentions geographical areas which have since changed names.

An old encyclopedia can stir your imagination with fresh ideas as these entries from *Encyclopaedia Britannica* (3rd edition, 1798) demonstrate: BREAD, AEROSTATION (balloon or dirigible), MEDICINE, MEXICO, MICROSCOPE, MIDWIFERY.

But how hard is it to find an old set? It's surprising how many are sitting on the shelves of large (usually academic) libraries. I found the two

---

[1]The article implies that the "divers Nations" are the American Indians; but in 1813, the reader undoubtedly would have known that.

mentioned above in the UCSD library stacks, and I was able to check out individual volumes. Book sales are another place to turn up old sets for as little as $30.

ENCYCLOPEDIAS ON MICROFILM

Though microfilm is often used to preserve print material (as we have seen with magazines and books), there is no strong evidence that encyclopedias are being considered for this format. Though space conservation and the preservation of old volumes seem noble reasons to consider the option of putting encyclopedias on microfilm, it has not yet caught on.

As with specialized magazines, however, specialized encyclopedias that have limited audiences are more economical if issued exclusively in microform. This is the case with the 16-volume *Encyclopedia Antarctica* (University Microfilms International). It was originally compiled in the late 1940s and early 1950s by Arctic explorer Vilhjalmur Stefansson and his staff. It includes articles on the region's plant life, unique climate and conditions, and explorations. In short, the encyclopedia covers the science and history of the region.

ELECTRONIC ENCYCLOPEDIAS

Though microform encyclopedias are not extremely common, electronic encyclopedias are gaining enthusiastic support. In fact, the texts of most encyclopedias are already in computers for easier editing. Those same texts are being developed for information retrieval and manipulation in ways not possible with a printed encyclopedia.

In 1980, OCLC, Inc., conducted an experiment in Columbus, Ohio, in which they offered a variety of home information services known as videotex (banking, access to local library catalogs, educational games, etc.) to the public. Of all the on-line services available in this particular experiment, the encyclopedia was the most popular. However, in experiments conducted in other cities, the on-line encyclopedia was not always the winner. Electronic banking was the most popular service overall.

Nevertheless, the interest is there, and on-line encyclopedias are the wave of the future. Once demand is up and home information services are common (with computers in the home and suppliers ready with such services as banking, classified ad information, theater and sports schedules, etc.), on-line retrieval of information from a person's home "information center" will be common.

The early videotex experiments offered encyclopedia articles much like those you'd get in a print encyclopedia. The user consulted an index of terms on his TV screen and then selected the article he wanted to read. When two-way, interactive home information services (see more on this in Chapter 13 [on computers]) are more fully developed, you'll be able to search for information in encyclopedias in a far different way: by key word. That kind of on-line encyclopedia will allow you to extract information anywhere in the text by using key words alone or in combination.

Contrast this system with the way we currently look up subjects in the print encyclopedia. We now search a subject by alphabetical order, or we check the index in case a term is mentioned within another article. Unfortunately, the index to a printed encyclopedia does not include every term or item of information in the encyclopedia itself. We miss much valuable data that is scattered and submerged within the articles.

For example, you might not be able to use a print encyclopedia to answer the question "When did the infamous 'march on Rome' take place?" because there might not be an entry for MARCH ON ROME in the index. In an on-line encyclopedia, you'd simply key in the phrase "march on Rome," and you'd find it wherever it happened to be mentioned. In this case, it might be buried in the general article on Italy. Similarly, with an on-line encyclopedia you could easily find out which President's wife was named Eliza by keying in the name *Eliza* in combination with the word *president*.

Some of the questions you might ask the on-line encyclopedia could generate a list or chart that did not appear in the printed encyclopedia (although the information for such a list was actually there). The computer would pull information from throughout the encyclopedia to answer these questions: "In which countries of the world is French spoken?"; "How many state legislators are black and what is the percentage of the black versus nonblack population in those states?"; "When did each state enter the Union?"; "What are the winter high and low temperatures of the 10 largest cities in the United States?"; "How many national parks offer camping facilities?" The possibilities seem endless.

Because information, wherever it is, will be easily extracted from an on-line encyclopedia, this version may actually replace a number of different reference books such as dictionaries of geography (cities, states, countries, rivers, mountains, etc.); animals; world leaders; artists; explorers; authors; presidents; and also chronologies of American history, inventions, or aerospace highlights, to name a few.

But for all its versatility and speed, an on-line encyclopedia offers one problem yet to be resolved. Unlike a print encyclopedia, the on-line version has the ability to continuously update information in the data base as it changes. Normally, this would be considered a positive feature, but ponder the implications.

If information does not retain some permanent, nonchanging form at some time, where will our record of history come from? How will researchers of future generations know the life we lived in the late 20th century? For this reason alone it would be foolhardy to dispose of printed encyclopedias and books.

Incidentally, people in the information field don't really believe that will happen anyway. On the contrary, computers have already led to the publishing of *more* and different kinds of reference books than currently exist. Computers can give us the kinds of statistics and lists that hand compiling has made nearly impossible. Now that computers can easily do what we could not do by hand, the newly collected information is being published.

Our need for "encyclopedic" information will continue to grow as will our options for getting it. Whether you're a serious researcher or an expert in finding answers quickly, you'll still use encyclopedias in one form or another.

READY REFERENCE ALMANACS

Almanacs and Bibles were the first books to come to the United States. At a time when there were few newspapers, the settlers used almanacs for a mélange of valuable information and entertainment. Almanacs predicted the weather for the coming year; gave advice on crops and planting; listed home remedies, multiplication tables, interest charts, and even stagecoach schedules. They also included inspirational verse and stories.

Almanacs today have evolved into one-volume, annual reference books that cram tidbits of information into as many as a thousand pages. Like encyclopedias, the information they include may be general or specifically geared to some subject or discipline.

Despite their low quality paper, tiny print, and skimpy binding, general almanacs are the best research bargain for the money.

They are largely a reprint medium, a collection of countless fleeting facts and statistics that we often need, but can't always find quickly: weights and measures, mathematical formulas, sports and Olympic records, population figures, Nobel and Pulitzer prize winners, government officials, etc. For the most part, general almanacs are books of lists adapted largely from other reference books.

Q. On which day of the week did Christmas 1940 fall?

A. Wednesday. Most almanacs have perpetual calendars in them, as do some telephone books. (The location seems to change from time to time from the White Pages to the Yellow Pages and back.)

Though all general almanacs have the world as their subject matter, they are not all alike. Their differences are due mostly to what their compilers choose to include. Once you use almanacs regularly, you'll start to develop an intuition for what *should* be there. As a rule, check more than one before you give up your search.

Q. I've gotten into the calendar business and need information about movable holidays, such as Easter and the Jewish holidays, and also the dates of federal holidays. I need information on the tides and moon phases for the coming years as well.

A. *Information Please Almanac* and the *World Almanac* list legal holidays with the days on which they fall, so you can compute them as far ahead as you wish.

They also list Christian and Jewish movable holidays for the coming decade. Other almanacs give skimpy holiday information.

For tides and moon phases, see the *American Ephemeris and Nautical Almanac* and a book called *Sunrise and Sunset Tables for Key Cities and Weather Stations in the United States.* These references are in large libraries.

Everyone should have a general almanac in his personal library. It's the best research bargain for the money -- nearly 1,000 pages packed with facts and figures for about $5. General almanacs in print include:

1. *Hammond Almanac.* Hammond, Inc. 1979-date.
2. *Information Please.* Simon & Schuster. 1947-date.
3. *Reader's Digest Almanac.* Reader's Digest Assoc. 1966-date.
4. *World Almanac.* World Almanac. 1869-date. (Issued on microfilm from 1869-1974 by Bell & Howell.)

The *Whitaker Almanack* (1869-date) is the British counterpart to the American general almanacs listed above. It covers popular information in Britain such as events of the year, museums and art galleries, income tax information, athletic records, colleges, tides, immigration statistics, and Parliamentary constituencies. It's a standard resource in large libraries.

Subject Almanacs

As with encyclopedias, the word *almanac* is used freely in the titles of many reference books: *Massee's Wine Almanac, Country Music Almanac,* etc. These reference books usually contain a conglomeration of facts, figures, addresses, and commentary on a single topic and are extremely useful for information in a particular field. Whether the word *almanac* in their titles actually makes them almanacs is difficult to answer, since many other kinds of reference books do the same thing. For a researcher's purposes, as usual, it's getting the information that counts.

The following is a list of subject almanacs available in large libraries. (Don't forget, when you find a reference book with "almanac" in the title, just think of it as a general or a subject reference book.)

1. *Almanac of American Politics.* Barone & Co. Biennial. 1972-date.

Describes every Congressional District in the country; provides profiles of every member of Congress and each Governor; gives ratings of performance of special interest groups; includes many election statistics.

2. *Catholic Almanac.* Our Sunday Visitor. 1904-date.

Contains information about the church: religious news events for the year, a list of popes since early times, the dates of ecumenical councils, events in church history, U.S. Bishops, procedural rules for sacraments, information on church tax exemption, etc.

Q. Our celebration of St. Valentine's Day is an outgrowth of the old Roman feast of Lupercalia, but I'd like to know the procedure the Roman Catholic Church follows in ascribing a particular day to a particular saint.

A. The *Catholic Almanac* says, "The calendar of the Roman Church consists of an arrangement throughout the year of a series of liturgical seasons and feasts of saints for purposes of divine worship. This is explained in sections 102-105 of the Constitution of the Sacred Liturgy, issued by the Second Vatican Council." This publication should be available in theology libraries for further study.

---

3. *Dow Jones-Irwin Business and Investment Almanac.* Dow Jones-Irwin. 1977-date.

Lists include a chronology of business news for the year, large corporations and brief statistics on them, top performing stocks and funds, military procurement programs, etc.

Q. I'm doing research for which I'll need the expiration dates of certain union contracts. Must I write to labor union headquarters, or is there some reference book that gives this information?

A. *The Dow Jones-Irwin Business and Investment Almanac* lists labor contract expiration dates for the year for more than 350 unions from Rubbermaid of Wooster, Ohio to the National Football League Management Council. Also included is the number of union members.

Labor contracts covering 1,000 workers or more are on file in the Bureau of Labor Statistics Office of Wage and Industrial Relations. According to the *DJ-I Almanac,* the expiration dates also appear in the bureau's monthly magazine called *Monthly Labor Review.*

---

4. *Places Rated Almanac: Your Guide to Finding the Best Places to Live in America,* by Richard Boyer and David Savageau. Rand McNally Co. 1981.

Provides data on weather, taxes, education, recreation, the arts, crime, health care, transportation, employment, and other points of interest to people looking for The Perfect Place to live.

5. *Texas Almanac.* 1857-date; *Ohio Almanac.* 1967-date; *Canadian Almanac and Directory.* 1848-date. (*CAD* is issued on microfilm for 1848-1970 by Micromedia Ltd.)

Geographical almanacs such as the three mentioned here include legal, commercial, statistical, religious, political, social, financial, educational, and general information about their particular area. Many addresses of hospitals, associations, colleges, and government offices are also included. Few geographical areas have almanacs, but those that do issue them annually or biennially. Two other states that have almanacs are Florida and Louisiana; theirs are published by Pelican Books.

Out-of-Date, Not Out-of-Use

Old almanacs don't die. Their uses are just redefined. Their research potential remains valid, and they can usually be checked out in large libraries. If you find a recent or old edition at a book sale for a bargain price, grab it. Like encyclopedias, they contain certain information that is static and rarely changes: biographies of the presidents and their wives; overviews of each presidential administration (except the recent ones, of course); histories of the nations of the world; chronology of U.S. history; birth-death dates of historical figures; the history of U.S. space efforts; prize winners (academy awards, Pulitzer and Nobel prizes, Olympic events), etc.

Judgment plays a part in how you'll use an old almanac. Obviously you can't use a five-year-old edition as an accurate reflection of current prices, addresses, and other data subject to constant change. But consider the kinds of information you can reap from these interesting lists in the *1896* edition of the *World Almanac*:

1. Survey of world news of the year.
2. Chronology of events in the United States for the year.
3. Astronomical phenomena for the year (eclipses, planetary configurations, etc.).
4. State legislations for the year.
5. The names of members of Congress.
6. Statistics abridged from the census and other sources on topics such as education, agriculture, and population.
7. U.S. military strength.
8. Sporting events records up to 1895.
9. Postal information and rates.
10. Principal railroad systems of the United States and Canada.

Of course, not every almanac currently in print dates back to the 19th century. (See the list on page 116 for dates when the currently available general almanacs started publication.) The next time you are shelf browsing, look for other old almanacs which are no longer in print. Their historical research value will likely be worth the effort.

THE WORD ON DICTIONARIES

Dictionaries are another type of reference book whose resources may be both over- and underestimated. As with encyclopedias and almanacs, dictionaries, too, have personalities and specialties. Though you may find one that serves your needs most of the time, it's likely you will have to switch from time to time to accommodate your particular project.

There have been frequent debates on the dangers of equating the biggest dictionary with the best. But my favorite general dictionary *is* the biggest. And the heaviest. It's *Webster's Third New International Dictionary*, published by Merriam Co.

It's not an average shelf dictionary in either size (more than 2,600 pages) or price ($80), but it can be used faithfully for years, even decades.

I like it because its definitions seem more complete, and its contents include more words than some other popular dictionaries. And it also contains bonuses—lists of weights and measures, Indo-European languages, the Braille alphabet, principal ocean currents, constellations, cattle brands, consanguinity (family relationships—aunts, uncles, cousins twice removed, etc.), a perpetual calendar, radio frequencies, ranks of the armed forces, a summary of grammar rules, and appendices giving forms of address, and rules of punctuation and spelling. With all these extras, *Webster's Third New International* resembles a reference book more than a dictionary.

(Since everyone's research needs vary, it's difficult to recommend dictionaries. The best approach to selecting the one best for you is to compare entries in a variety of dictionaries. It's revealing and sometimes surprising to see how each dictionary treats a word. The lengthy historical evolution of the word *nice* as it appears in the *Oxford English Dictionary* is far different, for example, from the coverage it gets in a standard desktop dictionary. But if you have no need for etymology or the history of a word, the *OED* would not be appropriate for your use. Kenneth Kister's *Dictionary Buying Guide*, available in large libraries, can also help you choose your favorite.)

Word and Phrase Books

Not every term you'll ever read is defined in every general dictionary. Some words are common only to a particular country, dialect, or region; others are used only by hobbyists or word enthusiasts. Any of these may not be included in a popular dictionary. To accommodate them, we have special word and phrase books usually compiled around a theme. Some are:

1. *Dictionary of Afro-American Slang*, edited by Clarence Major. International Pubs. Co. 1970.
   Sample Entries: "cow express" - shoe leather [from the 1940s]; "foxy" - a female beauty, especially black.

2. *Dictionary of American Slang*, by Harold Wentworth and Stuart B. Flexner. 2nd ed. T.Y. Crowell. 1975.
   Sample Entries: "pig iron" - inferior, homemade, or bootleg whiskey; "comma counter" - one who exaggerates minor details.

3. *Dictionary of Foreign Terms,* by C.O. Mawson. 2nd ed. Barnes & Noble. 1979.

Sample Entries: "ipso jure" - by the law itself; "parbleu" - by jove, egad.

4. *Language of the Underworld,* by David W. Maurer. University of Kentucky Press. 1981.

Sample Entries: "paperhanger" - a professional check forger; "live cannon" - a police term describing a pickpocket who steals from moving victims.

5. *Mountain-ese,* by Aubrey Garber. Commonwealth Press. 1979.

Sample Entries: "Eye-way" - Iowa; "everone" - everyone; "eats" - food.

6. *Mrs. Byrne's Dictionary of Unusual, Obscure and Preposterous Words,* by Josefa Heifetz Byrne. University Books. 1974.

Sample Entries: "furfuraceous" - covered with dandruff; "infare" - a housewarming given by a recently married couple.

7. *-Ologies and -Isms: A Thematic Dictionary,* edited by Laurence Urdang and Charles Hoequist. Gale Research Co. 1981. Defines words ending in a variety of suffixes.

Sample Entries: "Alcoranist" - a strict follower of the Koran; "steleography" - inscribing or chiseling inscriptions on stone tablets or pillars.

8. *Soldier and Sailor Words and Phrases,* by Edward Fraser and John Gibbons. Reprint of the 1925 edition. Gale Research Co. 1968.

Sample Entries: "hot stuff" - a heavy shell; "hand grenade" - the Army water-bottle.

Q. Why were American infantrymen called doughboys during World War I, and why were British soldiers called Tommies?

A. *Soldier and Sailor Words and Phrases* explains various theories. One theory suggests doughboy came from a kind of dumpling called doughboy which resembled the globular brass buttons on Civil War infantry uniforms. The name stuck and later became associated with the soldiers themselves.

The term was also used 50 years before in the Battle of Talavera in Spain. A soldier used the expression in his diary in reference to the cornbread the men fashioned with their hands from corn they found in the fields.

Tommy Atkins was a British equivalent of the hypothetical John Smith. The name first appeared in 1815 when sample forms for soldiers showed where their signatures should appear. Tommy Atkins was the name chosen for the sample, and it continued to be used for decades on military forms. Rudyard Kipling helped popularize the term "Tommy" in his verses.

9. *Western Words; A Dictionary of the American West,* by Ramon F. Adams. University of Oklahoma Press. 1981.

Sample Entries: "necktie party" - a hanging; "cookie pusher" - a cowboy's name for a waitress.

SUBJECT DICTIONARIES

Subject dictionaries take care of the rest of the language not found in general dictionaries or word and phrase books. They cover terms unique to particular fields, subjects, or professions. If you don't find a word in a general English language dictionary, it might just be a special term belonging to a specific discipline such as astronomy, dance, or geology.

Q. What's the difference between baking powder and baking soda?

A. Van Nostrand's two-volume *Scientific Encyclopedia* says both baking powder and baking soda produce carbon dioxide gas which, when combined with a flour mixture and moistened and heated, makes the mixture rise. Baking soda (sodium bicarbonate) is one component of baking powder which consists of several chemicals listed in this dictionary.

To get an idea of the huge number of subject dictionaries in print, flip through the pages of *SGBIP.* Not only are there countless dictionary titles for every subject, but they cover different time periods and languages as well. Some of the dictionaries sport definitions that are one line long; others are as long as half a page. Here's a random sample of titles:

LAW—DICTIONARIES (over 70 in print)
(These dictionaries define words, phrases, and names in the legal context. Covered are such terms as Coupled with an interest, Court calendar, Court of Civil Appeals, Court of Common Pleas, Criminal conspiracy, Criminal intent, and Cruce signati.)
Black, Henry C. *Black's Law Dictionary.* 5th edition. 1979.
West Publishing Co.
Cowell, John. *The Interpreter: or, Book Containing the Signification of Words.* 1970. Reprint of the 1607 edition. Walter J. Johnson.
Egbert, Lawrence D. *Multilingual Law Dictionary: English, French, Spanish, German.* 1978. Oceana Publications.

MATHEMATICS—DICTIONARIES (over 30 in print)
(These dictionaries define words, phrases, and names in a mathematical context. Entries include: Form; Formula; Four; Fourier, Jean Baptiste Joseph Baron de (1768-1830); Fractional; Fulcrum; and Function.)

Eisenreich, G., and Sube, R. *Dictionary of Mathematics.* 2 vols.
1982. Elsevier.

Sneddon, I. N., ed. *Encyclopedic Dictionary of Mathematics for Engineers.* 1976. Pergamon.

MEDICINE—DICTIONARIES (over 100 in print)
(These dictionaries define words, phrases, and names in a medical context: for example, Hernia, Heroin, Herpangina, Herpes Simplex, Herpes Zoster, Hesperidin, Heterograft, and Hexachlorophene.)

Carpovich, Eugene. *A Russian-English Biological and Medical Dictionary.* 2nd ed. 1960. Technical Dictionaries Co.

Sliosberg, A. *Elsevier's Medical Dictionary.* 2nd ed.
1975. Elsevier.

Tabery, Julia J., et al. *Communicating in Spanish for Medical Personnel.* 1975. Little, Brown & Co.

MUSIC—DICTIONARIES (over 75 in print)
(These dictionaries define words, phrases, and names connected with music, including Boutade, Bow, Bowed harp, Braille music notation, Brass instruments, Brazil, Buffo, and Bugle.)

Ammer, Christine. *Harper's Dictionary of Music.* 1972. Harper-Row.

Emery, Frederic B. *The Vioi n.s . Encyclopedic Dictionary.* 1979. Reprint of the 1928 ed. Longwooc Press.

Pulver, Jeffrey. *A Bibliographical Dictionary of Old English Music: Old English Music and Musical Instruments.* 1970. Reprint of the 1927 ed. Burt Franklin Pub.

Some reference books may use the word "dictionary" in their titles, but they may not be definition books in the accepted sense. For example, the *Dictionary of United States History: Alphabetical, Chronological, Statistical* combines statistics, chronologies, and information not normally found in dictionaries (except as small charts). As with encyclopedias and almanacs, the word "dictionary" is liberally used in some reference book titles. If you look at the five-volume *Dictionary of the History of Ideas* and the eight-volume *Dictionary of American History,* you'll see that they more resemble encyclopedias than dictionaries.

DICTIONARIES IN HISTORICAL RESEARCH

Reprinted dictionaries, like some of those mentioned above, define words according to the accepted definition of the day. These may be useful if you are trying to capture the speech of a particular era.

For a comprehensive look at the evolution of the English language, however, there is one giant resource. It is the standard dictionary researchers use often in large libraries, namely, the *Oxford English Dictionary* (12 vols. and supplements. Oxford University Press. 1933). It allows you to trace a word's early history and use. Depending on your research project, this could be a valuable tool. Imagine your embarrassment at finding out that you have used a slang word in your historical novel before it was even coined!

You'll find many annotations for each word you look up in the *OED*. These annotations give the year of publication, author, and title of works in which the word was first seen in print with a particular meaning. In addition, the entries give the sentence in which the word appeared. If you check the *noun* BUS, for example, you'll find this: (occas. buss; a familiar shortening of omnibus). 1832 HT. Martineau. *Weal & Woe*. 14. If the station offers me a place in a buss. (After the word's definition comes the book in which the word appeared with that meaning. In this case, *Weal & Woe in Garvelock; a tale,* by Harriet Martineau. C. Fox, London, 1832. The sentence ran on page 14. Other historical examples of the word's use are also included.)

If you check the *verb* BUS, you will find a similar arrangement: definition, year, author, title, sentence example. For its historical value in studying the evolution of the English language, the *OED* is unparalleled.

CHRONOLOGIES

According to its simplest definition, a chronology is a reference book that lists events in the date order in which they occurred. Beyond that, chronologies are as individual and different as the compilers who select the items to include in them.

Perhaps because chronologies are so varied, researchers don't use them as much as they might. Besides allowing you to pinpoint the date of a particular event (by using the subject index), chronologies let you scan the events—historical, cultural, political—of a year or period of years. This gives you a quick overview of that era without reading extensively in books.

As with other reference books, the quality of different chronologies varies. Some are more detailed than others. Most include a certain amount of insignificant minutiae that may not be useful at all.

The following list shows a selection of chronologies and how you might use them.

1. *Cyclopedia of Classified Dates,* by Charles E. Little. Funk & Wagnalls, 1900; reprinted by Gale Research Co., 1967.

This chronology is a monumental publication that records all manner of events from prehistory to 1900. It's arranged alphabetically by country (Austria, Borneo, Cape Colony, Egypt, etc.); then by period of years (varies for each country); and finally subarranged by topic (Army-Navy, Art-Science-Nature-Letters, Births-Deaths, Church, Society, State, etc.).

Some events you might find mentioned under "FRANCE: State", include:

1719 — Jan. 10. — France declares war against Spain.
        Dec.   — Spain sues for peace; the allies demand the
                   dismissal of Alberoni.
1720 — Jan. 25. — Spain accepts the terms of the Quadruple
                   Alliance.

To find the date of a particular event, check the index. In this publication of 1,454 pages, the index runs 289 pages.

2. *Day by Day: The Forties*, compiled by Thomas M. Leonard. Facts on File, Inc. 1977.

Day by Day: The Fifties, compiled by Jeffrey Merrit. Facts on File, Inc. 1979.

Day by Day: The Sixties, compiled by Thomas Parker. 2 vols. Facts on File, Inc. 1982.

These are very detailed chronologies considering the short time span covered by each one. Information is arranged by day rather than by year as in other chronologies. Each volume covers over a dozen categories of information, including World affairs; Europe; The Americas; U.S. Politics & Social Issues; Economics; Science, Technology and Nature; and Culture. Subject indexes are also included.

Events reported read like newspaper headlines. On May 26, 1952, under the category "The Americas," you can read that the Toronto Symphony dismissed six musicians accused of Communist activities prior to a U.S. tour as a result of pressure from the U.S. State Department. On that same day in "Science, Technology and Nature" Dr. Paul Wermer of the AMA reported that a new drug, Benemid, increases the efficiency of penicillin by causing the body to retain it longer.

3. *People's Chronology; A Year-by-Year Record of Human Events from Prehistory to the Present*, edited by James Trager. Holt, Rinehart & Winston, 1979.

This hefty chronology is arranged first by century, then by year, then by 30 categories: theater, everyday life, crime, energy, political events, transportation, consumer protection, literature/publishing, etc. It also includes an extensive subject index.

By consulting this resource, you would learn that in 1876 New York's Central Park was completed after 17 years of work and that the A & P grocery chain opened its 67th store.

PC also mentions many "firsts": In 1967, the first compact microwave oven for home use was introduced in the United States; in 1965, Cranapple fruit juice was introduced by Ocean Spray Cranberries, Inc., and Diet Pepsi was introduced by Pepsi-Cola; on May 15, 1940, the first nylon stockings went on sale in the United States; in 1939, the food stamp program was introduced by the Department of Agriculture; and in 1850, the first women's rights convention, organized by Lucy Stone, was held in Worcester, Massachusetts.

Q. I'm doing some research on the Gold Rush period in the mid-19th century and would like to know if there's a reference book that can give me a glimpse of what was going on in the country and the world at that time.

A. A chronology would do that. *People's Chronology*, by James Trager, is an excellent one to check. It covers events in all fields. Here are some things that happened in 1850: President Taylor died of typhus after 16 months in office and was succeeded by Vice-President Millard Fillmore; China's T'ai Ping Rebellion began with the southern peasants rebelling against the Manchu government in a civil war that killed 20-30 million people in the next 14 years; Congress abolished flogging in the Navy; tenement construction began in New York City lasting for 50 years; Wells & Co., Livingston, Fargo & Co., and Butterfield, Wasson & Co. merged to form American Express.

With *People's Chronology*, you can also get an overview of the important events that occurred in a particular field. You can, for example, trace a 10-year stretch of political happenings from 1845 to 1855. You can do the same for literature, drama, and even food, since those are categories covered in the book.

Some chronologies are arranged like calendars. They list major events that occurred on a particular day (June 1, November 8, etc.) regardless of the year in which the event took place. For example, on May 26, 1445, King Charles VII of France added 15 new companies to his army. On May 26, 1799, Russian poet Alexander Pushkin was born; and on May 26, 1864, Montana became a state. The two references below are arranged in calendar fashion from January 1 to December 31:

1. *Almanac of Dates*, by Linda Millgate. Harcourt Brace Jovanovich. 1977.

2. *Book of Days; A miscellany of popular antiquities in connection with the calendar . . .*, by Robert Chambers. 2 vols. 1862. Reprinted by Gale Research Co. 1967.

CHRONOLOGICAL CHARTS

In addition to the chronologies above, chronological charts are often a feature of other reference books. General almanacs usually include a chronology of major national and international news events of the year as well as a complete list of space achievements. The *Dow Jones-Irwin Business and Investment Almanac* (see page 117) includes a chronology of the year's business and finance news.

A reference book that links publishing with other cultural/political/economic factors is *Eighty Years of Best Sellers, 1895-1975*, by Alice Payne Hackett and James H. Burke. (R. R. Bowker Co. 1977). Though its major focus is on book news of the year, the book provides a chronology of some major world events along with a list of annual best sellers. For example, in 1922, when the fiction list included *The Sheik*, by Edith Hill; *To the Last Man*, by Zane Grey; and *Gentle Julia*, by Booth Tarkington, it was also the year of waistlines at the hip, Mah-Jongg, Rudy Vallee, the Castle and Astaire dancing teams, and *Babbitt*, which introduced a new word into the language (middle-class businessman).

In similar fashion, *Variety Music Cavalcade, 1620-1969: Chronology of Vocal and Instrumental Music Popular in the U.S.* mentions popular songs of each year with major cultural and world events that occurred at the same time.

When you consult almanacs and subject reference books, also check to see if they have chronology charts within their pages. They are sometimes a large portion of a reference book.

Q. A friend and I were discussing the increase of the Filipino population in the United States. She said Filipinos have been in America for years and first settled in Florida. I said they've only been in this country since World War II. Who is correct?

A. According to *The Filipinos in America, 1898-1974: A Chronology and Factbook*, Filipinos started arriving in this country in sizable numbers as students during the first two decades after the United States acquired the Philippines from Spain in 1898.

The present population of Filipino ancestry is the result of two separate waves of immigration. The first began in the mid-1920s. The Exclusion Act of 1924 reduced the numbers of cheap Japanese labor, a particular hardship for California farmers and Northwest canners. They therefore turned to the Philippines and Mexico for a new source of labor. The second wave of immigration started in the mid-1960s. The 1965 Immigration Act repealed the national-origin quota system used since 1924.

By 1975, the Filipino population in this country numbered half a million.

YEARBOOKS

Yearbooks are mini-encyclopedias. The only difference is that they confine their information on the general or specific topics they cover to the latest developments of a particular year. General yearbooks are usually arranged alphabetically by subject. Sample subjects might be AFGHANISTAN, AFRICA, ARCHAEOLOGY, CHILD WELFARE, CHINA, CHURCH MEMBERSHIP, CHILE, DANCE, EDUCATION, ENVIRONMENT, FOOD, and LITERATURE. Most yearbooks are published by encyclopedia publishers, and they can be used as supplements to the encyclopedias to update information in certain subjects. Some general yearbooks are:

1. *Americana Annual.* Grolier, Inc. (1923-date).

2. *Britannica Book of the Year.* Encyclopaedia Britannica, Inc. (1938-date).

3. *World Book Yearbook.* World Book-Childcraft. (1962-date).

Yearbooks are also published in specific subjects—maybe just one of the topics covered by a general yearbook. Whether their subject is law or education, a subject yearbook notes the latest developments and research in that field. (Yearbooks are sometimes reference books in disguise, as they may list a collection of facts, figures, and even addresses.)

Some yearbooks of current developments are *Yearbook of Astronomy, Yearbook of Drug Therapy, Yearbook of Higher Education, Yearbook of Medicine, Yearbook of School Law,* and *Yearbook on International Communist Affairs.* Most of these are shelved in libraries with other books on the subject, but since they usually start with the word *yearbook,* they're easy to identify through a library catalog or in the title volume of *Books in Print.*

General yearbooks no longer in print are available in large, usually academic, libraries and are often on circulating shelves. The brief sampling below suggests the historical information on general topics (politics, consumer affairs, education, etc.) available within these older volumes.

1. *The American Year Book: A Record of Events and Progress.* D. Appleton & Co. 1910-50.

Sample topics from the 1931 volume include: Advances in Science; Agriculture; American Relations Abroad; Astronomy; Automotive Engineering; Books; Business Conditions; Defense and the Military; Foreign Exchange; National Budget; Painting; Religion; Theater; U.S. Debt.

2. *Appleton's Annual Cyclopaedia.* D. Appleton & Co. 1861-1903.

Sample entries from the 1861 volume: Army Operations with a railway map of the South (over 150 pages); Astronomical Phenomena and Progress; Austria; Ballooning; Baton Rouge; Blockade; Building Materials; Cochin-China; Colt, Samuel; Commerce; Confederate States.

3. *The New International Year Book.* Dodd, Mead & Co. 1907-65.

Sample entries from the 1917 volume include Fire Protection; Flax; Flood Prevention; Food and Nutrition; Formosa; France; Friends, Religious Society of; Garbage and Refuse Disposal; Gas Poisoning; German Literature.

It's easy to take standard reference books for granted and to assume that they're all alike—and just like the ones you used in high school or college. Look again. As a researcher, you are constantly sharpening your skills of observation. Don't forget to notice all the extra information the "old regulars" give you. It's not just chance that they have long survived and continue to thrive as ready-reference sources.

—————————— *CHAPTER SUMMARY* ——————————

  I. Encyclopedias are familiar reference books with conventional and unconventional uses.
     A. Multivolume general encyclopedias answer questions, provide subject overviews, and recommend further reading. But not all encyclopedias are alike. (page 104)
     B. Subject encyclopedias provide in-depth coverage of a particular topic. They may be one volume or multivolume. (page 107)
     C. Old encyclopedias are useful for historical research. (page 112)
     D. Electronic encyclopedias are the wave of the future. They both replace and create reference books. (page 113)
 II. Almanacs are books of lists, facts, figures, and formulas adapted from other sources. (page 115)
     A. Subject almanacs are subject reference books providing a compendium of information on a special topic. (page 116)
     B. Old almanacs enable you to capture the important stats, events, and names of a particular year. (page 118)
III. Dictionaries provide word definitions, pronunciations, and spellings. They may also include charts and appendices containing bonus information. (page 118)
     A. Word and phrase books cover special language: slang, foreign terms, the vocabulary of ethnic groups, etc. (page 119)
     B. Subject dictionaries cover the vocabulary of professions and specific disciplines: botany, medicine, sports, etc. (page 121)
     C. Old dictionaries define words as they were used in a particular period. The *Oxford English Dictionary* is the best "historical" dictionary. (page 122)
 IV. Chronologies vary from collections of specific dates or events to calendar arrangements that tell what happened on a particular day of the year, regardless of the year. (page 123)
  V. General yearbooks summarize (often in alphabetical order by event) the spectrum of happenings in one year. (page 126)
     A. Subject yearbooks capsulize the year's highlights in a specific profession or special interest. (page 127)
     B. Old yearbooks are useful in reconstructing events of the past. (page 127)

9

More Finding Tools:
SPECIAL INDEXES AND
A DIRECTORY

*Research is to see what everybody else has seen
and think what nobody has thought.*
—Dr. Albert Szent-Cyoryi

More than a century ago, Dr. Thomas Horne, a so-called *eccentric* British Bible scholar, counted (in his spare time over a period of 17 years) the words, letters, books, chapters, and verses in the Old and New Testaments and The Apocrypha. To preserve his three solid years of labor, he published the statistics in his book, *Introduction to the Study of the Scriptures* (1813).

I hope Horne wasn't considered eccentric because of this single task; librarians do this sort of thing routinely. This kind of meticulous activity, this indexing and organizing of information for easy retrieval later on, has always been a part of library work—and researchers are richer for it.

To show you just how much richer, this chapter focuses on finding tools—specifically, special indexes and one remarkable directory that can lead you to other books . . . and the information you need.

SPECIAL INDEXES

Indexes are the important, often unheralded, volumes on library shelves. The special indexes allow you to retrieve book and film reviews, poems, plays, songs, speeches, and other pieces of information which are not individually recorded in library catalogs. They let you know the whereabouts of countless essays and short stories invisible to the library catalog user, because they're tucked away in scores of anthologies. (Library catalogs list magazines, not the articles in them; poetry books, but not the individual poems in them.)

It's true that some of these individual items are included in periodical indexes (which will be covered in the next chapter on magazines), but the coverage is meager. To find the lyrics to a childhood song or the clincher from a President's speech, you must look systematically; and special indexes give you direction.

These special indexes originate in many ways. Librarians and other researchers often create homemade indexes in card-file form. These files may help them locate frequently used data—anything from specific songs in songbooks to poems in poetry anthologies that are not recorded in published indexes and reference books. A unique file, developed over a 20-year period at the Newberry Library in Chicago, contains surnames librarians extracted from published city, county, and family history books, vital records, and other Midwestern genealogical publications. Without the effort of those who contributed to this file, many genealogical researchers would not know of ancestors' names buried within the pages of long-forgotten publications.

Many homegrown files eventually result in published reference books as did the Newberry Library's file. It's called *The Genealogical Index of the Newberry Library*, and it was published in four volumes by G.K. Hall & Co. of Boston in 1960. Through distribution to other libraries, it enables researchers all over the country to share its valuable information. Indexes such as the Newberry file are here to stay, and they'll exist as long as information must be unearthed from within the depths of books and other printed matter. (You recall Dr. Watson's dismay—not to mention Marston's—at discovering his medical book had no index to help him locate the antidote for Marston's implied poison.)

Here are some standard special indexes you should know about. They are among the most popular and heavily used indexes. Housed in large libraries, each one includes a key to its abbreviations. (Those indexes which list anthologies include the full bibliographic citation in the front or back of the volume.)

1. *Book Review Index*. Gale Research Co. 1965-date.

BRI locates book reviews published in approximately 200 periodicals since 1965. Check by author. (There's a separate title index at the end of each volume.) Book reviews are especially useful to get a general idea of a book's contents before deciding whether you want to borrow it through interlibrary loan.

An author entry looks like this:
> IRVING, John—*The Hotel New Hampshire*
>   *Am Spect*-v15-F '82 p4
>   [*American Spectator*, vol. 15, Feb. 1982, page 4.]
>
>   *Comt*–v73–Je '82–p59
>   [*Commentary*, vol. 73, June 1982, page 59.]

(See also #2, #4, and #5 for other book review indexes.)

2. *Book Review Digest*. H.W. Wilson. 1905-date.

BRD looks much like BRI except that BRD includes summaries of original book reviews as well as references to them. BRD covers approximately 100 popular and scholarly periodicals from 1905 to date. Annual volumes which are arranged alphabetically by author also provide a separate subject and title index. If you don't know the year a book was originally reviewed, check *BRD*'s cumulative author/title index, 1904-1974. After that, unless another cumulative index is issued, you must check the index in each annual volume. (If you don't find your book at all, it means it wasn't reviewed by any of the sources *BRD* covers.)

Note that each entry in *BRD* includes the word count of the original review (e.g. 500 w), so you can distinguish long reviews from short ones. (In some cases, *BRD*'s summary is almost as long as the original review.) When there's a choice, you might prefer to select long (300 words or more) rather than short reviews (100 words or less).

3. *Chicorel Index to Poetry in Anthologies and Collections in Print.* 4 vols., Chicorel Library Publishing Corp. 1974; suppl., 2 vols., 1979.

Chicorel lists poems by title and poet. If you're looking for a particular poem, this index will tell you which poetry anthology it's in. *Chicorel* locates some 100,000 poems in over 1,000 anthologies. It also includes a separate anthology, subject, author, and editor index. Entries look like this:

> THE EVE OF ST. AGNES, by John Keats. In: *Romantic Poetry.*
> > [poem title entry]
> EVERWINE, Peter. Routes. In: *The New Naked Poetry; Recent American Poetry in Open Forms.*
> > [poet entry]

Check the index of anthologies covered in *Chicorel* to get the editor or compiler, publisher, and date of the anthology in which the poem appears. (See #7 for another poetry index.)

4. *Combined Retrospective Index to Book Reviews in Scholarly Journals, 1886-1974.* 15 vols. Carrollton Press. 1979-1982.

This historical index locates book reviews in approximately 400 scholarly periodicals such as *Economic and Social Review, Florida Historical Quarterly, Hungarian Review,* and *Russian History.* The sources covered here are generally not duplicated by the other book review indexes in this chapter. Twelve of the volumes in the *CRI* set are arranged by author, and three volumes provide a title approach. Note the index's coverage dates—1886-1974. A sample author entry:

> Fox, Vernon
> > *Violence Behind Bars; Crime & Delinq,* v3 1957 p334.
> > [*Crime & Delinquency,* vol. 3, page 334.]

5. *Current Book Review Citations.* H.W. Wilson. 1976-date.

CBRC indexes book reviews in approximately 1,000 general and scholarly periodicals not covered by *Book Review Digest.* Included here are *American Archivist, Art News, Flying, Geophysics, Microwaves, Transportation Research, Travel/Holiday,* and *Yale Law Journal.* The index is arranged by author and includes the reviewer's name. A separate title index appears at the end of each volume. A sample author entry:

> Kerby, W.F. *Proud profession*
> > *Barrons* 61:22+ Jl 13'81. M. Gordon.

[*Barrons*, vol. 61, pages 22+, July 13, 1981, reviewed by M. Gordon.]

6. *Essay and General Literature Index.* H.W. Wilson. 1900-date.

Books of collective essays contain individual chapters (essays) written by different authors. Library catalogs list only the book's overall title and author or editor, not the individual essays and their authors. *EGLI* identifies these essays by author and subject and gives the titles of the anthologies in which they are found. This index is especially useful in finding essays on one subject in books that seem to be, according to their titles, on another subject.

EGLI covers anthologies published since 1900 in all subjects from abortion to film; it should be used as a supplement to periodical indexes. A sample subject entry looks like this:

Nurse and patient [subject entry]
　　Jackson, E.E. Effective communication in nurse-patient
　　relationships. In Henderson, G. ed. *Human relations in the
　　military* p203-17

Q. I am doing research on Alfred Hitchcock. But the books I need never seem to be "in" at the library. Is there any way to quickly get additional materials such as articles of criticism (not the articles that ran in *Time* magazine, for instance) instead of waiting for books through interlibrary loan?

A. Interlibrary loan doesn't take as long as it used to, so you might consider it. Also, try indexes to film magazines. These cover the kind of articles you need. *Film Index* started publication in 1973, but an earlier index to check might be *Social Sciences and Humanities Index*. It covers some film magazines. Also try *Essay and General Literature Index*. *EGLI* guides you to chapters in books of essays. For example, some of the essays mentioned in the 1965-1979 volumes of *EGLI* are "The Rhetoric of Hitchcock's Thrillers," by O.B. Hardison, in *Man and the Movies*, edited by W.R. Robinson (Louisiana State University Press, 1967) and "Alfred Hitchcock: To Catch a Thief," by Francois Truffaut in *The Films in My Life*, by Francois Truffaut (Simon & Schuster, 1978).

---

7. *Granger's Index to Poetry; Indexing Anthologies Published from 1970 through 1981.* 7th ed. Columbia University Press. 1982.

This index helps you locate thousands of poems in 248 poetry anthologies. Check by first line or title. Separate subject and author indexes appear in the back of the volume with an abbreviations list for the anthologies covered. A sample poem title entry:

Coming On to Winter. Doug Flaherty. HeS
　　[HeS = *Heartland II: Poets of the Midwest.* Lucien Stryk, ed.
　　(1975) Northern Illinois University Press.]

Each edition of *Granger's* indexes poetry anthologies published in the past decade. Therefore, the references for a poem included in two succeeding editions may not necessarily be to the same anthology. (To researchers it doesn't matter where a poem is anthologized, as long as they can find it.) Both old and new editions include mention of age-old and classic poems, since these are continuously reprinted in new anthologies; in addition, the recent editions include the newer poets.

8. *Index to Fairy Tales, 1949-72, Including Folklore, Legends and Myths in Collections*, by Norma Ireland. F.W. Faxon Co. 1973; suppl. for 1973-77. 1979.

This index helps you locate individual fairy tales, legends, and myths of all countries that have appeared in anthologies published since 1949. It's arranged by subject and title with complete information under the title entry.

Entries look like this:
CHRISTMAS [subject]
    Why the sea is salt
WICKEDNESS [subject]
    Yukiko and the little black cat
(In both of these cases, you would check the titles in the title index to find the bibliographic information needed to retrieve the stories themselves.)
Title entries look like this:
The story of Atlantis [legend title]
    Higginson–*Tales* p. 1-4
    [*Tales of the Enchanted Islands of the Atlantic.* Thomas Wentworth
    Higginson. NY, Macmillan. 1898. Rptd, Core Collections 1976.]
Why the sea is salt [legend title]
    Rugoff–*Harvest* p. 672-676
    [*A Harvest of World Folk Tales.* Milton, Allan Rugoff, ed. NY:
    Viking Pr 1949; rptd, ibid 1968.]

9. *New York Times Film Reviews*. New York Times/Arno Press. 1913-date.

This multivolume reference set reproduces, in full, every film review that has run in *The New York Times* since 1913. It includes a personal name index and a film title index. Be sure to check the cumulative index for 1913-1968. Indexes appear in individual volumes after 1968. A sample film entry looks like this:
Member of the Wedding, The
    1952, D 31, 10:2
    [The review ran in the December 31, 1952 edition. 10:2 = page
    10, column 2. The page and column information refers to the
    location of the review in the newspaper only. It is not needed to
    find the review reproduced in this set.]
(For a broad selection of film reviews that have run in a variety of magazines, see issues of *Reader's Guide to Periodical Literature* under the subject heading MOTION PICTURE REVIEWS-SINGLE WORKS.)

10. *Play Index*. H.W. Wilson. 1949-date.

PI includes an author, title, and subject index that helps you locate individual plays published in collections such as *Best Plays of the Modern American Theatre*. Full information appears under the author entry only and includes a brief summary of the play and a cast analysis. *PI* is published continuously but is slow to come out. Entries look like this:

> Satire [subject]
>> Feiffer, J Little murders
>>> The terrible revenge of Fred Fumanchu, by S. Milligan [play title]

(In both cases above, the next step would be to check the author index for a complete citation.)

> Shepard, Sam [author]
>> The holy ghostly
>>> Confrontation between spiritually dead but mechanically alive father who unsuccessfully resists ghost of death and disaffected son who fears same death. Singing. 1 act 3 m 1 w extra 1 exterior. In *Best short plays of the world theatre, 1968-1973* [3 men, 1 woman, an extra, and 1 exterior are needed for production]

11. *Popular Song Index.* Scarecrow Press. 1975; suppl. 1978.

PSI has title and first line approaches to finding folk songs, hymns, pop tunes, sea chanteys, etc., in over 350 songbooks published since 1940. It covers such songbooks as *Welk's Sing-A-Long Book, Songs of the Cowboys,* and *Songs of the 20's and 30's. PSI* also includes composer and lyricist indexes. A sample title entry looks like this:

> 'Papa Hobo' Paul Simon. FL: It's carbon monoxide, the ole Detroit perfume. 60
>> [single quotes indicate a song's title. Paul Simon is the composer. FL = the first line of the song. Book no. 60 = Paul Simon. *The Songs of Paul Simon as Sung by Simon and Garfunkel and Paul Simon Himself.* Knopf. 1972.]

12. *Short Story Index.* H.W. Wilson. 1953-date.

SSI indexes (by author, title, and subject) short stories published since the early 50s in over 4,500 short-story anthologies and magazines. Some magazines currently covered are *Ladies' Home Journal, Esquire, McCall's, New Yorker, Hudson Review,* and *Yale Review.* Full information appears under the author entry. Check the appendix for the anthology's publisher and date. Sample entries look like this:

> HASIDISM [subject]
>> Singer I.B. The boy knows the truth.
> He who searches. Valenzuela, L. [short story title]

(Either of the entries above would lead you to the author index to find out where the short story appeared.) An author entry appears below.

> Harvey, Steve [author]
>> Play ball, you sporeheads
>> Lewis, J.D. ed. *Great baseball stories*

Q. I recently met someone who said she's had short stories published in *Good Housekeeping* and other women's magazines. How can I find out which issues her stories ran in so I can read them?

A. *Short Story Index* covers many top women's magazines including *Good*

Housekeeping. Back issues of the magazines should be in a large library; if not, borrow them through the library's interlibrary loan service.

---

13. *Song Index.* H.W. Wilson. 1926; suppl., 1954. Reprinted by Shoe String Press. 1966.

Here is an index to 19,000 American and foreign songs appearing in 281 songbooks published before 1934. *Song Index* provides approaches by first line, composer, author, and title in one alphabet. (The Shoe String Press edition includes two volumes in one. Look for the supplement at the end of the volume.) A song title entry looks like this:

The Widow Malone ("Did you hear of the widow Malone?")
    Irish air. Words by C. Lever. MMI
    [MMI = Moffat, A. *The minstrelsy of Ireland.* 4th ed. Augener n.d. (no date)]

14. *Speech Index: An Index to Collections of World Famous Orations and Speeches for Various Occasions, 1935-1965;* suppl. 1966-80. 4th ed. Scarecrow Press.

SI traces contemporary and century-old speeches made by little-known and well-known people—from educators to Richard Nixon. Coverage includes 115 books and anthologies. Full bibliographic citations for anthologies are included apart from the regular entries. Speeches are arranged alphabetically by subject and orator and cover such items as inaugural addresses and Nobel prize speeches. Sample entries:

Thoreau, Henry David [orator]
    Civil disobedience. BOORA 1:318
    [BOORA = Boorstin, Daniel J. ed. *American primer.* Chicago: University of Chicago Press, 1966. 2 vols.; 1:318 = volume 1, page 318.]
TORIES - ENGLAND [subject]
    Beaconsfield, B.D. Tory democracy. JAE: 139.
    [JAE = Jackman, Sydney W., ed. *English reform tradition, 1790-1910.* Magnolia, Mass., Peter Smith, 1967; 139 = page 139.]

15. *Words and Phrases Index.* 4 vols. Pierian Press. 1969-70.

This reference indexes articles and brief items in four journals and publications—*American Speech, American Notes and Queries, Britannica Book of the Year,* and *Notes and Queries*—from the turn of the century to 1969. These publications discuss the purported origins of words and phrases such as "I'll be jimjammed," "passing the buck" and "easy as falling off a greasy log." Many of the slang expressions cited in *WPI* refer to books where they've been seen in print that are even earlier than those cited by the *Oxford English Dictionary.* (See Chapter 8). *WPI* is useful when dictionaries of word and phrase origins don't have what you need. Sample entries:

CURTAIN, NYLON—
    AS, vol 30, Oct 1955, p 185.

DAMPERS, PUT ON THE—
　　AS, vol 30, May 1955, p 94.
　　[AS = *American Speech*]

FOOTNOTE TO INDEXES

Indexes cover almost any area where an astute compiler sees an unfilled need. Some special indexes are not really indexes at all, but instead are bibliographies or reference books that happen to use the word *index* in their titles. Some of these bibliographic kinds of indexes are *Index to Multilateral Treaties*, *Index to Periodical Literature on Christ and the Gospels*, *Index to Top-Tune Hits*, *Index to Spanish American Collective Biography*, and *Index to Scientific Articles on American Jewish History*.

Norma Ireland's *Index to Indexes* (1942) covered a large selection of the varied indexes (and non-index types) published before 1942, but it has not been updated since that time and no other has replaced it. The indexes in the list above are among the most popular and heavily used special indexes. They're easy to find in large libraries along with many others that are usually shelved with them.

NOT ALL RESEARCH TOOLS ARE ALIKE

In my discussion of research tools, I covered a wide range of indexes, bibliographies, and reference books. It would seem that there can't be any left to mention. But there are. Many more. So many that it would be impossible to include them in a book you could put on a shelf. Aside from the space limitation, there's another good reason I don't mention many other reference titles.

Some reference books are just too comprehensive to be effective research tools. They include more information than most of us need, and a reference book's scope can sometimes work against it. It often makes the book hard to use because it forces you to wade through much unnecessary information to get to the items you want. Much of the information is likely duplicated in other reference books anyway.

You can easily find whatever your research demands by using the systems and tools I've outlined in this book. If you want to know about other reference books not covered here, you'll be able to find them, too, by using your newly learned research skills.

If you're already a researcher, you've probably noticed that I've omitted some reference books that might be considered standard and familiar. One popular book I've excluded, for example, is Sheehy's *Guide to Reference Books* (also known as Winchell's, after an earlier compiler). Sheehy's has become such a sacred cow that it's almost blasphemy to denigrate it. It became popular, I suspect, because some researcher long ago discovered it and passed the word on to others who continue to recommend it. Tools like this may become popular, not because they're the best ones to use, but because researchers are unaware that there are other books which, in fact, may be more appropriate and easier to use.

In truth, I never use Sheehy's, because it covers many foreign language resources, and I don't want to sort through them while trying to find what I *can* use. That's not to say *you* won't use it to death. There are many books that some researchers use and others don't. We favor certain tools, because we're different people, and because the duplication among reference books allows us this flexibility.

Using One Tool to Find Others

There are some reference books, however, that deserve special mention because they do far more than they seem to do. Since I strongly advocate self-help research techniques, I want to emphasize the versatility of one important reference tool. I've already touched on it in earlier chapters, because it's an important signpost to other reference books. That tool is *Directory of Directories(DOD)* (Information Research Enterprises, 1980-date). In Chapter 3, I mentioned five guides to finding reference books by subject (*Finding the Source*, etc.). I've also stressed the value of using *SGBIP* to locate books on your topic.

DOD is in the same class of multiuse references as these resources, because it does far more than its title implies. It not only identifies valuable directories, it also lists bibliographies. No matter what your subject, it's probably covered. It offers something akin to one-stop shopping in the research world. It's easy to use and has an excellent subject index to its contents.

A directory of directories isn't a new concept, and there are others out there that try to do the same thing. But *DOD* does the job best. *Directory of Directories* is arranged in subject categories such as Science and Engineering, and Arts and Entertainment. It has a separate title index in addition to its subject index; but in most cases, you'll want to start at the back of the volume with the subject index.

Let's look closely at *DOD* to see the variety of other useful reference materials it identifies. (Chapter 16 discusses another valuable use for *DOD*.)

BUSINESS REFERENCES

Business is just one of the many categories of reference materials *DOD* covers. It's impossible, of course, to name all the potentially useful reference sources for business people. There are hundreds. I'll name just a few from *DOD* to show you its broad scope.

1. *Directory of Foreign Manufacturers in the United States*, edited by Jef-

frey S. Arpan and David A. Ricks. Georgia State University Business Publications. Rev. Ed. 1984.

This directory lists some 3,400 companies in alphabetical order in approximately one dozen broad manufacturing categories (electrical and electronic equipment, rubber and plastic products, machinery, chemicals, transportation equipment, etc.). It includes the names and addresses of the firms abroad that own each company listed.

2. *International Directory of Importers*. Blytmann International. 4 vols. 1981-date. Annual.

The volume entitled "Asia/Pacific" includes 10,000 importers; "Europe" includes 32,000; "Middle East" includes 13,000; and "North America" includes 20,000 importers—with addresses and brief company statistics.

3. *Major Companies of the Arab World; Major Companies of Argentina, Brazil, Mexico & Venezuela; Major Companies of Nigeria; Major Companies of Europe*. Graham & Trotman Ltd., London.

Each annual directory lists a company's name; address; officers; telephone; telex and cable numbers; subsidiaries; activities; branches; profits; other figures; and related information.

4. *Standard Rate and Data*. Standard Rate and Data Service. 1919-date. Monthly.

This set of books gives advertising rates, circulation, audience composition, and other marketing data on magazines, newspapers, radio, and television stations.

5. *The Thomas Register of American Manufacturers*. Thomas Publishing Co. 1905-date. (In microform from 1905-77).

The Thomas Register lists thousands of products manufactured by approximately 115,000 American manufacturers. Doilies, dolls, dolly rollers, dowelpins, and a variety of doors (bullet proof, cemetery vault, corrosion resistant, animal access, cooler, etc.) are just a sampling of the products listed in the product index. The multivolume, annual set also includes a brand-name index, an alphabetical list of companies, and catalogs of some 1,100 manufacturers.

(*DOD* also lists individual state manufacturers' directories in the subject index under the name of the state.)

The list goes on. *DOD*, and sometimes *SGBIP*,[1] list some important broad-based tools to other business books and serials. Consider these:

1. *Encyclopedia of Business Information Sources*. Gale Research Co., 1983. (Issued every 3-5 years.)

This is a research guide much like Sheehy's but easier to use. It is high-

---

[1] *SGBIP* does not always list new editions of an annual directory after the initial listing of a first edition.

ly underrated, because its title implies a narrower scope than it actually covers. It's arranged by topic: CONSUMER PRICE INDEXES, COSMETIC INDUSTRY, COUNTRY CLUBS, COURTS MARTIAL, DETECTIVES, DIET, DIPLOMATIC AND CONSULAR SERVICE, etc. Under each, you'll find categories of reference books: encyclopedias and dictionaries, bibliographies, handbooks and manuals, indexes, biographical sources, statistical sources, periodicals, and more—with the titles of reference sources recommended. Use this excellent guide to reference books to help you find the many others you'll need in various business- and nonbusiness-related subjects.

Q. As a member of the insurance committee for a national organization, I need information on various insurance companies and policies available in other states. Also, what reference sources exist on the insurance business?

A. Each type of insurance—health, life, accident, marine, casualty, etc.—has its own corresponding reference publications. A book that identifies many is *Encyclopedia of Business Information Sources*. For example, under HEALTH INSURANCE, you'll find the titles of handbooks and manuals such as *Life and Health Insurance Handbook* (Dow Jones-Irwin). Also listed is a free annual called *New Group Health Insurance Policies Issued* giving the coverage of selected group policies; trade journals such as *Health Insurance Underwriter;* statistics sources such as the *Source Book of Health Insurance Data;* and the names of related professional or trade associations, including Health Insurance Institute of America.

---

2. *Where to Find Business Information,* by David Brownstone and Gorton Carruth. 2nd ed. John Wiley & Sons. 1982.

The subject index (called "Source Finder") in this reference lists over 2,500 subjects such as FOREIGN TRADE, FRANCHISES, FREEDOM OF INFORMATION, GEORGIA, GLIDERS, GOLD, HOME REPAIRS AND ALTERATIONS, IMPORT AND EXPORT COMPANIES, etc., and refers to 5,000 specialty business magazines, newsletters, and newspapers in those fields. For example, some of the publications listed under CURRENCY EXCHANGE RATES are *Dow Jones International News Wire, Euromoney Currency Report, Green's Commodity Market Comments, International Trade Newsletter,* and *The Wall Street Journal.* Subscription information is also given.

REFERENCE BOOKS FOR WRITERS AND JOURNALISTS

Reference books for writers are diverse. Some books, like this one, teach the basics of research. Other books may focus on the how-tos of a type of writing—songs, poems, articles, fiction, plays, etc. Still others list the potential outlets for your writing. If you're ready to sell your writing, the guides below from *DOD* (and many in *SGBIP*) should help you find an appropriate home for it. (Be sure to check for the most recent edition of any book you use.)

1. *Ayer Directory of Periodicals*. Ayer Press. Annual.

This volume lists 21,000 newspapers and magazines published in the United States and Canada. The directory is arranged alphabetically by state, then city. Beneath the city name is an alphabetical list of the magazines and newspapers published there. Special appendices arrange publications by category (foreign language, college, labor, etc.) and newspapers by circulation. A special feature of the latter list is that it identifies departments within a newspaper (food, travel, book review, etc.) and gives the editor's name.

Q. Is there a master list of the major newspaper in the major city of every state in the country? If so, where would I find it? The only way I've figured out to do it thus far is to cull the names from out-of-state phone directories at the phone company offices—and that has become cumbersome.

A. There are several directories of nationwide newspapers in large libraries according to the *Directory of Directories*. The most familiar are *Editor and Publisher International Yearbook*, *Working Press of the Nation*, and *Ayer Directory of Publications*.

---

2. *Directory of Small Magazine/Press Editors and Publishers*. Dustbooks. Annual.

This volume lists 3,500 small publishers and literary magazines. Each entry includes the requirements for publication so that prospective writers may submit their work according to identifiable guidelines.

3. *Fiction Writer's Market*. Writer's Digest Books. Annual.

FWM lists over 1,400 magazines, book publishers, and small presses that buy short stories and novels for adult and youth markets. It includes articles offering instruction and writing tips.

4. *How to Enter and Win Fiction Writing Contests. How to Enter and Win Nonfiction and Journalism Contests*. By Alan Gadney. Facts on File, Inc. 1981.

Listed in each book respectively are some 500 and 400 contest sources with rules and qualifications for entry by writers.

5. *International Directory of Little Magazines and Small Presses*. Dustbooks. Annual.

This is a guide to about 3,500 poetry markets, also literary and essay magazine markets and small publishers, many of which are not in other guides. Many of the publishing companies are tiny ventures operating on a shoestring. Though they give bylines, they may not offer pay for freelance material.

6. *Literary Market Place*. R.R. Bowker Co. Annual.

LMP is considered one of the basic tools for writers. It covers a number of varied services in publishing: over 1,430 book publishers and organizations that issue three or more books per year; book printers and binders; syndicates; periodicals; radio and TV stations that do book reviews; literary agents; literary organizations; and more.

7. *Publisher's Trade List Annual*. 5 vols. R.R. Bowker Co. Annual.

PTLA, found mostly in large libraries, is a list of the current and backlist in-print books issued by over 1,800 publishers. Not every press is included since listings are by subscription. A writer can use *PTLA* to find the most appropriate publishers for his proposed book. (For a company's most recent releases and projected titles, send directly to the publisher for a current catalog.)

8. *Working Press of the Nation*. 5 vols. National Research Bureau. Annual.

Volumes list syndicates, daily and weekly newspapers, radio and TV stations, magazines and internal house organs (company publications), and names of freelance feature writers and photographers. Many of the lists offer potential markets to whom writers may submit freelance work.

9. *Writer's and Artist's Yearbook*. A & C Black Publishers Ltd. Annual.

Market listings of book publishers, book clubs, magazines, syndicates, poetry markets, broadcasters, photography libraries, etc., in the United Kingdom, Australia, Canada, India, Ireland, and New Zealand, that buy freelance material or offer services to freelancers. *WAY* also includes information on selling screenplays and getting an agent in Britain.

10. *Writer's and Photographer's Guide to Newspaper Markets*, by Joan and Ronald Long. Helm Publishing Co. Published irregularly.

This guide lists the kind of freelance articles and photographs major newspapers buy, with information on how to submit your work.

11. *Writer's Market*. Writer's Digest Books. Annual.

WM lists more than 800 book publishers and 3,000 magazines, syndicates, agents, script buyers, gag and filler markets, and greeting card publishers with purchasing requirements and general pay rates.

Q. Where can I get information on making and marketing crossword puzzles?

A. The August 1975 issue of *Writer's Digest* magazine ran two articles on puzzles. One was an interview with the crossword puzzle editor of *The New York Times* in which he tells how to construct a puzzle. The other article tells how to create a word maze.

The back issue should be in a large library. Also check the games and puzzles section in the current *Writer's Market* for submission requirements to magazines that buy crossword puzzles.

Reference Books for Students

DOD suggests many useful and diverse college and career titles for students.

1. *Association for Intercollegiate Athletics for Women Directory.* AIAW. Annual.

This volume lists two- and four-year AIAW member colleges and their athletic programs and scholarships.

2. *Barron's College Profiles In-Depth Series.* Barron's Guides, Inc. Published irregularly.

The profiles describe 80 large colleges and universities. In addition to standard information such as tuition, costs, aid, etc., the guide includes information on social life and academic environment.

3. *Barron's Handbook of Junior and Community College Financial Aid.* Barron's Education Series, Inc. Published irregularly.

This directory lists approximately 1,000 junior and community colleges offering financial aid.

4. *Grants for Graduate Study Abroad.* Institute of International Education. Annual.

Included here are grants and exchanges offered by foreign governments, universities, and private groups in 50 countries. Specific information is given on language requirements, degrees offered, eligibility, selection procedure, etc.

5. *Insider's Guide to the Colleges.* Congdon & Weed. Annual.

The guide offers a personal glimpse at housing, leisure and recreational activities, student body characteristics, faculty/student ratio, etc., for 230 American colleges and universities.

6. *Internships: On-the-Job Training Opportunities for All Types of Careers.* Writer's Digest Books. Annual.

This directory describes internship opportunities with 850 corporations, social service agencies, government agencies, and recreational organizations such as national parks.

7. *Need a Lift?* The American Legion. Annual.

This annual lists scholarship, loan, and career assistance sources with requirements for each.

8. *Peterson's Annual Guides to Graduate Study.* 5 vols. Peterson's Guides, Inc. Annual.

Peterson's describes 1,350 institutions offering graduate degrees in the humanities, arts and science fields. Entries include costs, admission requirements, etc.

9. *Randax Education Guide: A Guide to Colleges Which are Seeking Students.* Education Guide, Inc., Annual.

This guide indentifies over 200 two- and four-year colleges and trade schools actively recruiting students.

10. *Study Abroad.* UNESCO. Biennial.

The international guide lists more than 200,000 scholarships and educational exchange programs in 107 countries with sponsoring organization, type of aid offered, and eligibility requirements.

REFERENCE BOOKS IN MICROFORM

Besides reference books in print, there are other kinds of reference materials (including books) that come out simultaneously in microform. You may, in fact, have a choice between microform and hard copy. Often, the microform version includes the entire back run of a reference work, such as the annual *Thomas Register of American Manufacturers, 1905-1977.* Sets like this fill a particular research need. Since they are now historical tools rather than current reference books, you can use them to trace addresses and former locations of businesses or the financial development of a particular company or industry.

Information about what reference books exist in microform is included in publishers' sales catalogs. You might pick up another clue from *SGBIP,* even though it doesn't include microform materials as such. If you find mention of a printed guide to a particular reference book in *SGBIP,* that means a microform set exists. Since they're becoming increasingly available, watch for complete runs of reference books that would suit your needs.

Though reference books with microform counterparts are mentioned elsewhere in the book, there are a few sets not covered. Demand for this kind of resource seems especially strong in the business sector, as evidenced by the selection below.

1. *Annual Reports of the Major American Companies.* Pergamon Press. 1844-1973, with annual updates.

This set includes the annual reports of the Fortune 500 industrials and 25 additional companies from each of the Fortune 50 lists of top commercial banking, life insurance, diversified financial, retailing, transportation, and utility companies. If you want to trace the financial development of a company or industry, this handy cumulation of annual reports will help you do it.

2. *Fisher Manual of Valuable and Worthless Securities.* Vols. 1-12, 1926-57. Microfilming Corp. of America.

This reference set gives the ultimate fate of more than 100,000 companies that issued stock no longer listed on a stock exchange. If you own securities of companies you can't trace, this directory is a major tool to help you determine if a company still exists, and consequently, if the securities still have value. (Current volumes of the manual are in hard copy.) (Also check *Directory of Obsolete Securities* for this kind of search.)

3. *Pick's Currency Yearbooks, 1955-73.* Pick Publishing Corp.

These are statistical yearbooks which include charts, figures, and graphs reflecting the economies of various countries. *Pick's* is arranged alphabetically by a country and its currency—Icelandic Krona, Italian Lira, Lebanese Pound, etc. An entire run of this reference book will help you trace the changes, developments, and trends in a country's foreign trade. You can also compare balance of payments, national incomes, gold production and gold prices, and much more from 1955 to 1973.

4. *Moody's Manuals, 1909-1978.* Moody's Investor Service.

This microform set includes the financial statements and histories of companies in *Moody's Transportation Manual, 1909-1978; Moody's Public Utility Manual, 1914-1978; Moody's Municipal and Government Manual, 1918-1978; Moody's Industrial Manual, 1920-1978; Moody's Bank and Finance Manual, 1928-1978;* and *Moody's OTC Industrial Manual, 1970-1978.* Researchers can use this set in conjunction with annual reports to trace a company or industry's growth. (The Moody's manuals include far more companies than the annual report microform set.)

One of the interesting things about doing research (and at the same time, one of the funniest and perhaps the oddest) is noting the existence of indexes to indexes and directories of directories. (So far I haven't seen a "guide to guides" or a "handbook of handbooks," but they're undoubtedly on the way.) What these special finding tools point out is the phenomenal number of publications that exist. By using these book-finding tools, you'll literally have access to all of them.

CHAPTER SUMMARY

I. Besides indexes to periodical articles, there are special indexes useful in locating book reviews, poems, plays, essays, film reviews, songs, short stories, and speeches. Included here is a list of widely used special indexes. (page 129)
   A. A reference book with the word "index" in the title may actually be more of a bibliography than an index. (page 136)
   B. There is no recent index to indexes. (page 136)
II. Not all researchers use the same reference books. But a certain book-finding tool that most researchers agree is an excellent resource is *Directory of Directories (DOD).* It will lead you to references in hundreds of subjects.
   A. Business references found in *DOD* (page 138)
   B. References for writers listed in *DOD* (page 140)

    C.   References for students listed in *DOD* (page 142)

III. Dozens of reference books come out simultaneously in microform and hard copy. (page 143)

10

Quick and Timely Information Sources:
MAGAZINES

A week is a long time in politics.
—Harold Wilson,
British politician

M agazine articles are like newspaper articles. They report, they entertain, they inform. They're also fleeting, and when you cut them out for future reference, they often get lost. Furthermore, if you want a duplicate, you can never remember in which issue of what magazine the article ran. Sound familiar?

Magazines are such a casual part of our lives that we don't often think of them as "research" material. Yet, articles are one of the ways we find out what's new and trendy in health care, home building, parent-child relationships, and Swiss bank accounts. They may even tell you how to grow potatoes in a barrel, or how to finance your medical school education. Articles contain valuable information on *everything*. And, they're very easy to get.

There's only one problem. If you don't need the information from an article on cataracts when you read it, the information is almost worthless. Like other research, articles come to us hit or miss. The real challenge is to get that article—or another on the subject—exactly when you need the information it contains.

MAGAZINES GALORE

First, you should know that there are far more magazines than the 200 or so popular, mass-market magazines (*TV Guide* and *Woman's Day*, for example) sold in supermarkets, drug and chain stores. Those represent only a fraction of the thousands of magazines published. Where do you find out about the others?

Bookstores and specialty shops (sporting goods stores, kitchenware shops) may carry magazines you never knew existed: *Camera Arts*, *Skin Diver*, and *Audio Amateur*, for example. These are written for readers with special leisure, work, or life-style interests. There are also magazines for hobbyists such as *Miniature Collector* and *Antique Trader Weekly.*

You'll find other magazines in your doctor's office, a neighbor's garage sale, the local flea market, or a friend's coffee table: *Maryknoll Magazine, Vegetarian Times, Soldier of Fortune,* and *Scandinavian Review,* etc.

Many companies publish magazines for their employees or customers. *Friendly Exchange* for example, is published by the Farmer's Insurance Group for its policy holders. *Silver Circle* and *Gemco Courier* are each issued by a particular bank and member department store for their customers. Airlines provide free copies of magazines they publish for their passengers.

Trade and professional people subscribe to both technical and newsy publications in their fields: *Journal of the American Psychological Association, Brain, American Cinematographer,* and *Hardware Retailing.*   (Physicians alone have as many magazines covering their field as you'll find on any supermarket's general magazine rack.) If you have a special interest or expertise, there's undoubtedly a magazine that covers it.

Small public libraries subscribe to perhaps one or two hundred magazines which are likely to appeal to the greatest number of patrons. But if you check a large library, you'll find hundreds, even thousands of special interest and technical, as well as broad-appeal magazines. Large university libraries may subscribe to well over 5,000 magazines, a combination of popular, scholarly, and professional magazines published in English and numerous foreign languages. A rundown of the broad categories of magazines will help you decide which are most appropriate for your information search.

USING POPULAR MAGAZINES IN RESEARCH

Articles in general are appropriate for solving *some* research problems. A short term paper or report, for example, may not justify checking anything longer. Since articles are short, they're easier than books to scan for quick answers. Like newspapers, they report the latest breaking developments, new trends, and research. (That's something that books, because of their long production schedules, cannot do as well.)

Articles from popular newsstand magazines are fine for solving certain research problems, but not for others. In an article I wrote for a magazine called *18 Almanac,* I gathered all my information from interviews and popular magazine articles. (The assignment called for a summary of tips to graduating high school seniors on how to live on their own.) My research project called for current, timely information, so popular magazines were a logical resource. Likewise, if you're looking for nontechnical information about your back problem, you won't need articles from the *Journal of the American Medical Association.* An article from *American Health* may do just fine.

Not long ago I was in my neighborhood branch of the public library working on my "Reference Librarian" column. I was checking an index to magazines to identify some articles on the topic of the question I was then researching. My teenage daughter was with me, and she was anxious to leave.

Recalling that she had previously asked me for advice on a minor acne problem, I suggested that while we were there we check for appropriate articles in current popular magazines. After all, I told her, I didn't know a thing about acne, nor did I know which drugstore preparations were best. In short, I couldn't advise her. We recalled having seen many articles in the past when we didn't need them.

Not surprisingly, my daughter was no longer in a hurry to leave the library. With my help, she checked the periodical index under ACNE and found several articles. We chose two: one in *Newsweek* which reported on startling results from a new prescription drug; and another in *Prevention* magazine which suggested a certain dietary supplement. We read the *Newsweek* article and found that the information didn't pertain to us, but we decided to follow the advice of the second article and try some of the supplement it suggested.

Not only did these popular magazine articles give us valuable information we did not previously have, the magazines were also accessible. Moreover, we knew where to find more information if we needed it. And as a bonus, it helped accustom my teenager to some research routines which, when done in the name of homework, had been much less interesting.

USING SCHOLARLY MAGAZINES IN RESEARCH

In some instances, researching scholarly magazines is more appropriate for your search than using popular publications. For example, a writer once asked me to find recent statistics on infidelity for an article she was writing for *Harper's Bazaar*. The information she needed had to be new, not secondhand; if the studies I found had already been reported in the popular magazines like *Family Circle* or *McCall's*, then it was too late for her to sell the information back to them.

A writer's requirements for selling articles to these magazines are to report NEW research and NEW ideas and trends. She needed recent data from psychologists and other professionals studying infidelity. I found several appropriate articles in scholarly magazines. The articles were written by qualified researchers and carried titles like "Multivariate Model of the Determinants of Extra-marital Sexual Determinants." This particular study ran in *Journal of Marriage and the Family*.

Graduate students and professional researchers must usually go beyond the popular magazines for information. For them, it's a natural research tactic. They regularly refer to articles that document original research, studies, surveys, and experiments. The "publish or perish" syndrome, a source of paranoia for some academics, actually benefits researchers who use scholarly journals. Articles in such magazines are written by experts for other experts and students. The language may often be pedantic or technical, but these studies are conducted by creditable professionals as part of their own research.

Q. About 10 years ago I saw an experiment on television demonstrating people's instinctive demands that justice be done. It involved several persons (in two different rooms) who were given false information by the psychologists conducting the experiment. Do you know of a similar experiment? I tried *Reader's Guide to Periodical Literature* and *Psychology Today* magazine but could find nothing.

A. Although *Reader's Guide* indexes *Psychology Today*, it doesn't cover the majority of magazines you need for this kind of information. Use an index to psychology journals such as *Psychological Abstracts* in large public and academic libraries. Every article referred to is based on experiments conducted by psychologists and other researchers, and has been published in a psychological journal or as a doctoral dissertation.

Check the term "justice" in *Psychological Abstracts*. There are dozens of articles. Two that I found at random in the 1977 edition are "Belief in a Just World and Trust" in the September 1977 issue of *Journal of Research in Personality* and "Innocent Victim, Deserved Victim and Martyr: Observer's Reaction" in the October 1977 issue of *Psychological Reports*.

USING INDEXES TO FIND ARTICLES

Where to begin hunting for articles is a big question. Magazine indexes provide the answers and give your information search a direction. They'll help you find exactly where you saw that article on cataracts and even direct you to others you didn't know existed.

When I was a beginning writer, I frequently used magazine articles to answer my own questions about the writing life. Even though I had begun selling articles, there was still much I didn't know. Since there wasn't always someone knowledgeable to ask for help, I developed self-help techniques.

One question I repeatedly asked myself concerned query letters to editors. (I wasn't sure what a good query letter was, and I wanted to see samples.) Other questions included "Where can I find out about agents?" and "What's the market for short stories?"

I had already read articles on these topics but needed to reread them, because now they were relevant to my interests. I tracked down the articles on writing the same way I found the background and statistics I needed to write the articles I sold: I checked periodical indexes for articles in magazines.

Some of the relevant article listings addressing my questions I found in *Magazine Index*[1].

SHORT STORIES—AUTHORSHIP
> Guest editor's column (collecting subject matter for stories)
> by Frayne, Karen. il *Teen* v26 Sept '82 - p14 (2).
> [(2) tells the number of pages in the article]

LITERARY AGENTS
> Taking a flier (find a literary agent). *Writer's Digest*
> v60 March '80 - p64 (2).

LETTER WRITING—TECHNIQUE
> How (and why) to write a query letter. *Writer* v95 Oct '82 - p22 (4).

Other questions I had later concerned copyright, newsletters, and taxation for authors. These were some of the related articles listed in *Magazine Index:*

COPYRIGHT—LAW AND LEGISLATION
> Last rights. (the importance of copyright laws).
> *Writer's Digest* v62 Oct '82 - p10 (2).

NEWSLETTERS—PUBLISHING
> Earn big money in your spare time with no money down, no real
> estate, no talent! by Lyons, James. *Washington Monthly* v12
> Nov '80 - p26 (7).

AUTHORS—TAXATION
> New authors caught in IRS roadblock. *Jet* v59 Nov 20 '80 - p21 (1).

The true value of a magazine index, whether your research takes you to popular or scholarly publications, is that it tells you exactly where to find an article ON ANY SUBJECT when you need it. If you happen to read an article about how to sue in small claims court and you don't need that information at the time, you probably won't remember how to do it when you *do* need to know. The ability to successfully relocate articles for any purpose, any time, puts you at the controls of the research game.

Q. I've noticed some windmills attached to homes in this area. Where can I get information on the uses for and the cost and construction of windmills?

A. Check *Reader's Guide to Periodical Literature* or *Magazine Index* (on microfilm) in the library under WINDMILLS. There are many articles listed under various subheadings such as DESIGN AND CONSTRUCTION, PURCHASING, and ECONOMIC ASPECTS. Some articles I found were "Wind-solar system could provide uniform energy output" in the November 1980 issue of *Countryside* magazine and "How to erect your own water pumping windmill" in the June 1979 issue. A

---

[1]*Magazine Index* is explained on page 155. For easier reading, magazine titles here and in other magazine entries mentioned in the book may be spelled out. Magazine titles are abbreviated in most periodical indexes, however. Check for their full spelling in the list that appears in the front or back of the particular index. If you can't find the abbreviation there, check *Periodical Title Abbreviations*, compiled by Leland G. Alkire. (3d ed., Gale Research Co. 1981).

buyer's guide to 35 windmills appears in the July 1982 issue of *Popular Science* magazine.

There are also many books on windmills. Check *Subject Guide to Books in Print* under WINDMILLS. One title is *Windmills: An Old-New Energy Source*, by Lucile McDonald.

USING POPULAR PERIODICAL INDEXES

Reader's Guide to Periodical Literature (RGPL) is the index familiar to most of us. It's the one we grew up with, as it's the index most schools and neighborhood libraries subscribe to. It was also one of the first published indexes (now past its 80th year). For many of us, checking *Reader's Guide* is a reflex action. We don't really know why we're checking it when we do article research; we know only that it's "what you're supposed to do." In truth, this periodical index has been credited with more than it can deliver. *Reader's Guide* doesn't cover every magazine published, by any stretch of the imagination. It presently indexes about 180. You'll have some idea just how few that is when you contrast that number with the nearly 3,000 magazines listed in *Writer's Market*, the annual guide to freelance writing opportunities, and the more than 6,500 magazines identified in Bill and Linda Katz's directory called *Magazines for Libraries*.

Some researchers use *Reader's Guide* as if it does everything. When college students ask a librarian "Where's the *Reader's Guide?*" she's often tempted to ask in reply, "What are you researching?" In fact, librarians often do ask. And if the student replies, "I'm researching the significance of African masks in the rituals of West African tribes," the librarian quickly steers him to *Anthropology Abstracts* and other anthropology-related indexes. After all, what can the student expect to find on African masks and rituals in *Good Housekeeping, Field and Stream,* or *Ms.* magazine? It's popular magazines like these that *Reader's Guide* covers. *Reader's Guide* may work in high school, but more varied research demands more varied magazines, and the indexes that lead you to them.

Periodical indexes are almost as numerous as diet books. Some good ones have existed for years in addition to several which have recently started publication. These other indexes can be used with or in place of *Reader's Guide*, depending on your purpose or the topic you're searching.

Very small libraries may carry only *Reader's Guide* and perhaps a few others. Libraries of similar size may carry a slightly different selection, so check them, too. Generally, the larger the library, the more indexes it carries.

The following list includes those indexes that cover popular newsstand and newsstand-type magazines. Use it to select the indexes to popular magazines that are most relevant for your search. This list includes most of the popular magazine indexes currently in print. (Scholarly indexes are covered later in the chapter.)

(NOTE: You'll notice that abstracts are also mentioned in this list. An abstract is an index that includes a summary or abstract of the article it refers to. Abstracts are generally more informative than a straight index entry, since the abstract tells you exactly what the article is about.

They're different in other ways, too. Indexes are arranged alphabetically by subject. Abstracts are arranged by broad categories with a subject index in the back of the volume.

Some indexes have an author as well as a subject approach; some don't. The best way to find out if the one you're using has this arrangement is to cross-check the author of any article to see if he's listed. [This information may also be mentioned in the index's introduction.] Abstracts usually have separate author indexes.)

Since indexes and abstracts use many abbreviations to save space, check the key, usually at the beginning of the volume, to decipher them.

1.*Abstracts of Popular Culture*. Bowling Green University, Popular Press. Issued quarterly. 1976-date. (Covers rock stars and music, avant-garde art, TV, books, Hollywood, the underground culture, and related subjects, in approximately 300 magazines.)

Indexes such magazines as *After Dark, Berkeley CA Barb, Blade Sunday Magazine* (Toledo, Ohio), *Car and Driver, Country Music Magazine, Dance Magazine, Flying Saucer Review, Good Housekeeping, Gourmet, Successful Farming, TV Guide*, and *TWA Ambassador*.

2.*Access*. John G. Burke, Inc. Issued three times a year. 1975-date. (Covers popular fields—health, family life, hobbies, jobs, consumer issues—in approximately 150 magazines similar to those indexed by *RGPL*. *Access* advertises itself as the supplement to *RGPL* and covers only magazines not indexed there.)

Indexes such magazines as *Bicycling, Early American Life, Family Circle, Modern Maturity, Penthouse, TV Guide, Woman's Day*, and over 75 city and regional magazines.

(*Access* is divided into author and subject sections. To search a subject, say ASTROLOGY, be sure you're checking the subject section. It mentions all bibliographic information [author, magazine, issue, date], about an article that appears *except* the article title. This is listed under the author's name in the author section.)

3. *Alternative Press Index*. Alternative Press Center, Inc. Issued quarterly. 1969-date. (Covers approximately 200 magazines representing the left-of-center viewpoint.)

Indexes such magazines as *Big Mama Rag, Briarpatch, Capital and Class, Dollars and Sense, Direct From Cuba, Fag Rag, Longest Revolution, Militant, New International Review, Puerto Rico Libre*, and *Radical America*.

4.*California Periodicals Index*. Gabriel Micrographics. Issued three times a year. 1978-date. (Covers approximately 30 magazines published in California about Californians, their life-styles and interests. The magazines which are covered by this index also come in a microform set called *California Periodicals on Microfilm*.)

Indexes California's city magazines (*Santa Barbara Magazine, San Francisco, San Diego Magazine, Orange Coast,* etc.) and such magazines as *California Garden, California Nurse, California Senior Citizen, High Country, Skin Diver, Surfing, West Art,* and *Westways.*

5.*Catholic Periodical and Literature Index.* Catholic Library Association. Bimonthly. 1930-date. (Covers approximately 130 magazines on Catholic life-style, family living, faith, education, culture, and other topics of interest to Catholics.)

Indexes such magazines as *America, Diakonia, Etudes, Living Light, Listening, National Catholic Report, St. Anthony Messenger, Sisters,* and *Thomist.*

6.*Children's Magazine Guide: Subject Index to Children's Literature.* The Guide, Inc. Ten issues a year. 1948-date. (Covers approximately 55 children's magazines devoted to nature, animals, holidays, family, crafts, current events, health, history, and other general subjects.)

Indexes such magazines as *Boy's Life, Children's Playmate, Co-ed, Cricket, Jack & Jill, Junior Scholastic, My Weekly Reader, Ranger Rick's Nature Magazine, Wee Wisdom,* and *Young Athlete.*

7.*Consumer's Index to Product Evaluations and Information Sources.* Pierian Press. Issued quarterly. 1973-date. (Selectively indexes articles that review consumer products and services from approximately 110 magazines.)

Indexes such magazines as *Audio, Backpacker, Camera 35, Caveat Emptor, Consumer Reports, Datamation, Modern Maturity, Model Railroader, Office, Outdoor Life, Parents Magazine, QST, Trailer Life,* and *Vintage.*

Q. Has there been a comparative study of the techniques and successes of the Berlitz versus the Lozanov language schools? I am about to invest time and money in conversational Spanish, and since both courses are costly, I would like information on them.

A. I found two articles rating foreign language study programs in *Consumer's Index to Product Evaluations and Information Sources.* One is called "Take Your Pick of Language Lessons" in the October 1982 issue of *Changing Times,* the other "Language Courses: Good, Better, Best" in the April 1982 issue of *Money* magazine. Back issues of these magazines are in the library.

8.*Index to Free Periodicals.* Pierian Press. Issued semiannually. 1976-date. (Covers approximately 55 free periodicals and free company magazines in a variety of topics such as tourism and travel, family life, human interest, hobbies, investing, consumer issues, as well as other general-interest topics. Most of these magazines are not in libraries.)

Indexes such magazines as *American Baby, Exxon USA, Ford Times, Kiwanis Magazine,* and *Rotarian International.*

9.*Index to How-To-Do-It Information.* Norman Lathrop Enterprises. Annual. 1963-date. (Covers approximately 55 magazines that feature how-to articles in arts and crafts, from woodworking and metal work to needlework and dough art. This index also covers the how-to articles in selected general magazines.)

Indexes such magazines as *Better Homes and Gardens, Boy's Life, Early American Life, Family Circle, Modern Photography, Mother Earth News, Popular Science, Radio-Electronics, Sky and Telescope, Woodworker,* and *Workbasket.*

10.*Index to Jewish Periodicals.* Index to Jewish Periodicals. Semiannual. 1963-date. (Covers approximately 35 popular and scholarly magazines mostly published in the United States and focusing on Jewish interests in education, psychology, religion, current events, culture, etc.)

Indexes such magazines as *ADL Bulletin, Commentary, Forum, Hadassah Magazine, Journal of Psychology and Judaism, Midstream, Moment, National Jewish Monthly,* and *Response.*

11.*Index to New England Periodicals.* Atlantic Indexing Co. Issued quarterly. 1977-date. (Covers New England history, politics, life-styles, economics, culture, and residents, in approximately 20 popular and scholarly New England magazines.)

Some of the magazines included are *Boston Magazine, Connecticut Magazine, Down East, Maine Times, New England Outdoors, New Hampshire Profiles, Vermont Life,* and *Yankee.*

12.*Index to Periodical Articles By and About Blacks.* G.K. Hall Co. Issued annually. 1950-date. (Covers approximately 25 popular and scholarly magazines in education, medicine, music, theater, civil rights, discrimination, and other topics relating to black Americans.)

Indexes such magazines as *Black Collegian, Black Enterprise, Ebony, Essence, Freedomways, Jet, Phylon,* and *Review of Black Political Economy.*

13.*Magazine Index.* Information Access Corp. Issued monthly. 1977-date. (*MI* is on microfilm and duplicates everything covered by *RGPL* and *Access.* It's totally cumulated and updated monthly with a new reel of microfilm. The publications covered by this index are listed at the beginning and end of the microfilm reel.)

In addition to articles, *MI* indexes new product evaluations, major editorials, short stories, poems, recipes, book reviews, and biographical pieces in over 400 magazines.

14.*Physical Education Index.* BenOak Publishing Co. Issued quarterly. 1978-date. (Covers fitness and nutrition, injuries, training and coaching, sports psychology, sports biographies, and individual sports from rugby to gymnastics in approximately 175 magazines.)

Indexes such magazines as *Australian Journal of Sports Medicine, Black Belt, Journal of Sport Medicine, Racquetball, Today's Jogger,* and numerous state physical education journals and newsletters. Approximately half the magazines are uniquely covered here and not duplicated by *Physical Education/Sports Index* below.

15.*Physical Education/Sports Index.* Marathon Press. Issued quarterly. 1973-date. (Covers approximately 100 professional and popular sports magazines in the same topics as *Physical Education Index.* About 28 journals in this index are duplicated by *PEI.*)

Indexes such magazines as *Coaching Clinic, Golf Digest, Journal of Sport and Social Issues, Journal of Sport History, Runner's World, Tennis Magazine, Volleyball,* and *Wilderness Camping.*

WHICH INDEX TO USE

Periodical indexes are not equally useful for very current articles. In the list above, *Reader's Guide* comes out most often, biweekly. Many indexes come out quarterly. Other indexes come out less frequently, semiannually or annually.

You'll also discover quickly that some magazines are covered simultaneously by several indexes. This is good. The juxtaposition of magazines by a subject or region that some indexes provide gives a unique perspective, something a general index doesn't always offer. For example, if you want to check *Yankee* magazine on a strictly New England topic such as life on Nantucket Island, you'd check *Access,* because it indexes *Yankee* magazine. In this case, it would also be useful to check *Index to New England Periodicals* which also covers *Yankee.* In this way, your search will reveal what other New England magazines have written on the subject.

As you use periodical indexes regularly, alert yourself to new indexes that come out and current ones that cease publication. Indexes are born and die much like the magazines they cover (and for the same reasons— lack of investment capital and/or profit).

You may also run into the situation where you don't know whether the magazine you need is indexed *anywhere.* The reference books below will help you find out.

1.*Chicorel Index to Abstracting and Indexing Services.* Chicorel Publishing Corp. 2nd ed. 1978.

This volume alphabetizes some 50,000 popular and scholarly magazines followed by a list of the indexes covering each.

2.*Ulrich's International Periodicals Directory.* R.R. Bowker Co. Annual.

This reference is a category arrangement of 65,000 international magazines and newsletters. *Ulrich's* main uses are to find the address, editor, and subscription price of magazines and to identify magazines in a certain field. One of the bonuses it includes is a line near the end of an entry that tells where a magazine is indexed.

3.*Magazines for Libraries*, by Bill Katz and Linda Stern Katz. 4th ed. R.R. Bowker Co. 1982.

The actual purpose of this reference book is to describe approximately 6,500 magazines recommended for small- and medium-sized libraries. As an extra, each magazine entry includes the index that covers the magazine.

Let's say you want to find out who indexes *American Rifleman*. The indexes listed with its entry in *Chicorel* are *Consumer's Index*, *Writings on American History*, and *Art and Archaeology Technical Abstracts*. (*Chicorel* is current only to the date of its publication. New editions come out approximately every five to ten years.)

Use *Ulrich's* magazine title index in the back to locate *American Rifleman* within the directory. The indexing information, when it appears, is on the last line of the entry.

In *Magazines for Libraries*, the index which covers each magazine listed appears just below the magazine title.

Neither *Ulrich's* nor *Magazines for Libraries* lists any indexes for *American Rifleman*.

Be sure to use the latest edition of *Ulrich's* and try all three reference books when checking to see where a magazine is indexed, because they don't all cover the same magazines. Also, two of the three books provide this information as a bonus, and when you use a book for a purpose other than its intended one, you may find coverage spotty.

INDEXING INFORMATION FOUND IN MAGAZINES

Many magazines themselves offer clues as to where they're indexed. Look in the masthead, the section listing the magazine's staff, near or on the table of contents page. The indexing information, if it appears, will be in the fine print. According to the fine print in *Changing Times* magazine, the publication is indexed in *Reader's Guide to Periodical Literature* and is available on records from Regional Libraries for the Blind.

If you want to relocate a specific article in a particular magazine, you may not need a general index, and you may not have to flip randomly through issue after issue hoping to find it. Some magazines print an annual index in their December or January issue. To look for an article on children's fiction in my personal collection of *Writer's Digest* magazine, I simply checked the magazine's annual index in the December issue. Finding it was a lot quicker than going to the library and plowing through *Magazine Index* which covers more than 400 magazines.

A very small number of magazines publish a cumulated index covering years or decades of issues in individual book-like volumes. *Scientific*

American and *National Geographic* are two magazines that issue cumulated indexes. In some libraries, these are shelved next to the bound back-issues of the magazine. In other libraries, they're kept in the reference section.

USING SCHOLARLY INDEXES AND ABSTRACTS

The only difference between scholarly and popular periodical indexes and abstracts is the type of magazines they cover. Popular indexes, as we've already seen, cover magazines appealing to the general public; scholarly indexes cover professional and research-oriented magazines (more typically called journals or periodicals). If you don't know where or *whether* a particularly scholarly journal is indexed, check the three sources (Ulrich's, Katz, Chicorel) described on page 156.

Academic libraries own many scholarly indexes and abstracts. But you shouldn't make any assumption about who owns what. Large libraries don't own everything simply because they're large. As I've already mentioned, academic libraries have individual subject strengths which you can check in the college catalog. It is in these subjects (astronomy, business, theater arts, etc.) that they own the largest selection of related indexes and magazines.

The main or central library on campus won't duplicate many of the indexes the department libraries own, so an index you need may be in another building. Call the main university library if you're not sure which library branch has the indexes and magazines in your subject.

Indexes are like books, because they cover more subjects than their titles imply. In addition to the scholarly indexes which are obvious for your particular research topic, you'll also find it helpful to use some indexes that are apparently unrelated. You will learn how to manipulate scholarly periodical indexes to cross fields and sometimes reveal the unexpected.

To determine the appropriate indexes to search, think in categories. For example, to research electronic music, think "electronics" and "music." This will lead you to *Music Index* and also to *Electrical and Electronics Abstracts*, where the topic is also covered. For an article on food or diet, you'd expect to look in *Nutrition Abstracts and Reviews;* but for unusual examples from folklore and history, check *Abstracts of Folklore Studies* and *Writings on American History*. The following is the entry for an article on food from *Abstracts of Folklore Studies:*

Yorkshire Cheese-making. Kate Mason. *Folk Life, pp. 7-17. Vol. 5, 1967.*

The article below comes from *Writings on American History:*

Pilgrim Cookery and Food Supplies of the 17th Century.

Helen T. Biggs. *American Cookery,* pp. 214-217. Vol. 60, 1935.

The topic of computers can touch many fields. That means you'd search other indexes besides *Computing Reviews.* For an article on computers in the field of architecture, you'll find this in *Art Index* (which covers architecture):

How a California Firm Grew up with the Computer.
B. Willis. *American Institute of Architects Journal.*
Vol. 65, p.48+, Jan. 1976.

Here's an article from *Index to Legal Periodicals* on the computer's connection with privacy:

Privacy, Law Enforcement and Public Interest:
Computerized Criminal Records. *Montana Law Review.*
Vol. 36, pp. 60-79, Winter 1975.

You would check *Education Index* for information on computerized teaching machines; *Communications Abstracts* for articles on computers in newspaper publishing.

The following examples show the broad coverage possible in some apparently narrowly focused scholarly indexes. Take the index *Writings on American History*, for example. What subjects would you think this index covers? If you said American history, go stand in a corner. It actually covers literature, theater, art, religion, medicine, conservation, race relations, economics, industry—in a word, EVERYTHING in American history. A source like this is especially rich for people who want information on a specific topic without getting bogged down in lots of books and heavy reading.

These articles from *WAH* show its broad approach to American history:

The Criminal Patterns of Boston since 1849. Theodore N. Ferdinand.
American Journal of Sociology. Vol. 73, July 1967. pp. 84-99.
First of the Gold Rush Theaters. Charles Hume.
California Historical Quarterly. Vol. 45, Dec. 1967, pp. 337-44.
Lincoln's World Image. Herman Blum. *Lincoln Herald.* Vol. 65,
Summer 1967. pp. 49-50.
The Sex Radicals in High Victorian America. Hal O. Sears.
Virginia Quarterly Review. Vol. 48, Summer 1972. pp. 377-92.

Similarly, these diverse entries from *Applied Science and Technology Index* show you its broad scope:

Inflatable Buildings. *Aircraft Engineering*, Vol. 49, pp. 23-24, Aug. 1977.
Tobacco May be Food Source, says USDA. T.C. Tso. *Food Engineering.*
Vol. 49, p. 25, July 1977.
Holograms Help to Print on China. *New Scientist*,
Vol 74, p. 275, May 5, 1977.

To use any scholarly index effectively, be sure you know the answers to the following questions.

How is the index or abstract arranged? Scholarly indexes are arranged like popular periodical indexes—alphabetically by subject. The abstracts, arranged by broad categories, print their subject index in the back or front of a volume.

Does the index or abstract cover articles alone? In addition to periodical articles, many scholarly indexes also mention books in their field, chapters in books, conference proceedings, and government documents. The type of research material, as well as subjects covered, is quite broad. This information is obvious from the text, and it may also be mentioned in the introduction.

Does the index or abstract include an author approach? As with popular indexes, cross-check by the author of an article to determine which scholarly indexes include an author approach (or check the introduction). Abstracts provide separate author indexes.

What periodicals does the index or abstract cover? You may want to note the publications each index covers. The list usually appears in the front or the back of a volume (though not necessarily *every* volume). Don't forget to check the abbreviations in the key.

Are "cumulations" available? Many indexes come out four to twelve times a year and cumulate into an annual hardcover volume. Searching annual volumes is tedious in cases where you must check articles over a five- or ten-year period. Look for cumulative volumes. Many indexes issue a five-, ten-, even twenty- or thirty-year cumulation in one set of books. These are easier to search than the individual volumes.

What are the limitations of abstracts? Although abstracts are extremely helpful for the article (and book) summaries they provide, their subject indexes are frequently too broad to be useful. For example, I recently searched for information on municipal carpooling programs in *Sage Urban Studies Abstracts*, and while I accidentally found an article on carpooling within the volume, it wasn't under CARPOOLING. When I checked the subject index for other articles, I noticed that CARPOOLING was not even used as a subject. Information was buried under the general topic of TRANSPORTATION.

Where can I find science and technical indexes? Because of the overlapping coverage offered by the scholarly indexes that are included here, I've omitted many highly technical indexes and abstracts from the list below—publications such as *Abstracts on Hygiene, Aerospace Medicine and Biology, Chemical Abstracts, Food Science and Technology Abstracts, Gas Abstracts, Oceanic Abstracts,* and *Solar Energy Index.* Although many of the highly technical indexes and abstracts may include some articles useful in your research, you'll have to do much screening to find them. If you want to check them for yourself, these technical indexes are available in science libraries.

Start your in-depth search with the following scholarly indexes and abstracts. The list covers about half of those in print; but the indexes included cover most subjects. Indexes also overlap; that is, many cover the same periodicals. *Public Opinion Quarterly,* for example, is covered by over a dozen indexes. This suggests that you needn't search every index in a field to be thorough. You may not be able to locate every index in your area in any case.

1.*Abstracts in Anthropology.* Baywood Publishing Co. 1970-date. (Covers approximately 300 periodicals in archaeology, ethnology, language, physical anthropology, and related subjects.)

Indexes such periodicals as *BC Studies, Florida Anthropologist, Heredity, Iran, Journal of Sex Research, Man in India,* and *Primates.*

2.*Abstracts of English Studies*. National Council of Teachers of English. 1958-date. (Covers approximately 1,500 international periodicals in American and English literature and language, aesthetics, criticism, theory, women in literature, black studies, and related subjects.)

Indexes such periodicals as *Arts in Society, Renaissance Quarterly, Rocky Mountain Review, Southern Literary Journal, Studies in American Humor, Theatre Annual,* and *Thomas Wolfe Newsletter*.

3.*Abstracts of Folklore Studies*. American Folklore Society, 1960-1975. (Covers approximately 175 periodicals in mythology, wit and humor, legends, superstition, folk songs and dances, customs, riddles, and the folklore of physical objects and costume. *AFS* ceased publication in 1975, but it's still useful. Other indexes such as *Humanities Index* cover folkore studies to date.)

Indexes such periodicals as *Bluegrass Unlimited, Grit, Kentucky Folklore Record, Names, Relics, Scottish Studies,* and *Sports Afield*.

4.*Air University Library Index to Military Periodicals*. Air University Library, Maxwell Air Force Base. 1949-date. (Covers approximately 75 periodicals in military training, air accidents, foreign air forces, unconventional warfare, military tactics and strategy, national security, preparedness, and other subjects related to air military science.)

Indexes such periodicals as *Air Force Times, Armada International, Defense Electronics, International Security, Military Engineer, Signal,* and *Soviet Military Review*.

5.*America: history and life:* part A, Article Abstracts and Citations. ABC-Clio, Inc. 1964-date. (Covers approximately 2,200 international periodicals and serial publications on all aspects of U.S. and Canadian history, from the history of theater to the history of education.)

Indexes such periodicals as *The American West, Civil War History, Journal of Southern History, Military Affairs, Montana,* and *Virginia Cavalcade*.

6.*Applied Science and Technology Index*. H.W. Wilson Co. 1913-date. (Covers approximately 180 periodicals in space science, computers, energy, fire technology, food industry, geology, mathematics, mineralogy, metallurgy, oceanography, oil and gas, plastics, transportation, and other industrial and mechanical arts.)

Indexes such periodicals as *Adhesives Age, American Metric Journal, Audio, Cryogenics, Energy Conversion, Fire Technology, Microwaves, Monthly Weather Review, Public Roads, Rock Products, Surveying & Mapping, Textile World,* and *Wireless World*.

Q. Please furnish me with resources to find an electric wheelchair for a quadriplegic who can move only her neck. The wheelchair must move by breathing or speaking into a device.

A. An article in the November 1979 issue of *Mechanical Engineering* magazine which I found through *Applied Science and Technology Index*, describes a sensor device which allows wheelchairs to be controlled by eye movements. A small lamp in a sensor directs a low intensity beam at the eye. A photo cell/lamp combination mounted on an eyeglass frame catches the reflected beam, and when the wearer moves his eyes in different directions, he can start, stop, or turn the chair.

The device was originally developed for astronauts to control a spacecraft during certain kinds of maneuvers. It can also be adapted to allow the user to dial telephones, turn pages, and control appliances.

For further information, contact Marshall Space Flight Center, Code ATol, Huntsville, AL 35812. Attention: MFS-25091.

7.*Art Index.* H.W.Wilson Co. 1929-date. (Covers approximately 140 periodicals in photography, film, archaeology, graphic arts, industrial design, interior design, fine arts, city planning, crafts, architecture, and related subjects.)

Indexes such periodicals as *African Arts, Boston Museum Bulletin, Camera, Craft Horizons, Japan Architect, Journal of Egyptian Archaeology, Museums Journal, La Revue du Louvre et des Musées de France,* and *Sight and Sound.*

8.*Biography Index.* H.W. Wilson Co. 1946-date. (Indexes biographical articles from about 2,000 popular and scholarly periodicals covered by other Wilson indexes. Also indexes biographical books and chapters from collective biographies. People included fall into all fields—politics, the arts, education, literature, the military, science, etc.)

9.*Biological and Agricultural Index.* H.W. Wilson Co. 1913-date. (Covers approximately 200 periodicals in animal husbandry, botany, conservation, food science, pesticides, veterinary medicine, zoology, and related sciences.)

Indexes such periodicals as *Cereal Chemistry, Evolution, Forest Science, Molecular Biology, Oceans, Pest Control, Plants & Gardens,* and *Western Horseman.*

10.*Business Index.* Information Access Corp. 1979-date. (In microfilm only.) (Covers books and approximately 350 periodicals plus *The New York Times* financial section. This index duplicates *Business Periodicals Index,* #11, and covers approximately 70 more periodicals.)

11.*Business Periodicals Index.* H.W. Wilson Co. 1958-date. (Covers approximately 280 periodicals in accounting, advertising, banking, communications, computers, economics, industrial relations, international business, personnel administration, marketing, occupational health and safety, real estate, etc., as well as specific industries and businesses.)

Indexes such periodicals as *American Druggist, Arbitration Journal, Black Enterprise, Commodities, Consumer News, Editor & Publisher, Euromoney, Fleet Owner, Governmental Finance, Hotel & Motel Management, Nursing*

Homes, Public Relations Quarterly, Real Estate Appraiser, and *Social Security Bulletin.*

12.*Child Development Abstracts and Bibliography.* University of Chicago Press. 1927-date. (Covers books and approximately 175 periodicals in learning, perception, psychology, health, the family, education, and other aspects of child study.)

Indexes such periodicals as *Child Care Quarterly, Journal of Abnormal Child Psychology, Journal of Child Language, Journal of Pediatrics, Psychology in the Schools,* and *Young Children.*

13.*Combined Retrospective Index to Journals in History, 1838-1974.* 11 vols. Carrollton Press. 1977-78. (Covers approximately 600 international periodicals in the history of culture, politics, education, business, etc. This index is arranged by geographic region, then subdivided by period, broad topic, and key word in article title context. Note that unlike other indexes, article entries in the *CRIJ* indexes [also see #14 and #15] are arranged in columns. Periodicals are assigned a number rather than abbreviated. The key is on the inside front and back covers. Another unique feature of the *CRIJ* indexes is that they are not continuously issued as other indexes are. They're complete sets. They're also among the few indexes that cover pre-20th-century periodicals.)

Indexes periodicals such as *Aerospace Historian, Business History, Ethnohistory, Pharmacy in History, Labor History, Quaker History,* and *New Testament Studies.*

14.*Combined Retrospective Index to Journals in Political Science, 1886-1974.* 8 vols. Carrollton Press. 1977-78. (Covers approximately 200 periodicals in political thought, national minorities, multinational corporations, foreign political ideologies, electoral processes, the military, and related subjects from the 16th century to the present. The index is arranged by broad subject category such as international affairs; then articles are subarranged by key word.)

Indexes periodicals such as *Africa Today, Disarmament, Dissent, Kuwait, Problems of Communism, Scandinavian Studies, Social Security Bulletin,* and *UN Review.*

15.*Combined Retrospective Index to Journals in Sociology, 1895-1974.* 6 vols. Carrollton Press. 1978. (Covers approximately 125 periodicals in family planning, behavior, health, mass communication, group interactions, and related subjects. The index is arranged by broad category; then articles are subarranged by key word.)

Indexes periodicals such as *Family Law Quarterly, Human Relations, Journal of Cross Cultural Psychology, Journal of Leisure Research,* and *Soviet Sociology.*

16.*Communications Abstracts.* Sage Publications. 1978-date. (Covers approximately 200 periodicals in advertising, broadcasting, mass communications, journalism, public relations, radio, speech, and related subjects.)

Indexes such periodicals as *Brain and Language, Decision Sciences, Intermedia, Irish Broadcasting Review, Journal of Advertising Research, Public Opinion Quarterly,* and *Visible Language.*

17.*Criminal Justice Abstracts.* National Council on Crime and Delinquency. 1968-date. (Covers approximately 160 international periodicals in crime prevention, genetics and crime, juvenile offenders, the insanity defense, attitudes on firearms, and related subjects.)

Indexes periodicals such as *Journal of Probation & Parole, Criminal Law Bulletin, FBI Law Enforcement Bulletin, Justice System Journal,* and *Crime and Public Policy.*

18.*Current Index to Journals in Education.* Oryx Press. 1969-date. (Covers approximately 780 educational and education-related journals on adult education, vocational education, counseling, higher education, testing, and individual subjects that are taught. This largely duplicates *Education Index.*)

Indexes periodicals such as *Bilingual Review, Chinese Education, Com-College Review, Counseling Psychologist, Journal of Aesthetic Education, Journal of Basic Writing, Journal of Moral Education,* and *Nurse Educator.*

19.*Education Index.* H.W. Wilson Co. 1929-date. (Covers approximately 200 periodicals in preschool-to-adult education, school administration, audiovisuals, counseling, curriculum materials, and teacher education, as well as subjects taught in the schools: languages, social studies, mental health, religion, etc.)

Indexes such journals such as *American Biology Teacher, Gifted Child Quarterly, Journal of American Indian Education, Journal of Learning Disabilities, Jewish Education, Music Journal, Psychology in the Schools, School Shop, Urban Education,* and *Western European Education.*

20.*Engineering Index.* Engineering Index, Inc. 1884-date. (Covers technical reports, conference proceedings, books, and approximately 1,400 journals in the design, construction, maintenance, and durability of buildings, bridges, dams, roads, various modes of transportation and equipment, and related subjects.)

Indexes periodicals such as *Air Force Engineering and Services Quarterly, Earthquake Engineering & Structural Dynamics, Engineering in Medicine, Industrial Robot,* and *Nuclear Engineering & Design.*

21.*Film Literature Index.* Filmdex. 1973-date. (Covers approximately 135 periodicals in technical aspects of film, festivals, unreleased films, avant-garde films, instructional materials, producers, wages and salaries, women in film, and related subjects.)

Indexes periodicals such as *Bilingual Review, Chinese Education, Com College Review, Counseling Psychologist, Journal of Aesthetic Education, Journal* includes selective indexing of magazines such as *Gypsy Scholar, Harper's Bazaar, School Arts, Sports Illustrated,* and *Variety.*

22.*General Science Index*. H.W. Wilson Co. 1978-date. (A montage of approximately 90 selected periodicals from other comprehensive science and technical indexes issued by Wilson. It is useful primarily in smaller libraries that may have no need for the more complete Wilson indexes but who want representation in several sciences. Subjects covered are astronomy, biology, botany, chemistry, earth science, nutrition, genetics, mathematics, medicine and health, oceanography, physics, physiology, zoology, etc.)

Indexes such periodicals as *American Biology Teacher, Audubon, Evolution, Horticulture, International Wildlife, Journal of Heredity, Nature, Oceans, Psychology Today, RN Magazine, Science Digest, Sky and Telescope,* and *Weatherwise.*

23.*Hispanic American Periodicals Index*. UCLA Latin American Center Publications. 1974-date. (Covers approximately 250 American and Spanish-language periodicals in Hispanic humanities and social sciences such as literature and criticism, politics, social conflict, labor unrest, land reform, migration, and theater in the United States, Mexico, the Caribbean, Central and South America.)

Indexes such periodicals as *The Americas, Caribbean Quarterly, Cuban Studies, Cultura* (Brazil), *Guatemala Indigena, Latin American Theatre Review,* and *Nueva Sociedad* (Costa Rica).

24.*Historical Abstracts*. ABC-Clio, Inc. 1955-date. (Covers approximately 2,000 international periodicals in all aspects of history. Part A of *HA* covers modern history, 1450-1914, and Part B covers 20th-century history, 1914-date.)

Indexes such periodicals as *Arctic, Baptist Quarterly, Carolina Lifestyle, History of Agriculture, Islamic Culture, Nigeria Magazine, Sea History, War & Society,* and *Youth and Society.*

25.*Hospital Literature Index*. American Hospital Assn. 1945-date. (Covers approximately 550 English-language periodicals in hospital planning, administration, equipment, staffing and economics, nursing homes and other health-care institutions, and the general field of health and patient-care delivery.)

Indexes such periodicals as *Early Human Development, FDA Consumer, Food Management, Geriatrics, Infection Control Digest, Intensive Care Medicine, Journal of Music Therapy, Michigan Hospitals,* and *Pharmacy Times.*

26.*Human Resources Abstracts*. Sage Publications. 1966-date. (Covers approximately 325 periodicals in manpower problems, the labor market, earnings and benefits, employment and unemployment, equal employment opportunity, career development, etc.)

Indexes such periodicals as *Amerasia Journal, Bureaucrat, Employee Relations, Journal of Family Issues, Modern China, Small Group Behavior,* and *Soviet Sociology.*

27.*Humanities Index*. H.W. Wilson Co. 1974-date. (This index split off from *Social Sciences and Humanities Index* in 1974. Covers approximately 210 periodicals in archaeology and classical studies, folklore, history, language, literary and political criticism, performing arts, philosophy, theology, etc.)

Indexes such periodicals as *African Literature Today, American Speech, Church History, Civil War History, Dance Scope, Ethnomusicology, Hispanic Review, Journal of Mexican American History, Novel, Opera, Review of Metaphysics, Slavic Review, Victorian Poetry,* and *Yale Theater.*

28.*Index Medicus.* National Library of Medicine. 1960-date. (Covers approximately 2,600 international periodicals in disease control, genetics, psychiatry, dentistry, veterinary medicine, sports physiology, and transplants.)

Indexes such periodicals as *Advances in Virus Research, Annals of Allergy, Blood, Bulletin of the Menninger Clinic, Currents in Alcoholism, Journal of Antibiotics, Nursing Forum,* and *Vascular Surgery.*

Q. I am looking for the latest research on menstruation. Though this information is likely to be found in medical journals, I'm afraid they might be too technical for my purposes. Can you suggest any other sources?

A. The topic is covered well and from many viewpoints in a number of indexes. I checked several, and besides the obvious one that covers medicine (*Index Medicus*), you'll also want to check *Psychological Abstracts, Applied Science and Technology Index,* and *Social Sciences Index.* Many of the articles cover the medical, social, and psychological aspect of menstruation. The only way to find out if they're too technical for you is to check some. One article I found in *Biological and Agricultural Index* is entitled "Nutrition-fertility interaction in lactating women of low income groups," in the May 1981 issue of the *British Journal of Nutrition.* (The topic is covered in even more indexes with other focuses—*Women Studies Abstracts* and *Religion and Theological Abstracts,* etc.)

29.*Index to Legal Periodicals.* H.W. Wilson Co. 1908-date. (Covers approximately 350 journals in all aspects of military, civilian, and international legal matters from corporation law to family practice.)

Indexes such journals as *Air Force JAG Law Review, Atomic Energy Law Journal, Black Law Journal, Criminal Law Quarterly, Duquesne Law Review, The Irish Jurist, Journal of Maritime Law & Commerce, Performing Arts Review, Tax Advisor, Trusts & Estates, Unauthorized Practice News,* and *Women Lawyers Journal.*

30.*Index to United States Government Periodicals.* Infordata International, Inc. 1974-date. (Covers approximately 170 government-published periodicals in government scientific and sociological research, aerospace, law, national defense, the arts, wildlife and conservation, consumerism, and other subjects relating to the work of various governmental agencies and departments.)

Indexes such periodicals as *Aging, Endangered Species Technical Bulletin, Fish and Wildlife News, Mine Safety and Health, Postal Life, Recombinant DNA Technical Bulletin,* and *Tree Plant Notes.*

31.*International Index to Periodicals.* H.W. Wilson Co. 1907-74. (*IIP* was known as *Social Sciences and Humanities Index* from 1965 to 1974. In 1974 it split into two separate indexes: *Social Sciences Index* and *Humanities Index.* Send entries #27 and #52 for coverage information.)

32.*International Political Science Abstracts.* International Political Science Association. 1951-date. (Covers approximately 700 international periodicals in public opinion, political ideology, foreign policy, military institutions, international relations, etc.)

Indexes such periodicals as *Arab Studies Quarterly, Australian Outlook, Continent, Government Opposition, Indonesia, Journal of Developing Areas,* and *Yearbook of Finnish Foreign Policy.*

Q. I'm looking for confirmation that the United States years ago agreed to cede the Panama Canal to Panama very shortly. Will Panama make concessions to America's shipping after it takes over?

A. The government has issued copies of the 1977 treaty hearings which I found through an index called *Public Affairs Information Service Bulletin.* The treaty provides for the transfer of the administration of the Panama Canal from the United States to Panama in stages, and it should be completed by 2000. The hearings are rather complicated to wade through. Articles I found through *International Political Science Abstracts* suggest that this may be due to the fact that some important terms of the treaty are obscured to the point of incomprehensibility. The hearings do state, however, that the Canal plays a key role in international commerce, and the United States intends to negotiate for its use.

One of the articles I mentioned above, from the *Yearbook of World Affairs* (1981, page 181 +), also criticizes the United States for ignoring continuing obligations to Panama under the Hay-Pauncefote Treaty of 1901.

Another critical article in the *Journal of Contemporary History* (April, 1980, page 299 +) accuses the United States of "imperial hangover." The author says that America must get over the ownership mentality imbedded in its national psychology concerning the Canal.

I suggest that you examine these articles and the treaty hearings to fully understand the problem. Apparently, the treaty has not, according to its critics, provided a simple, or satisfactory, solution.

33.*Language and Language Behavior Abstracts.* Sociological Abstracts, Inc. 1967-current. (Covers approximately 1,000 international periodicals in audiology, linguistics, educational psychology, phonetics, communication, psychology, and related topics.)

Indexes such periodicals as *Brain and Language, Cleft Palate Journal, Journal of Auditory Research, Language Problems and Language Planning,* and *Oceanic Linguistics.*

34. *Legal Resource Index.* Information Access Corp. 1980-date.(microfilm only.) (Covers approximately 600 periodicals and four legal newspapers, overlapping with *Index to Legal Periodicals, #29.*)

35.*Library Literature.* H.W. Wilson Co. 1921-date. (Covers approximately 220 periodicals in publishing, map and picture librarianship, research, censorship, on-line data bases, book preservation, book selling, etc.)

Indexes such periodicals as *American Archivist, Catholic Library World, Film Library Quarterly, Indexer, Law Library Journal, School Libraries,* and *Virginia Librarian.*

36.*Music Index.* Information Coordinators, Inc. 1949-date. (Covers approximately 260 periodicals in music from classical to rock; also covers music education, concerts, music abroad, innovative music techniques, composition, music celebrities, and related subjects.)

Indexes such periodicals as *American String Teacher, Billboard, Church Music, Composer, English Dance and Song, Jazz Report, Journal of Music Therapy, Record Collector,* and *Southern Folklore Quarterly.*

37.*Nineteenth Century Reader's Guide to Periodical Literature, 1890-99.* H.W. Wilson Co. 1890-1899. (Covers approximately 55, mostly defunct, late-19th-century magazines in general subjects such as the military, motion pictures, religion, Indians, economics, transportation, farming, family life, travel, politics, foreign relations, etc.)

Indexes such magazines as *Appleton's Popular Science Monthly, Catholic World, Education, North American Review, Overland Monthly, Political Science Quarterly, Scientific American,* and *Yale Review.*

Q. Some time ago I saw a newspaper reference to a school for the study of lost antiquities, located on Point Loma in San Diego. Can you tell me what this school was and where the materials from it are? Also, what kind of antiquities were studied? I need this information for an article I am writing.

A. According to the San Diego Public Library, the present site of Point Loma College housed (from 1897 to 1941) the headquarters of a flourishing world movement called Theosophy. The School for the Revival of the Lost Mysteries of Antiquity, later shortened to the School of Antiquity, was part of the complex of buildings. The school served as a literary repository and offered public lectures and correspondence courses.

Originally organized as a utopian community, the Theosophists believed in Eastern and occult philosophies. Financial problems, power struggles, and the death of the leader, Katherine Tingley, led to the end of the school in 1941.

UCSD houses the largest collection in this area of books, magazines, and unpublished papers generated by the group. Articles about the group also ran in *Outlook* and *Arena*, national magazines of the day. These can be traced through *Nineteenth Century Reader's Guide to Periodical Literature, 1890-99*, with some also listed in *Poole's Index to Periodical Literature, 1802-1907* and early editions of *Reader's Guide to Periodical Literature*.

38.*Nutrition Abstracts and Reviews*. Commonwealth Agricultural Bureau and John Wiley & Sons. 1931-date. (Covers approximately 500 international periodicals in food processing, feeding programs, agriculture, malnutrition, vitaminology, and related subjects.)

Indexes such periodicals as *Diabetes, Gerontology, Journal of Food Science, Nestle Research News, Journal of the National Cancer Institute*, and *Kidney International*.

39.*Philosopher's Index*. Bowling Green State University. 1966-date. (Covers books, dissertations, and approximately 300 international periodicals in aesthetics, epistemology, language, metaphysics, anthropology, political philosophy, religion, science, etc.)

Indexes such periodicals as *Algebra and Logic, Aquinas, Criminal Justice Ethics, Free Inquiry, Journal of Indian Philosophy, Research in Phenomenology*, and *The Thomist*.

40.*Pollution Abstracts*. Cambridge Scientific Abstracts. 1970-current. (Covers technical reports, government documents, and approximately 2,500 international periodicals in air, water and noise pollution, land pollution, recycling, public health, environmental policies and programs, legislation, etc.)

Indexes such periodicals as *American Nuclear Society Transactions, Coastal Zone Management Journal, High Speed Surface Craft, Radiation Research, Toxicology*, and *Undersea Biomedical Research*.

41.*Poole's Index to Periodical Literature, 1802-1907*. Houghton Mifflin. 1887-1908. Reprinted by Peter Smith, 1938. (Covers approximately 175 defunct magazines in general subjects such as hunting, transportation, pop psychology of the day, education, child rearing, politics, travel, etc.)

Indexes such magazines as *Jewish Quarterly Review, Knowledge, Methodist Review, Pall Mall Magazine, Quarterly Journal of Economics*, and *Sunday Magazine*.

42.*Population Index*. Office of Population Research, Princeton University and Population Association of America, Inc. 1913-date. (Covers approximately 500 periodicals and serial publications in population trends, political and sociological aspects of world population, family planning, demographic studies, and related subjects.)

Indexes such periodicals as *Advances in Planned Parenthood, Demography India, Nigerian Journal of Economic and Social Studies, Pakistan Development Review*, and *Social Science and Medicine*.

43.*Predicasts F & S Index: United States*. Predicasts, Inc. 1960-date. (Covers special reports and approximately 750 periodicals, business newspapěrs, and trade magazines. The index is divided into two sections: Industries and Products, and Companies.)

Indexes such periodicals as *Beverage World, Capital Investments of the World, Petroleum Industry, Fishing News International, Lloyd's Mexican Economic Report, Marketing in Hungary, Seatrade,* and *Vending Times.*

44. *Psychological Abstracts*. American Psychological Assoc., Inc. 1927-date. (Covers dissertations and approximately 850 international periodicals in animal psychology, parapsychology, personality development, marriage and the family, mental disorders, sex roles, and related subjects.)

Indexes such periodicals as *Alternative Lifestyles, Death Education, Intelligence, International Journal of Group Tensions, Journal of Black Psychology, Pain, Rural Sociology,* and *Sleep.*

45.*Public Affairs Information Service (PAIS) Bulletin*. Public Affairs Information Service, Inc. 1915-date. (Covers approximately 425 periodicals in international relations, economics, current events, commerce, industry, government affairs, law, and related fields.)

Indexes such periodicals as *African Business, Aging, Arab Economist, Capital Goods Report, Journal of Criminal Justice, Military Review, Police Chief, San Francisco Business, Ukrainian Quarterly,* and *World Marxist Review.*

46.*Religion Index One*. American Theological Library Assoc. 1949-date. (Covers approximately 200 international periodicals in church history, sociology and psychology of religion, liturgical reform, the Bible, women in religion, religious current events, and related topics.)

Indexes such periodicals as *American Protestant Hospital Association Bulletin, The Biblical Archaeologist, The Greek Orthodox Theological Review, Indian Journal of Theology, Judaism, Lutheran World,* and *Radical Religion.*

47.*Resources in Education*. Government Printing Office. 1966-date. (Covers reports sent to Education Resources Information Center (ERIC), an information network. The reports cover such subjects as education, psychology, family living, career guidance, literacy, and counseling. Documents are available from ERIC Documents Reproduction Service, or you can read them on microform if your library subscribes to the ERIC collection.)

Use this index by subject. Each entry has an ED number. When you check the entry by its ED number in another section of the index, you can read a summary of the report.

48.*Sage Family Studies Abstracts*. Sage Publications. 1979-date. (Covers approximately 260 periodicals in childhood development, foster care, death, family life, divorce, remarriage, family violence and abuse, and related subjects.)

Indexes such periodicals as *Adolescence, Generations, Journal of Abnormal Psychology, Journal of Homosexuality, PTA Today, Stepfamily Bulletin*, and *Suicide and Life Threatening Behavior*.

49.*Sage Public Administration Abstracts*. Sage Publications. 1974-date. (Covers approximately 275 periodicals in city budgeting and finance, the public interest, policy making, bureaucracy, and related subjects.)

Indexes such periodicals as *American Journal of Public Health, Arizona Review, Charities USA, Government Executive, Journal of Psychoactive Drugs,* and *New Society*.

50.*Sage Race Relations Abstracts*. Sage Publications. 1975-date. (Covers approximately 130 periodicals in integration, discrimination, attitudes, education, employment, family relations, health, women, culture, identity, etc.)

Indexes such periodicals as *Afro American in New York Life and History, Civil Rights Alert, Contemporary Marxism, Journal of Ethnic Studies, Klanwatch, Patterns of Prejudice,* and *Southern Exposure*.

51.*Sage Urban Studies Abstracts*. Sage Publications. 1973-date. (Covers research reports, dissertations, pamphlets, and approximately 180 periodicals in employment, economic development, crime, law enforcement, public welfare, taxation, and related subjects.)

Indexes such periodicals as *Citizen Participation, Connecticut Government, Environment and Behavior, Governmental Finance, Landscape, Small Town,* and *World Politics*.

52.*Social Sciences Index*. H.W. Wilson Co. 1974-date. (This index split off from *Social Sciences and Humanities Index* in 1974. Covers approximately 260 periodicals in anthropology, economics, environmental studies, geography, law, criminology, political science, public administration, psychology, sociology, etc.)

Indexes such periodicals as *Armed Forces & Society, Corrections Today, Futurist, Journal of Housing, Rural Sociology, Social Work,* and *Western Political Quarterly*.

53.*Sociological Abstracts*. Sociological Abstracts, Inc. 1953-current. (Covers approximately 1,300 international periodicals in rural and urban sociology, the family and socialization, poverty, violence, culture, education, religion, and related subjects.)

Indexes such periodicals as *Audio-Visual Language Journal, Black Sociologist, Contemporary Marxism, Drugs in Health Care, Family Relations,* and *Radical American Spelling Progress Bulletin*.

54.*Women Studies Abstracts*. Rush Publishing Co. 1972-date. (Covers books, reports, and approximately 500 periodicals in psychology, public affairs, women and education, law, mental and physical health, government, family, etc.)

Indexes such periodicals as *American Journal of Clinical Nutrition, Child*

Development, New Directions for Women, Off Our Backs, Psychology of Women Quarterly, and *Research Quarterly for Exercise and Sport.*

55.*Writings on American History.* American Historical Association. 1903-date. (Covers approximately 400 international American history periodicals in the history of culture, business and industry, religion, labor, theater, etc.)

Indexes such periodicals as *Alabama Review, Detroit in Perspective, Film & History, Journal of Religious History, Kansas History, Railroad History, Swedish Pioneer Historical Review,* and *Tampa Bay History.*

OTHER SCHOLARLY INDEXES

The two directories below offer another picture of the total number of scholarly indexes and abstracts in print. They're both arranged by broad topic (biological sciences, for example). You can check the indexes in the back of each volume for the name of the scholarly index you want, and then flip to the actual index entry for a description of how it's arranged, what it covers, etc.

Scholarly indexes generally increase the number of magazines they cover each year. You can keep alert for new indexes, or indexes that change titles, by consulting the most recent edition of these directories which are updated every five to ten years:

Abstracts and Indexes in the Sciences and Technology, by Dolores B. Owen and Marguerite M. Hanchey. Scarecrow Press. 1974.

Periodical Indexes in the Social Sciences and Humanities: A Subject Guide, by Lois Harzfeld. Scarecrow Press. 1978.

A FINAL TIP ON SCHOLARLY PERIODICALS

One unique thing about scholarly periodicals is the way you must look up some of them in catalogs and printed lists. Be aware of this simple filing rule:

Periodicals that include in their titles an association or organization name, whether it's a bank, a social club, or a university, are filed under the organization's name. That's why *Journal of the American Psychiatry Association* is found under *A,* while *Journal of Psychiatry* is alphabetized under *J.* This kind of arrangement keeps all of an organization's publications together.[2]

American Musicological Society. *Bulletin.*
American Musicological Society. *Journal.*

[2]This is one of those rare instances when catalogers may take liberties with the word order in the title of a publication. Even if the cover says *Journal of the American Medical Association,* it will be cataloged and filed under *A.*

American Musicological Society. *Papers.*

In all other cases, periodicals are filed as they are worded, such as *New Jersey History* under *N.*

MAGAZINE RESEARCH BY COMPUTER

Thanks to new technology, you can now search magazine indexes by computer instead of by hand. The service is offered by a growing number of large libraries and independent firms. If you've searched magazine indexes manually for any time at all, you'll appreciate the time *this* method saves.

To search magazines by computer, a desktop computer terminal is connected by your telephone to a huge data bank which may be hundreds of miles away. (Two of the three major data base suppliers are located in California; the third is in New York.) Data bases that store magazine indexes are called bibliographic data bases. Today, there are more than 125 periodical indexes you can search by computer. *Psychological Abstracts, ERIC, Pollution Abstracts, Reader's Guide to Periodical Literature,* and *Magazine Index* are all available on-line as are most of the indexes mentioned in this chapter.

Many corporate libraries search indexes by computer. They do this to carry out company research just as they would do with printed materials. Because of the costs involved, information industry experts expect the business sector to be the primary user of computerized data base searching. Average search costs presently range from $10 to well over $300 an hour depending on the charge of the individual data base. A completed search can average $30 for 10 minutes (including royalties, a charge per citation, and the services of an experienced researcher). Companies can offset these costs more easily than can individual researchers. And as the greater access to information may increase a company's profits, businesses find the service is worth the price. Besides, for businesses, it's a taxable expense.

You, too, may be willing to pay a library or commercial service to do a computer search for magazine articles. If time is at a premium for you, the costs involved may be worth it.

Let's say you want to search for information on the kind of parenting problems uniquely experienced by a racially mixed couple. You'll find that the term most suitable to search through indexes is INTERRACIAL MARRIAGE. There are several indexes at your disposal for this search: *Psychological Abstracts, Social Sciences Index, Index to Periodical Articles By and About Blacks,* and many others listed in this chapter.

When you begin your manual search, however, you run into the same problem in all the indexes you try. The topic is too broad. You'll have to sort through much material to find articles specifically mentioning the problems of interracial couples raising their children. (The phrase PAR-

ENT AND CHILD is also too broad and requires a similar amount of scanning.)

What's your next step? You already know that a search through several indexes will take some time, because you'll have to scan article titles closely and also read article abstracts. Perhaps there hasn't been much written on the subject. Or, the information may be buried in some of the articles on INTERRACIAL MARRIAGE. Maybe you'll have to read some of them completely.

The dilemma this search presents makes it a perfect candidate for a computer search. When you want two or more distinct topics to cross, the computer can quickly extract key words from the computer abstracts of the pertinent articles and list the articles for you. (The computer includes more subject terms per article than printed indexes; therefore, your choices are considerably expanded, and your ability to be precise is enhanced.)

In general, the more involved or complicated your research project, the more seriously you should consider a computer search. Perhaps your manual searches through printed indexes suggest to you that an article, dissertation, or book is long overdue. A computer search of magazine articles would pick up what you missed in a manual search.

Unfortunately, there's no way to determine the cost of a computer search in advance. Certain costs are fixed—the cost of the searcher's time in the presearch interview and connect time, for example—but you can't know ahead of time how many citations the search will yield and how long it will take.

The longer your project, the more worthwhile the computer search will be. As time goes on and more people do computer searches, the costs will likely drop. In academic libraries, the trend is definitely toward computer magazine searching.

HOW DOES IT WORK?

Once you decide that you want a computer search, the real planning begins. First, you must make an appointment with a searcher to discuss your research problem. The purpose of this meeting is to select the primary and alternate terms you want to search. (This kind of meeting has other benefits. It helps a researcher define or narrow his topic. It's surprising how many people start researching before they've refined their topic.)

Furthermore, you must select, in advance, the indexes you want to search. Since each index on computer is published by a different firm, it's billed separately and so must be searched separately. (The indexes are not integrated into a single alphabet, although the technical capability to do so is there.)

The major incentive for this meeting therefore is to contain the cost of the search. The entire search strategy—from defining your topic to selecting the search words and terms from a data base thesaurus that each data base (index on-line) will recognize—is mapped out. By planning the entire search in advance with alternatives to try if your first choice of terms or index doesn't work, the time spent on the computer, and your cost, are kept to a minimum. There's nothing so unnerving as having a little chat about what you're going to do next while computer costs are ticking away at $1 per second.

When your presearch interview is over and the searcher is ready to go on-line, she connects the telephone to the computer via a rubber attachment on the computer. She calls the data base whose service she subscribes to, logs on the computer, and begins. She selects the index you want her to search, then feeds in the preselected words or terms to find out how many articles include them in their titles or abstracts. (You must select which one you want scanned: titles or abstracts.)

We'll assume that INTERRACIAL MARRIAGE is an acceptable term to search through the index you've selected. The computer may then scan five or ten years (you must preselect time limits) of articles, and very quickly it will print the number of articles during that period with INTERRACIAL MARRIAGE in the titles or abstracts. Perhaps it will be 273. The searcher may then feed in the word CHILDREN to see how many articles include that word in the titles or abstracts. That would probably elicit many entries, say 1,500. After the searcher feeds in as many related terms as you have preselected, she starts to combine them. For example, she'll ask the computer to search articles with INTERRACIAL MARRIAGE *and* CHILDREN in the title. The result of this search might then be 10 citations.

Now, to get the articles. As speedy and precise as computer searching is, it's still at an embryonic stage, and it only provides a citation to an article, not the article itself. You still must retrieve the article in the usual way. On foot. Document delivery *is* available commercially for about 10 times the cost per page of a photocopy you can make yourself, and it's rather slow since the article must be mailed. Industry experts predict that article texts will eventually be printed out on demand.

Though many large libraries offer computerized search services to the public for the same fees as commercial information brokers, they may offer the service only during limited hours of the day. Commercial brokers are popping up in large cities nationwide and are listed in the Yellow Pages of the phone book under LIBRARY RESEARCH, INFORMATION BROKERS, or other similar terms. The library may also be able to recommend independent information brokers in your area. (See Chapter 13 for more on computerized searching.)

RESEARCHING MAGAZINES IN MICROFORM COLLECTIONS[3]

User studies in libraries show that current issues of magazines are the most heavily used. Still, the trend toward preserving back issues of maga-

[3]See Chapter 14 for information on how to find magazines in microform.

zines on microfilm has snowballed in recent years. Many large libraries continue to carry magazine subscriptions in the print version, but they also buy a permanent copy on microfilm. Not only do these copies take up less room, but they also save bindery costs. Special photocopy machines are available to make paper copies from microfilm for about 15¢ per page.

Among the popular magazines available on microfilm are *Family Circle*, *McCall's*, *Mother Earth News*, *Photoplay*, *Golf Digest*, and *Changing Times*. Countless scholarly magazines such as *Developmental Psychology*, *Early Childhood Education*, and *Journal of Natural History* are also issued in microfilm. Micropublishers, in most instances, have also gone back to volume one of current periodicals so that a complete run is available on microfilm. In time, all published magazines and newsletters will undoubtedly be microfilmed.

Microform is also the perfect medium for making available very old magazines. As century-old and subject-specialized magazines slowly deteriorate or disappear, it becomes expensive to reprint them, not to mention the problem of finding shelf space for them. Microform is the answer. The lower cost of microform and the reduced space it consumes have made it possible for many large libraries to buy old magazines, something most of them would not do if they were simply reprinted.

The microform collections mentioned below number approximately three-fourths of those in print at this writing. Researching magazines in microform is similar to searching them in their print counterparts. Since they derive from print versions, many have already been indexed. Those which are not indexed will likely have coverage in the future, so you'll be able to use them with little problem. (Where there's a need for coverage in research, someone eventually fills it.)

■ *American Periodicals, Series 1-3, 1741-1900.* University Microfilms International.

These combined series include more than 1,000 periodicals depicting life and thought in the United States from 1741 to 1900. You'll find the issues of the nation's first scientific journal, *Medical Repository* (1747-1800) plus other periodicals such as *Musical Magazine*, *Thespian Oracle*, *Southern Quarterly Review* (a magazine which upheld slavery), *Godey's Lady's Book*, *The Youth's Companion*, and *Water-Cure Journal*.

Two printed publications will help you use this microform magazine collection. One is *American Periodicals, 1741-1900, An Index to the Microfilm Collection*, edited by Jean Hoornstra and Trudy Heath (University Microfilms International). It contains a subject, title, and editor index to the magazines by name, but NOT to the articles in them. You can use *Poole's Index to Periodical Literature, 1802-1907*, to identify articles by subject. It indexes many (though not all) of the magazines in this microform collection.

■ *English Literary Periodicals.* University Microfilms International.
This microform magazine collection covers 200 journals from the 17th

to the 19th centuries featuring the work of the important writers of the time: Steele, Defoe, Addison, Eliot, Lamb, Tennyson, Mill, etc. Besides serialized fiction, the magazines include moral commentary, humor, poetry, essays, literary criticism, and lists of newly published books.

The print companion is *Accessing English Literary Periodicals, A Guide to the Microfilm Collection*, edited by Grace Puravs, Kathy Kavanagh, and Vicki Smith. (University Microfilms International. 1981.) Once again, the hard copy is an index to the magazine titles only, not the articles in them; but the subject list of the magazines can help guide you to general topics you want to research.

■ *Missionary Periodicals from the China Mainland.* Greenwood Press.

Eleven periodicals, including *Anking Newsletter* (1937-48), *The China Medical Journal* (1887-1921), and *West China Missionary News* (1899-1943) cover the conditions in China in the 19th and 20th centuries under the rule of the Protestant missions.

The set comes with a reel guide.

One of the publishers issuing many specialty periodical collections in microform is Greenwood Press. Some of the publisher's other offerings include: *Periodicals on Women and Women's Rights* (13 mid-19th- and early-20th-century magazines), *Radical Periodicals in the United States, 1890-1960* (48 periodicals), and *Radical Periodicals of Great Britain, 1794-1881* (33 18th- and 19th-century magazines).

■ *Nineteenth Century Reader's Guide, 1890-1899.* University Microfilms International.

This collection of 51 complete periodicals, the leading magazines of the 1890s, includes everything indexed by H.W. Wilson's printed index, *Nineteenth Century Reader's Guide to Periodical Literature, 1890-1899.* It covers a period just prior to the advent of the *Reader's Guide to Periodical Literature.*

The century-old magazines in this collection feature articles on topical issues: slums, prostitution, birth control, women's rights, the war with Spain, the Chicago World's Fair of 1893, free trade, money and credit, and more.

Use the printed index to identify articles by subject. If your library has the microform collection, you'll be able to read the articles quickly instead of having to send for them through interlibrary loan.

■ *Periodicals By and About North American Indians on Microfilm, 1923-78* and annual updates. Microfilming Corp. of America.

Approximately 90 Eskimo, American, and Canadian Indian periodicals are microfilmed covering a broad range of issues such as arts, crafts, poetry, archaeology, education and schools, and religion. Some of the magazines covered are *American Indian Law Newsletter, Choctaw Community News, The Flandreau Spirit, The Indian Historian, Journal of American Indian Education,* and *Three Tribes Herald.*

The only print accompaniment to the index is a reel guide which comes with the microfilm collection. (The reel guide helps you locate individual magazines on the microfilm, since they are not arranged in any logical [e.g., alphabetical] order.)

■ *Two Centuries of British Periodicals*. University Microfilms International.

This is a collection of 22 complete periodical runs. They reflect the politics, economics, religion, and art of Britain between 1732 and 1914. They include Parliamentary debates, biographical sketches, stock prices, labor news, military reform, book reviews, and news of the day in such magazines as *Political Register* (1802-35), *The Midwife* (1750-52), and *The Literary Magazine* (1756-58).

The companion print guide is *Two Centuries of British Periodicals*, by Daniel Fader and George Bornstein. The volume contains useful background essays and a bibliography of periodicals, but it is *not* an index to the articles in the periodicals. The essays in the book should help you learn the concerns of the period and how they were covered by the periodical literature. In the absence of a printed periodical index to the magazines, this technique will give you some direction in how to use the magazines in this collection.

Magazine research, once you know the ins and outs of using periodical indexes and abstracts, is one of the most popular ways to look for information. Researchers often begin their information searches hunting for the succinct, straightforward formats of magazine articles. What you find may answer your immediate question or provide valuable background necessary for continuing your search.

CHAPTER SUMMARY

I. Magazines are plentiful; so much so, that we often overlook them as research tools. There are about 200 popular magazines sold in stores, yet there are thousands of others read by professionals, hobbyists, and other persons with special interests. (page 147)

    A. Popular magazine articles report on the latest developments in health, child care, fitness, education, politics, relationships, and other concerns. These are useful not only for researching light articles or short term papers or reports, but also for answering personal questions. (page 148)

    B. Scholarly or specialty magazines are appropriate for in-depth looks at a subject. They help you find experts and

catch trends and new developments before they're reported in popular magazines, in newspapers, and on TV. (page
148)

II. Indexes are the keys to unlocking magazines for research. Periodical indexes give your information search a direction.

   A. Popular periodical indexes go far beyond *Reader's Guide*. In-
       cluded here are 15 periodical indexes covering popular and
       special-interest magazines. (page 153)

   B. There are over 100 scholarly abstracts and indexes in print.
       Included here is an annotated list of more than half of
       them. Most of these indexes are in large public and aca-
       demic libraries. (Remember that scholarly periodicals with
       an organization's name in their title are filed in a unique
       way.) (page 160)

III. Magazine research may be conducted by computer. Certain subjects are easier to search via computerized indexes than through
printed indexes. If you're working on a lengthy project, you may
want to consider a computerized search, even if the costs average
$25 or more. (page 173)

IV. You can also research magazines in microfilm collections. Old magazines have been microfilmed and assembled into collections that
many large libraries own. To research these older magazines, check
the collection guides or printed indexes that cover them. (page 175)

11

Research Tools for Daily Living:
NEWSPAPERS

Journalism allows its readers to witness history . . .
—John Hersey

Newspapers record the fine print of our daily lives. As research tools, they record facts, figures, trends, and even commentary about the history we make today. Much of the timely information they provide is not readily available anywhere else.

Newspapers report the cost of individual consumer goods from housing and automobiles to food; they describe or picture fashions; they reveal economic conditions through headlines and classified advertising, and discuss the public mood and the political atmosphere in editorials; they provide clues to our religious beliefs and the educational and cultural setting of the day. In short, newspapers portray the intimate details of life.

Q. When, for how much, and under which President did the United States pay Mexico for portions of our present states, and which states were they? Also, how would that amount compare with today's inflated money?

A. In 1848, under the 11th President, James Polk, the United States ended the Mexican War. Most portions of Texas, New Mexico, Arizona, and California were ceded to the United States for $15 million.

Through countless economic charts in old almanacs, and the advertisements in old newspapers, you can learn the monetary values of the day. President Polk's annual salary was $25,000; his vice-president's salary, $5,000. (Today, the President and vice-president earn $200,000 and $91,000 respectively, not counting expense allowances.) An army colonel's starting base salary averaged $2,100 in the mid-1800s; today it's more than $20,000. The total cost of attending Harvard for one year was $90; today it's over $14,000.

The New York Times, in 1851, was a five-page tabloid costing 1¢. Its pages show that an average book cost 50¢; carpeting averaged $1 a square yard, and a salesman for Brother Jonathan's patented furniture polish could earn from $5 to $10 a day ($1,320 to $2,600 a year). According to the 1980 *World Almanac and Book of Facts,* Procter & Gamble spent $550 million on TV advertising in 1979.

Even more than books and magazines, newspapers report the kind of minutiae that allows you to absorb the texture of the times.

Q. In reminiscing about the old days, I was wondering where Rex imitation jelly was made and how much it cost in the late 1930s.

A. In checking the back issues of today's *Consumer Bulletin Annual*, I found a Za-Rex jelly rated in the September 1937 issue. Its grape jelly and cherry preserves were not recommended, because they contained lead in excess of government standards.

The current *Trade Names Dictionary* shows that the brand name is still around. S. C. Clayton Co. of Marlboro, Mass., the company that uses it, makes fruit products.

According to food ads in microfilmed back issues of *The San Diego Union*, one pound of preserves sold for about 20¢ in 1937.

NEWSPAPER INDEXES

To find information buried in back copies of national newspapers, researchers depend on indexes.

A friend of mine once mentioned a coworker who claimed to have lived in a haunted house. Situated in a local suburb, it was built in the 1940s and was well known for its innovative construction. Several stories had since emerged concerning the house and its various occupants, contributing to its attention and folklore. My friend's coworker mentioned that the newspaper had run an article about the house shortly after it was built, but that he didn't know how to find it.

The story piqued my curiosity, and I wanted to read the article to check the facts as they were documented *then* against the mixed stories that had since evolved. (I thought it might make an interesting Halloween story for the newspaper.) But first, I had to find the article.

It was easy. I checked the index to *The San Diego Union* at the public library. It told me exactly where to look. There's no way I could have found the article without the index except to flip tediously through countless back files of the newspaper.

An index does for newspapers what it does for books and periodicals. It leads you to a precise bit of information without your having to flounder fruitlessly in a time-consuming search that does not guarantee success.

Q. A series of concerts, known as Community Concerts, ran in San Diego between about 1930 and 1950. Who ran them and in which years were they given?

A. The index to the back issues of *The San Diego Union* available in large local libraries mentions several community concert associations (CCA): the Clairemont CCA, the Coronado CCA, the Grossmont CCA, the San Diego CCA, and the La Jolla CCA, with the dates the articles ran. The CCAs all started at different times, with the earliest one forming in the late 1940s. The Grossmont and the San Diego associations are still active, according to the index. Contact them for more information. The phone book lists a P.O. box and phone number under "Community Concert Association of S.D."

Newspaper indexes vary in the forms they take and the material they cover. Some are simply typed on 3x5-inch cards and compiled by a reference librarian. They may cover only local news and exist in a single copy. Others are published in book form and cover international, national, and local news. These are sold commercially to libraries.

Although there are hundreds of city newspapers in microform, large local libraries will likely own none but their hometown newspaper and major newspapers, such as *The New York Times* and *The Washington Post*. The reasons are limited space, limited demand, and high cost.

In 1978, for instance, the microfilm edition of *The San Diego Union*, 1871-1975, cost about $20,000. Few libraries outside San Diego would need that newspaper, nor could they afford it.

In any case, libraries needn't own every newspaper. Once you find in an index the reference to a particular newspaper story, it's just a matter of tracking down that issue. And you can usually get information from any newspaper anywhere by writing to the public library in that community. (See page 196 for information on borrowing newspapers in microform.)

Q. When my father (born in 1929) was growing up, he read a comic strip in a Cleveland, Ohio, newspaper. He can't recall the character's name, and the family doesn't remember either. The characters in the strip used to roller skate through town, and one guy would have a little fellow on his shoulders. How can I research this comic strip without a name?

A. Check two reference books called *World Encyclopedia of Comics* and *World Encyclopedia of Cartoons*. Cartoons and cartoonists are arranged in alphabetical order in these books, so this could make for cumbersome searching.

It may be faster to write the Cleveland Public Library and ask them to check back issues of city newspapers. Their address is 325 Superior Ave., Cleveland, OH 44114.

If you're interested in national newspaper coverage, you will find *National Newspaper Index* (Information Access Corp. 1979-date) helpful. It jointly indexes five major newspapers: *The New York Times*, *The Christian Science Monitor*, *The Wall Street Journal*, *The Los Angeles Times*, and *The Wash-*

ington Post. This research tool in microfilm is available in many large libraries.

These major newspapers are also indexed individually in printed indexes, but a file that indexes several newspapers jointly often saves search time and provides more information with the same amount of effort as checking one newspaper's index. The *National Newspaper Index* is especially useful if you eventually plan to read and compare the coverage these newspapers gave to a particular national or international event. If you find an article you want to read in *The Christian Science Monitor* and a similar one in *The Los Angeles Times*, but your library subscribes to neither of these, you can get the edition you need in microform through interlibrary loan.

CLIPPING SERVICES AND NEWS DIGESTS

Most libraries can't afford to subscribe to major newspapers from every state. Clipping services and news digests that select and organize newspaper articles according to broad topical areas help to fill that void. *NewsBank* (NewsBank, Inc., 1970-date), on microfiche, is one such service. For a fraction of the cost of individual subscriptions, it offers material from some 200 newspapers in over 130 U.S. cities.

NewsBank doesn't have the kind of newspapers you sit down and read. And that's *not* because it's in microform. The newspapers in the collection have been clipped, and their articles rearranged and microfilmed according to 13 topics: Business and Economic Development, Consumer Affairs, Education, Employment, Environment, Government Structure, Health, Housing & Urban Renewal, Law & Order, Political Development, Social Relations, Transportation, and Welfare and Poverty. (Separate sets are available for Film & TV, Fine Arts and Architecture, Literature, and the Performing Arts. These include many reviews and criticisms.)

Though *NewsBank* gives you the convenience of complete articles (as opposed to an index citation which you must use to get to the actual article), it does have one limitation. Because the newspapers it includes are not reprinted in their entirety, all the advertisements are excluded. Thus, the unique societal and economic perspectives that ads provide are missing. These can, of course, be easily filled in through other complete newspapers on microfilm your library may own.

NewsBank recognizes newspapers for their information value. By using *NewsBank*'s printed indexes to guide you by subject to certain articles (regardless of the newspaper in which they originally appeared), you can get a regional perspective of national issues. You can also observe attitudes, moods, and trends in different parts of the country.

This is precisely the perspective that enabled John Naisbitt to write his best-selling book, *Megatrends* (Warner, 1982). (Naisbitt owns a clipping service that services major corporations. His firm repackages newspaper information to detect trends and attitudes.) His book is based on his observations of the news gathered from 10 years of reading 200 major newspapers from different parts of the country.

Q. A few months ago my husband and I were watching a TV show that talked about the mysterious lights of Marfa, a town in Texas.

The report said that strange balls of lights mysteriously appear over the mountainous horizon above Marfa. They've never been explained, although scientists and even the Army have sent out teams to investigate. The lights have been documented for over 100 years.

I've tried to find out more about this phenomenon at my local library but could get nowhere.

A. *NewsBank*, a microfilm collection of articles clipped from newspapers nationwide, featured an article on Marfa's mysterious lights from *The Dallas Morning News* of July 4, 1982. (Marfa is a tiny ranching community of about 2,500 people in West Texas.)

The article said the lights were first reported in 1883. Scientific explanations suggesting that swamp gas and car lights tunneling around the mountain account for the lights don't hold, because the nearest swamp is too far away, and there weren't any cars to speak of in 1883.

The lights come out at dusk and can be seen year round on clear, still nights. Although the University of Texas McDonald Observatory is 26 miles northwest of Marfa, the light phenomenon has not been the subject of serious scientific study.

According to the article, resident Elton Miles wrote a book called *Tales of the Big Bend* (A & M University Press) with a chapter on the Marfa lights. The book should be available through your library's interlibrary loan service.

Other collections of clipped newspaper articles, as well as digests of the news and current events, exist in book form. The ones listed below cover most of those in print. They are usually issued in small pamphlets weekly, biweekly, or monthly, and are often kept in a loose-leaf binder. (Some are replaced annually with bound volumes.) To find individual articles within the volumes, check their indexes.

Large libraries should have most of these clipping services and news digests; they will likely be found in a periodicals or reference section. Because they are reference tools, it's likely they won't circulate, even the back issues.

FOR AMERICAN NEWS

■ *Comité de México y Aztlán (Comexaz)*. News Monitoring Service. 1972-1980.

The newspapers from seven major Western and Southwestern cities (Albuquerque, Los Angeles, Denver, El Paso, San Francisco, San Antonio, and Phoenix) have been clipped for Mexican American news, filmed, and reproduced in book form. Local and national topics cover all aspects of Mexican American life. Articles report on population growth and local shootings and accidents involving Mexican Americans; also included are personality profiles and editorials on such issues as Americans in Mexican jails and traffic between El Paso and its sister city, Juarez, Mexico. The subject index appears in the front of each volume. (*Comexaz* ceased publication in December 1980, but it's still useful for Mexican American news and views of events that occurred between 1972 and 1980.)

■ *Editorials on File*. Facts on File, Inc. 1970-date. (Also comes in microform)

Each 125-page booklet issued monthly offers editorial coverage of eight to ten major American news topics (TV in courtrooms, curbing news leaks in the White House, small car safety, the Equal Rights Amendment, cuts in student loans, etc.). Some foreign issues—Canada's proposed press law, Nicaragua's peace overtures, and the Beirut suicide bomb attack, all of which occurred in 1983—may also be included.

Editorial opinions representing different political views are reprinted from an average of two dozen of the 150 or so newspapers covered that made comment on that particular issue. (Publication lags by one month.)

FOR INTERNATIONAL NEWS

■ *Facts on File: World News Digest With Index*. Facts on File, Inc. 1941-date.

FOF is a 10-15-page weekly summary of major national and international news events in economics, the military, banking, agriculture, law, the arts, etc. *FOF* includes bonus charts giving major speeches such as the President's State of the Union address; and tabulations such as annual bestseller book and record lists, top box-office film successes, and top rated TV programs. The cumulated subject index helps you find the particular topical issues covered as well as those features which do not appear every week. (Lags by one month.)

■ *Keesing's Contemporary Archives: Record of World Events*. Longman Group, Ltd., London 1931-date. (Also comes in microform.)

KCA, issued weekly, focuses primarily on politics and economics: elections, coups, treaties, etc., Its April 10, 1981 issue featured 6 ½ pages on the adoption of Vietnam's new constitution; the August 7, 1981 issue had 11 pages on the background and course of the Iran-Iraq war, including world opinion as reported in various sources around the globe. Other issues covered have been the U.S.-Norwegian agreement on stockpiling military equipment, a cabinet change in Tunisia, a coup attempt in Rwanda, and a summary of economic developments in Japan, 1979-1980. The index is arranged by country, then subdivided by major subject. (Lags by about three months.)

FROM THE FOREIGN PRESS

The foreign press and broadcast media in English or in English translation cover much international news with opposing ideologies and views hard to find in U.S. newspapers and broadcasts. In addition, the sets of clipped articles below cover many newspapers that libraries don't normally carry.

■ *African Recorder: A Fortnightly Record of African Events*. New Delhi: Recorder Press. 1962-date.

Information for this loose-leaf set is gathered from African newspapers, periodicals, radio, embassies, and government sources. Some newspapers whose articles are reprinted are *The Egyptian Gazette* (Cairo), *The Hindu* (Madras), *Gulf News* (Dubai), *Ghanian Times* (Accra), *Baghdad Observer*, *Statesmen* (New Delhi), *The London Times*, and *The New York Times*. In a random search, I found reports on Palestinian autonomy, the renewal of the 1981 Moroccan trade pact with India, the 1983 Libyan/Chad struggle and its discussion in the UN, and the role of oil in Cameroon's economy. (Lags by about four months.)

Q. Where can I get information about South African apartheid policies and world opinion of them?

A. African news from *The New York Times*, *The Washington Post*, *The London Times*, major African newspapers, and a few others is summarized in a publication called *African Recorder*, available in many large libraries. A random copy I checked from 1983 included many items: summaries of a study on apartheid published in Johannesburg showing features of the country's apartheid policy (from *The Washington Post*); a report on the first anti-apartheid policy conference concluded in Manila (from the *UN Newsletter*); and an apartheid-in-sports statement made as a result of observations on apartheid at the 1976 winter Olympic games in Montreal (from *ILO Information*).

■ *Asian Recorder; Weekly Digest of Asian Events*. New Delhi, Recorder Press. 1955-date.

Information is gathered and summarized from many of the same sources as the *African Recorder*, plus some Asian newspapers such as *The Korea News* (Seoul), *Dawn* (Karachi), *Japan Times* (Tokyo), and *The Bangkok Post*. Stories I discovered included the Soviet Union in Afghanistan, the appointment of the Bishop of Peking (the first Catholic prelate to be named in China since the cultural revolution), and the reestablishment of full U.S.-China diplomatic relations in 1978. (Lags by about four months.)

■ *Canadian News Facts: The Indexed Digest of Canadian Current Events*. Marpep Publishing Ltd. 1967-date.

Issued biweekly, *CNF* summarizes such stories as British Columbia's coal deal with Japan, living cost increases in 1980, the Reagan-Trudeau talks, and the issue of Canadian unity. The information is gathered from 20 of the country's leading newspapers and national news gathering agencies.

■ *Current Digest of the Soviet Press*. American Association for the Advancement of Slavic Studies. 1947-date.

Every week, *CDSP* features a selection of articles translated from Soviet newspapers such as *Pravda* and *Izvestia*, as well as from magazines. The news covers everything from arms control, industry, and the press, to child care, domestic affairs, and the arts. Articles in past issues have tackled such topics as "What's wrong with Soviet health care?" ("Polyclinics offer slow, rude service"); martial law in Poland in 1981 through 1983; prospects for developing the Arctic; and Leonid Brezhnev's 75th birthday celebration.

■ *Survey of People's Republic of China Press*. Issued by the National Technical Information Service, a division of the Department of Commerce. 1950-77. (Also comes in microform.)

SPRC was issued quarterly and reporting came from foreign news agency transmissions, foreign radio broadcasts, and newspaper and periodical articles. Topics included China's wheat crops and drought, Tibetan women today, and activities of the counterrevolutionary Gang of Four. One 1976 issue reports on a friendly visit between Palestine's Al Fateh delegate and Foreign Minister Huang Hua. The article, in unsurprising rhetoric, refers to the Israeli aggressors and the U.S. imperialists, and also remarks that "the Soviet social imperialists, self-styled 'natural ally' of the Arab people, are even more insidious."

Survey of People's Republic of China Press ceased publication in 1977 and is continued as part of the following service.

■ *U.S. Foreign Broadcast Information Service. Daily Report*. 1978-date. Issued by the National Technical Information Service. (Also comes in microform.)

In addition to reporting news from China, this series also translates news of wars, daily life, politics, commerce and culture from Latin America, Eastern Europe, and the Soviet Union. (Lags by about two months.)

Q. Where can I get news from the Iran media?

A. Many large libraries once received Tehran's two English-language newspapers but both ceased publication in March 1979 when the Ayatollah Khomeini took over.

A government publication sent to the documents sections of large libraries is called *U.S. Foreign Broadcast Information Service Daily Report*. It is a translation of news from various sources abroad. *FBIS* comes in both print version and microform. It's promptly translated, but libraries may receive their copies as much as two months late.

Another digest of news about Iran is the weekly *Asian Recorder*, usually found in academic libraries. It summarizes news items from radio broadcasts and the major newspapers of Japan, Egypt, Afghanistan, India, and other countries. This may be as much as four months late.

HISTORICAL CLIPPING FILES

Some clipping sets provide a historical look at the news as it happened in ways that history books cannot. The following sets organize the news from over a period of decades by subject.

■ *Great Contemporary Issues Series.* Ayer Pub. Co.

This is a series of published books featuring the original articles that appeared in *The New York Times* as far back as a century ago. Each volume focuses on a particular topic and through the articles selected, forms a complete history as seen through the pages of a major newspaper. The volume on *Big Business*, for example, starts in 1866 with *Times* coverage of the tyranny of corporations. Other articles trace the growth of American industry through events in the business world of the mid-1970s.

The volume on *The Presidency* starts with original articles on Teddy Roosevelt and progresses to 1975. It's arranged in chapters such as Congressional-Executive Relations, Party Politics in the Nominating Conventions, Foreign Policies, and Administration Scandals.

Many titles in the 30-volume-plus *Great Contemporary Issues* series were published over a decade ago and have since been supplemented with updates. Some of the titles include:

■ *Black Africa*, edited by Hollis Lynch. 1973. Articles in this volume span the 1880s to 1972 and cover the forces that shaped Africa's recent history. They show how Africa's role in World War I led to its quest for independence, how Ghana became Africa's first independent Black nation, and other significant events such as uprisings, wars, and apartheid policies in South Africa.

■ *China*, edited by O. Edmund Clubb. 1972. Articles report on such events as the Boxer Rebellion, China's struggle with imperialist Japan, the rise of Communism, and Nixon's historic visit. Through this volume, you can trace China's growth as a 20th-century world power.

■ *Crime and Justice*, edited by Ramsey Clark. 1974. The articles cover everything from organized crime in the 1920s to prison riots in the 1960s. They examine changes in criminal activity over the years and our attitudes towards it through film reviews, opinion polls, and news stories.

■ *Drugs*, edited by James Fixx. 1971. This volume covers the evolution of the use and abuse of various drugs from the 1920s to the 1970s and their social, medical, criminal, and legal implications.

■ *Education USA*, edited by James Cass. 1973. This volume covers the changing nature of American education through reportage of teacher strikes, student activism, school busing, etc. from the early 1900s to 1972.

■ *The Family*, edited by David J. Rothman and Sheila M. Rothman. 1979. Features, news stories, and advertisements reflect new child rearing patterns and the changing role of wives, mothers, and fathers in the 20th century.

■ *Labor and Management*, edited by Richard Morris. 1973. Events are reported from post-Civil War days to 1972. The coverage begins with the rise of industrial capitalism and follows through the formation of the American Federation of Labor, child labor laws, New Deal programs, and farm labor movements led by Cesar Chavez.

■ *The Mass Media and Politics*, edited by James Fixx. 1971. These articles published between 1936 and 1972 show the impact of television on our political processes, the evolution of the presidential press conference, and the rights and responsibilities of the media in a free society.

■ *Popular Culture*, edited by David Manning White. 1978. This volume demonstrates America's popular taste through articles on vaudeville, radio, early talking pictures, television, and other forms of culture. Popular culture is reflected in reviews of popular books, plays, movies, musical performances, and television programs as well as interviews with performers and authors from 1900 to the mid-1970s.

■ *Terrorism*, edited by Michael Wallace and Gene Brown. 1979. Interviews, essays, editorials, and news stories report on terrorism in the United States and abroad. They examine ethical and political issues and consequences involved in individuals and groups pressing for justice.

■ *Values Americans Live By*, edited by Gary Wills. 1974. Articles show the influence of the church, politics, business, etc., on our social values. This volume covers everything from Herbert Spencer's theory of Social Darwinism in the late 19th century to Watergate in the 1970s.

Some other volumes in this series include *Central America and the Caribbean; Childhood, Youth and Society; The Cities; Energy and Environment; Ethnic Groups in American Life; Food and Population; Japan; The Middle East; Medicine and Health Care; Religion in America; Science in the Twentieth Century; Southeast Asia; Sports and Society;* and *Women: Their Changing Roles.*

■ *Tuskegee Institute News Clipping File, 1899-1966.*Microform Corporation of America.

Gathered from more than 300 national newspapers, magazines, religious and special interest publications, and foreign newspapers, this microform collection of individual clippings is based on an actual file compiled at the Tuskegee Institute in Alabama. The collection forms a complete history of black America, documenting primary news coverage of black issues such as lynchings, Jim Crow laws, and voter registration in the South.

The set consists of many subseries such as Soldiers File, 1918-1920; Emancipation Celebrations File, 1913-1965; and the Lynching File, 1899-1966. Its printed guide is called *Guide to the Microfilm Edition of the Tuskegee Institute News Clippings File*, edited by John W. Kitchens (Tuskegee Institute, 1978).

TELEVISION NEWS BROADCASTS

You may already have noticed that most of the clipping services above gather their news from a combination of sources. Besides newspapers, they also use news magazines, news agency transmissions, and television/radio broadcasts.

Broadcasts are, of course, a legitimate but often overlooked source of news and opinion. Though researchers usually focus on print sources to interpret current events because they're more accessible, news broadcasts are available in print. Some transcripts of TV news broadcasts and news programs have been in print for many years, but researchers are often unaware of it. Recently, even more have been issued in microform; these are usually in large or academic libraries. I've included some of them so you'll be aware that these alternative news sources exist.

■ *CBS News Television Broadcasts*. Microfilming Corp. of America. 1975-date. (In microfiche only. Comes with a printed index. Backfiles to 1963 are also available.)

This compilation features the verbatim transcripts of every CBS news broadcast, *60 Minutes*, *CBS Reports*, and other CBS public affairs programs since 1963. The set allows you to read the TV accounts of John F. Kennedy's assassination, the coverage of the first moon flight, skyjackings, political controversies, economic news, etc. Also included are the in-depth and investigative features on fraudulent business ventures, municipal scams, etc., covered on news programs such as *60 Minutes*.

■ *Face the Nation*. Microfilming Corp. of America. 1954-70 (base set). Issued annually from 1970. (Comes in print and microform editions and reproduces the complete transcript of each program. The print index provides approaches by subject, guest, and date of program.)

Hundreds of prominent figures have been interviewed since *Face the Nation* first aired on November 7, 1954 with Senator Joseph McCarthy. The program has treated political and social issues in interviews with Mustafa Amin, Menachem Begin, Fidel Castro, Nikita Khrushchev, Tom

Hayden, Robert Kennedy, Martin Luther King, Jr., Golda Meir, Eleanor Roosevelt, Anwar Sadat, Adlai Stevenson, George Wallace, and Harold Wilson among others.

■ *MacNeil Lehrer Report*. Microfilming Corp. of America. 1976-date. (Issued quarterly in microform. An accompanying print index includes program titles, featured guests, program dates, program subjects, and organizations discussed.)

The MacNeil Lehrer Report has explored important issues such as teenage alcoholism, women's rights in Iran, nuclear proliferation, Three Mile Island, the death penalty, and welfare reform, with such luminaries as Bella Abzug, Woody Allen, Jimmy Carter, the Shah of Iran, Andrew Young, and others.

■ *Summary of World Broadcasts by the British Broadcasting Corp.* University Microfilms International. 1973-date. (In microform only. Back files to 1939 are available. Comes in weekly or daily subscriptions.)

This set includes transcribed news broadcasts monitored and translated into English by the BBC, covering the Soviet Union, Eastern Europe, the Far East, the Middle East, and Africa. It features key speeches by national leaders, official war communiqués, propaganda messages, civilian news, etc.

NEWSPAPER RESEARCH BY COMPUTER

Experiments have been conducted nationwide to test the market for home information services via interactive, two-way television reception called videotex. Along with news abstracts, videotex may provide home banking and shopping capabilities, classified advertising, movie theater advertising, weather reports, sports scores, encyclopedia access, and even educational games. Does this mean that the traditional newspaper is doomed?

That's the question many newspapers are trying to answer. They evidently believe computers will infringe on their domain to some extent. This is one reason why many newspaper chains are investing heavily in the emerging home information market. If vital sources of revenue, like classified and movie theater advertising, switch from newspapers to videotex, newspapers will lose money.

How does this threat to traditional newspapers affect researchers? Not as much as you may think. Newspaper research involves much more than looking for current information, and using videotex won't be much different from using today's newspaper, at least in the amount of information you receive. Fleeting weather reports, sports scores, and want ads are not the stuff for which researchers usually hunt. The real value of research in newspapers comes from older and often out-of-town newspapers. Neither of these categories is accommodated to any appreciable extent by videotex.

However, many current newspapers *are* offered through on-line computer services—the same services you would use to search magazine indexes on-line. Here the computer can play a definitive role in your research. Although the newspaper data banks currently available do not provide broad newspaper coverage or go back more than about 10 years, they are probably more useful to the researcher than the current or proposed videotex offerings.

The data bases below are some of those presently on-line. Some provide full text or abstracts; others provide only a citation to the original. Most specialize in business and financial news. They may find that their most profitable markets are businesses and people needing this specific information.

With the proper computer setup either at home or through a library, you can connect with a service that specializes in providing news on-line. Of course, there is always the question of cost. Is it worth it to do your newspaper research on-line where costs mount by the minute; or are you better off using microform? As these services become more known to the public, their special uses and their demand will become more obvious.

The following list shows some of the newspaper data bases currently available.[1]

1. *New York Times Online Data Base*. New York Times Co. 1980-date. Offers the full text version of *The New York Times*.

2. *The Information Bank*. New York Times Co. 1969-date. Abstracts and citations of articles in *The New York Times* and approximately 90 other newspapers and general-interest magazines. (Some were added after 1969.) Information is searched by subject regardless of the source in which it originally appeared.

3. *National Newspaper Index*. Information Access Corp. 1979-date. This is the on-line version of the microform newspaper index covering five major newspapers mentioned earlier in the chapter. As in the microform version, it provides citations only, not full text.

4. *Newspaper Index* (NDEX). Bell & Howell. 1976-date. Citations (not full text) from 10 major U.S. newspapers serving black America. Eleven newspapers were added in 1979. The newspapers come from Chicago, Los Angeles, the District of Columbia, New Orleans, San Francisco, Detroit, Denver, Houston, and St. Louis, among other cities.

5. *NEXIS*. Mead Data Central. 1977-date. Provides the full text of various newspapers including *The Washington Post, The Christian Science Monitor,* and *American Banker;* also, various BBC summaries, seven Latin American newsletters, and some business and world events magazines.

---

[1]These newspapers are not currently available in this depth through CompuServe or The Source, two popular home information services.

THE VALUE OF OLD NEWSPAPERS

To this point, we've looked mostly at newspapers of the recent past as research tools. But old newspapers, too, are valuable resources for digging out forgotten facts and reconstructing the atmosphere of any period.

Newspapers are cameras; they give us snatches of time that has stood still long enough to be recorded. Yet, we take them for granted. We gloss over items in the morning paper—the President's latest pronouncement on Latin America, a possible cure for AIDS, a school bus that ran off the road. These same stories may well look old-fashioned and quaint, and maybe insightful, a century from now when the President's name is ancient history, no one recalls AIDS, and children use jet backpacks instead of buses to get to school.

It's no different from the way we view the news of 150 years ago. Consider these brief notices that appeared in *The New York Evening Post* of Tuesday, July 10, 1832. "The Merchant's Fire Insurance Co. declares a dividend of 3 ½ percent on their capital stock for the last three months"; Hy. & Geo. Barclay Co. advertises lampblack, grindstones, Persian berries, shoe thread, madeira, and sherry, among other things; the Rev. E. D. Barry's Academy promises "No exertions are neglected by him and his assistants to promote the moral and literary improvements of his pupils." (One of the terms of admission to the academy is that his pupils provide their own quills.) In these newspaper accounts, even the language and expression of the time is captured!

The possibilities for researching old newspapers are endless. A Philadelphia tabloid published at the time the Declaration of Independence was signed is a resource, as are the newspapers of Nathaniel Hawthorne's age. A Missouri newspaper of 1862 reflects the outlook appropriate for your Civil War research of that region. Barnaby Conrad's book, *A Revolting Transaction* (Arbor House, 1983) describes his research both in family papers and newspaper accounts of his great-grandmother's murder in Denver in 1891. I know a medical professor who borrowed certain issues of his hometown newspaper to read about his mother, a former Ziegfeld Follies girl. Another professor researching the Duchess of Windsor used various newspapers of the 1920s and 1930s on microfilm to supplement clues he found through his other research.

Old newspaper obituary notices and articles on personalities of the day may even help you complete your genealogical research.

Q. Was the post office in downtown San Diego operating from 1888 to 1891? I am interested because I've learned that my mother (I've enclosed her name) was the money-order clerk there at that time.

A. In the November 6, 1890 issue of *The San Diego Union*, there was an item announcing your mother's resignation, and I've sent you a copy of the text. In mid-1888 the main post office moved from a building at Sixth and F streets to rented quarters at Fourth and C streets. The present building on E Street, between Eighth and Ninth streets, opened in 1938.

HISTORICAL NEWSPAPER COLLECTIONS IN MICROFORM

For all their worth, newspapers were not originally thought of as having much research value. When this nation first began, one of their major purposes was to shape democracy.

It quickly became apparent, however, that even the smallest newspapers published in the remotest towns filled a great research void. After all, they were frequently the only source of recorded regional events; thus, they provided valuable information available nowhere else.

Despite their important research potential, however, newspapers have traditionally been printed on the poorest, least-durable-quality paper. Therefore, their use in research had been severely limited—at least until microfilm came along.

Because of the activity of microfilm publishers, libraries now not only have access to *The New York Times* and *The Washington Post*, but to newspapers of every circulation, frequency, and subject from cities around the world. Any organization can purchase an entire back run of a newspaper and store it compactly in a few cabinets. Today, the actual print copy of a current newspaper is purchased for convenient reading, is usually kept for about three months, and is eventually thrown away. The microfilm copy is purchased for permanence.

Among the top newspapers on microfilm which have been standard in large libraries for years are *The New York Times* (1851-date), *The London Times* (1790-date), *The Christian Science Monitor* (1908-date), *The Wall Street Journal* (1889-date), and *The Washington Post* (1877-date).

The following list consists of more than half of the English-language newspaper collections currently available in microform. In addition, there are hundreds of individual city newspapers currently reproduced. And that probably includes the major newspaper from your city.

■ *Canadian Newspapers on Microfilm*. Canadian Library Assn. More than 300 19th- and 20th-century Canadian newspapers are fully reproduced in this collection.

■ *Civil War Newspapers on Microfilm*. Bell & Howell. This set includes 301 newspapers representing 30 union and confederate towns and cities in 33 states and territories, published between 1861 and 1865.

■ *Contemporary Newspapers of the North American Indian*. Bell & Howell. Forty-nine newspapers from the 1960s and 1970s covering 23 states and the District of Columbia are represented here.

■ *Early American Newspapers, 1704-1820.* Readex Microprint. When filming is completed, this collection will include all existing newspapers listed in Clarence Brigham's *History and Bibliography of American Newspapers, 1690-1820.* The newspapers come from 29 states and the District of Columbia. There is no index to individual articles in the papers, but an accompanying catalog names all newspaper titles in the collection. You can use the papers successfully by time period, region, and coverage of particular historical events.

■ *Negro Newspapers on Microfilm.* Library of Congress. This is a collection of complete or partial files for most of the 200 well-known black American newspapers covering the mid-1800s to the mid-1900s.

■ *The Newspapers of Ireland.* Memo Ltd., Dublin, distributed in the United States by Bell & Howell. This set includes 25 Irish newspapers from the 19th- and early 20th-century.

■ *Underground Press Collection.* Bell & Howell. 1965-date. This set consists of more than 550 American and 28 foreign radical newspapers. Some are the *Berkeley* [CA] *Barb,* the *L.A.* [Los Angeles] *Free Press,* the *Hot Potato* [Indianapolis], the *Daily Planet* [Coconut Grove, Florida], and the *Old Mole* [Cambridge, Mass.].

Q. I wrote a series of articles for a small alternative newspaper called the *Philadelphia Drummer.* I have since had a disagreement with the editor and doubt if I can now get tear sheets of the articles from him. Do you know how I could get copies?

A. The *Philadelphia Drummer* is part of a series of alternative newspapers on microfilm called the *Underground Newspaper Collection.* It should be in large libraries. (Photocopies can be taken from microfilm.)

Another option is to write the Free Library of Philadelphia, Logan Square, Philadelphia, PA 19103. They should have the *Drummer* and may be able to photocopy the articles for you.

BORROWING NEWSPAPERS

Most of the 20th-century newspapers in the collections above are also recorded by their individual titles in two standard reference books: *Newspapers in Microform: U.S., 1948-72* (and supplements) and *Newspapers in Microform: Foreign Countries, 1948-72* (and supplements). They are both arranged alphabetically by state (or country), then by city. If you want to borrow a Missouri newspaper from 1958, check *Newspapers in Microform: U.S., 1948-1972* under MISSOURI, and scan the list by city for a newspaper that falls into the specified time period. (You recall this is one of those resources whose title does not reflect the scope of its contents. Newspapers going back to the 18th century are included here.)[2]

The codes at the bottom of each entry list the U.S. libraries that own the newspaper, but you may not need this information. If your library doesn't have the microfilmed newspaper collection you want, you can borrow individual issues in microform through interlibrary loan. (The librarian will use the library's computer to locate copies.)

WHAT ABOUT NEWSPAPER LIBRARIES

Though some newspaper libraries continue to handle certain mail or phone queries, many of them have closed their doors to the public in recent years. As local public libraries usually subscribe to their city's newspaper and often have an index to it, many newspapers refer queries they receive to the library.

Admittedly, a newspaper library that arranges clipped articles by subject provides a different and often more useful approach for a researcher than that offered by microfilmed articles he finds through the newspaper's index at the public library. But the newspaper library's primary purpose is not to serve the public; it is to assist its staff. When a reporter writes about a person or topic, he must know if anything related has run in past issues.

Reporters at large newspapers now use VDTs, video display terminals (computers), to compose and edit their articles. With minor adjustments, the articles already in the computer can be recalled and printed out. Essentially, this is a newspaper library on computer.

At this early stage, many newspapers using computers have yet to decide how far back they will keep their newspaper in that form. At *The San Diego Union*, for example, there is a chance that the data base will include only the newspapers for the latest five years. Librarian Sharon Reeves adds that a second data base may be created for anything older than five years. "It all depends on storage costs," she says. "Who knows what they'll be in the future? Maybe we'll have better computers by then, or the method of storing data may be different."

At present, clippings of *The San Diego Union* go back over 40 years, and the microfilm edition extends back over a century. A survey conducted by the *Union's* library staff shows that, like magazines, the most heavily used editions of the newspaper are the most recent ones. The cost of convert-

---

[2]*Newspapers in Microform*, 1948-1972 does what very few publications do. The dates in the title refer, not to the coverage of the material listed, but to the date the material was cataloged or received at the Library of Congress. *Newspapers in Microform* started publication in 1948. Each edition had a different closing date, e.g., 1948-1952 (1st ed.); then the second edition became 1948-1956, etc. The present edition, 1948-1972, is the 7th edition. Annual supplements are included; and the material in the 1973 volume refers to material, no matter how old, that was cataloged in 1973. When the 8th edition comes out, it will become 1948-?, perhaps 1985, or whatever. At that time, all the cumulatives since 1973 can be discarded.

ing the older, microfilmed issues of the newspaper to computer would be prohibitive—especially for a resource that, considering its journalistic context, would rarely be used. This new approach to "collecting" news-papers, however, may eventually herald improved service to the public.

Should you wish to query a newspaper in your research, nationwide newspapers are listed in the annual *Ayer Directory of Publications* (Ayer Press). Newspaper libraries appear in the *Directory of Newspaper Libraries in the U.S. and Canada* (Special Libraries Association), revised every three to four years. Also check the annual *American Library Directory* (R.R. Bowker Co.). If a newspaper shows no library in the appropriate directo-ry, write to the public library in that community. Sometimes the indexing of a local newspaper is an activity assumed by the local public library rath-er than the newspaper library.

━━

Newspapers are not appropriate for every kind of research. You wouldn't consider them the latest word in nuclear physics, for example. But when you need documentation of a notable event or the comings-and-goings of a notable person, or a sense of what people did "for fun" at the turn of the century or during the Depression, newspapers offer spe-cial—and often unique—rewards.

━━━━━━━━━━━━━ *CHAPTER SUMMARY* ━━━━━━━━━━━━━

I. Newspapers capture minute details of daily life and are useful as re-search tools.
- A. Newspaper indexes are used to locate specific newspaper articles. Some indexes may be strictly local files compiled by librarians. (page 182)
- B. Other indexes, like *The Los Angeles Times Index*, are commer-cial publications. Still others, like the *National Newspaper In-dex*, which covers five major city newspapers, come in mi-croform. (page 183)

II. Clipping services and news digests collect newspaper articles and arrange them by subject.
- A. Published in pamphlet, book, or loose-leaf formats, clip-ping services cover American and international news, as well as world events as covered by the foreign press. (page 184)
- B. Historical clipping sets organize newspaper articles by sub-ject over a period of decades. (page 189)

III. Television broadcasts are another news resource available in print. (page 191)

IV. Computers can now play a role in newspaper research.

    A.   Videotex is basically a screen version of a daily newspaper available in your home by subscription. (page 192)

    B.   Newspapers on-line are a more useful service for researchers. Newspaper searching is possible through the same computer services that provide access to magazine indexes on-line. (page 193)

V. Many individual city newspapers are available on microform. Some newspaper collections have also been organized in sets with a particular focus (Early American, Civil War, etc.) If your library doesn't own a certain microform collection, you can request a newspaper through interlibrary loan. (page 195)

VI. Because their main purpose is to serve their own staff, newspaper libraries generally limit service to the public. The public library in a city usually subscribes to the city newspaper and often its index. (page 197)

12

Tools from
the Nation's Largest Publisher:
GOVERNMENT DOCUMENTS

*Two characteristics of government are
that it cannot do anything quickly,
and that it never knows when to quit.*
—George Stigler,
The New York Times, July 27, 1975

———— PART 1 ————

THE BROAD PICTURE

Despite various Presidents' promises to control the size of the U.S. government, it still adheres to its own law of nature: growth. As it expands, so, too, do its publishing activities.

In the early 1970s, Andy Rooney hosted a television program during which he investigated this snowballing phenomenon. He discovered that many government offices, when created to investigate or resolve a particular issue, continued to exist after their mission was completed. Rooney's candid interview with one noncommittal civil servant finally exposed the truth: The only thing this particular worker's office had done for the past few years was to write books, pamphlets, and brochures—because it didn't have anything else to do.

This could be part of the reason the U.S. government is the largest publisher in the country. It could also explain why the diversity of subject offerings in its list rivals that of commercial publishers.

Indeed, the government needs statistics, studies, and reports to better serve the people in some 18,000 cities, 3,000 counties, and 50 states. At the same time, it also generates information *about* the nearly 240 million people who live here. For better or worse, the federal government analyzes us, our needs, and our interests. It reaches into subject areas covered by its myriad departments: health, consumer affairs, business, economics, industry, agriculture, the military, and so on. The result is a staggering amount of published material.

WHO CARES WHAT THE GOVERNMENT SAYS?

The country does. Not only do researchers seek out the various publications of the government, but every citizen has a stake in knowing what goes on from the White House to the National Weather Service. A glance at a large city newspaper will quickly show that much of the news we read comes from or revolves around our constant interest in the activities of the federal government. Consider these headlines from *The San Diego Union*:

"TVA Abandons Work on Four N-Reactors." (The Tennessee Valley Authority is a government-owned corporation.)

"Antique Engine, Solar Energy a Powerful Team." (The Jet Propulsion Laboratory in Pasadena, California, is developing an energy system through the Department of Energy's Solar Thermal Technology Program.)

"Teen Prostitution: A Survival of the Least Fit." (Results of a study by the General Accounting Office.)

"New Sierra Volcano Still Not a Certainty." (Predictions made by federal scientists of the U.S. Geological Survey of the Department of the Interior.)

Because the government plays such a large role in our lives, it makes sense that we should be informed of its functions—hence the large number of publications issued to record government activities, be they congressional probes or courts-martial. And some of the records are substantial. The hearings dated September 9-11, 1981 on the nomination of Sandra Day O'Connor, the first woman justice of the Supreme Court, issued by the Senate Committee on the Judiciary, resulted in a 414-page report documenting O'Connor's background, qualifications, views on judicial responsibilities, and her legal philosophy. The Nuremberg trials held in Germany from October 1946 to April 1949 resulted in 15 volumes of transcripts issued by the Department of Defense (Adjutant General's Corps., Army).

WHAT IS A GOVERNMENT DOCUMENT?

The average American assumes that government documents are just that: documents, official papers, committee reports, hearings, statistics, and other items of government business. But that's only part of the picture. Other "documents" that run off government presses are publications we don't expect: cookbooks, national park guides, posters, employment directories, dictionaries, magazines, and more.

A Where can I find records of daily weather reports for a specific month over a period of several years in San Diego County?

A. The U.S. Weather Bureau issues a series of pamphlets called *Climatological Data.* Each pamphlet covers one state and gives temperature, precipitation, and wind velocity for several weather stations in each county. Ask for this reference in a science library or a large library housing government publications.

The expression "government document" is actually a misnomer. Documents are varied. They're not just official publications, but anything printed by the government or a contractee at government expense. The magazine *American Education,* which accepts articles from freelance writers, is a government document; so is the *Zip Code Directory,* used in offices and post offices nationwide; so is the *West Point Catalog,* sent to prospective students. These three "documents" are printed by government agencies: the Department of Education, the Postal Service, and the U.S. Military Academy, respectively.

Though "documents" is a misleading term, we are nevertheless stuck with it. In reality, we have government-published dictionaries, indexes, bibliographies, directories, magazines, handbooks, histories, textbooks, cookbooks, exhibition catalogs, and just about everything that commercial publishers issue, except fiction.

Q I understand that the Daughters of the American Revolution publish informative pamphlets which include questions useful in preparation for the citizenship examination. Where might I obtain them?

A. The DAR issues several citizenship study manuals. Their address is 1776 D St., NW, Washington, DC 20006. There are other similar publications in libraries and bookstores. *Twenty-five Lessons in Citizenship,* by D.L. Hennessey is highly rated. This and other commercial publications are listed in *Subject Guide to Books in Print* under CITIZENSHIP.

The Department of Immigration and Naturalization also issues home study books in a series called *Federal Textbook on Citizenship.* Ask for them at large libraries.

DOCUMENTS AND SUBJECTS GALORE

You'll notice that this chapter is one of the longest in the book. That's because government documents incorporate many of the various types and forms of research material—indexes, magazines, books, directories, statistics, experts—covered in other individual chapters. Diversity abounds under the umbrella of that single term, *documents.* It takes some understanding of where documents come from (and why) to begin to tap their richness.

Many agencies of the government produce publications for internal use whether or not comparable commercial publications already exist. *Recipes for Quantity Service*, over 1,800 recipes on 3x5-inch cards issued by the Armed Forces Recipe Service, is produced for the benefit of military cooks. The recipes-for-groups concept is not unique in publishing—*Subject Guide to Books in Print* lists almost four dozen books and some recipe card sets under QUANTITY COOKERY. But this particular set is geared for the needs of the military, and because it's published by the Department of Defense, it's a government document.

Q. There are a few road atlases that give travel distances between about two dozen major cities, but is there any source that does this for a greater number of cities?

A. The Departments of the Army, Navy, and Air Force jointly issue an 800-page book that they use to compute mileage for the transportation allowances of military personnel. It's called *Official Table of Distances: Continental U.S., Alaska, Hawaii, Canada, Canal Zone, Central America, Mexico, and Puerto Rico.* It should be in the government publications section of a large library. Using the table, you can compute the distance from Grants Pass, Ore., to Bayonne, N.J.; but follow the instructions in the introduction to see how, since there are several possible routes.

Some critics of government spending can't justify the volume and variety of publications the government issues. Consider these: *The World of David Gilmour Blythe, 1815-1865* (the catalog of a traveling exhibition of Blythe's paintings), *The Nurse Practitioner in an Adult Outpatient Clinic* (the results of a study), *Super Me, Super Yo* (a Spanish-English activity book for young children), and *Career Opportunities in Art Museums, Zoos and Other Interesting Places.* Although the arguments as to their worth continue, you should be aware of the research wealth in government materials that not only supplement commercial publications, but are also unique and not duplicated elsewhere. (The *U.S. Navy Diving Manual,* for example, is acknowledged around the world as one of the most authoritative reference works on the subject.)

A Random Sample

To better show you the breadth and scope of government publications, I've randomly selected the following in various publication categories. Many of these are issued regularly and are updated every few years. (In Part Two of the chapter, I'll offer a list of document-finding tools to help you locate these and other important titles.)

Publications for Consumers and Taxpayers
Federal Benefits for Veterans and Dependents. Issued by the Veterans Ad-

ministration. 1982. 72 pages. (Summarizes eligibility and federal benefits for veterans, their dependents, and their beneficiaries.)

Find and Fix the Leaks. Issued by the Department of Energy. 1981. 28 pages (A step-by-step guide to reducing costly air leaks in your home.)

How to Buy Surplus Personal Property from the Department of Defense. Issued by the Department of Defense. 1978. 23 pages. (How you may be notified to bid on government surplus tools, furniture, office equipment, vehicles, etc.)

Posters

Snakes: Poisonous and Nonpoisonous Species. Issued by the U.S. Army Corps of Engineers. 37x28 inches. 1981. (A color poster depicting 18 species of snakes.)

Voyager's Encounter With Jupiter and Its Moons. Issued by NASA. 1980. (A set of six posters, each measuring 36x24 inches.)

Pamphlets and Brochures

Family Planning Methods of Contraception. Issued by the Department of Health and Human Services. 1980. (A brochure that describes contraceptive devices for men and women.)

When Your Child First Goes to the Hospital. Issued by the Department of Health and Human Services. 1979. 36 pages. (Tips on how to prepare your child for hospitalization, and how to select a doctor and a hospital.)

Your Trip Abroad. Issued by the Department of State. 1982. 30 pages. (Information on passports, visas, vaccinations, customs, legal aid, help from American consuls, etc.)

Bibliographies

Bibliography on Smoking and Health. Issued by the Public Health Service. 1981. 533 pages. (Refers to articles and books addressing the effects of smoking on individuals and society.)

Arms Control and Disarmament: A Quarterly Bibliography with Abstracts and Annotations. Issued by the Library of Congress. 1965-73. (Lists books and articles concerning arms control and disarmament in English, French, German, Russian, and other languages where an English translation was available.)

The College Presidency, 1900-60, by Walter Crosby Eells and Ernest V. Hollis. Issued by the Office of Education. 1961. 143 pages. (Lists 700 writings on the college president, his duties, responsibilities, administration, qualifications, etc.)

Directories and Guidebooks

Anglers Guides to the U.S. Atlantic Coast. Issued by the Department of Commerce. 1974-79. (Eight pamphlets giving information and charts on where to find various types of game fish.)

National Solar Energy Education Directory. Issued by the Department of Energy. 1980. 279 pages. (Lists solar energy and related courses offered in 900 colleges throughout the country.)

Directory of National Unions and Employee Associations. Issued by the Department of Labor. 1980. 139 pages. (A directory of addresses.)

Handbooks and Manuals

European Trade Fairs: A Guide for Exporters. Issued by the Department of Commerce. 1981. 75 pages. (Tips on how to choose a market in Europe, how to attend a fair and make it profitable.)

NOAA Diving Manual. Issued by the National Oceanic and Atmospheric Administration. 1979. 548 pages. (Information on diving technology and the techniques used in scientific diving tasks.)

Passive Solar Construction Handbook. Issued by the Department of Energy. 1981. 584 pages. (Instruction for homebuilders on how to adapt standard building practices to passive solar applications.)

Dictionaries and Glossaries

A Handbook of Heart Terms. Issued by the Department of Health and Human Services. 1978. 68 pages. (Defines terms that refer to the physiology of the heart.)

Dictionary of Mining, Minerals and Related Terms, compiled by Paul Thrush. Issued by the Bureau of Mines. 1968. 1,269 pages. (A comprehensive source for the mining industry listing 55,000 technical and layman's terms from the entire English-speaking world. Also notes the word's country of origin.)

International Relations Dictionary. Issued by the Department of State. 1980. 84 pages. (Defines terms, phrases, acronyms, catchwords, and abbreviations used in foreign affairs.)

Magazines

Aging. Issued bimonthly by the Department of Health and Human Services. 1951-date. (Features articles on activities and programs directed to the more than 33 million Americans over 60 years of age.)

Navy Lifeline. Issued bimonthly by the Department of Defense. 1974-date. (Features articles on safety and occupational health and stress experienced by Navy personnel in their work.)

Business America. Issued biweekly by the Department of Commerce. 1978-date. (Gives American exporters information on trade opportunities and ways of doing business abroad.)

Indexes and Abstracts

Sport Fishery Abstracts. Issued by U.S. Fish and Wildlife Service. 1955-date. (Covers articles and reports on pollution, fish diseases, geographical distribution, growth, spawning habits, genetics, etc.)

Selected Water Resources Abstracts. Issued by the Department of the Interior. 1954-date. (Indexes articles and reports on water-quality management, pollution, water law, harbor management, flood control, etc.)

A VARIETY OF ISSUING AGENCIES

Government publications do not emanate from one agency or department of the government any more than McGraw-Hill issues all new books published in the United States each year. The majority of documents are commissioned, written, and contracted by the hundreds of subdivisions in the 13 departments of the government's executive branch. These publications correspond to the interests and responsibilities of each agency. (A description of their specific duties appears in the *United States Government Manual,* a standard library directory familiar to many researchers, and *Information USA,* by Matthew Lesko. Viking Press. 1983.)

One way to better understand the scope of government charges (and, therefore, publishing topics) is to look briefly at the departments themselves and their particular domains.

1. Department of Agriculture

Of approximately 40 subordinate units, more than half in the DA issue publications available to depository libraries. (See page 212 for a definition of depository libraries.) Some DA divisions are the Forest Service, Soil Conservation Services, Economics and Statistics Service, and the Office of Environmental Quality.

Titles generated from these agencies include the *Agricultural Research Monthly* (technical articles on the results of research projects in livestock management, poultry, crops, etc.); *Soil Survey Reports* (soil maps with a description of the area they cover and productivity estimates); *Fire Management* (a quarterly magazine describing forest fire control techniques); and *Portfolio of American Agriculture* (a group of 20 photos and paintings that capture the picturesque quality of American agriculture).

Instructive handbooks are also a by-product of the DA. Titles include *Guide to Alaska Trees, Fire-Weather Observer's Handbook,* and *Avalanche Handbook.*

Q. Please send me the title of a book that gives the nutritional value of fresh fruits and vegetables.

A. Charts appear in those wallet-size booklets you often find near the supermarket checkout stands, but one of the most comprehensive publications I've ever seen is a 190-page book issued by the Department of Agriculture, called *Composition of Foods,* by Bernice Watt and Anabel Merrill. The last issue sold for about $6. (I have recently learned that this volume has been split into about 10 pamphlets organized by food group: e.g., *Composition of Foods: Sausages and Luncheon Meats; Composition of Foods: Soups, Sauces and Gravies.* These are not reprinted every year; the most recent edition is 1981.)

A librarian can check the current price and newest edition of the pamphlet best suited to your needs. You can buy the pamphlets from the Government Printing Office, Washington, DC 20402.

---

2. Department of Commerce

Publications emanate from the DOCs 20 major and minor units including the National Bureau of Standards, Bureau of the Census, Patent and Trademark Office, Maritime Administration, National Technical Information Service, and National Oceanic and Atmospheric Administration (including subagencies like the National Weather Service and the Environmental Data and Information Service).

Some of their titles are *Overseas Business Reports* (booklets giving information on world economics and international trade for exporters, importers, investors, manufacturers, and researchers); *Government Reports Announcements and Index* (biweekly abstracts of published reports on government sponsored research); *United States Earthquakes* (an annual that documents earthquake activity in the United States and its possessions); and *Survey of Current Business* (a monthly outlook and survey of current trends in business).

Q. What is California's cotton production and its ranking among other states?
A. *American Statistics Index* (under COTTON) shows that the Bureau of the Census issues statistics on major cotton producers in a publication called *Cotton Ginnings*, available in the government publications section of large libraries. Production is given in bales (average weight 500 pounds). The publication shows that in 1979, California produced almost 3 million bales, second only to Texas with 5½ million bales. These two states account for almost half of U.S. cotton production.

---

3. Department of Defense

Divisions in the Departments of the Army, Navy, and Air Force include the National Guard Bureau, the Naval Observatory, Air Adjutant General's Office, and the Office of Military History. They issue such publications as *American Practical Navigator* (the basics of navigation, piloting, and dead reckoning, electronic and celestial navigation, oceanography, and the weather); the *U.S. Army in World War II* (a 23-volume set arranged chronologically by campaign, with maps and charts); *The Army Air Forces in World War II: Combat Chronology 1941-1945* (a day-by-day record of the war); *Soviet Military Power* (an examination of Soviet military strength and the scope of Soviet military buildup); and *Edible and Hazardous Marine Life* (a booklet offering survival techniques in various marine environments).

4. Department of Education

Formerly part of the Department of Health, Education and Welfare, this department and its offices such as the National Center for Education Statistics, Office of Student Financial Assistance, and the National Institute of Education issue such publications as *Education Directory* (lists public schools throughout the nation); *Doing Your Best on Aptitude Tests* (a pamphlet of tips for taking tests); *Digest of Education Statistics* (a statistical handbook); *Your Responsibilities to Disabled Persons as a School or College Administrator;* and *Education and Training for Older Persons: A Program Guide* (a guidance booklet for educators).

5. Department of Energy

The Office of Conservation and Solar Applications, Office of Energy Research, Office of Energy Technology, and other DOE subdivisions issue such publications as *Fuel From Farms: A Guide to Small-Scale Ethanol Production* (teaches farmers and others how to convert farm crop waste into ethanol); *Electric Power Monthly* (a magazine that summarizes data on electric power production and consumption); *A Guidebook to Renewable Energy Technologies* (a nontechnical guide to 23 techniques for renewing energy); *Emergency Handling of Radiation Accident Cases* (a series with separate volumes for physicians, nurses, hospital administrators, ambulance rescue squads, police, sheriffs, and firemen); and *Solar Energy for Heating of Greenhouses and Greenhouse-Resident Combinations.*

6. Department of Health and Human Services

Once part of the former Department of Health, Education, and Welfare, this department includes the Social Security Administration, Public Health Service, and National Institute of Dental Research, among others. Some of its publications include *Pocket Guide to Babysitting* (a 48-page pamphlet of child care for teenage babysitters); *No Easy Answers: The Learning Disabled Child* (advice on how to help the learning disabled child understand his problems); *How to Select a Nursing Home* (how to select and evaluate a nursing home); and *The Industrial Environment—Its Evaluation Control* (an industrial hygiene textbook that shows how to evaluate the working environment).

7. Department of Housing and Urban Development

Some of HUD's subdivisions are the Federal Housing Administration, the New Communities Administration, and the Federal Disaster Assistance Administration. They issue the monthly report, *House and Urban Development Trends; Solar Dwelling Design Concepts* (a general guide for builders and homeowners); *Innovative Zoning: A Local Official's Guidebook; Minimum Property Standards* (four volumes, each by type of dwelling); *Guide to the Inspection of Existing Homes for Wood-Inhabiting Fungi and Insects* (a handbook for controlling insect infestations); and more.

8. Department of the Interior

The U.S. Geological Survey, Bureau of Indian Affairs, National Park Service, U.S. Fish and Wildlife Service, Bureau of Land Management, and other DI offices offer such titles as *The 1980 Eruptions of Mount St. Helens, Washington* (an 872-page report with 470 illustrations and 117 tables); *Earth Manual: Index of the National Park System and Related Areas* (a state-by-state guide to National Park Service areas including historic sites, seashores, preserves, and monuments); *Prospecting for Gold in the United States* (reviews areas in which gold has been found, with maps); and *Beehives of Invention* (an inside glimpse of Thomas Edison's research laboratories).

9. Department of Justice

The Federal Bureau of Investigation, Bureau of Prisons, Immigration and Naturalization Service, Drug Enforcement Administration, and other agencies issue *How to Crimeproof Your Home* (a pamphlet of tips for homeowners); *Judges of the United States: 1789-1978* (a biographical directory); *Illegal Corporate Behavior* (an examination of white collar crime); *Crime Scene Search and Physical Evidence Handbook* (a procedural text for investigating officers); and *Finding the Law: A Workbook on Legal Research for Laypersons* (designed to help government surveyors research property disputes). By the way, the last title listed here is one of those "you-can't-tell-a-book-by-its-title" varieties.

10. Department of Labor

The Bureau of Labor Statistics, Women's Bureau and Occupational Safety and Health Administration publish such items as the *Consumer Price Index* (a quarterly statistical guide measuring the cost of living in various cities); *Opportunities in Job Corps: A Directory of Job Corps Centers and Courses; Employment Projection for the 1980s; The Earnings Gap Between Women and Men* (a statistical report); and *Women and Business: A Directory of Women-Owned Businesses in Washington, Oregon, Idaho, and Alaska.*

11. Department of State

The Agency for International Development, Arms Control and Disarmament Agency, International Development and Cooperation Agency, and other subdivisions issue *World Strength of Communist Party Organizations* (an annual analysis); *Foreign Service Institute Basic Language Courses* (language instruction booklets in Spanish, French, Hebrew, German, and several other languages); and *Foreign Area Studies* (a series of 16 books—each analyzes a particular country's economic, military, political, and social systems).

12. Department of the Treasury

Among the agencies of this department are the Bureau of Customs; Internal Revenue Service; Bureau of the Mint; U.S. Secret Service; and Bureau of Alcohol, Tobacco and Firearms. Publications emanating from these offices include *Customs Bulletin: Regulations, Rulings, Decisions, Notices on Customs Matters* (a legal resource); *World's Monetary Stocks of Gold, Silver and Coins in [year]* (coinage statistics of various countries); *International Income and Taxes: Foreign Tax Credit Claimed on Corporate Income Tax Returns*, etc. (a report); and the *Internal Revenue Bulletin* (a weekly listing of regulations, procedures, and legislation affecting IRS operations).

Q. Where can I get the regulations that govern buying a car abroad and bringing it back to this country?

A. Any Office of the U.S. Customs Service will send you a pamphlet called *Importing a Car*. Check the phone book under UNITED STATES GOVERNMENT—TREASURY DEPARTMENT for an office in your area.

The points in the pamphlet are too numerous to mention here, but you'll get details on the forms needed, fees and taxes to be paid, tax-free situations, how to get your plates and permits, safety emission requirements, etc. A large library with a government documents section may also have the pamphlet.

---

13. Department of Transportation

The Federal Highway Administration, Federal Aviation Administration, Transportation Safety Board, Coast Guard, etc., issue *Basic Flight Manual and ATC* [Air Traffic Control] *Procedures* (a handbook for trainees); *Recycling Historic Railroad Stations: A Citizen's Manual* (a guide to restoration); *Emergency Medical Services: First Responder Training Course* (a how-to guide for emergency paramedics); *Truck Tire Cornering and Braking Traction Study* (the results of this study); *Private Pilot-Airplane, Written Test Guide*; and *Drugs and Driving* (a booklet for citizens on one of the dangers of drug use).

In addition to the 13 executive departments above, several dozen independent and regulatory agencies also issue publications. Some of those agencies and a sample of their publications include: Federal Trade Commission (*Franchising and Business Opportunities*); Civil Aeronautics Board (*List of U.S. Air Carriers*); Federal Communications Commission (*Purchasing a Broadcast Station: A Buyer's Guide*); Arms Control and Disarmament Agency (*World Military Expenditures and Related Data*); Atomic Energy Commission (*Nuclear Safety: A Bimonthly Technical Progress Review*); U.S. Postal Service (*A Guide for Mail Bomb Security*); and Small Business Administration (*Export Marketing for Smaller Firms*).

Q. I am interested in books giving details of space exploration since the 1950s, but my local library seems to be devoid of a decent selection. Do you think the local college libraries would have more to choose from, and would I be able to borrow books from them?

A. NASA issues a staggering number of publications on every aspect of space exploration such as *Results from Skylab, Comet Kohoutek, Skylab: A Guidebook,* and *Evolution of the Solar System.* The San Diego Public Library receives many government publications (there's even a special card catalog for them) issued by various governmental agencies, like NASA. However, because of the space problem, they're not in open stacks.

You're right that college libraries have a larger selection of astronomy books than the small library branches, and they offer fee cards to the public. But before you check them, try the government publications in the downtown library.

Besides the scores of documents published by the agencies noted above, the legislative and judicial branches of the government issue their own publications: myriad committee hearings, legislation, and documents of official business that are available to the public.

Some divisions of the legislative branch of the government are the General Accounting Office, the Copyright Office, and the Congress itself. They issue such items as *Central States Teamsters Fund: Hearings,* issued by the Subcommittee on Oversight of the Committee on Ways and Means, House of Representatives (1978); *Emerging Food Marketing Technologies: A Preliminary Analysis,* issued by the Office of Technology Assessment, U.S. Congress (1978); and the *Congressional Record,* issued by the Congress.

The Judiciary, including the Customs Courts, the Tax Court, the Supreme Court, and other federal courts, issues the *United States Codes Annotated* (the federal laws) and court reports such as *Cases Decided in the United States Court of Claims* (an ongoing series).

WHO COLLECTS GOVERNMENT DOCUMENTS?

A large amount of government-generated information is available in libraries. By law, it is distributed without cost to more than 1,300 libraries in the United States.

Libraries that receive government publications free are called depository libraries. They include each state library located in the state capital; two libraries in each Congressional District (including large public and academic libraries totaling more than 850 nationwide); two libraries chosen by each senator in any part of the state (totaling about 200); and others in U.S. territories, land grant colleges, military academies, and departments of the government.

Depository libraries do not receive *every* publication issued by the government, however. They receive only those which are defined by legislation as having educational value and public interest. This is a sizable amount but only a fraction of the total output.

In 1983, the inventory of the Government Printing Office was approximately 25,000 titles in print. (Compare this with the 35,000 to 40,000 new, commercially published books issued from several hundred U.S. publishers annually.) Many of these documents are scientific reports and technical publications with limited appeal for the general public. The public is not, in fact, the largest purchaser and user of government documents. Rather, state and local governments, and companies that do business with the government, buy and use government documents most.

Nevertheless, it is the depository library's responsibility to make documents of public interest and educational value available to any researcher. And they *are* available—so long as you know where to look.

―――――――――――――――― PART 2 ――――――――――――――――

FINDING GOVERNMENT PUBLICATIONS

Or, Everything You Always Wanted to Know
about the Government but Didn't Know You Could Find

The government publishes "finding tools"—indexes and bibliographies—through which you can identify a government document by subject, agency, or personal author. In recent years, commercial publishers that specialize in reprinting government documents, have issued their own indexes. These indexes have bettered the government's own finding tools, and access to documents has improved immeasurably. Nevertheless, the process of finding these documents requires an understanding of their idiosyncrasies before you dive in.

Government documents are different from commercial publications in two major ways—at least as far as libraries are concerned. These have to do with the way they're cataloged and the way they're shelved.

Documents do not follow either the familiar Dewey Decimal or the Library of Congress subject cataloging systems. A typical government document "call number" (also called Superintendent of Documents or Sudocs number) looks like this:

A 13.52:33/3.

The first letter in most cases stands for the issuing agency. Here, "A" stands for the Department of Agriculture. (J stands for publications issued by the Justice Department; S, the State Department; VA, the Veterans Administration, etc.) The other parts of the Sudocs number represent types of publications like handbooks and annual reports. Sometimes a year is noted in the call number along with a publication's volume number. Even though the components have some meaning to people who work with documents, they are not the kind of aids that help you find the items on the shelf. So, except for the first letter denoting issuing agency, the other numbers have no meaning for your purposes.

As a result of their different call-number system, documents are not arranged on the shelf by subject. Instead, they are arranged by issuing agency. (This is as logical for researchers as arranging books by publisher.) You might assume that this would not cause any problem; that if the Department of Education issues materials only in the field of education, then those publications will be together on the shelves. Unfortunately, it isn't that simple.

A subject usually consists of numerous subdivisions. For example, the DOE issues books on educating the mentally handicapped, for teachers; and guides on financial aid, for college administrators. In large libraries, even though books on these topics are still in the field of education, they would be shelved too far apart to be easily found by shelf browsing.

Another quirk in this setup is that many government agencies publish material in diverse subject areas. The Library of Congress has issued a book on children's poetry, as well as a guide to the official publications of Swaziland. Despite their diverse topics, these books may sit near each other on the shelf, because all LC publications are kept together.

The problem is further compounded because government agencies frequently reorganize or change their names. As a result, their "call numbers" change, which further means that books and especially runs of continuously issued publications (like magazines or annual reports) then become separated. A magazine published since the 1920s by the Federal Aviation Administration, for example, would appear in five separate locations under five separate call numbers, because the Federal Aviation Administration has undergone five name changes since 1926: the Aeronautics Branch (1926-1934), the Bureau of Air Commission (1934-1938), The Civil Aeronautics Administration (1938-1959), and the Federal Aviation Agency (1959-1966).

For researchers, the logic in this system compares to separating issues of *McCall's* magazine on library shelves each time its parent corporation changes hands. Granted, this would preserve the integrity of corporate change, but researchers don't look for books on library shelves by the name of their publishers.

Some libraries try to bring divergent parts of split sets back together on the shelf, but keeping up with the quantity of changes creates an added burden for library staffs in a system that is already cumbersome.

Because of their shelf arrangement by issuing agency rather than subject, shelf browsing in open stacks of documents doesn't work. And, since documents have their own unique call numbers, they're kept in their own section or department of the library where a separate catalog is maintained. (This separation contributes to the mystique of government documents even though it arose from purely practical considerations. Libraries don't have the resources to recatalog and integrate into the regular collection the vast quantity of documents they receive. Therefore the volumes must be kept separate.)

Despite these apparent roadblocks, there is a way to find documents successfully and easily. And that's by starting with the finding tools.

DOCUMENTS-FINDING TOOLS

As with other research situations, you normally begin your documents search through catalogs, indexes, and bibliographies. The only difference with documents searches is that it's easier to remember that you *must* use these finding aids. One attempt to shelf-browse the documents will convince you of that.

I should mention, too, that new technology and the need to save money have not bypassed government publications or their finding tools. Many documents are now available in microform; and since about 1981, more and more items sent to depository libraries have been in that format. (Paper copies are still sold to the public, however, through direct mail from the Government Printing Office, its agencies, and some two dozen documents bookstores nationwide. The locations of the government's bookstores appear on the inside back cover of recent issues of *Monthly Catalog*.)

Microfilm has also enabled commercial publishers to reprint documents as they are not bound by copyright. Since the 1970s several publishers, notably Congressional Information Service, Inc., unearthed, filmed, indexed, and packaged huge sets of documents containing thousands of out-of-print and nondepository items most libraries did not own.[1]

The indexes to these commercially published sets (even without the accompanying microform documents which can always be borrowed on interlibrary loan) are exquisite reference resources by themselves. Not only do they identify many nondepository documents, they also improve on the government-issued finding tools. For example, the *CIS Index and Abstract* set, published since 1970, duplicates much of the government's *Monthly Catalog*, but the *CIS* index has a better subject index with many more access points. It also indexes parts of documents, and each item listed is annotated, which the *Monthly Catalog* does not do.

As a result of these commercially published indexes and accompanying microform collections, there are thousands of once scarce and hard-to-get documents available in libraries all over the country.

You may have already noticed that some commercially published indexes and bibliographies include documents. Although there is some coverage in commercial sources, it's meager. For example, of the approxi-

[1]Remember, depository libraries receive only depository items, those publications defined by law as being of public interest and having educational value—only a small fraction of the government's total output.

mately 170 magazines currently issued by government agencies, *Reader's Guide* presently indexes only seven: *Aging, American Education, Children Today, Department of State Bulletin, FDA Consumer, Monthly Labor Review,* and *Smithsonian.*

Public Affairs Information Service (PAIS) *Bulletin,* is the most useful commercial index for identifying Congressional committee reports and hearings, but it, too, covers only a fraction of the output. (More on this later.)

The following list of indexes to government documents covers not only the ones received automatically by depository libraries but also the new commercially reproduced sets of old and nondepository documents. These indexes are normally kept in a library's documents department.

Note one important thing. Though many of the printed indexes listed here come with full sets of documents in microform, not all libraries own them.[2] Many libraries have purchased just the index (many cost between $500 and $1,000), and because of their high cost, they share the microform documents with other libraries. Check with a librarian about your library's access to the microform documents themselves. (You can always borrow the documents in microform through interlibrary loan.)

1. *Monthly Catalog.* Issued by the Superintendent of Documents. 1895-date. (Readex Microprint Corp., a commercial publisher, has microformed all depository publications from 1953 and nondepository publications from 1956 as listed in the *MC.* Many libraries carry these microform documents, and the *MC* serves as an index to them.)

Early government publishing was not as profuse as it is now. Publications that *did* exist covered the deliberations of Congress. Later, as the number of agencies and their functions grew, so did the scope and quantity of government publishing.

Prior to the first issue of the *MC* in 1895, there were several avenues of access to government material—all of them inadequate. And the complexities of using them grew with the numbers of documents published.

Since its inception, the *MC,* with its numerous title and format changes, has been the major tool for identifying government publications. But it's not the only one, and it does have many omissions. In fact, it is estimated to exclude from 55 to 90 percent of the federal output. Here's why:

(a) The Government Printing Office alone does not issue all government documents. Because of the volume of the government's output, there are over 300 additional presses under government contract. Even with the publishing reductions and cutbacks of recent years, it's obvious that the patterns of distribution and control are scattered rather than centralized.

---

[2]This list of indexes is not in alphabetical order; rather the order of the resources corresponds to how you might search them in an actual research project: See page 230 for a sample search of government documents.

(b) Just as commercial publishers send copies of their new books to the Copyright Office, universities, research institutions, and industries performing research under government contract are supposed to send copies of their completed publications to the Superintendent of Documents in Washington, DC for listing in the MC. Despite mandatory legislation, the practice is spotty, and many research groups do not submit their publications. This results in many omissions in the MC. (A survey of 102,000 publications issued by the government between January 1977 and June 1978 showed that only 66,000 were recorded in the MC.)

(c) Technical reports generated from government-sponsored research carried on in public and private industry are recorded in indexes issued by the National Technical Information Service (NTIS) and its subdivisions. This means they are listed in indexes other than the MC. The major index covering NTIS reports is *Government Reports Announcements and Index*. The MC records only a fraction of the technical literature.

In addition to the above omissions, the MC is actually a bibliography, not an index. It doesn't index articles in government-published periodicals or serials. It does, however, cover brochures and pamphlets of a few pages.[3]

Items in the MC are listed by issuing agency (Interior Department, Geological Survey, Heritage Conservation and Recreation Service, etc.) which is a rather useless approach for researchers' purposes. More often you'll use the subject approach. Check the subject index in back of monthly volumes or in the cumulative volumes for one, five, and sometimes ten years. (Or check item #2 on page 218.)

Entries in MC's subject index look like this:

INTERSTELLAR COMMUNICATION

> *Extraterrestrial intelligence research:* hearings before the Subcommittee on Space Science and Applications of the Committee on Science and Technology, U.S. House of Representatives, Ninety-fifth Congress, second session, September 19, 20, 1978., 79-9123
>
> [79 refers to the 1979 volume, 9123 is the chronological number for the full entry of this 89-page report.]

INTERVIEWING

> *The oral interview as a selection technique:* some suggested formats and guidelines for structuring the interview process/, 79-7329
>
> [A 111-page book issued by the Civil Service Administration.]

INVESTMENTS, FOREIGN—UNITED STATES

> *Foreign investment in United States agricultural land/,* 79-8762
>
> [A 292-page report issued by the Senate Committee on Agriculture, Nutrition, and Forestry.]

Note also the title key-word index in the back of each volume (published since July 1980). It provides still another access point and looks like this:

---

[3]In checking for government publications in the MC and other finding tools, note the number of pages. You may not want to pursue a document if it's only a brochure.

> *Global atmospheric background monitoring for selec* 83-23543
> *Global autovon telephone directory*   83-880
> *global environment: The consequences of nuclear*   83-21508

Key-word indexes seem confusing since you can't tell where to begin reading the document title. Most key-word indexes use some kind of mark such as / to indicate the break. In this index, look for the capitalized word. If there is none, then the entry starts with the key word itself. Also note that some entries (like the first one above) seem incomplete. Entries are cut off after a certain number of spaces even if the title isn't completed. Use the *MC* number—83-23543—to see the full entry.

Q. Where can I get a book naming all the Medal of Honor heroes with their feats, home states, etc.?

A. The Medal of Honor, the highest military award for bravery, was first conceived in the early 1860s and presented in 1863. There are several books which tell the stories of the best-known winners. *Men of Valor*, by Donald Ross, is one of these; but the most complete list is the one compiled by the government itself. It's called *Medal of Honor Recipients, 1863-1978* (found through both the *Monthly Catalog* and the Government Printing Office's *Publications Reference File*).

This 1,113-page book includes the full historical background of the award, extracts from the statutes which authorize it, charts showing the number of awards in each branch of the service, and other information.

Both books should be available in large libraries.

Items in the *MC* which are marked with a solid black dot indicate that they are depository items and are for sale. Those without the marking indicate that the document is not for sale.

2. *Cumulative Subject Index to the Monthly Catalog of United States Government Publications, 1900-71.* 15 volumes. Carrollton Press. (Comes with a microfilm collection of documents.)

This index arranges by subject, and in one alphabet, all the documents in the 72 annual issues of the *MC* (1900-71). Since entries are shortened, you must check the particular annual volume of the *MC* to get the full citation (number of pages, issuing agency, Sudocs call number, etc.). If the item is not in the library in the print version, ask about borrowing the microform copy. Listings in the cumulative subject index look like this:

HANDICAPPED EMPLOYMENT
    workshops, 1961 directory (62) 12777
        [62 = 1962, the year of the *Monthly Catalog* in which the full citation
        appears; 12777 is the chronological number of the item in the *MC*.]
HANDICRAFTS (04) 634
    Guatemala, industry (49) 1145
    Industries, Communist China (61) 2282
    North Vietnam Industry, reform and development (61) 4442

HANDLEY, WILLIAM J., nomination, hearing (69) 8065
HANDLING:
   hazardous materials (65) 1989
HANDWRITING (12) 844
   analysis and code of criminal procedure, West Germany (64) 10816
   criminological distinction of similar handwritings by computers, USSR
      study (66) 14864

The greatest asset of the *Cumulative Subject Index* is the time it saves by offering one lookup point instead of up to 72.

3. *Cumulative Title Index to United States Public Documents, 1789-1976.* 16 volumes. United States Historical Documents Institute. (Comes with a microform set of documents.)[4]

This index interfiles into one alphabet all document titles listed in past issues of the *MC* and some of its pre-1895 predecessors. If you have a document title but no date or Sudocs number, the *Cumulative Title Index* will help you find it quickly. Otherwise, its usefulness, as a title-only approach, is somewhat limited. Entries look like this:

Baccalaureate degrees conferred by American colleges in 17th and 18th centuries, 1958. FS 5.4:528.
   [FS 5.4:528 is the Sudocs number of this 71-page circular issued by the Office of Education, Dept. of Health, Education, and Welfare. FS is an old Sudocs number for this agency. It is not used for new Department of Education documents.]
Bach, Beethoven or Bacharach in Air Force band, 1973.
   D 301.2:B22/2. [issued by the Defense Dept.]
Back-country travel in national park system, 1971.
   I 29.9/2: B12. [issued by the Interior Dept.]
Background Berlin, city between two worlds, 1960.
   S 1.74:61. [issued by the State Dept.]
Background information on butter roll-back, 1943.
   A 21.18:18. [issued by the Agriculture Dept.]

4. Government Printing Office (GPO) Sales *Publications Reference File.* Issued by the Superintendent of Documents. 1977-date. (On microfiche only).

Called *PRF* for short, this file functions as a books-in-print to government documents, some more than 20 years old.

The approach to the *PRF* is by key word or phrase, subject, title, series, and personal author interfiled in one alphabet. Sample entries are:
   AEROBIC BIOLOGICAL WASTEWATER TREATMENT FACILITIES
      Process Control Manual for Aerobic Biological Wastewater Treatment Facili-

---

[4]Many of the individual microform sets of documents mentioned in this chapter cover the same material, so there's heavy duplication. As a result of the duplication libraries don't own all microform sets of documents. One may be enough. The duplication of filmed documents occurs because packages are offered by different publishers acting independently of each other.

ties. Issued by the Environmental Protection Agency. 1977. 343 pages.
AEROBIC EXERCISES
   *Physical Fitness Programs for Law Enforcement Officers: A Manual for Police
   Administrators,* by Clifford S. Price. Issued by the Justice Department.
   1978. 415 pages.
AEROBIC FITNESS
   Fitness and Work Capacity, by Brian Sharkey. Issued by the Department
   of Agriculture. 1977. 81 pages.

All documents in the *PRF* also appear in the *MC* (although not everything in the *MC* appears in the *PRF,* because not everything listed in the
MC is for sale). It pays to check both sources, but since it's easier and faster to use *PRF,* check that first.

Q. I need the cost-of-living figures for San Diego from 1974 to the present.
Where might I get them?

A. Cost-of-living figures are averaged in several ways: by product, service, or
geographical area. Almanacs give partial data, but their quotes are one to two
years behind. The figures in the *Statistical Abstract of the United States* are also
somewhat delayed.

For the most up-to-date figures, check a government-published monthly entitled *Consumer Price Index - Detailed Report,* which I found by checking the phrase,
COST OF LIVING in the *PRF (Publications Reference File).*

---

5. *Index to United States Government Periodicals.* Infordata International,
Inc. Quarterly. 1973-date. (All magazines covered by this index are also issued in microform.)

This index (arranged by subject) covers the approximately 170 magazines published by Uncle Sam for chaplains; military lawyers; government employees in public health, gerontology, consumerism, education,
energy, etc.

The articles in government periodicals cover the same ground as those
in commercial and scholarly magazines. Subjects run the gamut from advertising to anchovies. Entries in this index look like this:

ADVERTISING
   Greek magazine offers free advertising space. *Bus Amer* 4 24 31 N 30 81-
   216.
      Bus Amer = *Business America;* [4 24 = volume 4, number 24; 31 =
      page; N 30 81 = November 30 1981; 216 stands for an order number
      assigned by the Microfilming Corp. of America for buying the mag-
      azine on microfilm]
AERIAL PHOTOGRAPHY
   Continuous monitoring of Mount St. Helens volcano. Henry Spall, il
   Earth Info Bull 12 6 220-227 N-D 80-034.
      [*Earth Info Bull* = *Earthquake Information Bulletin*]

AERIAL WARFARE
  Airmobility in the 1980s. William R. Richardson. il *U.S. Army Avia Dig* 27 8 2-5+ Ag 81-107.
  [*U.S. Army Avia Dig* = *U.S. Army Aviation Digest*]
AFGHANISTAN
  Reported use of chemical weapons. Walter J. Stoessel, Jr. *Dept Sta Bul* 81 2056 79 N 81-29.
  [*Dept Sta Bul* = *Department of State Bulletin*]
ALASKA PIPELINE
  Putting it all together: Alaskan pipeline weld criteria. Collier Smith, il gr *Dimen NBS*, 64 9 2-5 N 80-102.
  [*Dimen NBS* = *Dimensions NBS*] [NBS = National Bureau of Standards]
AMUSEMENT PARKS
  Theme park employment. Connie Desaulniers, il *Trends* 17 3 17-19 Sum 80-241.

6. *Public Affairs Information Service* (PAIS) *Bulletin.* Public Affairs Information Service, Inc. Biweekly. 1915-date.

PAIS is one of the few commercial periodical indexes listing government publications. It merits mention, because it includes reports of governmental investigations and documents citing activities of social and political significance. It covers only a small number of documents and government magazines, but it's an easy way to locate many relevant items.

Most entries for government publications in *PAIS* start with the corporate author, UNITED STATES. The entries below are samples of a commercial periodical and a government publication, respectively.

  GUIDED MISSILES
    [personal author entry for a magazine article]
    Collison, Robert. The new threat of nuclear war: there are now actually people who think you can win one. (nuclear strategy and implications of the MX supermissile program) il *Saturday Night* 95: 15-18+ My '80.
    [corporate author entry for a government document]
    United States. House. Committee on Armed Services Status of the MX missile system: hearings, May 1, 1980. '80 ii + 46p diags map (96th Cong., 2d Sess.) (H.A.S.C. no. 95-96) - Washington, D.C. 20515.
    [H.A.S.C. = House Armed Services Committee]

PAIS is especially useful in the early stages of research for government documents, because it's only about three weeks behind in its indexing. Computerized text processing now enables commercial publishers to issue their indexes faster—the former average lag time was 6-8 weeks. But many government publications and indexes are still slow to come out, and often a report will appear in *PAIS* before it appears in the *MC*.

Another plus for *PAIS* is that because it's an index, it covers the articles in government periodicals and serial publications. You'll recall that *MC* is a bibliography, and it doesn't index individual articles in government magazines or serials. In the 1982 issue of *MC*, for example, there is little in the subject index under President Ronald Reagan's name. In *PAIS* for that

same period, however, there are countless references to him in government serial publications—particularly documenting his speeches and addresses which were reprinted in them.

Q. Margaret Thatcher of England visited President Ronald Reagan in early
1981, and I'd like to find some information on her visit and what the two leaders
discussed. Where should I begin my search?

A. Check *The New York Times Index* under Thatcher's name (there are too many
entries under Reagan's name to sort through).

Also check *PAIS Bulletin* for 1981. It mentions two items. One (under Thatcher)
is "Visit of Prime Minister Margaret Thatcher of the United Kingdom" [an exchange between President Reagan and Prime Minister Thatcher, Feb. 26-27, 1981]
published in the March 2, 1981 issue of a government serial called *Weekly Compilation of Presidential Documents.*

Under Reagan's name in *PAIS*, there's a long list of all his speeches and addresses in 1981 publications; surprisingly, there's an entry different from the one
under Thatcher's name. It's "Visit of British Prime Minister Thatcher; remarks,
Ronald Reagan and Margaret Thatcher," in the April 1981 issue of the *Department
of State Bulletin.*

---

7. *CIS/Index and Abstracts to Publications of the U.S. Congress.* Congressional Information Service, Inc. 1970-date. (Comes with a microform set
of documents.)

This CIS set abstracts all publications of Congress including press releases. CIS offers approaches by subject, witness, corporation or company name, subcommittee, popular names of bills, laws, and reports.

Though congressional publications also appear in the *MC, CIS* coverage is more detailed, and it also indexes parts of documents. In addition
to the greater number of access points, entries include a summary. Entries
in the *CIS Index* (1980 issue) look like this:

NATIONAL FUNERAL DIRECTORS ASSOCIATION
    Funeral Industry, FTC regulation, H501-125.9
      [H = House document; 501-125.9 = CIS's accession number]
NATIONAL HOCKEY LEAGUE
    Cable TV sports program transmission impact on sports leagues,
    H521-12.3
NATIONAL GASOHOL CORP.
    Alcohol and alcohol fuel production programs, S161-39.3
      [S = Senate document]
PREGNANCY
    Drug addiction during pregnancy, effects and treatment, H961-16

By cross-checking the accession number (e.g. H501-125.9) in the index
volume with its matching entry in the abstracts volume, you'll find, in addition to the document summary, a Sudocs number. This number allows

you to retrieve the complete publication from library shelves and to read it in full if the library doesn't own the item in microform.

Congressional Information Service, Inc., has also filmed retrospective Congressional publications in three microform sets, each of which is accessed by multivolume printed indexes. They are the next three resources in this list (numbers 8 through 10).

8. *CIS/U.S. Congressional Committee Prints Index from the Earliest Publications through 1969.* Congressional Information Service, Inc. (Comes with a microform set of documents.)

Much of the work of Congress takes place in hearings, committees, and subcommittees, where proposed legislation is deliberated prior to final action on the floor of Congress. Committee prints are background studies of an issue under investigation by various Senate and House committees. This background is vital in helping the committees make a decision.

The prints provide more in-depth data than is generally given through witness testimony in Congressional hearings, and this information is frequently not found in other documents. The prints add a dimension to research on issues of the day, be they the purported Communist activities of Joseph McCarthy's era, or the space race.

Since Congressional committee prints are internal working documents not meant for public distribution (except as requested by constituents from the committees themselves while the supply lasts), they are printed in small quantities of approximately 1,000. They may range in length from a few pages to a few volumes. Until recently, depository libraries did not receive most of them, nor were they sold by the Government Printing Office.

The following is a selection from the Congressional Committee Prints index:

ARMCO STEEL CO.
> Refusal of certain steel companies to respond to subpoenas issued Apr. 12, 1962 (87/2/62) S1422
> > [87/2/62 = 87th Congress, 2d session, 1962; S1422 = Senate print number 1422]

ARMED FORCES RESERVE ACT
> Text of Armed Forces Reserve Act of 1952 (with Amendments to Dec. 31, 1955) (84/2/56) S0169

ARMENIA
> Communist takeover and occupation of Armenia (83/2/54) H5047
> > [H5047 = House print number 5047]

ARMS CONTROL AND DISARMAMENT
> Battleships, data regarding modernization of (68/2/25) H10927

ART
> Capitol Building, list of works of art in (60/1/08) J0884; (61/2/10) J0885; (82/2/52) J0076
> > [J0884 = print number 0884 of the set of documents entitled 'Journal']

Q. I would like to know what, if any, kind of government probes have been carried out concerning the American Nazi Party.

A. Though references may appear in commercially published books and magazines that you'll find through *Subject Guide to Books in Print* and appropriate periodical indexes such as *Magazine Index*, a more direct route is to check indexes to government publications. The *CIS/U.S. Congressional Committee Prints Index* and the *CIS/U.S. Congressional Hearings Index* both cover activities through 1969. (Prints are background studies of matters before Congressional committees.) An index called *CIS Index and Abstracts* continues those two sets from 1970 to the present.

There are a number of items, in the *Prints Index* and the post-1970 index, on the American Nazi Party as well as early Nazi groups in the United States. One item from the *Prints Index* may provide some background. The entry reads: Activities, Nazi, in U.S. Historical sketch on origin and extent of 73/1/33 H3823. (The numbers refer to the 73rd Congress, 1st session, 1933, House document no. 3823.)

The following item from the 1970 *CIS Index* may also be informative: Riots, civil and criminal disorders: sources of instructive literature (Sisco). The first part of the entry refers to the name of the document; the second part is descriptive; the last part is the name of the witness. The item refers to part of a 1970 Congressional hearing on civil riots. This particular testimony was given by Ronald Sisco, publisher of *Militants' Formulary* (a book on how to use and manufacture bombs), in a hearing to determine any relationship with the American Nazi Party.

Ask the librarian to help you find these items and other items in the *CIS* indexes, since most of them are on microfilm.

9. *CIS/U.S. Congressional Committee Hearings Index*, early 1800s-1969. Congressional Information Service, Inc. (Comes with a microform set of documents.)[5]

Congressional hearings represent the investigations conducted prior to final action on a piece of legislation. Any number of prominent, newsworthy people have appeared in Senate or House hearings—Ralph Nader, Frank Sinatra, James Hoffa, Cesar Chavez, Tom Hayden, Stokely Carmichael, Norman Cousins, Wernher Von Braun, and thousands of others commenting on anything from cocaine use in Hollywood to connections with underworld investments. Many of these hearings, in fact, are reported in the newspaper. (During the McCarthy era of the mid-1950s, for instance, the newspapers covered little else.)

Until 1865, there were few Congressional committees. Records of the early hearings, when they were printed at all, were inconsistently distributed. Like prints, they were considered internal working papers and were not distributed to libraries or constituents, except for the most im-

---

[5]This set is a counterpart to the *CIS/U.S. Congressional Committee Prints Index*. Current hearings and prints issued since 1970 are indexed by the *CIS/Index and Abstracts*, #7.

portant ones. After the 1930s, the publication and distribution of hearings became more consistent.

These entries appear in the name index volumes of the *Hearings Index* covering 1965-69. They represent the witnesses who appeared before committee hearings during that time.

CARROLL, VINCENT A.
> Pornographic materials distribution to unsolicited addresses (90) H2283-4
>> [(90) = 90th Congress, H = House print no 2283-4]

DEAN, SIDNEY W., JR.
> Pay TV programs prohibition (91) H2479-9

MOORE, TAYLOR
> Electronic surveillance devices used in industrial espionage and by IRS (89) S1785-1-A
>> [S = Senate print no. 1785-1-A]

From the subject index covering 1965-69:

EPISCOPAL CHURCH
> School prayer constitutional amendment (89) S1767-4

EQUITABLE LIFE ASSURANCE SOCIETY
> Alcoholism, prevention and treatment (91) S1980-4

ESCALANTE, UTAH
> Capitol Reef Natl Park, estab (91) H2535-5

ESPIONAGE
> Communist activities in Caribbean (89) S1697-3

10. *CIS Serial Set Index, 1789-1969.* Congressional Information Service, Inc. (Comes with a microform set of documents.)

Just what is the *Serial Set?* Of the four types of Congressional publications, hearings and prints are just two. Reports and documents (the word *documents* is used here as the title of a publication rather than in the descriptive sense) are the other two. They appear in an ongoing numbered set called the *Serial Set.*

House and Senate *reports* are essential to legislation. After a bill is introduced, it is referred to committee. If the committee chooses to act positively on the bill, they issue a written report as to why it should pass.

House and Senate *documents* are less defined and not necessarily essential to the legislative process. They can be almost anything Congress puts its imprint on that is not a print, a hearing, or a report. Included in this category are annual reports from various governmental agencies.

Beyond prints, hearings, reports, and documents, the definitions of Congressional publications start to blur. For our research purposes, it's enough to know they exist and are available.

Q. I'd like to get a copy of the trial of John Charles Frémont, explorer and statesman. To whom would I write in Washington for this?

A. Frémont, 1813-1890, instrumental in opening the Far West and in the conquest of California during the Mexican War, was charged by the Army in 1847 with mutiny and disobedience to superior officers. He resigned his post after his court martial.

Transcripts of the trial were printed by the government. According to the *U.S. Serial Set Index*, the transcript appears as Senate Executive Document 33, 30th Congress, 1st Session, 1848.

It was also reprinted in the supplement of Donald Jackson and Mary Spence's book, *The Expeditions of John Charles Frémont* (University of Illinois Press, 1973). The document and the book should be in large libraries.

The *Serial Set* is voluminous. It has generated more than a third of a million publications since it began in the late 18th century. The hard-copy volumes for just one Congress occupy approximately 20 feet of shelf space. With the *Serial Set* now available in microform, 14 Congresses in that format occupy the same amount of space as one Congress in hard copy. Seventy-six Congresses in microform occupy approximately 85 feet of space or slightly over one foot per Congress. The cost of the microfiche collection is just over $100,000.

The following is a selection from the 1857-1879 volume of the *Serial Set Index:*

CAVALRY
>   Clothing lost by enlisted men of Third Cavalry
>   >   H.exdoc. 28 (43-2) 1644
>   >   [H.exdoc. 28 (43-2) 1644 = House executive
>   >   document 28, 43rd Congress, 2d session, item no. 1644]

(You would use this document number to access the material in microform.)

>   Memorial from cavalry and artillery officers on pay of blacksmiths
>   >   H.exdoc. 183 (41-2) 1418

CENTENNIAL
>   Centennial Exhibition and Celebration of 1876. Message of President of United States
>   >   S.exdoc. 74 (45-3) 1831
>   >   [S.exdoc = Senate executive documents]

CESSION
>   Payments due and lands ceded to Ute Indians
>   >   S.misdoc 6 (45-2)1785
>   >   [misdoc = miscellaneous document]

CHARACTER
>   Information on character of Indians killed or captured by United States troops under command of General George A. Custer
>   >   S.exdoc. 36 (40-3) 1360

CLEARY, WILLIAM G.
>   Assassination of Abraham Lincoln; implication of Jefferson Davis and others in crime of treason; letters relating to policy of rebel government towards Negroes bearing arms, rebel prisons, etc.
>   >   H.rp. 104 (39-1)1272
>   >   [H.rp. = House of Representatives document]

To show how valuable the material in the *Serial Set* can be to researchers, consider how they were used by writer Dee Brown. In 1970, Brown saw his *Bury My Heart at Wounded Knee* rise to the top of the best-seller charts.

Wounded Knee, as well as the nearly 20 other books Brown has written about the American Indians, reveals (in its notes and footnotes) his heavy reliance on old government documents as original background sources. Admittedly, Brown has a slight edge over other researchers in his knowledge of documents. Besides being a writer, he is also a documents librarian. His books, however, are proof that government documents are rich resources for research, in this case, for books on popular subjects.

And Brown publicly identified them as such. In the early 1980s at a conference of documents librarians, he told the story of a reporter who asked him to name the books he would most like to have on a desert island. His reply? The *U.S. Serial Set*. He called it a gold mine of living history detailing the social condition of almost every group that ever populated this country. In this voluminous set, he noted that one could trace the development of child labor, women's suffrage, industry, and the history of social security, to name a few.

Before the *CIS Serial Set Index* and microfiche collection were available, the documents they contain were scattered. Many were unavailable, and access to the printed set was through seven separate indexes.

The Congressional Information Service has filmed and indexed all the *Serial Set* documents up to 1969. (Many large libraries still have some of the originals.) Additions to the *Serial Set* after 1969 are both in print and in microform in libraries.

11. *Federal Index*. Predicasts, Inc. 1977-date.

The *Federal Index* covers several dozen magazines and newspapers. Most are commercially published such as *The Washington Post, The New York Times, Barron's, Advertising Age,* and *Natural Rubber News*. Also indexed are some government documents including these:

(a) *The Congressional Record*. Includes the daily activities of Congress and the views and remarks of its members.

(b) *The Federal Register*. Assembles largely the rules and regulations of the individual executive departments and agencies of the government. (Published five days a week.)

(c) *The Code of Federal Regulations*. Compiles the daily regulations from the *Federal Register* into a code.

(d) *The Weekly Compilation of Presidential Documents*. Records the news releases, views, remarks, speeches, and final actions on legislation reported by the President.

Q. Can a naturalized U.S. citizen of Japanese origin return to Japan to live permanently and retain U.S. citizenship?

A. The latest *Code of Federal Regulations*, available in large public, academic, and law libraries, says (Title 8 - "Aliens and Nationality," Paragraph 343b.1): "A naturalized citizen who desires to obtain recognition as a citizen of the United States by a foreign state shall submit an application on form N-577. The applicant shall be required to appear in person before an assigned officer for interrogations under oath or affirmation upon the application."

It also says that if the application is denied, the applicant will be notified of the reason and of his right to appeal.

Contact the local office of Immigration and Naturalization under U.S. Government listings in the telephone book or the *United States Government Manual* for the forms.

---

12. *Declassified Documents Reference System*. Research Publications. 1975-date. (Comes with a microform set of documents.)

This set, accessed through its subject index, includes federal documents which have been declassified under the Privacy Act of 1974. The set is purchased not only by academic libraries but also by some large newspapers and such foreign nations as the Soviet Union and the People's Republic of China.

The documents include telegrams, correspondence, field reports, minutes of cabinet meetings, national security policy statements, and intelligence estimates. Some of the following items are included:

(a) *Psychological Aspects of United States Strategy,* a 236-page secret document prepared after the 1955 Geneva Conference.

(b) *Foreign Intelligence Activities of the United States Government*, a 137-page report written in 1960 for the director of the CIA.

(c) 3,500 pages of CIA and FBI documents on the assassination of John F. Kennedy, including the personal diary of Lee Harvey Oswald.

(d) 100 top secret, secret, and confidential CIA, State Department, National Security Council, and White House documents tracing Iran's domestic and foreign affairs from the 1940s through the 1960s.

Since these documents have only recently been in circulation, researchers exploring events especially since World War II should examine the set to fill in information gaps.

13. *Transdex*. Bell & Howell. 1974-date. (Index and microform collection.)

Because your information search could take you beyond American shores, access to foreign resources is important. Finding original materials from Communist and Third World countries isn't as difficult as finding them *in English*, but the U.S. Joint Publications Research Service (JPRS) offers at least partial assistance. *Transdex* is a commercially published, monthly printed index of the JPRS, a subagency of FBIS, the Foreign Broadcast Information Service described in Chapter 11. (Though the monthly index comes in a print version, it is cumulated annually and reproduced in microfiche.)

JPRS collects items from foreign newspapers, periodicals, news agency transmissions, broadcasts, and other foreign media sources, and contracts with over 2,000 translators to convert them into English. The source of the news item is included in *Transdex* entries, but the reference is not precise: Zambia Daily Mail 3/79, Hanoi Domestic Service 5/79, etc.

Depository libraries haven't always received all JPRS translations. They've been listed fairly consistently in the *MC* since about 1963, but it has only been since the late 1970s that the quantity of translations sent to depository libraries has grown to substantial numbers.

Transdex has come to the rescue in one important way. It provides better indexing to these translations than you'll find in the *MC*. As a bibliography rather than an index, the *MC* indexes JPRS translations by series title, not by the individual items in them. *Transdex* indexes the items within the series much as a periodical index lists articles in magazines.

(Because of the varied indexing procedures used earlier, and because *MC* only began mentioning translations in the 1960s, there are problems with searching translations before then. If you want to search for pre-1960 translations, ask a knowledgeable and patient documents librarian to help you through the tools used at that time.)

These samples from the key-word section of *Transdex* show both the specific and the general terms that are used:

ACCUSED
    Romania
        writer accused of denigrating personalities in works on
        interwar period
                80960   0054
        [80960 is the JPRS document number; 0054 is the page number (54)
        on which the translation starts.]
ACQUISITION
    India
        Pakistan missile acquisition threat to India.
                81100   0005
AEROSPACE
        USSR aerospace and electronic systems determination of coordinates
        of moving object by airborne detection and ranging system.
                81060   0005B
ANGOLA
    Angola
        need for restructuring of economy seen officially admitted.
                80964   0001
APARTHEID
    South Africa
        Black trade unions set pace in antiapartheid struggle.
                81120   0122

You may find it useful to use *Transdex* in conjunction with the foreign news digests mentioned in Chapter 11.

A SAMPLE SEARCH

Now's a good time to catch your breath and lift your aching jaw off your chest. What's next is a proposed research project in which you could use most of the finding tools I've just described.

Let's say you are interested in writing the definitive work on organized crime in the United States. According to a newspaper article you've read, the government started monitoring the activities of organized crime in this country in the 1950s. The resources for your in-depth investigation might be newspaper accounts, magazine articles, interviews, and books (or a good bibliography) on the subject. Let's not forget to add government documents.

We'll trace the finding tools already covered in this chapter to see how they might enter into this information search. (To find the items mentioned in the sources below, copy the Sudocs number they list. If your library doesn't have an item, ask the documents librarian if you can borrow it through interlibrary loan. If it's in any of the microform collections of documents, it shouldn't be difficult to get.)

1. *Monthly Catalog.* 1895-date.

Searching the MC[6] from 1972 to the present under ORGANIZED CRIME—UNITED STATES, I find several publications listed. One item from the 1981 volume is entitled *Waterfront Corruption: hearings . . . February 17, 18, 19, 25, 26, and 27, 1981,* 493 pages. It was issued by the Senate Committee on Governmental Affairs, Permanent Subcommittee on Investigations.

2. *Cumulative Subject Index . . .,* 1900-71.

Several documents are listed under CRIME AND CRIMINALS—ORGANIZED CRIME. One item appears under the subheading: 'in interstate commerce, investigation - hearings 50 (24952)'. It's called *Investigation of organized crime in interstate commerce, hearings, 81st Congress, 2d session,* issued by the Senate Armed Services Committee. (Two vols. totalling 944 pages, 1950.)

3. *Cumulative Title Index . . .,* 1789-1976.

This tool is not relevant to this topic, because we're searching by subject, not document title.

4. *Publications Reference File.*

One of the publications listed under the heading ORGANIZED CRIME is *Rackets Bureaus: Investigation and Prosecution of Organized Crime,* by G. Robert Blakey, issued by the Justice Department. (160 pages. 1978.)

5. *Index to United States Government Periodicals.*

Articles on organized crime are included under the general heading

---

[6]Since many of the tools listed here overlap, you'll notice duplicate mention of some items.

CRIME AND CRIMINALS and can only be recognized by pertinent words in the titles. One article from the 1981 volume is:

> Criminal Division focuses on organized crime vulnerability . Phillip B. Heymann, por *Nav Civ Eng* 19 2-3 N80-077.
>
> [por = portraits; *Nav Civ Eng* = *Navy Civil Engineer;* 19 2-3 N80 = volume 19, pages 2-3, November 1980; 077 = the magazine's microform order number from Microfilming Corp. of America]

6. *Public Affairs Information Service Bulletin. (PAIS)*

Under the heading ORGANIZED CRIME are listed several hearings such as *Organized Crime and Use of Violence; hearings,* issued by the Senate Committee on Governmental Affairs, Permanent Subcommittee on Investigations. (Two vols. totaling 628 pages. 1980.)

7. *CIS/Index and Abstracts.* 1970-date.

The 1977 index lists 12 subtopics under ORGANIZED CRIME and ORGANIZED CRIME CONTROL ACT. One is "Foreign bank accounts use." CISs accession number is H 401-4.4, which refers to a publication called *Hearings on the administration of the Bank Secrecy and Reporting Act, June 28, 29, and July 1, 1976.* (338 pages.) Citation no. H401-4.4 refers to the testimony of John Keeney, Dept. Asst. Attorney General, Criminal Div., Justice Dept. which runs on pages 71-129 of the hearings.

8. *CIS/U.S. Congressional Committee Prints Index to 1969.*

Several items are listed under ORGANIZED CRIME. Two subheadings leading to publications are 'Kansas City area, strikes and racketeering in' (leading to a 1953 House document) and 'Labor racketeering activities of Jack McCarthy and National Consultants Associated, Ltd.' (leading to a 1967 Senate document).

9. *CIS/U.S. Congressional Committee Hearings Index to 1969.*

Some of the Senate hearings in the 1945-1952 volume under ORGANIZED CRIME are "Fla organized crime, investigation" and "Nev-Calif organized crime, investigation."

10. *CIS/Serial Set (to 1969).*

There is no heading for organized crime. Under the general term CRIME, however, there are dozens of items. Those on organized crime are not obvious unless that term is in the title. One is "Gambling and organized crime" for a 1962 Senate report.

11. *Federal Index.*

Since this index also covers commercial publications, many items are listed. The term used is CRIME, ORGANIZED. One item in the February 5, 1980 issue of the *Federal Register* is 'DOJ-LEAA: announces competitive long-term research program to increase understanding of organized crime problem in U.S.; applications by 4/4.' [DOJ-LEAA = Department of Justice-Law Enforcement Assistance Administration; 4/4 = April 4.

12. *Declassified Documents Reference System.*
This tool does not cover organized crime according to its subject index.

13. *Transdex.*
This tool is not relevant, because it reports on foreign, not American, events.

As this sample search shows, you can extract a great deal of information on certain topics by using the major finding tools described in this chapter. Government publications can and should be used in conjunction with commercially published material in many research projects.

How to Get the Documents You Need

The process of using documents for research involves two major steps: identifying them and getting them. The indexes described in the preceding pages will help you identify them. Once you have done this, ask the librarian to help you get the items. She'll tell you if they're already in the library (in the print version or in microform), or if you should borrow them through interlibrary loan.

As with many research tools, these indexes go beyond the scope, purpose, and budget of small libraries. Therefore, many such libraries won't have them, let alone the sets of documents they index. On the other hand, few large libraries, particularly academic libraries, will want to be without them.

As finding tools, indexes are not available for loan. *SGBIP* may come to the rescue, however, by naming commercially published subject bibliographies listing dictionaries, atlases, handbooks, pamphlets, books, bibliographies, indexes, etc., by subject which are published by the government. These bibliographies and some of the documents they name may be available through interlibrary loan. To find them, check *SGBIP* under UNITED STATES—GOVERNMENT PUBLICATIONS—BIBLIOGRAPHY. Some of the items you'll find include:

1. *A Bibliography of United States Government Bibliographies, 1968-73*, by Roberta Scull. Pierian Press. 1975. 1974-76; 1979.
Arranged by broad category, this book refers only to bibliographies. A full range of topics is covered. Use the subject index to locate specific bibliographies within the book.

2. *Government Reference Books*, 1968/69-date.
Published every two years by Libraries Unlimited. Covers pamphlets, books, bibliographies, directories, and other government publications in all subjects. It's arranged by broad category with separate subject and title indexes.

3.*Guide to U.S. Government Directories, 1970-1980,* by Donna Rae Larson. Oryx Press. 1981.

Lists only directories published by the government in topics such as divorce records listings, educational opportunities, and endangered species. Arranged by Sudocs call number. Use the subject index to find specific directories within the book.

4. *New Guide to Popular Government Publications for Libraries and Home Reference,* by Walter Newsome. Libraries Unlimited. 1978.

Covers a wide range of government publications, books, and pamphlets in consumer and business subjects: Eskimo arts and crafts, export opportunities, proper and improper use of drugs, the benefits of space exploration to mankind, mulch tilling, first aid, American Indians, civil rights, etc.

5. *A Popular Guide to Government Publications,* by W. Philip Leidy. 1st-4th editions, Columbia University Press. 1953-76.

Covers the same areas as #4.

6. *A Subject Guide to Government Reference Books,* by Sally Wynkoop. Libraries Unlimited. 1972.

Covers the same areas as #2.

Two other finding tools may help you identify government publications if your library does not have the indexes described earlier in this chapter. The first is *U.S Government Books: Recent Releases,* a quarterly publication available by subscription. Until December 1981, a free monthly bibliography called *Selected U.S. Government Publications* was available for the asking. It was a booklet of approximately 20 pages listing over 100 popular government publications for sale each month. This pamphlet became a victim of budget cuts, and has since been replaced by the quarterly. Each entry in the publication is accompanied with the Sudocs call number, so you can easily borrow the items in the library or through interlibrary loan, or purchase them by mail.

Another government publications list is not as attractive, but it's useful nevertheless. You can get it free, or use it and the back issues at a large library. It's called simply, *Subject Bibliography.* This index to more than 250 subject bibliographies (average length is 10 pages) of government publications covers a variety of topics: America in space; aging, aircraft, airports and airways, and the American Revolution. The Sudocs call numbers are always mentioned, so you can borrow items from the library.

MICROFORM SUBJECT SETS

In addition to the printed finding tools and accompanying sets of documents on microform, there are other collections of government-generated material assembled by subject. These collections make it easier to carry on systematic research, because you don't have to seek out the individual publications that comprise them. Here's a sampling of what's available:

1. *Hearings and Reports of the House Committee on un-American Activities, 1945-54.* Brookhaven Press.

Researchers can trace HUAC's investigations on routine cases as well as the more famous ones such as the Alger Hiss case and 1950s inquisition into Communist influence in the motion picture industry, with testimonies given by well-known celebrities and film executives of the era.

2. *Nixon Administration: A Comprehensive Microfiche Library with Analytic Indexes.* Johnson Associates, Inc., and National Educational Consultants, Inc.

This set consists of 100,000 pages of printed hearings, staff reports, judicial decisions, transcripts, press releases, and other documents covering Watergate and the events leading up to it.

3. *Prisoner of War Operations in the United States During World War II.* Library of Congress.

This document collection is valuable for research on Japanese American internees during World War II. The collection also covers the administration of prisoner of war matters in the United States during the war. The documents originally came from the Center of Military History in the Department of the Army.

4. *United States Department of the Air Force. Project Blue Book.* National Archives and Records Service.

The Air Force began its investigations of UFO reports in 1947 with disc-shaped objects sighted by Kenneth Arnold. The project was closed in 1969 with negative reactions to a controversial government-sponsored report by Edward Condon (*Final Report of the Scientific Study of Unidentified Flying Objects.* Reprinted by Dutton, 1969). All the material collected on reported sightings is now in the National Archives and in this microform set.

Government documents are additionally valuable to researchers in one unique way: They often fill in a library's subject weaknesses. I mentioned earlier that a university with no business or education major will likewise have a library collection weak in those fields. By checking the government documents section of that academic library, however, you'll find hundreds of useful materials (published by the Departments of Commerce and Education) you might not have expected.

――――――――― *CHAPTER SUMMARY* ―――――――――

I. The government publishes a variety of documents, brochures, pamphlets, books, dictionaries, bibliographies, directories, catalogs, indexes, atlases, magazines, posters, etc., as well as official hearings, technical reports, statistics, and items of official business. Indeed, the U.S. government is the largest publisher in the country. (page 201)

II. Government documents do not originate from one agency.
   A. The majority are commissioned and written by hundreds of subagencies, bureaus, and offices of the 13 major executive departments (Labor, Education, Transportation, etc.) in their area of responsibility. (page 207)
   B. Documents are also issued by several dozen independent and regulatory agencies such as the Atomic Energy Commission and the Securities and Exchange Commission; the federal courts, and Congress itself. (page 211)

III. There are more than 1,300 depository libraries in the U.S. that receive at no cost a large selection of government publications of educational value and public interest. (page 212)
   A. Government documents are assigned a call number called a Superintendent of Documents (Sudocs) number, based on the agency issuing them. This is also how they are arranged (by issuing agency) on library shelves. (page 213)
   B. Documents are usually kept in their own section of the library with a separate catalog.

IV. Government documents are accessed through various indexes; you can't shelf-browse for the material you need.
   A. Though some documents are included in commercially published indexes, the majority are found in specific indexes such as *Monthly Catalog* and *CIS/Index and Abstracts to Publications of the U.S. Congress*. A list of documents-finding indexes is included. (page 215)
   B. If your library doesn't own these finding tools, *SGBIP* may help you identify commercially published bibliographies that cover government documents. (page 232)
   C. Subject bibliographies issued by the government are also helpful in identifying government-published resources. (page 233)
   D. Some documents have been coordinated and microfilmed in subject collections by commercial publishers and government agencies. These collections save you time by eliminating the need to search individual publications for related subject materials. (page 233)

13

The Great Research Machine:
THE COMPUTER

A computer does not substitute for judgment
any more than a pencil substitutes for literacy.
—Robert McNamara,
The Essence of Security, 1968

The computer is fast gaining a reputation for regurgitating information on demand. And in research, on-line data bases seem to be the miracle of the moment. (In earlier chapters, I've already mentioned some ways to use the computer in research, especially for magazine research.) Can computers *really* do all your research effortlessly and automatically? If they can, you'll undoubtedly want to know how to tap these rich resources as quickly as possible.

From articles you've read on the subject, you may have the impression that a computer can do just about everything, from cook your meals to balance your checkbook. If it can't do that by now, time will certainly tell what it can do. Indeed, there's much to know about this multifaceted machine.

An essay by IBM's chief scientist, Lewis Branscomb[1], summarizes the present situation. "In the words of that great philosopher, Pogo," he wrote, " 'There is no heavier burden than a great potential.' "

THE IMPACT OF THE COMPUTER

Before we can fully appreciate how the computer might help us gather information (the second half of this chapter deals with computer research in the library), we must first understand the potential this machine has to affect our daily lives.

Despite the burden of its potential, few people believe the computer is just another appliance. Frank Herbert, author of the *Dunes* science fiction series, said, in a May 14, 1982 interview in *The San Diego Tribune*, that he believes the computer will have a greater impact on our lives than fire or

[1]"Video Disc Technology and the Book," in *Books, Libraries and Electronics,* edited by Efrem Siegel et al. Knowledge Industries Publications. 1982.

the wheel. British journalist/politician Anthony Wedgwood Benn feels that of the three great scientific developments of the last four decades, the invention of the computer, though less spectacular than the development of nuclear energy and space travel, outranks them both in importance.

The computer already touches our lives daily: at the library, the grocery store, the bank. And it will continue to do so. According to a 1982 study of computerized information systems, the National Science Foundation has predicted the following:

■ Information retrieval is expected to become the top use of computer data base services by business; and transaction services (banking, shopping, movie schedules, etc.) are expected to be the top use by the home market.

■ An electronic Yellow Pages (a one-way, noninteractive service) may be in use by 39 percent of all homes by the end of the century. The two-way, interactive, computerized information and transaction services requiring the use of a home computer may be in use by 38 percent of all homes by the end of the century.

■ Major social changes will occur. Homes will become the working area for information personnel (stock brokers, computer programmers, insurance adjusters, etc.) who will be the majority of the work force.

■ On-demand production systems will develop in home shopping. Manufacturers and publishers will make only what customers order.

These predictions may seem farfetched to us now, but the impact of computers will undeniably be substantial, widespread, and permanent.

There are currently two kinds of information services emerging. They are (1) videotex (banking, catalog shopping, video newspapers, educational games, encyclopedias, etc.) piped into homes through specially adapted TV sets for a monthly subscription fee; and (2) on-line data base searching of reference material (such as magazine indexes) through a computer/telephone/data base connection for a per-search fee presently used via a library or a commercial search service.

VIDEOTEX

As I mentioned in earlier chapters, experiments with videotex via TV sets have been conducted for several years in selected homes in various cities throughout the country. These experiments have been a technology in search of a market. Suppliers wanted to know if people would pay for TV extras, and if so, what kind. Since the potential of the home market is huge, many companies want to develop it. One question yet to be resolved is whether it will be developed through television cables or telephone lines.

Although this has not been settled, the videotex experiments have shown that the services home customers are most willing to pay for are banking and financial services. (In one Columbus, Ohio, experiment, the encyclopedia was the most popular videotex service.) For the most part, however, financial services are forming the basis of the first broad-scale home information systems. Television ads are already appearing in different parts of the country to sell these videotex services.

What exactly is videotex and how does it work? If you take a telephone, a television set, and a small microcomputer that allows you to call a larger remote computer storing information, you have a videotex system. Stand-alone videotex terminals are also available at a greater cost. (At the turn of the 21st century, the hardware we use now will resemble model-T's.)

Videotex, first developed in England in the early 1970s, is a two-way interactive system that allows you to talk back to your TV set. The system displays both graphical and textual information—pages or frames of information (airline schedules, ads for merchandise, encyclopedia entries, etc.) on the screen. (This is in contrast to teletext which is a one-way system offering Yellow Pages- or classified advertising-type information, but not allowing you to respond as you might need to in ordering tickets or merchandise or making a banking transaction.)[2]

With videotex, you select the information you want by using a numeric keyboard, almost like a channel selector; or you can use a typewriter keyboard. A table of contents or a "menu" appears on the television screen with pages or screen numbers which you then select to read.

Some simple videotex systems that present pages (frames) of information for scanning use an inverted pyramid structure to help you select what you're looking for. You get a broad choice of terms such as "A. Business" and "B. Theater Schedules." If you select "Business," you will be presented with another menu of terms from which to choose: "A. Stock Quotes" or "B. News Briefs." Each time you make a choice, you are presented with another narrower range of selections. More elaborate videotex systems such as *The Source* and *CompuServe* require a home computer and allow you to "do" much more. For example, you can use key words to find information buried within the text of *The New York Times*. If you need a recipe that cooks a roast with a mixture of water and instant coffee, for example, you would search for it by using relevant key words.

Though the convenience and speed of videotex make it an attractive tool, there is still the issue of privacy which must be addressed (see page 241). Banking and shopping by computer mean that your responses and transactions are made electronically—and that means they could be monitored by anyone else using the system. Protecting users' privacy will undoubtedly be an important feature in the further development of videotex.

Cost is another important issue which customers themselves are help-

---

[2]Ceefax and Oracle are names for the British teletext system. Videotex is called Viewdata in Europe and Prestel in England. Other countries use still other names.

ing to influence. It's likely that videotex will be a less-expensive service—perhaps between $15 and $40 a month—than on-line searching services. As videotex gains more subscribers, prices may drop or at least stabilize, and even more information and services will be offered.

As you can see, videotex systems are varied. Different data bases offer different amounts of information. Some services offer local information (ads by local merchants), and others, such as *The Source*, allow you to search for information in certain national newspapers and magazines. (These are actually scaled-down versions of the more sophisticated, less user-friendly, on-line data bases used in business and libraries.) Marketers believe that videotex—information services in the home—will first become popular with people who already own personal computers, since they're familiar with the hardware the systems require. How much information will be provided, however, depends on consumer demand.

ON-LINE SEARCHING

Despite the novelties of videotex capabilities, the most attractive use for computers, as far as researchers are concerned, is on-line data base searching. Computerized data bases yielding both specific information and references to articles are actually an outgrowth of computer use in publishing. Once information from a reference book, encyclopedia, magazine article, or newspaper is in a computer for editing and typesetting purposes, the publisher has inherited a data base from which information can be retrieved. Now that capability is available for consumers.

There are two specific kinds of data bases available to researchers: (1) full text (files containing numerical data such as financial and demographic statistics; newspaper articles; other kinds of information such as résumés listed with on-line career placement registries; and material from certain reference books such as *Who's Who in America*, *Books in Print*, and *Ulrich's International Periodicals Directory*); and (2) bibliographic (citations—not the full text—of book titles, book reviews, government reports, government publications, dissertations, magazine and newspaper articles, patents, conference papers, and Congressional publications).

Though researchers, who have used on-line searching, recognize its potential, there are roadblocks to the rapid development of computer information banks. (If you're not yet clear about what a data base and a data bank are, here's an analogy to something familiar. A data base, a file of information, is like a chapter in a book. A data bank is the book itself, consisting of many chapters, or data bases.)

One problem is that on-line data bases do not yet have a large enough market to make them profitable for their suppliers in ways they envision. Not only are too few of us familiar with computers and their growing capabilities, but those of us who *do* know something about them don't often use these more sophisticated information systems in our homes. In most cases, a librarian or a trained searcher at a commercial search service does the actual information search. These people have the hardware and the know-how to conduct a computer search. As a result, we're neither familiar with nor accustomed to a hands-on use of these machines. Not enough of us have adequate access to computer searching to enable us to embrace the idea.

The irony is that even though advances now being made are outstanding, suppliers will not likely invest huge sums of money in more elaborate information systems at reduced prices (where more people could afford them) until they see evidence of a large enough demand. This will come in time, but it doesn't exist on a large scale just yet. (For more information on on-line searching, see the computerized literature searching section of this chapter.)

THE PRIVACY ISSUE

One of the computer's outstanding features is its ability to help us streamline paperwork. Whether you use a home computer to catalog your stamp collection, or you use the more sophisticated service on *The Source* in which you search the text of *The New York Times* for a recent article, or you tap the less user-friendly on-line services through a commercial searcher to find articles on the architecture of 19th-century British music halls, the Great Machine saves us precious time. What could possibly be wrong, then, with converting paper files and records to the efficiency of the computer?

The answer to that question is closely tied to some potential problems blocking the way of widespread acceptance for both videotex and on-line searching. The issue is privacy. Consider the situation of doing your banking through a videotex system. If personal information such as bank account records go on-line, they will no longer remain in the privacy of your bank. Other confidential information in data bases—records of credit, criminal activity, and income tax, for example—is also subject to potential tapping by others hooked into the system.

With a variety of such personal information in computer files, abuse is possible. It may ultimately be very easy for people with access to use the confidential information in these files for purposes other than that for which it was originally intended. It's possible, for example, that firms could create personality profiles on individuals (without their knowledge) from random bits of information collected from various files. Such "profiles" could then be sold in the same way mailing lists are sold. What happens when this information, skewed or not, is used (also without a person's knowledge) when he applies for a job, or tries to enter college, establish credit, or even get a liquor license for his new restaurant?

Q. I'd like to find an article that appeared in *The San Diego Union* a few months ago referring to drug abuse and alcoholism in the Marine Corps. The article reported that the Corps used a secret code on a serviceman's fitness report to indicate this problem. Is there a quicker way to find the article than looking through each newspaper at the library?

A. Many newspaper indexes, including that of the *Union*, cover only regional news. Furthermore, the newspaper's "clippings" library is closed to the public. But there are other ways to confirm the information in this story.

While there is a government report called *Drug Abuse in the Military* (it's in libraries with government documents sections), it hardly seems the place such an admission would appear. Not surprisingly, it wasn't there. But since the practice described in the article violates personal privacy, I checked books on that subject and found it mentioned in Robert Ellis Smith's book *Privacy: How to Protect What's Left of It*, published in 1979.

Smith says the armed services used to put a numerical code on each discharge certification that indicated the reason for discharge: homosexual tendencies, alcoholism, insubordination, slovenly habits, physical disability, etc. He adds that the military now admits that this information can cause discrimination against the individual, since many employers ask to see the discharge report, DD Form 214. It appears, according to Smith, that the practice still exists, and substitute codes may be used. However, these do not appear on the copy given to the veteran.

A serviceman is entitled to a description of the code upon discharge and to have these Separation Program Numbers (SPN) deleted. Addresses for each branch of the service are given in Smith's book and are also in the *United States Government Manual* in the library.

By now, you've no doubt read about computer hackers who have broken into confidential government data bases through their home computers. The same computer systems that enable us to store references to research materials also store confidential personal information which could be misused. Before we open the floodgates, we must be sure that safeguards are firmly established to protect our personal privacy.

The government recognizes this threat and also the speed with which computer technology has developed without guidelines. In his article on the future of telecommunications ("Information Overload") in the January, 1981 issue of *Special Libraries*, former California Congressman Lionel Van Deerlin remarked that technology has outstripped the ability of federal policy to guide and control its uses and abuses. Federal regulations, he said, must be formulated.

THE BENEFITS OF COMPUTERS IN RESEARCH

Despite the problems which have yet to be resolved in the computer's future, no one can deny its potential as an information resource. Whether or not it lives up to its full capabilities remains to be seen.

Television is a perfect example of a medium that never reached its full potential. Though TV can be used to educate masses of people, it instead has become an advertising medium. Its programming offers entertainment which, according to advertising studies, appeals to people (under 25) who are most influenced by advertising. Many technical experts predict a similar fate for computers, because unless a computer research service is profitable, it won't be developed.

In his 1971 book, *The Information Machines,* Ben Bagdikian writes, "In guessing the direction of technology, it is wise to ask who is in the best position to profit most." The computer's future will be determined by profits—and profits depend on public demand. Though little-used research functions may never develop because of poor profit potential, it's hard to predict how far research by computer will go, because the market is still being formed.

Nevertheless, the computer already performs many useful research functions. As an information seeker, how can you use The Great Research Machine?

Specialists who once craved easy access to worldwide information now can't keep up with the output of literature even in very narrow fields. Computers can easily identify research material we never knew existed. This benefits researchers, as well as business people and consumers, by conveniently providing them with information they ordinarily wouldn't have or couldn't easily get. Will an analyst's report on the potential development of a foreign market be more complete if he follows up on the 20 magazine and newspaper citations the computer generated than if he sorts through the randomly gathered information he already had? You bet it will.

Other benefits and uses for computers will become clear as you use the machines more often. For example, computers don't answer "how-to" questions ("How can I go to Europe for as little as possible?"); but if you ask one to retrieve articles using the key words EUROPE and COSTS in its abstracts, you'll get references to articles that *do* answer the question.

Once you discover how to get to Europe at the lowest cost, you must plan your trip. In which cities are accommodations chronically in short supply; and where are they the cheapest? Which cities have the worst traffic problems? What is the typical weather for various seasons? What is the current monetary exchange rate? This information is available in books and magazines now, but it's much easier to extract from a data base—especially if it's accessible through a home computer.

Another genuine benefit of computerized services is the publicity they give to printed resources. Through computers, we are learning about the vast amounts of published material that exist. As a result, we'll use both computers *and* print resources more. And we're learning enough about the printed sources to which computers expose us to determine when to use a print resource and when to use an on-line data base for maximum efficiency and completeness.

REALITIES OF ON-LINE SEARCHING

To get information from a data base, you need a computer (or a search service that has a computer) with an attachment called a modem (modulator/demodulator). A modem is a rubber cup (connected to the computer terminal) into which a telephone receiver is inserted. After you call the data base supplier to which you subscribe and request a search through a specified data base, the search can begin. This is done by typing prescribed commands into the computer via the keyboard. (See page 173 for a specific description of a magazine index search on-line.) Right now, *Knowledge Index* offers only about two indexes to search (*Magazine Index* is one). The language required to search it is simply key words alone and in combination.

Though on-line searching is the information service of greatest use to researchers, it is presently limited by the fact that relatively few people have computer terminals in their homes. Personal computers costing in the range of a thousand dollars and more aren't needed nor are they affordable by most people for home use. (Since data base costs are computed by the minute, the cheaper computers, which take longer to transmit, wind up costing more in connect time than the faster, more expensive computers.)

At least for the present, the majority of on-line research services allowing you to research the scholarly as well as the popular periodical indexes are used through a library or commercial service and are conducted by a trained searcher.

The majority of these on-line data bases are not yet "user friendly," that is, not just anyone can use them immediately. The command language demands that the searcher have some training and experience. Different data bases use different search terms which must be determined through a data base thesaurus. More subject terms can be searched through an on-line data base than through the traditional card catalog, but the researcher must still consult a thesaurus for that data base before starting to search on-line. As explained in Chapter 10, the more you preplan a search, the less the search will cost, since deciding your next move while the computer is running is very expensive. (When computer response time is speeded up, this, too, may change.)

Unless you use computer services often, however, you can't learn the full extent of their information capabilities. This is something a trained searcher learns by constantly performing computer searches. The high cost of data base searching makes it difficult for a novice to practice and subsequently learn both tips and pitfalls of the process. (If you learn how to search now using a popular service such as *Knowledge Index*—which costs about $5 for a four-minute information search—you'll be prepared to handle more sophisticated systems later.)

Of all the reasons why researchers don't widely use on-line data base searching, the biggest is cost. Since each index on computer is published by a different publisher, it must be paid for separately and therefore searched separately. The indexes are not yet integrated into a single alphabetical list—although the technical capability to do so is there. That's why a 10-minute search of magazine indexes yielding a list of 15 citations could cost you $30 or more.

As demand and interest soar, competition among vendors will increase, and costs will drop. The public interest in computer searching *is* growing; ever-increasing numbers of searches are performed annually at universities, and more and more commercial search firms are emerging nationwide. If you already have a personal computer, it's likely you are benefiting from its capabilities in your own research, and you're probably telling other researchers about it.

COMPUTERS IN THE LIBRARY

For those of us who don't acquire home computers, libraries will, in fulfilling their role of providing access to information, increasingly offer data base services as well as access to conventional print resources. Libraries already use computers for many functions and that, too, will continue.

The first encounter with the computer for many libraries occurred when they cataloged their books jointly with other libraries nationwide through OCLC (see page 67). In the early years of OCLC, which began in the mid-1970s, libraries used the system to order customized catalog cards which they then filed into their own catalog. When the data base of library holdings grew substantially larger, libraries gradually began transferring to the on-line catalog. They will eventually phase out their card catalogs.

Major hurdles in the computerization of catalogs remain, however. More libraries must acquire the funds to convert to the new computerized systems, to continue developing standardization that links incompatible systems, and to resolve the new copyright issues which broad access to computer-stored data has introduced.

Despite the problems to be overcome, computerized library catalogs, circulation systems, and acquisitions functions are saving libraries from a paper crunch. Libraries are records-intensive organizations. Using computers to show what they own is enabling them to lift their systems out of the Dark Ages and bring their wealth to the public's attention. On-line library catalogs also allow remote access—terminals in dormitories or other library branches, and in the future, other locations such as your home. On the national level, catalog hookups between libraries allow enormous access to and mutual sharing of research material.

The most wonderful feature of a computerized catalog for researchers is that on-line catalog searches for books can be conducted successfully with surprisingly sketchy information. A computer search for a one-word title, say "space," would extract every book from the on-line catalog with "space" in its title. That could number hundreds of books from *Space Saving Closets* to *UFOs in Space*. But the computer also allows you to narrow the range of possibilities by providing an additional key word, an author, a publisher, a precise or approximate date of publication or even a decade. With each added piece of data, the range of choices to find that one book you need diminishes. Eventually, a few of the original hundreds of titles the computer has located remain on the screen for your selection.

COMPUTERIZED REFERENCE SERVICE—THE PLUSES

Besides offering you a computerized catalog to speed up your search for a title and tell you which library owns it, computers also make other valuable library services possible. One of these is computerized reference service, actually on-line searching of magazine, newspaper, and encyclopedia data bases. This service will be increasingly available in libraries.

In addition to these resources, the texts of many other reference books are also available on-line, and the number is growing. Text manipulation is perhaps one of the most exciting of the computer's capabilities. In searching a reference book on-line, all manner of information groupings are possible that didn't exist in the print version even though the information was essentially there.

In *Who's Who in America* on-line, for example, a researcher can request a list of all Harvard graduates named in that publication, or Harvard alumni who graduated between 1960 and 1965, or Harvard alumni who graduated between 1960 and 1965 and who are physicians (or just pediatricians), or all Harvard grads who live in St. Louis, or all women Harvard grads, or all women Harvard grads in a particular decade, ad infinitum.

A standard reference book like *Reference Guide to Fantastic Films, Science Fiction, Fantasy and Horror* on-line could give you the names of all the horror films produced in Mexico, or all horror films produced in Mexico by a certain producer, or all horror films starring Vincent Price—even all science fiction films based on books versus those based on original screen plays. Through full-text newspapers and reference books already on-line, as well as access to encyclopedias on-line, a great deal of "ready reference" information can be extracted, much of it that wasn't so easy to gather before.

SOME DRAWBACKS

Before we become too enamored with the wonders of computerized reference services, let's look at the limitations of full-scale computerized research.

First, the magical information box containing *all* the answers to everyone's questions is very much a myth. Computers are still an expensive way to get answers. To operate the *ultimate* computerized reference service means the full text-computer conversion of hundreds of thousands of publications. Not only is that enormously expensive, but accomplishing it would take an unbelievable amount of time. (Libraries with full-time staffs working full work weeks are taking years just to transfer their card catalogs into computers.)

To help you understand the unimaginable amount of effort it takes to convert books to an on-line format, consider this. Since beginning my *Reference Librarian* column in 1979, I've accumulated a sizeable amount of copy—probably enough to fill several books the size of this one. In writing the column, I must often refer to earlier questions when similar ones are asked. How easy it would be to find and read the previously asked questions and my answers to them if I had the full text of all those columns entered into my home computer. Transferring them into the computer, however, is something I just don't have the time to do. I'd consider making the effort if the number of times I search for previously asked questions justified the amount of time a paper-to-computer conversion would take—not to mention the expense of buying dozens of computer disks on which to store the copy. But the justification isn't there. So for now, at least, key words and a date reference to my paper files must do. (This example is similar to the present system [and justification of it] for having only citations to magazines on-line rather than the full text storage of all the articles cited.)

If the thought of entering all my column questions seems time-consuming, imagine converting the full texts of the 14-odd million books in the Library of Congress to computer with present-day technology. Even print scanners (devices for sensing recorded data and transferring it to another medium), if they could do the job gobbling up one page of text per second, would take 10 people five-and-a-half years working 40-hour weeks (or one person working 55 years) to complete the job.[3]

Many books are currently on-line, because they were written since computers have been used for editing and typesetting. If computer storage costs drop, perhaps these new books will form the basis of some future cache of full-text material. But to conceive of going back and adding all the old ones that aren't on-line? Suppliers won't consider it because of

---

[3] If the Library of Congress's 14 million books averaged 200 pages each, that would equal 2.8 billion pages to transfer, not to mention trucking them to and fro, reshelving them, then creating indexes and other access programs as needed.

the high cost of computer storage, insufficient demand, and therefore, lack of potential profit. Unless those things change, entering the full text of past published materials is out of the question. It may turn out that microform will remain the most viable format for old books, magazines, and especially newspapers, since most of them are already in microform. But even this remains to be seen. The driving force will be profit.

No one yet knows to what extent libraries will cancel subscriptions to printed indexes and reference books as they go on-line. Industry experts say that, for now, as print resources shift to computer, it's more likely that on-line costs will remain at their present high levels to allow publishers to recoup the lost revenue caused by the cancellation of subscriptions for their print products.

Perhaps the most sensitive issue shaping the future of computerized reference service in libraries has to do with the cost. Computer service is expensive, and many librarians believe that it has the potential to destroy fundamental library service by limiting access to information to those libraries—and library users—who can pay for it. The pressure to provide on-line services has resulted in a Fee vs. Free debate, something that may take some time to resolve. Librarians support free access to information. At the same time, they are struggling to find the money to pay for on-line services they are forced to consider.

COMPUTERIZED LITERATURE SEARCHING IN LIBRARIES

Libraries that now offer computer searching do so on a limited and selective basis. They may conduct searches from full-text data bases like *The New York Times Information Bank* or the data bases listing references to magazine articles, newspapers, etc. Some large public libraries such as the Cleveland Public Library advertise Facts for a Fee, their on-line data base service to the public, and charge for it (notwithstanding the emotional issue attached to fee-based library services) to offset some of the costs.

Many libraries now use computers to answer, usually at no charge, questions that are referred to them through the library system's research center (see page 75). Computer access may be available at some university libraries only to faculty and graduate students, because it is subsidized by the institution to encourage its use in scholarship. Commercial services are most used, at present, by companies which can offset the costs as business expenses.

WHEN TO SEARCH BY COMPUTER

When you find a library or commercial broker that offers a search service, you should know the special conditions under which a computer search will benefit you most (versus those times when a manual search may work just as well).

A computer search generating a list of magazine references should be considered in the following instances:

1. When the material you need was written approximately within the last 15-20 years; or when it has been published so recently (within the past two or three weeks) that the printed indexes aren't even out yet.

Q. As a college student in the Midwest about 15 years ago, I wrote a term paper comparing heredity and environment as determinants in developing behavior and mores in adults. One reference work I used detailed a well-known case history of a family named the Jukes. This family was interesting in that the overwhelming majority of them were criminals. I understand there was another family of similar persuasion known as the Kallikaks.

A friend of mine is now planning to update the research in this area and has not been able to find mention of these earlier books. (He has access to the Library of Congress, if you can develop any leads.)

A. I found several books through a library computer called OCLC. Richard Dugdale wrote a book called *The Jukes: A Study in Crime, Pauperism, Disease and Heredity* (1877). It was reprinted in 1975. A follow-up book published by the Carnegie Institution in 1916 is called *The Jukes in 1915*, by Arthur Estabrook. Henry Goddard wrote *The Kallikak Family: A Study in the Heredity of Feeble Mindedness* in 1919; it was reprinted in 1973. These books should be available through your public library's interlibrary loan service. (Interlibrary loan draws from the Library of Congress as well as other libraries in the country.)

To thoroughly update the topic, check psychology and related-subject indexes in a university library for articles in professional magazines. A faster, though more expensive, procedure yielding up-to-the-minute articles is to use a computerized literature search service offered commercially or in many academic libraries. A typical search might cost over $25.

---

2. When a library (or business) does not subscribe to the indexes you need to search.

3. When the search must link two or more concepts. For example, you might be researching the effects of an adolescent's home environment on the development of racial prejudice. The three topics you would have to check through a printed index—adolescents, home environment, and racial prejudice—are too broad, and finding the specific articles linking all three concepts by hand would be time-consuming.

4. When the search topic is relatively new, and the printed indexes have not yet adopted an appropriate term for it. This is something that can go on for more than a year without a resolution. Skyjacking, like many things, was a fact before it had a name. Until *skyjacking* was coined, you had to search for articles on it under general headings such as AIRLINES.

5. When the topic may be stated in so many synonymous ways that manual searching would take too long. For example, if you want to search for information on sports for the handicapped, instead of looking for information under the terms ATHLETICS or SPORTS or HANDICAPPED, you may have to search SWIMMING, BASKETBALL, PING-PONG, and other individual sports as well as QUADRAPLEGIC, AMPUTEES, MENTALLY RETARDED, etc.

Deciding whether you need a computerized search of the most up-to-date information on a topic will depend on your research task. In science, technology, and finance, it may be essential to have the latest facts and figures. In history, philosophy, literature, theology, folklore, and many other fields, material published decades and even centuries ago is often more important. It is here that the physical library plays its role with all its vast stores of research material. Technology offers no present alternative to these rich resources, but it does give us easier means of identifying them.

HOW MANY DATA BASES?

If you decide to use a computer search to help you identify the material you need for your research, you should know about the variety of data bases available for on-line searching. At present there are more than 1,800 publicly available data bases including those for periodical indexes and newspapers. And the number is still growing. (These are available through the libraries and commercial services offering on-line searching to the public.) Most of the public-access data bases are listed in *Omni's On-line Database Directory,* by Mike Edelhart and Owen Davies (Macmillan, 1983). The brief list below shows some full-text, numeric data bases (those which include statistical, quantitative data) and will give you an idea of their diverse scope and content.

■ *National Foundations.* Current year. The Foundation Center.

Provides data on approximately 22,000 nationwide foundations that award grants. Many small foundations are included in this list, while another data base—*Foundation Directory*—includes information on the large foundations.

■ *The Source.* Source Telecomputing Corp. and others. (Includes both full text and citations.)

A popular data base containing a sampling of many other data bases and some unique services. It encompasses a cross section of business and finance news (citations of sources), shopping services (identifies products for purchase), movie reviews, the text of several newsletters such as *Refundle Bundle,* airline itineraries, a restaurant guide to major cities, a variety of reference and education services including access to data on financial aid and scholarships, astrological charts, lists of the week's bestselling books, a guide to energy conservation for home appliances, etc. *The Source*, which emphasizes recent information, can best be described as several magazines in one.

■ *Spacecomps.* European Space Agency. 1970-date.
Describes more than 11,000 components that have been approved for use in European spacecraft. Includes the approved lists of parts for all major space agencies. Also includes citations to over 1,000 technical reports on component reliability and testing.

■ *Trade Opportunities.* 1976-date. U.S. Department of Commerce.
Provides leads to export opportunities for American businesses. Describes products and services of interest for sales leads, overseas representation opportunities, and foreign government calls for tenders from over 120 countries.

The vast majority of data bases that exist are private, and these already number in the thousands. An example of a private data base is included in the answer to the question below.

Q. I got a traffic ticket in another state, and I never paid it. What will happen?
A. It's likely that nothing will happen unless you're stopped for another violation. At that time the officer may discover the unpaid ticket when he checks your record via computer, according to Rod Dornsife's *The Ticket Book*. Departments of motor vehicles in different states exchange information and keep it on a central computer. The worst that may happen is that you'll have to pay the fine. Occasionally, Dornsife says, a traffic warrant may expire in five or ten years, but it's up to a judge to establish an expiration date.

A source that includes both public and private data bases in industry and government is *Encyclopedia of Information Systems and Services*, edited by John Schmittroth, Jr., published by Gale Research. (5th edition, 1983. Issued every 2-3 years.) The private data bases are simply paper files converted to computers. They have been created by businesses and different kinds of research organizations for their own use. Most do not now have a commercial market, but some may go on-line in the future. A sample of private data bases that could be useful to researchers is given below:

■ *Auto Parts Database (Audatex).*
If you've ever had to run around town gathering insurance estimates on the damage to your car from a minor fender bender, you'll appreciate what this data base offers. It lists all parts of an automobile likely to be involved in a collision and includes manufacturer's part number, price, and estimated labor hours to repair it.
The data base includes information on about 1,000 auto model years.

■ *Bicentennial Inventory.*

The *BI*, funded by Smithsonian's National Collection of Fine Arts and housed in the Archives of American Art in Washington, DC, records every known American oil, watercolor, fresco, pastel, and painting in any medium made before 1914. The list includes at least a million works of art. Besides the title and artist of the piece, the file records the date the work was created, the medium, material, dimensions, present owner if available, and location.

■ *Computer Museum Network.*

This data base, maintained at the State University of New York at Stony Brook, Long Island, houses information about works of art, artifacts, and other materials in 20 large museums that belong to this network. Included are the Museum of Modern Art in New York and the National Gallery of Art in Washington, DC. Terminals are set up at each institution to retrieve the information stored in the central data bank shared by the affiliates.

The information available on the computer includes the name of the work, artist, and location, as well as the physical description of the piece, the previous owner, and in some cases, the buying price.

■ *Real Estate Database.*

Realtors throughout the United States now have nationwide access to listings, office exclusives, financial data, open house information, prospect files, and management reports. The system includes a profile sheet on each piece of property, which enables the agent to better match it with a suitable buyer.

The broker can also use the system to compute amortization figures, mortgage schedules, and other financial data.

The data bases described here are just the appetizer. Imagine any type of industry, organization, or institution making its files available to data base vendors nationwide so that you can subscribe to them. Access to some private data bases may materialize in time if a public demand develops. Then you'll have an idea of the computer's enormous potential for providing limitless information.

COMPUTER VS. PRINT RESOURCES

One clue to any successful information search is the careful choosing of resources. With print and computer aids at your disposal via the library, your choices are greater, and your chances of finding what you need are better than ever. To make optimal use of both print and computerized resources, you should recognize the unique strengths of each.

Traditionally, we've used print material for consulting and reading. Consulting means a quick check. We look up a definition, a phone number, an address, a statistic, a formula. This function is actually the one that the computer handles very well; for such research, the computer is superior to a book. It's quicker and simpler to call up on the computer screen an answer from an article, chart, or directory, than to search for it through a paper copy.

The book is superior to the computer, however, for reading or studying at length. Experts in the information and publishing fields seriously doubt that people will enthusiastically choose to read extensively from a screen. In addition, computers are not as portable as books. They are irksome to read at length, and they rack up a charge like a taxi meter. (Even microfilm, without the negative side effect of mounting costs per second, is a nuisance to read for prolonged periods.)

Books and computers with their individual strengths can be used separately or together. Data bases deal with parts, not the whole. They are best for quick reference and pulling together stray bits of information. Books are best for extended reading and study. Both functions are part of many research projects. Industry experts expect that computers will fill in or complement services where print is not efficient and add services that books cannot offer.

The two formats—computer and print—will go hand in hand in research. You may never throw away your dictionary. It's still cheaper to look up a word in a print dictionary than to look it up in a data base. Maybe it will always be cheaper to use a print dictionary, since a book is a one-time investment whereas a data base requires an individual charge each time you use it.

On the other hand, the computer will always be available to answer other kinds of questions. "Give me a list of hangover cures." "What have gasoline prices at the pump been for the past ten years?" "What is the latest information on treatments for herpes?" "What patents have been taken out in the past five years on gasoline-free engines?" The list of questions you'll think to ask will grow—simply because The Great Research Machine will be there to answer them.

As we and our children increasingly use computers at work and in school, we'll feel more comfortable with them. We'll learn what on-line information services offer, and this familiarity will lead us to accept them more readily in our homes. At the same time that we gain more computer savvy, data base publishers will make the systems easier to use. Both of these things are already happening. (At this writing, a new data base service has just been made available to owners of personal computers. Mentioned earlier in this chapter, it is called *Knowledge Index;* it is offered by Dialog Services and heralds user-friendly, but limited on-line data base services.)

It's safe to say that computers will not replace books. Even in the educational field where there's a growing market for disks and cassettes, these will enhance the printed texts rather than replace them.

There is no evidence to suggest that computers and print resources cannot coexist. In 1950, when computers and televison began to make inroads, some 11,000 new books were published in the United States. By 1970, with both TV and computers cheaper and in more widespead use, the book output had more than tripled. In 1980, with even more advances and improvements in electronics, approximately 40,000 new books were published. Statistics in academic libraries also show that as a result of the jump in data base searching, interlibrary loan use (which translates to book use) has soared.

In an age of high technology, the important thing to recognize is the individual strength of both computerized and print resources. Then you can use each of them when your research dictates. Undoubtedly, the library will continue to play an important role in encouraging the use of both.

———————— CHAPTER SUMMARY ————————

I. Computers are here to stay. As research tools, they have great potential. Home use of computers as research tools will increase when regulations protecting personal information in computers are formulated; when we become more familiar with the kind of information computers can provide; when the language by which we communicate with computers becomes easier; and when on-line costs drop. (page 237)

II. At present, the computer offers two emerging kinds of information services.

A. Videotex makes banking, catalog shopping, newspapers, educational games, and encyclopedia reference available via your TV screen. (page 240)

B. Data base searching of reference materials covers some indexes, reference books, newspapers, etc., published in the last 20 years.

1. One kind of data base available to researchers is full-text information (statistics, articles or abstracts of articles, and material from reference books such as *Who's Who in America*). (page 240)

2. The second kind of data base offers bibliographic information (citations to books, book reviews, government reports, dissertations, magazine and newspaper articles, patents, conference papers, and Congressional publications). (page 240)

C. Not all research material will likely be available through computer data bases (e.g., the full text of millions of books). Microform may fill this role more adequately. (page 247)

III. There are times when searching periodical indexes by computer is more fruitful than a manual search through print indexes.
    A. This may occur when the material you need was published so recently that the printed indexes aren't out yet. (page 249)
    B. Consider a computer search when the terms you must check aren't yielding results in the print indexes. (page 249)
    C. There are approximately 1,800 data bases available to the public from several hundred data base suppliers. You can search them through a library or firm that has the computer hookup and subscribes to them. (page 250)
    D. Private data bases number in the thousands; at present these do not have a commercial market, although some may develop commercially and go on-line in the future. (page 251)
IV. Computers and books complement eacn otner. Computers work best when they are used for quick lookups, and books work best when used in concentrated study. There is no reason why these two resources cannot coexist as research aids. (page 252)

14

Space Saver, Time Saver:
MICROFORM

Small is beautiful
—Title of a book by Ernst F. Schumacher

Research material available in microform[1] can be be anything from personal papers (the papers of some members of the U.S. Congress) to newspapers (major U.S. city newspapers). Various chapters in this book show you how to access and use microform as a research tool. But there's more to know.

Microform is actually just emerging as a research force despite the fact that some items listed in other chapters have existed for several years. Let's take a closer look at the medium, the reasons for the recent surge in micropublishing, and some of the tricks you can use to locate microform materials.

WHY MICROFORM IN LIBRARIES?

By the 1940s, thanks to improved technology, publishing had reached a feverish pitch. Presses rushed books and magazines into print faster than libraries could collect them. At that time, Wesleyan University librarian Fremont Rider calculated that academic libraries were doubling their collections every 15 years. According to those estimates, unless a solution were found, he foresaw a future that would bring us clogged, bulging, and unusable libraries. Microform seemed to be the solution.

In truth, inflation of the 1970s turned out to be, if not the solution, then an incentive to find alternatives. As book and periodical costs (particularly in the sciences) skyrocketed, librarians shifted gears to slow down purchasing. Library systems merged, branches closed, and academic libraries started subject-specializing and sharing acquisitions, not

[1]Microformats are microfilm, microfiche, and microprint. Microfilm is film on a roll or reel. Microfiche is film on sheets that measure 3x5 or 4x6 inches. Microprint is a trade name for a 6x9-inch opaque sheet of microfilm.

only to curtail spiraling book and processing costs but to control over-crowded buildings.

Librarians closely examined the apparent savior, microform. It was an attractive option for many reasons.

For one thing, a microform book is cheaper than its print equivalent. And, it occupies a fraction of the space. (A 200-page book fits on two slender 4x6-inch microfiche cards; an entire library of nationwide phone books fits into a 2-foot-long drawer.) The space factor makes it possible to buy even more publications in giant collections—material that would certainly be rejected if it were offered in the print format.

But the medium has its problems, too—user resistance, for one. Library staffs find that users complain of eye and back strain from prolonged reading on a screen. And microform isn't as portable as a book. Users dislike reading in a fixed location. To further compound those problems, microform is invisible without a machine to magnify it; therefore, shelf browsing to identify appropriate material doesn't work. Finally, the cost of cataloging the enormous influx of microfilm publications is a serious concern. Many individual microform items have not been cataloged at all; therefore, much of the material is not entered into library catalogs.

Despite the drawbacks, microform offers other attractions besides copying of books and magazines. It also substitutes for a library's catalog (see COMCATS in Chapter 6). And, in fact, when it is used for short periods of time or as a lookup medium, the disadvantages described above disappear.

When I worked as a reference librarian at the University of California-San Diego, the reference department labored over the wisdom of offering our patrons the library's serials holding list (a list of magazines, periodicals, and directories) in a microformat. Why not stick with the known, namely, the computer printout we were already using? (Each volume in the three-volume set was about 1½ inches thick.) Each three-volume printout was distributed to about 10 library departments and branches; at a cost of $35 for each printout, the total monthly investment was $350. Why switch to this stranger even though the microfiche (at $3 for a 12-card set) would replace the computer printouts at a tenth of the cost?

But we did switch. There was no question about savings. And the cost of the approximately one dozen microfiche readers we needed at various library stations (about $250 each) could be recouped in no time. Our real question was, would our users be as doubtful as we originally were?

We were amazed. The majority of them, young people in their late teens and early 20s, loved it. It wasn't quite so readily accepted by our older library patrons who, incidentally, were usually women. But the machines were easy to use, we discovered. And once we showed reluctant researchers how they worked, they adapted beautifully.

It was becoming clear to us and to other librarians nationwide that microform, especially for short, quick uses, had a place in the library.

WHY MICROFORM FOR PUBLISHERS?

Microform is economical not only for libraries, but for publishers as well. Many of them see it as the only way to issue low-demand, specialized, rare, or fragile items they could not otherwise afford to reproduce. Many publications are, in fact, issued exclusively in microform with no print counterpart. The periodicals *Aesthetic, Reconstructive and Facial Plastic Surgery* and *Architectural Psychology Newsletter* are two examples. *Wildlife Disease*, issued by the Wildlife Disease Association, has been an original micropublication since 1959. More than 35 percent of the published conference papers read at professional and scholarly meetings come out in microform only. At this moment, more than 25 percent of the holdings in academic libraries are in microform, and the figure is climbing.

During the 1970s, the microfilming fever accelerated further. And today there are hundreds of firms that film current magazines and newspapers as well as old and hard-to-get items. Because of microfilm, libraries can buy—on film—other libraries or complete special collections containing items they never expected to be available for mass purchase: 17th- and 18th-century books; magazines and newspapers; diaries; presidential compaign literature; personal notebooks of noted novelists and playwrights; old theater programs; and much more. The Library of Congress, for example, has filmed in their entirety a number of its special manuscript collections such as the papers of 23 Presidents. (Traveling to Washington is no longer the *only* way to do research in these manuscript collections since any library can now buy them in microform.)

It's not that this material could not have been reprinted; that option was always available. The problem was space. Libraries would not have bought, in print, sufficient quantities of the items currently offered in microform collections to make it profitable for publishers to reproduce them.

Actually hard-copy buying has not decreased by the amount microform buying has increased. Though budget cutbacks have made a dent in libraries' purchasing power, microform acquisitions have been added, by necessity, to their budgets.

WHAT'S AVAILABLE IN MICROFORM
AND HOW TO FIND IT

One of the biggest drawbacks of books and other microform material has been access to it. How do you identify and find things that are almost invisible? The titles of many microform books have not been entered into library catalogs, because the purchase of a single microform set adds hundreds, sometimes thousands, of new books to a library's collection all at once. So much new material cannot be easily or quickly cataloged in libraries, so, in most cases, it has not been done. (Card sets that are sold by the micropublishers often use different cataloging rules from those a library presently follows, so these cards, which are also very expensive, don't always help. Also, many early books were never cataloged by any library and micropublishers have determined that the cost of cataloging them for the first time would be higher than the microform collections themselves.) Therefore, many large libraries have owned microform material for a long time without researchers knowing it.

Contributing to the access problem is the fact that many microform sets consist of ephemeral material such as brochures, manuscripts, reports, clippings, notebooks, posters, playbills, etc. The microform collection entitled *The Papers of Daniel Webster, 1798-1852*, for example, consists of much correspondence, hand-written drafts, essays, poems, and other loose items. These are traditionally difficult and expensive to catalog even in the hard-copy form because of a lack of cataloging standards to follow and the time consumed by an item-by-item inventory. But a partial solution is imminent.

Grants have now been awarded to individual libraries so they can catalog, on behalf of every library in the country that owns a set, the individual book titles in microform collections. This means the job of cataloging these sets will be done only once. It also means that thousands of individual microform books will start appearing in computer catalogs nationwide. Libraries owning microform sets need only add this information to the computer and it will be shared on-line.

Until the access problem is at least partially solved, you must take the initiative to find the microform materials in your libraries. If you're working on a long or involved project, the effort you make to survey the libraries in your area now may save you untold time and money later on. Why travel to New York City to use the rare books and manuscript collection of the Library of the Jewish Theological Seminary of America under tight security if it's available in microform (339 reels of microfilm costing more than $8,000) and possibly owned by a library more conveniently located?

In the meantime, the following tips should help you identify and find microform materials in libraries where some microform material may only be partially recorded or not recorded at all.

1. Notice the symbols or abbreviations in library catalogs that indicate that a publication is in microform. They usually include the word 'micro' and often, a chronological number rather than a call number. (The chronological number corresponds to the way the microform is arranged on shelves or in cabinets. In many cases, microform is not arranged by subject.) As I've already mentioned, catalog cards are sold with some microform collections, but because they're very expensive and may require editing according to the cataloging rules of the purchasing library, many libraries do not buy them. The practice of buying catalog cards with microform collections is uneven in libraries across the country and even within a single library.

2. Don't expect much help from librarians until they've had time to work with the improvements in access (book authors and titles on-line) that are in progress. Since many microform holdings are not yet in library catalogs, few researchers presently use these collections. Therefore, there's little opportunity for library staffs to learn about them. The inadequate access is as much a disadvantage to library staffs as it is to you. (Recall the Azores example in Chapter 6.)

3. Only academic and some large public libraries are buying most of the microform collections of research material I've mentioned throughout the book, although you might use your neighborhood branch to borrow individual items in them through interlibrary loan (provided you can find a machine on which to read them). Small libraries can only afford a few general-use tools like *NewsBank* (page 184) and *Phonefiche*, a collection of nationwide telephone books in microfiche (page 293), if any.

4. Check to see if a large library you use has a separate microform department and/or catalog. Keeping the format, catalog, and printed collection guides together has advantages. A special staff that oversees the collection also learns more about the material the library owns than staff at other reference stations. They may be able to recommend certain collections for certain research projects as a result of their familiarity with them. Perhaps they issue a special list telling what their library owns in microform. The *Oregon Historical Society's Microfilm Guide*, issued by the Society (1973, 162 pages) is one such book.

Also, ask if the library owns a list (usually called a "union list") of regional microform holdings. Libraries in an area often join forces to print or mimeograph directories telling who has what. One of these is *Union List of Microform Sets in the Libraries of the California State University and Colleges*, edited by Janice Zlendich.

5. Check the printed guides that accompany the microform collections. These usually provide the best descriptions of a collection's contents. In many cases, the guides may be the *only* way to get information about the collections.

Many printed guides are mentioned in this book. If you find microform sets not discussed here, be sure to ask the librarian if they come with a printed guide. (Some do not.) Some libraries also buy printed guides to microform collections they do not own. The more guides you have to identify microform material, the better.

6. Ask to see the micropublishers' sales catalogs announcing their offerings in microform. These are not, however, the same as the printed guides that accompany individual collections. (*MTLA*, item #5 on page 255, lists individual titles in microform sets.)

Some of the largest micropublishers in the country are Microfilming Corporation of America, University Microfilms International, and Bell & Howell. General descriptions of the microform sets in their sales catalogs are often quite good. University Microfilm's 800-plus page sales catalog called *Serials in Microform*, listing their magazines and newspapers on film, is an important reference tool in its own right. Libraries often catalog it and keep it in the reference section. (Sales catalogs that are not cataloged are usually kept in a library's order department and using them should be no problem. You may also write to the micropublishers for your own copies.)

Many of the books selected for inclusion in microform collections are based on bibliographies that were published years ago. These bibliographies are usually mentioned in the micropublisher's catalog. Like the collection guides, the bibliographies are title-by-title lists. They not only tell you what the collection contains,[2] they may also help you identify other appropriate material for your project.

7. An easy way to think about what might be available in microform without knowing specific microform collections is to assume that every book and most magazines and newspapers published in this country before 1820, many after 1820, and a selection of foreign published materials are or soon will be in microform.

At the current rate and scale of micropublishing, this could one day be true. Therefore, ANYTHING published in the United States before 1820 mentioned in ANY printed bibliography should appear in SOME microform collection.

Many books, in fact, appear in several different collections. *Early American Medical Imprints, 1668-1819* is totally duplicated by the *Early American Imprints* series, the one which purports to be a total collection of ALL books published in America between 1639 and 1820.[3] Any microform collection which includes pre-1820 books in it, regardless of the subject focus (*American Prose Fiction* series, *Western Americana* series, etc.) would appear to be duplicated by the *Early American Imprints* series. The present lack of complete title access through library catalogs makes this difficult to confirm conclusively, but in random cross-checks, I've already verified duplicates.

8. Be alert to specialized microform sets consisting of a collection so comprehensive that you may be able to do much of your research in one place without having to track down the individual items in it or travel to a distant library or archive to use them. The *Genealogy and Local History* collection in microform, for example, consists of hundreds of books, magazines, and documents on genealogy that exceed the selection available in any but a few of the largest libraries.

---

[2]You'll soon discover that not all microform sets based on bibliographies reproduce every publication mentioned. Many publishers select only a portion of the titles to reproduce.

[3]The duplication of microform books is not necessarily bad. If a medical library wants only historical medical books, it shouldn't have to buy the entire *Early American Imprints* series to get it—it would mean a difference of many thousands of dollars.

Q. How can I research child labor in the early 19th century using original books and articles written at that time?

A. You can find many articles in print and reprinted books by checking CHIL-DREN - EMPLOYMENT and other related subject headings in *Poole's Index to Periodical Literature: Combined Retrospective Index to Journals in History, 1838-1974* and in *Subject Guide to Books in Print.*

To find additional material which may not be accessible through interlibrary loan in the print format, but which may be in microform, examine the various microform-finding tools. For example, the subject headings in *Guide to Microforms in Print* may be too broad to be helpful, but if you should find a relevant title, look for it in your library's catalog or borrow it through interlibrary loan. Then you might check *Dodson's Microform Research Collections: A Guide* and *Microform Review*, to see if any microform collections therein listed encompass your child labor topic. Microform collections such as *Women's History* and *Library of American Civilization*, for example, are likely candidates for further checking.

Scan the printed guides that come with these sets or the bibliographies on which they are based for relevant books that have been microfilmed. If your library doesn't own any of the appropriate titles, get them through ILL.

Remember that not all microform books are in all library catalogs. Also, some may have been reprinted as books. Looking for microform materials is still not like looking for printed books and articles which are better recorded and therefore easier to find. Check with a film librarian in a large public or academic library for resources she may know of in your area.

FOLLOW-UP TO A REFERENCE

Now for the specifics of connecting a reference to an early book or article with some microform counterpart. Let's say you've found a printed bibliography called *Travels in the Old South*, edited by Thomas D. Clark, in which you notice this book: *Views of Society and Manners in America; In a Series of Letters From That Country to a Friend in England, During the Years, 1818, 1819, and 1820.* By an Englishwoman. [Frances Wright D'Arusmont, 1795-1852]. London, 1821. 523 pages. You also find a footnote in a book mentioning an article in the April 1840 issue of *Mother's Magazine.* You want to get the book and the article, whether they're in microform or in hard copy.

The quickest way to get them is to do one of the following:

1. Check the library's catalog. The book or magazine may appear in the original, as a reprint, or in a microform collection the library has cataloged.

2. If the library doesn't own the item or it doesn't show up in the catalog for some reason, check one of the microform collections of books mentioned in Chapter 7, the microform collections of magazines cited in Chapter 10, or any of the others your library owns. Your library may actu-

ally own the item without the information showing up in the catalog.

3. Place an interlibrary loan request.

It's difficult to predict how well the steps above will work. Much of your success depends on the progress of the access program (the cataloging of individual titles in microform collections). It may take years to complete. In the meantime, there are other references to microform collections with which you'll want to be familiar in order to identify microform material:

1. *Guide to Microforms in Print* (subject and author/title volumes). Incorporates International Microforms in Prints since 1977. Meckler Publishing. 1976-date.

Similar to *Books in Print*, this annual guide lists various "in print" microforms for sale: books (*Babylonian Magic and Sorcery*, by L.W. King. London. 1896); journals (*Fifth Avenue Journal: A Mirror of Art, Literature and Society*, 1872-73; or, *Field and Stream*, 1977-date); newspapers (*Boston Evening Post*, 1735-1775); government publications (*Congressional Digest*); archival material (*Anderson Family Papers, 1802-1905*, in the Kansas State Historical Society), etc. Theses and dissertations are not included. (See *Dissertations Abstracts International* in Chapter 17 to get dissertations in microform.)

Many of the items listed are actually part of some microform collection though not named in the guide.

The subject volume of *GMIP* uses broad categories; therefore, it's not as useful in identifying microform materials as the *Subject Guide to Books in Print* is for identifying printed books.

The title volume lists books, magazines, and other publications in microform. If you find a book in *GMIP* that you'd like to see, follow the three steps mentioned on page 263 to get it.

2. *Index to Microform Collections*, edited by Ann Niles. Meckler Publishing. 1984.

This hefty guide is a title and author index to several thousand books in 26 microform collections that do not come with printed guides. There is no subject index, but the collections listed and the publications in them are subject-oriented, such as *British Architectural Library* and *History of the Pacific Northwest and the Canadian Northwest*. The guide tells you if a book exists in microform in one of the 26 collections covered.

3. *Microform Research Collections: A Guide*, edited by Suzanne Cates Dodson. Microform Review, Inc. 2d ed. 1984.

This handbook describes almost 200 microform collections (*Early American Imprints* series, *Western Americana* series, etc.) which started filming before 1978. It also includes the titles of the printed bibliographies on which they were based. It's one of the few comprehensive lists of microform collections in print.

4. *Microform Review*. Bimonthly. Meckler Publishing. 1972-date.

MR reviews microform collections, as other magazines review individual books. It tells librarians what's new in microform collections, and how they rate as far as legibility and arrangement are concerned. For researchers, it describes enough of a set's contents to indicate whether it may be useful in a particular research project.

MR, usually available in large public or academic libraries, comes out six times a year. Besides indexes in each issue, there is also an annual index in the December issue. The handiest thing to start with is the cumulative index covering volumes 1-10 (1972-81). Not all microform collections issued are reviewed, but *MR* manages to catch most of them.

5. *Micropublisher's Trade List Annual*. 1975-date. Meckler Publishing.

Available on microfiche only, *MTLA* is published annually with six-month supplements. It's a microform counterpart to *Publisher's Trade List Annual* and thus reprints micropublishers' catalogs which specify books, magazines, and other items they have microfilmed. *MTLA* offers a broad subject approach.

6. *National Register of Microform Masters*. Library of Congress. 1965-date.

NRMM exists merely to identify those books and magazines (and their publishers) reproduced in a microform copy. Its purpose is also purportedly to prevent duplicate materials from being filmed. The approach is by author or magazine title only. Individual items in microform collections are listed, though not the name of the collections in which they were reproduced. You may find this set to be of limited use unless you have a book's author or magazine title in hand and you simply want to verify that the item exists in a microform copy.

7. *Newspapers in Microform: U.S., 1948-1972* and supplements. Library of Congress. *Newspapers in Microform: Foreign, 1948-1972*, and supplements. Library of Congress.

These directories, covered in Chapter 11, list newspapers (geographically by state, then by city) which are available in microform.

THE FUTURE OF MICROFORM

Getting materials in microform is not hard if you're patient and know where to look. Using material in this format not only will save you time and money, it can also enrich your research with items you might not otherwise easily get. Unlike computers, with limited materials available and mounting charges per minute, the hundreds of thousands of microform items are available to use at your leisure.

Microform technology has already begun to penetrate the consumer market. In the October 3, 1979 edition of *The New York Times* (page C-10), Craig Claiborne wrote an article called "A Home Cookbook Library on Microfilm" in which he described a home microfiche reader and box containing, not recipe cards, but nine recipe *books*, on microfiche, with the potential of hundreds more to follow. This package, he reported, already sells for $325 in some department stores like Neiman-Marcus in Dallas and Bloomingdale's in New York City.

When microfiche becomes as acceptable in the home as computers are already becoming, we'll have access to complete libraries of crafts books, repair manuals, songbooks, and others for our personal use.

Though improvements in micrographics technology through the 1970s were tremendous, they were overshadowed by even more astounding developments in computer technology. Libraries were, therefore, not as taken with microform as expected.

During the 1980s, libraries of all sizes are introducing more material in microform—starting with COMCATS. Computer services are still expensive, and microform may meet the demand for information at a more reasonable cost. The larger libraries will continue to innovate and experiment with new information technology, and this will eventually affect service offered by small libraries.

According to predictions, once libraries have established full micrographic service, we may expect the following:[4]

■ Micropublishing will increase and offer a greater selection of material at lower prices.

■ Major reference books will come out in microform and be available as alternatives to on-line access for brief lookups in libraries of all sizes.

■ Microform packages consisting of items on popular topics such as home and auto repair, crafts, and recipes will be issued in packages and be available for loan along with portable readers.

■ The duplication of microform material will become common as more noncopyright and royalty-free materials become available.

■ Both computers and microform will be used to identify information, and microform will record the content.

■ Microfilm machines will become automated with greater storage capacity. Not only will we no longer have to load film, we will use the material from a compact unit and read through a video screen or terminal.

The negative stereotypes (hard to use, difficult to read) surrounding microform as a research tool are steadily falling away. Acceptance of the format is a clue that we will be using microform materials even more in the future. Like the computer, microform will not take the place of print materials as we know them; rather, it will provide yet another option for getting the research material we need.

[4]From: *The Microform Connection: A Basic Guide for Libraries*, by Ralph Folcarelli, Arthur Tannenbaum, and Ralph Ferragamo. R.R. Bowker Co. 1982.

_____ *CHAPTER SUMMARY* _____

I. Microform has emerged as an important research tool. It makes available many books, magazines, and entire collections of special material for mass purchase by libraries. The medium's pluses are conservation of space and costs. It is especially useful in looking up brief references. (page 257)

II. Because of problems with entering individual items in microform collections into a library's catalog, access to the medium through library catalogs is spotty. Until all microform book titles are in computer catalogs, you must take the initiative to find the items in your library. (It may help to know that everything published in America before 1820, and many items after that, are already in film.) (page 259)

III. The process of tracking down microform resources involves several steps.
    A. To identify microform materials, notice references to microform in library catalogs. Check for published guides and sales catalogs that correspond to microform collections, and ask librarians for union lists of microform holdings in area libraries. (page 260)
    B. To actually locate the material, first check your library's catalog; then try a microform collection in case your library really owns the item, but it doesn't yet show up in the catalog; finally, try interlibrary loan. (page 263)
    C. Certain reference tools report on and describe individual items and entire collections in microform. These tools range from title and subject guides, such as the *Guide to Microforms in Print*, to review journals such as *Microform Review*. (page 264)

PART THREE

WHERE TO LOOK FOR SPECIFIC INFORMATION

15

Dead or Alive:
LOOKING FOR BIOGRAPHICAL INFORMATION

If a man's life, like a piece of tapestry, is made up of many strands
which interwoven make a pattern; to separate a single one and look at it alone
not only destroys the whole but gives the strand itself a false value.
—Judge Learned Hand,
Proceedings in Memory of Mr. Justice Brandeis

Once upon a time, as all fairy tales go, I met a writer who recalled the good old days when she was working with one of the country's most popular authors before he started writing. (Both shall remain nameless to avoid possible embarrassment, I'm not sure to whom.)

When someone tells you stories about the early days of an author whose name is known around the world, you listen. I liked the nostalgia so much, in fact, that I decided to mention it in my Books/Writers column for *The San Diego Tribune*.

That evening, I made my weekly trek to the library to research my other column, The Reference Librarian. Mr. Bestseller was still on my mind, and for no other reason than curiosity I looked up some brief biographical information about him. Perhaps, I thought, some of his secrets would rub off on me.

What happened next can only be described as high drama. Both my jaw and the books I was checking fell. I charged for the phone to call my editor. "Kill the story," or words close to those, tumbled from my lips. Mr. Bestseller's biographies disagreed with two major facts my writer source had given me. In truth, the famous author didn't work in this particular field in the early days—nor could he have worked in any field then—because at that time he was a teenager. The conflict on these two points made everything else the writer told me highly doubtful, if not impossible.

What might have happened had I not, by chance, checked some printed sources in time? The information I had gotten would have run in the newspaper. Readers who didn't know better might have added that interesting vignette about Mr. Bestseller to their repertoire and perhaps reused it later on. Who would have doubted that it was true? It would have appeared in print, after all. (The truth is, I *still* don't know what went wrong. My source stood by her story, and the print sources disagreed.)

When you do research long enough (and it needn't be very long), you become a confirmed skeptic about anything you read. And when you interview enough people, you learn that "right from the horse's mouth" can be tinged with anything from poor memory to pure fantasy. (No one was more shocked than I, for instance, when I discovered that congressmen can change their remarks in Congress's daily log, the *Congressional Record*, before it goes to press.)

The Mr. Bestseller example illustrates one thing about biographical research that is unlike any other kind of research: Everyone has his own version of a story. It may not help you when you're trying to write about it, but where people are involved, there are bound to be interpretations, opinions, and differences.

WHO'S WHO

Regardless of the challenges that await you in biographical research, you must begin somewhere. The most obvious place to start in print resources is with the many "who's who" biographical directories.

To the uninitiated, "Who's Who" is one magical book, a bottomless pit of every name you'll ever need. The fact is, there are hundreds of "who's who" directories listing people by country (*Who's Who in France, Who's Who in Israel*), or by profession (*Who's Who in American Art, Who's Who in Insurance*). They may be issued annually (*Who's Who in Finance*), or only once (*Who's Who in World Aviation and Astronautics*, whose two volumes were published in 1955 and 1958).

They may include prominent people and be heavily used by researchers in libraries (*Who's Who in America*, published annually by Marquis Who's Who, Inc.), or simply be intended as an organizational or professional membership directory (*Who's Who in Barbed Wire*).

A few may be vanity publications compiled just to sell to the people whose names are included. These have no reference value and are seldom bought (knowingly) by libraries.

Q. My teenage son received a letter saying he had been selected to appear in a high school "who's who." We completed the questionnaire, even including both grandparents' names and addresses, and returned it. We were flattered—until we were asked to buy a copy which was quite expensive. Now we're wondering how people get their names in a "who's who" in the first place.

A. "Who's who" publications (and there are hundreds) generally have editorial boards that select the people to be included according to certain criteria. The board sends them questionnaires to fill out, and the information goes into the book.

Libraries buy many biographical directories of prominent people, such as *Who's Who in American Politics*, for their patrons' research needs. The kind of "who's who" to which you're referring is known by librarians and book people as a vanity publication. It gets its main revenues by selling copies to the people listed. Libraries usually don't buy these because they have no reference value. Libraries that do own them usually received them free.

Many people don't object to those kinds of "who's whos," because they like to see their names in print, but they should know what these books are all about. (A small percentage are outright frauds. Their publishers collect money but never publish the book.) You might note that admissions offices of local colleges say that the high school "who's whos" do not influence college admissions boards. Grades are the primary criterion for admission to college.

The glut of biographical directories, which don't all start with the words "Who's Who" (e.g., *American Architects Directory, Foremost Women in Communications, British Authors Before 1800,* etc.), presents awesome choices for anyone. Where do you begin a search for biographical information?

BIOGRAPHICAL DIRECTORIES

The first step in acquiring people information is to decide what kind of and how much biographical information you need. Are you looking for a current address, verifying one or two points of conflict about a person's life, or seeking an overview of his achievements? For most of these needs, biographical directories (BDs) are appropriate resources. Their information is generally brief, ranging in length from one paragraph to two pages. Entries usually include basic data and vital statistics: date of birth; parents', spouses' and children's names; education and degrees; career highlights; awards; and dates related to these events.

One point to note about BDs is that many of them (especially the well-known group published by Marquis Who's Who, Inc.) print biographical information provided by the person himself. You might think that coming from the individual, the information would be more accurate than secondhand sources. But not always. Kenneth Petchenik, president of Marquis Who's Who, Inc., confirms that occasionally it is not, particularly regarding academic credentials. I recently ran into just this kind of situation.

I read a book that said Eliot Janeway, well-known financial analyst and advisor to several presidents, has no academic credentials. This statement was hard to accept at face value despite the fact that it appeared in print. Further checking was definitely in order. (If *you* don't check further, your editor, instructor, or a critic will undoubtedly catch it.)

Who's Who in America said that Janeway has very prestigious credentials. He graduated from Cornell University and attended the London

School of Economics. With two opposing views, both in print, the situation is still in doubt. By scanning periodical indexes, I found an article in the November 21, 1978 issue of *Esquire* that clarified the point. It said that Janeway attended college for nearly four years but did not finish. (By this time, of course, you'll even be skeptical of the *Esquire* article. It's hard to say when to stop doubting and when to start believing. Even if the majority of your cumulated information supports one viewpoint, numbers don't make it true. Those sources might have copied their information from equally unreliable sources—perhaps each other. History books and biographies are riddled with many such contradictions and outright errors.) You can always verify information with the individual, but perhaps a contradiction might be denied, especially if the person provided the data himself.

Whether exaggerating one's academic credentials is justifiable in the face of a direct question or an ethical point is not the issue here. What such a distortion can do for you as a researcher is mislead you and cause you to make mistakes. And there's always a chance that the mistakes will be passed on to other researchers. Verifying and double-checking biographical information is a must.

MASTER INDEXES

When you ask a librarian for references to BDs appropriate for your search, she'll use some tricks from her repertoire and produce some biographies very quickly. (You'll likely want to know how she did it so you can learn where to look on your own.) Finding the most appropriate biographical resource (or selection of several, depending on your needs) is not difficult. Like most forms of research, finding biographical information follows a pattern.

Suppose you need a short biography of the late Truman Capote to double-check some facts about his early writing. Which BD would you consult?

The number of current and back-issue BDs has ballooned over the years, and libraries own an awesome quantity. (Academic libraries may own between 500 and 1,000 recent and old editions.) Someone like Capote is mentioned in almost three dozen BDs. How can you determine which ones? Should you hunt randomly through dozens of them? Even if you do, you'll likely stop far short of the total number your subject appears in, because you won't know to look further. Even though much of the information you find will be repetitive, you may also miss something new.

The ideal situation for a researcher is to be able to look up any name in a single alphabetical list that refers to all the BDs in print. Indexes that do this are available. They're called biography master indexes (BMIs). And you should begin your search with them.

BMIs interfile all names found in up to 500 different BDs into a single alphabet. They tell, through abbreviations, which BDs include information on any person listed. A partial BMI entry looks like this:

Capote, Truman 1924-1984
 AmAu&B, AmNov, AmSCAP66, Au&Wr 71, BiE&WWA, CasWL,
 CelR, CnDAL

The abbreviations stand for *American Authors and Books; American Novelists of Today; ASCAP Biographical Dictionary of Composers, Authors and Publishers; Authors and Writers in the West; Biographical Encyclopaedia and Who's Who in the American Theatre; Cassell's Encyclopaedia of World Literature; Celebrity Register;* and *Concise Dictionary of American Literature*. (You can decode all the abbreviations by checking them in the BMIs key.)

The following is a list of BMIs published by Gale Research Co. They are standard reference tools in large libraries. (There is some overlap among them. The complete list of BDs each BMI covers appears on both the inside front and back covers of the volumes. Also note that the first six in the list below are duplicated by one large set—#7, *Biography and Genealogy Master Index,* and its even larger microform counterpart, *Bio-base,* #8.

Specialized BMIs are often found in department or special libraries that don't want to buy the entire multi-volume set covering all BMIs but just want those that cover their field.

1. *Author Biographies Master Index.* 2 vols. 2d ed. 1984. Supplement. 1980. Interfiles the names from 140 BDs such as *American Women Writers, British Writers, Creative Canada, Dictionary of Irish Writers, Modern French Literature, Pseudonyms of Authors,* and *Who's Who in Spy Fiction.*

2. *Children's Authors and Illustrators.* 2nd ed. 1981. Interfiles the names from about 200 BDs such as *Black American Writers, Concise Encyclopedia of the Theatre, Dictionary of Oriental Literatures, Indiana Authors and Their Books, Puerto Rican Authors,* and *Who's Who in Graphic Arts.*

3. *Historical Biographical Dictionaries Master Index.* 1980. Interfiles the names from about three dozen BDs such as *Biographical Dictionary of the Confederacy; Biographical History of Medicine; Encyclopedia of American Agricultural History; Notable American Women, 1607-1950; Who was Who in America;* and *Who's Who in Military History.*

4. *Journalist Biographies Master Index.* 1979. Interfiles the names from about 200 BDs such as *Authors in the News, Current Biography, Foreign Press, Leaders in Education, Minnesota Writers, New Muckrakers, Who's Who in Advertising,* and *World Authors, 1950-70.*

5. *Performing Arts Biography Master Index.* 2nd ed. 1982. Interfiles the names from about 100 BDs such as *American Film Directors, Blues Who's Who, Creative Canada, Film Actors Guide, The Great Movie Comedians, The MGM Stock Directory,* and *Whatever Became of . . .?*

6. *Writers for Young Adults: Biographies Master Index.* 1979. Interfiles the names from about three dozen BDs such as *Anthology of Children's Literature, Book of Catholic Authors, Contemporary Poets, European Authors, Minnesota Writers,* and *Newbery Medal Books.*

7. *Biography and Genealogy Master Index.* 8-volume base set and 3-volume supplement. 1980-81. Interfiles the names from 350 BDs including all of those mentioned in items 1-6. If your library owns this set, skip those above and start here.

Q. I've recently found a watch fob from the championship fight between Dempsey and Gibbons, which took place on July 4, 1923 in Shelby, Montana, with a reference to Dempsey as the Manassa Mauler. Where did this nickname come from?

A. I checked the *Biography and Genealogy Master Index* which indicated that Dempsey has a listing in *Who's Who in Boxing.* The entry says he was born William Harrison Dempsey in Manassa, Colorado, in 1895, hence, the source of the nickname.

---

8. *Bio-base.* (microform). 1978. Updates issued. Interfiles the names from approximately 500 BDs and duplicates all of the above.

Two other especially useful Gale Research Co. BMIs are the following:

An Analytical Bibliography of Universal Collected Biography. 1980, reprint of the 1934 edition. Indexes 56,000 biographies in over 3,000 books published before 1933—books like *Biographical Dictionary of Modern Rationalists,* by Joseph McCabe (1920); *Judges of England,* by Edward Foss (9 vols., 1848-64); and *Historic Oddities and Strange Events,* by Sabine Baring-Gould (1891).

In Black and White: A Guide to Magazine Articles, Newspaper Articles and Books Concerning More Than 15,000 Black Individuals and Groups. 3d ed., 1980.

Some of the books indexed include *New Negro Renaissance,* by Arthur Dans; *Black Frontiersmen,* by J. Norman Heard; and *NAACP,* by Charles Kellogg. Some magazines and newspapers indexed are *Jet, Ebony, People, Black Enterprise, Down Beat, The New York Times, The Washington Post,* the *Detroit Free Press,* the *Chicago Tribune,* and the *Chicago Defender.*

The following BMIs are compiled by publishers other than Gale Research Co:

1. *Index to Artistic Biography,* compiled by Patricia Havlice. Scarecrow Press. 1973. Suppl., 1981. Interfiles entries from about 135 books and BDs such as *Dictionary of Italian Painting, Contemporary Japanese-style Painting,* by Tanio Nakamura; *Modern Austrian Art: A Concise History,* by Kristian Sotriffer; and *Who's Who in American Art* (all volumes since 1936).

2. *Index to Literary Biography,* compiled by Patricia Havlice. 2 vols. Scarecrow Press. 1975. Suppl., 2 vols., 1983. Interfiles entries from about 100 books and directories such as *Twentieth-Century American Science Fiction Writers,* by David Cowart and Thomas Wymer; *Chicano Scholars and Writers,* by Julio Martinez; and *American Writers in Paris, 1920-39,* by Karen Rood.

3. *Marquis Who's Who Publications: Index to All Books.* Marquis Who's Who, Inc. 1974-date. Interfiles the names from approximately 15 Marquis Who's Who publications for the year such as *Who's Who in America, Who's Who in the East, Who's Who in Government,* and *Who's Who in Religion.*

4. *Motion Picture Performers,* by Mel Schuster. Scarecrow Press. 1973. Supplement, 1976. Lists citations to articles in more than 250 magazines and selected books published between 1900 and 1974. (Newspapers are covered sporadically.) Some of the books indexed are *The Heavies,* by Ian & Elisabeth Cameron, and *Academy Awards Illustrated,* by Robert Osborne. Magazines covered are *After Dark, Cinema Journal, Good Housekeeping, Ms., Oui, People, Show, TV Guide,* and *Viva.*

Check your library for these BMIs, revisions, and new titles that may come out.

BOOKS AND ARTICLES BY THE PERSON

Yet another way to gather information about a person is to investigate his published credits. Has he written a book? The following sources will help you find out.

- *National Union Catalog.* Library of Congress
- *Books in Print,* Authors. R.R. Bowker Co. 1948-date.
- *Cumulative Book Index: A World List of Books in the English Language.* H.W. Wilson Co. 1898-date.
- OCLC
- Book reviews. (See Chapter 9.)
- Periodical indexes. (See Chapter 10.)

You may first want to check your local library's catalog to see what's immediately available on your subject. Then check to see what else has been published according to printed bibliographies. There are several comprehensive sources to check for books, whether they're in print or out of print. One is the Library of Congress's published card catalog entitled *National Union Catalog.* It consists of more than a thousand volumes, starting with a 750-plus-volume base set called *National Union Catalog, Pre-1956 Imprints,* published by Mansell. Later volumes are usually shelved nearby. (The years covered appear on the spine of the books. Look for five-or-more-year cumulations or a microform cumulative.) *NUC* is an author-only list of all books, American and foreign, cataloged by the Library of Congress.

You can also check *Books in Print* (author volumes) or *Cumulative Book Index*. *CBI* includes English language books published in other countries as well as in the United States. (It has a dictionary arrangement in which subject, author, and title entries are in one alphabet.) *BIP* covers only American published books. (Skip *BIP* and *CBI* if you have access to *NUC*.)

A shortcut that combines all the steps above is to ask a librarian to check OCLC, the library's on-line computer catalog. Don't forget to ask how far back OCLC goes. At this writing, it is complete only for approximately the last 10 years and uneven for books published before then. Until a program is under way to include all older books, you will still have to rely on printed sources to identify most of them. In situations where your subject's published books are all in the very recent past, OCLC may be all you need to check.

In the case of Truman Capote, the sources mentioned above cover his published books. *CBI* and *NUC* include editions published abroad.

Once you've compiled a list of books, you may want to borrow some through interlibrary loan. To help you decide what to borrow, try reading some book reviews. Reviews not only summarize the books but also give insight as to public reaction to them.

Has your subject written any articles? Truman Capote, for example, authored more than fiction. By checking periodical indexes (see Chapter 10), you may also find opinion pieces or autobiographical articles.

Q. I'd like to get a list of all articles, books, pamphlets, etc., written by Dr. Ivan Lindahl. He has been working in the Department of Animal Husbandry in Beltsville, Md. I think he's a geneticist and he could be a government employee.

A. Ivan Lindahl, a government researcher employed by the Agriculture Research Center in Beltsville, Md., appears in the current *Who's Who in the East*. He's a biochemist and animal nutritionist.

His numerous articles, which have been published in *Journal of Animal Science*, *Applied Microbiology*, and other technical journals, can be traced through *Bibliography of Agriculture*, published by the government. It's in large libraries with government publications sections or in a science library. Also try *Zoological Abstracts* and other related indexes and abstracts.

I know of no systematic and comprehensive way to find *everything* a person has written except this method—unless someone has compiled the information in a published bibliography.

If your subject is famous, don't forget to check for a bibliography on him. That would save you most of the work involved in the steps above. (More on bibliographies below.)

BOOKS AND ARTICLES *ABOUT* THE PERSON

Not only what a person writes, but also what others write *about* him is a source of biographical information. In addition to gaining valuable insights that other opinions offer, be prepared to sort the wheat from the chaff, the believable from the doubtful, and the subjective from the objective.

Some of the steps described earlier will draw out writings about the person as well as by him. Other sources to check for biographical and autobiographical information include the following:

- *Biography Index* (page 162) and other periodical indexes.
- *Biographical Books, 1876-1949 and 1950-80.* (2 vols. R.R. Bowker Co.) A two-volume compilation of American books published between 1876 and 1980 about people in all fields.
- *Subject Guide to Books in Print.* 1957-date.
- *Library of Congress Dictionary Catalog: Subjects* (1950-date). An alphabetical-by-subject list of all books cataloged by the Library of Congress since 1950. Use five-year cumulations, if your library has them, so you don't have to search each yearly volume.
- Bibliographies.

Biography Index covers many (but not all) scholarly and popular magazines. For example, *BI* does not index many literary magazines; yet these sources would be most appropriate to check for further information on someone like Truman Capote.

Therefore, you might check another periodical index. The 1975-1976 edition of *Abstracts of English Studies* (page 161) cites an article from a periodical called *Thought* (Winter, 1972, pages 569-86) in which the writer unfavorably compares Capote's *In Cold Blood*, written in 1966, with Theodore Dreiser's *An American Tragedy*. Another reference to Capote in this abstract is slight, but it could be significant in your research. It refers to an article on Vladimir Nabokov that mentions that he is an admirer of Capote. (Other scholarly indexes may also be helpful in your Capote search.)

Q. Where can I find information about sharpshooter Annie Oakley? I've only found one adult book about her by Walter Havighurst. The other books I've found are for children.

A. Articles about Oakley have been written in history magazines which can be traced through indexes that cover them. This search would be done best in an academic library, provided it allows public use of its collections without a card. There's an article on her in a 1966 issue of the *North Carolina Historical Review*, for example, which I found through an index to American history periodicals called *Writings on American History*.

Articles, especially those in scholarly magazines, may give you leads to other information sources—not only in the readings listed in their bibliographies, but also through important references they may make to the location of hard-to-find original materials such as personal papers, notebooks, and such.

If your subject lived long ago, other biographical articles may appear in low-circulation or specialty magazines published before *BI* began in 1946. Old issues of *Reader's Guide* may lead you to popular magazine articles written about newsworthy people at the time of an event such as the Lindbergh kidnapping or the death of Rudolph Valentino.

A single source like *Biographical Books* is the quickest to check. It's published by the same company that issues *SGBIP*. Since it draws from the same data base of information, it duplicates most of the books in *SGBIP* as well as the other sources.

Q. Please advise where I can find a biography of the life and film career of Richard Crenna.

A. Many celebrities have not yet had biographies written about them nor have they written their autobiographies. (For some, these things may never happen.)

Crenna is one of those celebrities on whom no biography yet exists. No articles on him appear in the magazines covered by *Biography Index*. A few (concerning his directing credits) appear in cinema journals in 1977 and 1981 which I traced through *Film Index*. His acting credits are listed in several standard film reference books such as *Motion Picture Almanac*. Also check the Library of the Academy of Motion Picture Arts and Sciences in Beverly Hills (8949 Wilshire Blvd.), which keeps more film- and celebrity-related material than any other library, much of it not in book form or previously published.

What about biographies/autobiographies for Truman Capote? It may be surprising to find through searching *Biographical Books* and *SGBIP* that biographies and autobiographies of Capote are scarce. Capote's aunt, Marie Rudisill, coauthored with James Simmons one book about Capote's younger years (*Truman Capote*, Morrow, 1983.) Research through magazine and newspaper articles might reveal Capote's reactions to his aunt's biography.

LOCAL OR REGIONAL SOURCES

Is your person local? If so, check issues of your hometown newspaper through its index. If the person was an important figure in city history, the local historical society or other local history collections may also have relevant files—including clippings from newspapers of the day. If he still has relatives living nearby, local collections may also contain a cache of family papers. If he is a native or former resident of your city, the library may have started a file of information on him and his activities.

If the person came from or later went to another city, write to the library and/or historical societies there. I recall one case where a researcher wanted to verify certain information about his great-grandfather who reputedly was a civil engineer on several important projects including the Erie Canal. The researcher wanted to know whether personnel records were kept for such construction projects and if so, where he might find them. Since local libraries and historical societies keep the most detailed information about their own areas, I suggested he start with research organizations there. In this case, Lee Ash's *Subject Collections* specifically mentions a collection of material under the heading ERIE CANAL in the Buffalo and Erie County Historical Society in Buffalo. I suggested that he contact them directly. (The addresses of libraries and historical societies are available in the directories mentioned in Chapter 2.)

PEOPLE IN THE NEWS

Depending on a person's repute, large newspapers may carry articles about him, and several sources can lead you to them.

■ Indexes to large city newspapers.

■*NewsBank, Inc.*

You might guess that Truman Capote would likely have been mentioned in *The New York Times* over the years. The *Name Index to The New York Times, 1851-1974* does, in fact, show approximately two dozen listings. (They appear in two separate entries: T. Capote and Truman Capote.) Consulting the *Name Index to the New York Times* is a must before checking for individual names in *The New York Times Index*. It makes names easier to find since many are submerged in the regular index under other headings such as OBITUARIES, and they might easily be missed. In other cases, people may be mentioned in scattered editions and the information is hard to find without a time-consuming search through individual annual indexes. The *Name Index* pulls all diverse entries together so you avoid the frustrations of a hunt-and-peck effort.

Since, however, the *Name Index* covers the *Times* from its inception in 1851 to 1974, you'll encounter references to different people who share the same name; or, as in the Capote example above, two separate entries for the same person (in this case, one entry using an initial and the other a full name). In such cases, you may have to check the *Times Index* to see who's who. (The *Times Index* includes a summary of most stories and can help you avoid going to the newspaper on microfilm unless you choose to do that.) In cases where there are too many names to check in the *Name Index* (often the case with a common name), it may be easier to check other reference sources to confirm some vital statistics about the person such as the date of his birth (and perhaps death).

Q. The father of former actress Grace Kelly died years ago and left a cleverly written will. At the time, the wire services picked it up, and it received wide publicity. I would like to read that will. Can you help?

A. You can't imagine how many John Kellys there are. The *Name Index to the The New York Times* lists dozens. Through magazine articles, I discovered that Princess Grace's father was John Brendan Kelly, Sr., 1890-1960. Although he appears as John B. Kelly in the *Name Index,* I was able to match the death dates to confirm the appropriate entries.

The June 29, 1960 issue (p.35) of *The New York Times* ran excerpts of the 12-page document which shunned legal language. One of the homespun directives was "Give my son 'Kell' all my personal belongings . . . except the ties, shirts, sweaters and socks as it seems unnecessary to give him something of which he has already taken possession." Consult the article for more.

A rich source for checking articles on people currently making the news in a variety of newspapers around the country (except *The New York Times)* is *NewsBank, Inc.,* described in Chapter 11.

Let's say you want to find out what San Francisco's first woman mayor, Dianne Feinstein, did during the first year she took office in 1979. Should you rummage through back issues of *The San Francisco Chronicle?* Even if you could get them, it wouldn't be the most practical or efficient approach. Of course, you could write to the mayor's office or the San Francisco Public Library. You could also try *NewsBank.*

The San Francisco Chronicle is one of the newspapers covered by *NewsBank.* Feinstein's name is listed in *NewsBank's* name index which leads to articles in the *Chronicle* specifically about her. Since *NewsBank* reproduces the newspaper article in full, you can read them without checking any other source.

OBITUARY INDEXES FOR PROMINENT PEOPLE

If the person you're researching was either famous or infamous in life, chances are he'll earn a write-up in death. If so, check these sources:

■ *The Annual Obituary.* 1980-date.

■ *Obituaries From The* [London] *Times.* 3 vols. 1951-75. Newspaper Archive Developments, Ltd.

■ *Obituary Index to The New York Times.* 2 vols. 1858-1978. New York Times Co.

Sometimes biographical information in BDs and articles is skimpy. But both *The New York Times* and *London Times* obituaries are often long and brimming with biographical information. In one search of a variety of art resources, I was unable to find information on a sculptor named Paul Herzel. The only thing I could uncover was his obituary which ran in *The New York Times.* It was accompanied by a lengthy article.

Also check *Annual Obituaries* (St. Martin's Press, 1980-date). It's a biographical dictionary that recaps a person's life, a sort of "who was who" of famous people who have died since 1980.

ORIGINAL (PRIMARY) MATERIAL

Though you can write a definitive biography from published books and articles, you may decide that something is missing. If your secondary sources repeat errors or are too subjective, you may need primary sources to inject memories and other facts that haven't yet appeared in print (though these, too, may have biases and subjective slants).

But the needed primary sources—diaries, notebooks, and correspondence—may still be in private hands, and the only way to find them is to make inquiries about their existence. Also, keep your eyes open for clues in print. Leads pop up in books and articles. Many researchers place ads in literary or book review magazines such as *The New York Times Book Review* in hopes of drawing out people who own caches of personal material. Though much private material is still just that, many personal papers have been donated to libraries and historical societies. These are recorded in certain reference books.

1. *Archives of American Art: A Directory of Resources.* R.R. Bowker Co. 1972.

Since 1970, the archives has been a bureau of the Smithsonian Institution. Its goal is to gather, preserve, and make available the papers of over 550 painters, sculptors, art dealers, critics, collectors, and curators. Everything in the archives is briefly annotated in this directory, and since it has all been duplicated on microfilm, anything can be borrowed via interlibrary loan.

2. *The National Union Catalog of Manuscript Collections.* Library of Congress. 1959-date. Annual.

This directory lists the photographs, diaries, account books and receipts, genealogies, correspondence, and other personal papers acquired by this country's several hundred archives, historical societies, and special collections. The people covered are known nationally or locally: governors, legislators, inventors, farmers, surgeons, land owners, war correspondents and journalists, authors, lumber merchants, playwrights, actors, soldiers, and others, representing all walks of life. This catalog also refers to the location of the papers of organizations, companies, and other groups such as symphony orchestras and churches.

A listing in this resource depends on the owning organization contacting the Library of Congress so the information can be included. While this is a very comprehensive source, as with other reference tools there are still omissions.

Q. In reading Martha Washington's biography, I learned that a frequent visitor in the Washington home was a Burwell Bassett. It was of interest to me in making my genealogical chart, and I suspect Burwell was given his mother's maiden name. Can you offer help regarding her ancestors, or refer me to a source so I can confirm a possible link to my family tree?

A. Bassett, a Virginia state legislator for 40 years, was born in Virginia in 1764 and died in 1841. He was married to Martha Washington's sister, Anna Dandridge.

According to the *National Union Catalog of Manuscript Collections*, Bassett's family papers are in two libraries. The Library of Congress, Manuscript Division (Washington, DC 20540) holds 2,000 items. Other family papers and a family genealogy are in the possession of the Virginia Historical Society, 428 North Blvd., Richmond, VA 23221.

---

3. *Subject Collections: A Guide to Special Book Collections and Subject Emphases as Reported by Universities, Colleges, Public and Special Libraries and Museums in the U.S. and Canada,* by Lee Ash. R.R. Bowker Co. Published every 5-7 years.

Entries are alphabetical by subject, and many mention a printed catalog for these collections that can be checked further. (Consult your library's catalog or borrow the catalog through interlibrary loan.)

Q. During World War II my uncle served aboard a merchant marine ship, the *W.C. O'Connors,* in the Great Lakes. The ship had a steam reciprocating machine shop aboard and was built to repair PT boats. The port of embarkation was Seattle. Is the ship in a museum now? Where can we find information about it?

A. There are many ship registers in print, but they do not mention a ship's disposition after it was decommissioned. Check with the library at the U.S. Merchant Marine Academy, Great Neck, NY 11024. According to Ash's *Subject Collections,* they own more than 85,000 books and special materials on the merchant marine.

By the way, *Subject Collections* also gives you a lead for your Truman Capote search. The entry shows that some of his personal manuscripts and papers are in the Library of Congress.

4. *Where Are Their Papers: A Union List Locating the Papers of 42 Contemporary American Poets and Writers,* compiled by Joanne Akeroyd. University of Connecticut Library. 1976.

This book locates the manuscripts and correspondence (as little as one postcard may be mentioned) in up to 15 libraries for each of 42 minor and avant-garde writers of the Beat era since World War II. Some of the writers included are Denise Levertov, Allen Ginsberg, Lawrence Ferlinghetti, William Burroughs, and Gary Snyder. (Where holdings are sparse, a library may be willing to photocopy the materials.)

5. *Women's History Sources: A Guide to Archives and Manuscript Collections in the U.S.* 2 volumes. R.R. Bowker Co. 1979.

The compilers of this huge resource have analyzed hundreds of published and unpublished guides to archives and created a single index of women's history sources. The index also includes references to men (Samuel Hale), societies (Halfhill Club), book titles (*Half a Century*), and family names (Hall Family), among other things, as long as there's some connection with women's studies. A typical entry looks like this:

> Goltra, Elizabeth Julia.
>> Papers. 1853. 21 pp.
>> U. of Oregon library, Special Collections.
>>> Journal describing a journey across the plains from Mississippi to Oregon. See Martin Schmitt, *Catalogue of Manuscripts in the University of Oregon Library*, (Eugene, OR: University of Oregon Press. 1971).

This resource also has a geographical index. You can use it to check the libraries and archives in your area to see what they own. If I wanted to get some idea of original resources on women's studies in San Diego, I'd check all listings under the heading SAN DIEGO.

There are, of course, other, more exotic directories of manuscripts and original material: *The French and British in the Old Northwest: A Bibliographical Guide to Archive and Manuscript Sources* and the *Census of Medieval and Renaissance Manuscripts in the United States and Canada*, for example. These can be found in large libraries. (See Chapter 18 on Original Research.)

A PERSON'S AFFILIATIONS

Writing to an organization or company with which a person is or was once affiliated often uncovers biographical information. I recall one researcher who was looking for background on Josephus Collett, one of the original incorporators and stockholders in a company that built the world-famous Hotel Del Coronado near San Diego about a century ago. He found almost nothing on Collett locally. Material in the San Diego Historical Society did mention, however, that Collett cofounded a college in Terre Haute, Indiana. When contacted, the college sent a great deal of biographical information, much more than the researcher had found in San Diego.

Contacting an organization that should know about a particular person, whether he's affiliated with the group or not, can likewise bring information. I remember being asked about an apparently well-known Israeli artist who unfortunately goes only by his first name. Several calls to art galleries finally found a dealer that knew of him. She provided a last name so a search could be conducted.

PERSONAL INTERVIEWS

Maybe your biographical needs go beyond the generally detached entries in biographical directories, the subjective thirdhand accounts in articles and books, and the mementoes collected in historical libraries. Where can you look for personal input? From other people. Insights from your subject's friends, relatives, enemies, supporters, associates, and acquaintances may offer subtleties about his personality and his work. And what about contacting the subject himself if he is currently available? Aside from the problems you'll encounter with biases, grudges, and other subjective viewpoints, people have an important place in biographical research.

Interviewing people is an art. Sometimes *getting* an interview is an art. When Bernice Kert decided to write *The Hemingway Women* (Norton, 1983), she did not call Hemingway's ex-wives and ask to drop by. She felt she could not impose on them, since she had few writing credits and, at one point, no book contract. In addition, some of the wives harbored bitter feelings about the past and not all of them were willing to relive it. Besides that, they were scattered all over the country.

The story of how Bernice won their confidence is a long one that spanned several months of patience and included the aid of an earlier Hemingway biographer who opened some doors. When she finally did get the coveted interviews, she confessed that they turned out to be less helpful than the colorful correspondence she found in library special collections that were open to the public. "People wrote letters in great detail, because at that time, they didn't use the telephone much. From the women, I got the authenticity of the person."

Indeed, conducting interviews is not an exact science, and you never know what or how much information they will yield.

Two fascinating books that will introduce you to the art of asking the right questions, as well as the problems involved, are *How to Talk with Practically Anybody about Practically Anything*, by Barbara Walters (Doubleday, 1983), and *The Craft of Interviewing*, by John Brady (Writer's Digest Books, 1976). Both are filled with anecdotes and real-life experiences not only about well-known people but also about categories of people including the bore, the handicapped, and the newly bereaved. If you are incurably shy, you might want to start with Alan Garner's delightful book, *Conversationally Speaking* (McGraw-Hill, 1981). Garner, who says he once talked only to parking meters, gives practical tips on starting and maintaining a conversation effortlessly in social situations.

BIOGRAPHICAL MATERIAL IN MICROFORM

Besides biographical resources in print and input from people themselves, there are microform sets that make available much historical information. Most of the microform sets described below reproduce material that also appears in print. However, using the microform sets can save you a great deal of sifting through individual issues of, say, *The Times*.

1. *American Autobiographies*, series 1, 1676-1850; series 2-5, 1851-1900. Northern Micrographics, Inc.

Of the 6,000 titles listed in Louis Kaplan's 1961 bibliography entitled *American Autobiographies* (University of Wisconsin Press), some 800 have been reproduced in full in this set. The autobiographies originally appeared in newspapers, manuscripts, periodicals, family histories, diaries, collected letters, and fictional autobiographies. They represent people in a variety of occupations, professions, trades, and ethnic groups from America's early history to 1900. The set also comes with a reel guide.

Sample titles from Kaplan are *The Life and Career of the Most Skillful and Noted Criminal of His Day*, by Charles Mortimer, published in 1873, and *AB-SA-RA-KA, Home of the Crows, Being the Experiences of an Officer's Wife on the Plains*, by Mrs. Margaret Carrington, published in 1869.

2. *City Directories of the United States*. Research Publications, Inc.

You may already be familiar with city directories. They're commercially compiled books which list the residents of a city or town much as the phone book does. City directories, however, provide more information. They list occupations and spouses' first names. They include a separate street address section in which all streets are arranged in alphabetical and numerical order with the name of the resident at each address. A third section is arranged in telephone number order, which helps in identifying a residence or business by a particular telephone number. Libraries usually keep city directories for their own community and maybe some recent directories for major cities.

The city directories in this microform set cover dozens of American cities for more than 100 years; the directories themselves are now scarce. Segment One of the collection covers city directories published as early as 1665 and going through to 1860. Segment Two covers those published between 1861 and 1881. Segment Three covers selected city directories from 1881 to 1901. (These are hand-gathered and -written lists with giant gaps of decades in the early segments. Better coverage is more common in the later years toward 1860.)

The advertisements in early city directories such as these are useful for determining prices of the day, methods of transportation, and dress—much like early newspapers, magazines, subject and reference books, and encyclopedias. The names listed are mainly to confirm someone's residence or business in a certain year.

The printed guide for this microform set is called *Bibliography of American Directories through 1860*, by Dorothea N. Spear, published by the American Antiquarian Society in 1961 and reprinted by Greenwood Press in 1978.

3. *Genealogy and Local History*. Microfilming Corp. of America. Part 1-3.

The broad scope of material in this set makes it a fairly complete genealogy library. Its comprehensiveness means you can do much of your genealogical research in one place. It consists of thousands of American family genealogies, regional histories, primary material such as records kept in the different states, and genealogy magazines. A printed guide comes with the collection. It's called *Genealogy and Local History: A Guide to the Microform Collection* (Microfilming Corporation of America, 1980).

4. *Great American Writers One and Two as Reported in The New York Times*. Microfilming Corp. of America. 1980.

This resource is a combination of articles, editorials, letters, news stories, obituaries, and other items which have run in *The New York Times* covering 81 famous poets, novelists, humorists, and philosophers, such as Sherwood Anderson, Louis Auchincloss, James Baldwin, Willa Cather, John Cheever, Sinclair Lewis, Edgar Allan Poe, Katherine Anne Porter, and Walt Whitman. (Truman Capote is also included.)

A printed guide, *Great American Writers as Reported in The New York Times: Program Guide*, published by Microfilming Corp. of America in 1980, is available.

Other microform sets of material reproduced from *The New York Times* have also been issued: *Great Black Americans as Reported in The New York Times* and *Great Personalities One and Two as Reported in The New York Times*. Each set groups people by category: politics, religion, sports and entertainment, literature, journalism and the arts, science, medicine and technology, and business.

5. *The New York Times Oral History Program*. Microfilming Corp. of America.

These oral memoirs, originally taped, are now also in microform. The collection consists of more than two dozen separate subsets covering people in all fields from religion to the arts. For example, the *American Film Institute Seminars and Dialogues* collection consists of the transcripts of weekly seminars conducted from 1967 through 1976 on every aspect of the film industry. Participants were Robert Altman, Lucille Ball, Bernardo Bertolucci, Peter Bogdanovich, Michael Caine, John Frankenheimer, Henry Fonda, Howard Hawks, Edith Head, Ernest Laszlo, François Truffaut, and hundreds of others. While these dialogues don't give direct biographical data, they do furnish insights on the participants' attitudes toward their profession.

The *Sangamon State University Oral History Collection* which is part of this set includes memoirs of individuals involved in coal mining, the Italian-American experience, and mental health care to name a few. For example, in one segment, miners, union members, and officials discuss coal mining and John L. Lewis; in another discussion, different ethnic groups recall their experiences and feelings as new immigrants. In still another, a local banker recalls his career and association with Sinclair Lewis.

Collections are quite diverse. Consult the various printed guides that accompany them for specific coverage. The overall printed guide is *The New York Times Oral History Program: Oral History Guide* published by Microfilming Corp. of America.

Biographical research is an intriguing process. We are naturally curious about our neighbors. It's important to remember, however, that whether you're researching a contemporary celebrity or an average citizen who lived 100 years ago, you are dealing with contradictions and people's perceptions of others. Using the biographical resources described in this chapter can become something of a scientific process, but interpreting the information you find is still an art.

CHAPTER SUMMARY

I. Biographical research may be a one-step or multistep process depending on the kind of information you need about a person. The important thing to remember about research into people's lives is that it may be more subjective, more complex, and more contradictory than almost any other kind of research. (page 271)

II. Biography master indexes help penetrate the hundreds of biographical directories in print. A list of several is included here. (page 274)

III. Books and articles are good sources of information about people.
   A. Writings *by* your subject can add to his profile. Several finding tools exist to show you what your subject has written. (page 277)
   B. Writings *about* your subject can be identified through tools such as *Biography Index*, other periodical indexes, and *Subject Guide to Books in Print*. (page 279)

IV. If the person you are researching is a famous personality, you have several options for finding information about him.
   A. Check local or regional sources like historical societies, libraries, and special collections. (page 280)
   B. Check *The New York Times* or any of the 200 newspapers covered by *NewsBank* since 1970. (page 281)
   C. Much biographical information is contained in obituaries for famous or infamous people. *The New York Times* and *The London Times* often carry lengthy obituaries for well-known people. (page 282)
   D. A subject's personal papers—diaries, notes, correspondence—often shed additional light on his feelings, dreams, and ideas. Some well-known people have donated a significant amount of personal material and letters to historical

societies and special libraries. (page 283)

V. Sometimes you have to go beyond printed sources to get the information you need.

    A. You can learn much about a person through the various organizational affiliations he keeps. (page 285)

    B. Personal interviews with the subject himself, his friends, enemies, and associates may also be revealing. (page 286)

VI. Much biographical information has been reproduced in microform: clippings from *The New York Times*, reproductions of early diaries and autobiographies, genealogical books and magazines, and oral histories. The techniques for retrieving microform material (described in Chapter 14) should help you find much of it. (page 286)

16

Anywhere, U.S.A.:
LOOKING FOR ADDRESSES

Smart is better than lucky.
—Titanic Thompson, hustler,
in *Fast Company* by Jon Bradshaw, 1975

As I mentioned in an earlier chapter, the question, "Where do I write for . . .?" is heard regularly by reference librarians. In fact, from my own experience, I would say that looking for addresses is the single most active use made of a public library's reference collection. People want to contact film stars, pop singers, scientists, manufacturers, banks, colleges, politicians, artists, and long-lost high school classmates. Still, many researchers use only a fraction of the finding tools at their disposal.

You might think that finding an address should be very simple. What could be more logical? People and groups have to be *somewhere*, right? The search becomes more challenging, however, when they change their names, move several times, leave a deliberately checkered trail, leave the country, or die. Nevertheless, it's reasonable to believe there's a way to track someone—anyone—given enough time to do it and provided he wants to be found.

Let's examine the finding aids most useful in looking for addresses, and also identify some important detours to avoid. Knowing a handful of places to look puts you way ahead of the researcher who has no plan of attack.

No matter who or what you're tracking, directories exist for most categories of people and organizations. Many current biographical directories described in the last chapter give addresses in addition to biographical data on the people they cover. People who belong to nationwide trade or collectors' organizations—societies of engineers, high school science teachers, or button collectors, for example—often appear in the group's membership directory.

Addresses given in directories available to the public are usually (though not always) business addresses. Many organizations will not give out members' addresses but will forward mail for you. You can also send mail to someone in care of an affiliation: a publisher, a network, a university, etc. Long after Richard Nixon left office, one of my readers asked if I could find his address. Since he had just written a book, I suggested she write him in care of his publisher.

Q. How can I get the address of a movie star?
A. Many movie stars are listed in general biographical directories such as *Who's Who in America* and *Who's Who of American Women*. An agent's rather than a personal address is usually given for the celebrity. If you're reasonably sure he lives in Beverly Hills, you could try reaching him with just a city address. The Beverly Hills postmaster says that of an average of 1,000 celebrity letters received monthly without specific street addresses, 95 percent are delivered.

Celebrity directories are listed in the *Directory of Directories*, but many of these either don't give addresses, or they're used mostly by people in the industry to keep up with celebrities' daily or weekly movements. (They're also very expensive. Earl Blackwell's *Celebrity Bulletin* costs about $45 a month; subscribers are interviewed before being considered for the service.)

TELEPHONE BOOKS

Large libraries carry a selection of nationwide telephone books and often give information from them through their telephone reference service. They provide addresses, phone numbers, and services listed in the Yellow Pages.

It may seem obvious to mention telephone books as address sources, but they do have important features we often forget. For example, national businesses such as hotel chains and commercial airlines advertise in phone books from Birmingham, Alabama, to Albuquerque, New Mexico. The phone book often comes to the rescue in serving basic human needs. The White Pages of many big city phone books include key words that lead to specific listings. In a police or fire emergency, you may not have time to look up a listing; but if you should, you'd find entries under the words FIRE and POLICE. Hotlines and associations are also frequently entered under key words—DRUG ABUSE TREATMENT or DRUG COUNSELING, for example. Other specific headings such as CHILDREN'S INFORMATION NETWORK or CHILDREN'S HOSPITAL may also lead you to a useful source. In some cities, if you want to make a consumer complaint, you can find the address and phone number of the appropriate agency to contact by simply checking the White Pages under CONSUMER COMPLAINT.

A wealth of information is also submerged in Yellow Pages ads. Here, a firm will elaborate on its range of services and provide more information than an address and telephone number. Mortgage companies may have a display ad that lists the number and kinds of loans they offer; a music store ad may mention the availability of private lessons on selected musical instruments; a television store may specify in a quarter-page ad the brands it sells.

The telephone books of major cities are especially valuable. The Manhattan telephone book shows so many services and products that researchers soon learn to routinely check its Yellow Pages early in a search. Likewise, the Washington, DC, White Pages is a miniguide to government agencies and the headquarters of many national associations (often listed by an association's key word).

Telephone books have been standard research tools in large and medium-sized libraries for years. Now, many libraries are trading their paper telephone book collections for *Phonefiche* (Bell & Howell), a set of some 1,400 nationwide telephone books on microfiche, covering thousands of cities and towns. The value of *Phonefiche* will grow as telephone books, whose paper editions were previously discarded each year, accumulate. Researchers of the future will find it much easier to trace a person or company, because phone books for previous years will be easy to get on microfiche.

THE *ZIP CODE DIRECTORY*

A quick and easy source from which to get general addresses is the *Zip Code Directory (ZCD)*. The first page of each city entry lists the actual street addresses and zip codes for the major hotels, motels, apartment buildings, hospitals, office buildings, colleges and universities, and government buildings in that city.

Copies of the *ZCD* are easy to find in large libraries, post offices, and many business offices.

Q. Is there a directory listing hospital addresses? I'm primarily interested in several in Indiana. The telephone operator won't give me addresses.

A. Some libraries have phone books from cities nationwide, so you might be able to get some addresses by calling the library. Also, the *Directory of Directories* lists a number of hospital directories. The library should own at least one. If that doesn't work, try the *Zip Code Directory*. It's arranged alphabetically by state and then by major city within each state. On the first page of the city listings, you'll find addresses for hospitals and other city-wide buildings such as hotels and universities.

A SELECTION OF DIRECTORIES

A library's reference section usually consists of a large selection of directories that contain addresses. The *Directory of Directories (DOD)*, published since 1980 by Information Research Enterprises (see Chapter

9), is the easiest source to use for identifying over 5,000 directories covering dozens of topics from convention centers and toy manufacturers to radio stations. Each entry describes the directory's contents and approaches (alphabetical, geographical, etc.). It also gives price information and the publisher's address.

Q. I would like to contact the highest-ranking individual in the research and development departments of the major American automobile manufacturers and, if possible, the foreign auto manufacturers with offices in the United States.

A. The address and top officers of American automobile manufacturers are listed in any directory of corporations, many of which can be found through the *Directory of Directories*. One specific directory *DOD* mentions is *Industrial Research Laboratories of the United States*, which includes laboratories in America, as well as foreign branches of American laboratories. This gives more precise information. For example, under Ford Motor Company's listing, there are nine laboratories carrying out different types of research and development operations with officers' names and addresses listed.

The following is a brief, but diverse, selection from *DOD*. Here you'll run the gamut of directories in print. Each *DOD* entry tells you how the directory is arranged: alphabetically, geographically, by subject, SIC number, product, etc. Some directories are published particularly for members of an industry, profession, or even hobby; others are more broad-based and are bought for general reference use in libraries. Whatever their focus, they should provide you with addresses you need. If you want to see any directory your library does not own, don't forget ILL. Some library in the country may have even the most specialized directory but lend you last year's copy if the current edition is in their reference section. (The *International Cemetery Directory* [#11 below] appears in *OCLC*, the nationwide on-line catalog which tells which libraries own a copy. In any event, the Library of Congress stocks all publications in the country because of the copyright law, and LC's materials are available through ILL.)

Each entry includes a rundown of what's included in the directory—addresses, contact people, etc. In searching for a directory in your field of interest, check *DOD's* subject index.

1. *American Art Directory.* Jaques Cattel Press/R.R. Bowker Co. (Biennial) Lists 2,900 art museums and organizations; 1,500 art schools; corporations with art holdings of public viewing; art fellowships and scholarships; national, regional, and state open art exhibitions. The directory is arranged geographically with separate indexes by personal name and institution.

2. *American Bank Directory.* McFadden Business Publications. (Semiannual) Lists 14,000 banks nationwide, with major personnel. Arranged geographically.

3. *Apparel Trades Book.* Dun & Bradstreet, Inc. (Quarterly) Lists about 125,000 apparel retailers and wholesalers in the United States in a geographical arrangement. A separate *Apparel Trades Book* is also published for each state.

4. *Directory of Conventions.* Bill Communications, Inc. (Annual) Includes 18,000 meetings nationwide with contact addresses. Covers trade and professional conventions and meetings, hobby shows, etc., in a geographical, then date arrangement. The directory also includes an index to conventions by category (giftware, educational tools, etc.).

5. *Directory of Medical Specialists.* Marquis Who's Who, Inc. (Biennial) Includes brief biographies and addresses of physicians in over 20 areas of medical practice from allergy to urology. Arranged alphabetically by medical specialty, then geographically. Also includes a personal name index.

6. *Directory of Nuclear Reactors.* International Atomic Energy Agency, Vienna, Austria. (Irregularly published) Locates 80 power and research reactors throughout the world. Arranged by type of reactor.

7. *Funparks Directory.* Billboard Publications, Inc. (Annual) A geographical list of over 1,500 amusement parks, zoos, kiddie lands, theme parks, caves, state and national parks, and other tourist attractions.

8. *Guide to North American Bird Clubs.* Avian Publications, Inc. (Frequency not established) Identifies the location of several hundred bird clubs in the United States, Mexico, Central America, Puerto Rico, the Virgin Islands, West Indies, Bermuda, and Canada.

9. *Horseman's Catalog.* McGraw-Hill. (Frequency not established) Arranged by subject category, this directory lists addresses of equine vets; veterinarian colleges; racetracks; riding schools; breed associates; publishers of related magazines; firms, manufacturers, and organizations associated with horses.

10. *Hotel and Motel Redbook.* American Hotel Association Directory Corp. (Annual) Identifies 8,500 hotels, motels, resort hotels, and condominiums with rental programs in the United States, Canada, Mexico, and the Caribbean. Arranged geographically.

11. *International Cemetery Directory.* American Cemetery Association. (Irregularly published) Lists geographically more than 8,000 cemeteries and their addresses.

12. *MacRae's Blue Book.* 5 vols. MacRae's Blue Book, Inc. (Annual) Covers 60,000 manufacturers in the United States. Volume 1 lists companies

in alphabetical order; volumes 2-4 are arranged by product category. Volume 5 includes selected company catalogs.

13. *Marconi International Register.* Telegraphic Cable and Radio Registrations, Inc. (Annual) Offers the addresses of 45,000 worldwide firms arranged geographically and by product.

14. *Moody's Transportation Manual.* Moody's Investors Service, Inc. (Annual) Presents facts, figures, and addresses for over 1,000 railroads, airlines, steamship companies, electric railways, bus and truck lines, oil pipelines, bridge companies, and truck leasing companies. Each company is arranged by class of business, and the directory includes an alphabetical company index.

15. *National Directory of High School Coaches.* Athletic Publishing Co. (Annual) A geographical list of over 158,000 coaches in approximately 19,500 high schools nationwide.

16. *National Faculty Directory.* 2 vols. Gale Research Co. (Annual) Names 450,000 teaching faculty at 3,200 junior colleges, colleges, and universities in the United States, and institutions in Canada which teach in English. Arranged alphabetically by name with a geographical list of schools.

Q. Can you help me find the address of Danske Nivfabrik, makers of Lundtofte stainless steel flatware in Denmark?

A. In *Bottin International*, one of several international business directories listed in *Directory of Directories*, I find the following in the section for Denmark called KITCHEN UTENSILS AND HOUSEWARES—manufacturers and wholesalers: Lundtofte Stall A/S, Sandvikenvej 3, Nakskov 4900, Denmark.

---

17. *Patterson's American Education.* Educational Directories, Inc. (Annual) Lists 19,000 high schools; 11,000 junior high schools; 2,000 parochial high schools; and 9,000 colleges, universities, trade, technical, private, and prep schools in the United States. Arranged by category of school; includes an alphabetical index of schools.

18. *Rand McNally Campground and Trailer Park Guide.* Rand McNally & Co. (Annual) Provides addresses for, and describes the facilities of, 20,000 public and private camp and trailer parks in the United States, Canada, and Mexico. Arranged geographically

19. *Standard and Poor's Register of Corporations, Directors and Executives.* 3 vols. Standard & Poor's Corp. (Annual) Volume 1 lists 37,000 U.S. corporations with key personnel in alphabetical order by company. Volume 2 lists directors and executives alphabetically. Volume 3 contains a geo-

graphical arrangement and a classified-by-product arrangement by SIC [Standard Industrial Classification] number.

20. *Sunflower Directory.* Sunflower Directory. (Irregularly published) Identifies 250 companies, trade associations, and government agencies, and over 400 persons concerned with sunflower agriculture and products in the United States and Canada. Organizations are first arranged as government/nongovernment, then alphabetically. Also includes personal name, geographical, and specialty indexes.

21. *Thomas Grocery Register.* 3 vols. Thomas Publishing Co. (Annual) Lists 1,800 supermarket chains, 4,300 brokers, 4,200 wholesalers and distributors in grocery lines (frozen foods, international foods, etc.). Volume 1 arranges companies by geographical location; volume 2 lists companies by product and source; volume 3 contains a straight alphabetical list of companies.

22. *United States Directory of Meat Slaughtering Plants* Food Industries Directories. (Irregularly published) Lists 3,600 plants across the United States and Canada. Arranged geographically.

23. *World Aviation Directory.* Ziff-Davis Publishing Co. (Semiannual) Lists aviation, aerospace, and missile manufacturers, and companies that provide support services such as fuel companies, airports and heliports, airlines, airline caterers, air freight companies, government agencies, associations in aviation, etc. Arranged by category with alphabetical indexes by company, product, and personnel.

24. *World Cement Directory.* European Cement Assn., Paris, France. (Annual) A list of manufacturers of cement and cement products in 140 countries. Also includes institutions and associations concerned with information and research in the field. Arranged geographically.

25. *World Wide Chamber of Commerce Directory.* Johnson Publishing Co., Inc. (Annual) Locates chambers of commerce in 7,750 localities in the United States and 275 abroad; also lists foreign diplomatic offices in the United States, and American offices abroad. Arranged geographically.

WHEN AN ADDRESS ELUDES YOU

Even though directories listing addresses abound, there are still times when you'll have trouble nailing down someone's whereabouts. Here are some things to keep in mind, whatever your latest address challenge.

■ You won't find all addresses using a one-step approach. Sometimes you may have to rely on a circuitous route. For example, you may first have to read a newspaper or magazine article for a clue to someone's home base. I once tried to find the address of Red Adair, whose name came to national attention when he helped control an oil-well blowout and fire near Mexico in June 1979. I checked *NewsBank* for articles on him and discovered that he came from Houston. This led me to the Houston phone book where his address and phone number were listed.

■ Sometimes, finding an address becomes an imaginative challenge. Perhaps you want to locate a foreign firm or manufacturer. I've learned from experience that many large overseas companies have American branches. This hunch is easy to confirm by checking American rather than European directories.

■ Beware of old directories. Though most are useful for identifying a company's existence, be sure to update the address in a current phone book (even though the phone book, like any print resource, is also somewhat out of date). Or, you may want to call information and match addresses and phone numbers. Letters sent to businesses which have moved are often not forwarded for a variety of reasons (forwarding order expired, the business has failed, etc.). Don't take a chance on an outdated address; it can be a time-consuming and costly gamble. (See page 340 for another view of using old directories in research.)

■ Take a few minutes to check any directory's arrangement by flipping through the pages and skimming the table of contents and index. Is the directory arranged in alphabetical order? By subject or geographical categories? Does it include separate appendices or addenda for late entries? Many directories are not arranged in a single—and simple—way.

Though many phone books interfile into one alphabet the names from each city covered by that book, other phone books have separate sections for each community covered. I once called the library for the address of a particular leather shop in Sierra Vista, Arizona. The librarian didn't find it in the White Pages of the Cochise County phone book. Since I was certain it was there, she checked the Yellow Pages and found it. That told me each community covered by the White Pages of that phone book appeared in a separate section.

Be sure to verify the arrangement of the telephone book or directory you're using so you won't miss what's really there. (This is a common research trap like many of those mentioned in Chapter 4.)

■ Another potential snag with telephone books and some other directories is that they may list names, organizations, and businesses without addresses. (Small organizations and self-employed people as well as other individuals can instruct the phone company to omit this information in the directory.) I recall one woman's frustration in trying to find the address of the California Genealogical Society in San Francisco. When she checked the phone book, only a telephone number was listed. She had to take one more step: either call the society for its address, or look it up elsewhere. It did turn up in the *Directory of Historical Societies and Agencies in the United States and Canada*.

■ Whenever possible, select a directory offering a specific rather than a general focus in your search for addresses. In 1970, a publication was issued called the *International Yellow Pages*. It purported to offer worldwide coverage, yet it was the same size as the San Diego Yellow Pages. Specific directories—subject, product, or regional—are usually more complete than general or all-encompassing directories. Far more information on clothing manufacturers (and more of them), for example, appears in *Fairchild's Textile and Apparel Financial Directory* than in the *Thomas Register of American Manufacturers*.

■ No reference book includes *everyone* or *everything* no matter how big or wonderful it seems. One mistake some researchers make is consulting only one directory, then abandoning their search. The *Thomas Register of American Manufacturers*, for example, is so large a set of directories that it's easy to assume it includes every manufacturer in the country.

In truth, the *Thomas Register* is short on entries for many industries— as the example above demonstrates. There are dozens of clothing manufacturers in Los Angeles, but the *Thomas Register* mentions fewer for the entire state of California than the Los Angeles Yellow Pages lists for that city alone. An incomplete list is sometimes more misleading than the absence of the category altogether.

Similarly, there's not one "best" way to find an address, nor just *one* list that has the information. In many instances there are several possible approaches to locating an address. Because reference books which seem alike can really be very different in the amount and quality of information they provide, large libraries with healthy book budgets buy several directories that seem to do the same thing. They may overlap and/or duplicate some material, but each is a potential information-finding tool.

Q. I've been searching for the address of the Society of American Travel Writers. Can you find it for me?

A. The address is given in several sources. Both the *Encyclopedia of Associations*, which lists associations in all categories, and *Literary Market Place*, which lists only writers' and publishing-related associations, show the address as 1120 Connecticut Ave., Suite 940, Washington, DC 20036. Active membership is limited to those regularly engaged as salaried or freelance editors, writers, broadcasters, or photographers in the travel field.

■ Not every business or organization is listed somewhere. There are several possible reasons for this: A business may consist of one person operating from his home; a group may survive only a short time and then disband; a business or organization may operate through a post office box—these are traditionally hard to find in directories; the phone book doesn't list them unless they have a telephone. Directories overlook such groups for any of these reasons, unless there's a systematic, reliable way for a compiler to determine their existence. Often there is not.

Another reason an address may not appear in a directory is that the individual or group has either just recently been catapulted into fame, or they've just become operational. People or groups escalating to overnight national attention may be too new to be mentioned in directories. If you're trying to locate a short-lived and temporary group—a presidential or gubernatorial candidate's headquarters, for instance—you may discover that it hasn't been established yet (or it's just closed camp).

Through perseverance and creative thinking, you might come up with a link, perhaps a person connected with that organization or business. You could call a CB shop for the address of a local CB club, for example. Finding an address in cases like these can depend upon unorthodox side trips and how far you choose to pursue the hunt.

■ If you've reached a dead end using all the traditional directories, remember this: Addresses often pop up in unexpected places. A publication not known primarily for giving addresses may include them anyway. Or a magazine article on learning disorders or on growing exotic plants may list related associations or companies and their addresses in a sidebar. When a specific source for an address evades you, take the general approach: think of the broad category into which your business or organization falls. It often works.

Q. How can I contact paper-doll collectors?
A. The chapter on paper dolls in the Time-Life *Encyclopedia of Collectibles* gives three collector's magazines in which classified ads appear. One is *Midwest Paper Dolls and Toys Quarterly*, Box 131, Galesburg, KS 66740.

A NEW USE FOR OLD ADDRESSES

Earlier in the chapter I cautioned you about sending anything to an unverified address. Old directories are certainly not appropriate for correspondence, but in the right context, they can be valuable research tools.

Q. How do you find a missing person?
A. Start with known factors. Speak to anyone this person knew, worked with, or lived near—the realtor who sold his house, the president of his union at work, a fellow member of a social club. Talking with them can provide leads for continued checking. Old telephone books and city directories in libraries are other possible sources of leads.

Remember that the police cannot help in these matters unless a law has been broken. In such investigations, only law enforcement officials have legal access to names in computer files and information from certain agencies such as motor vehicle registrations and schools. Even then, according to the local police department, it has become harder for them to gain access since the passage of the Privacy Act in 1974.

A private investigator doesn't have any more access to records than a private citizen—but he usually has more expertise and tricks up his sleeve.

A final suggestion might be to hire a registered genealogist who is skilled in records searching (divorce, marriage, death). Names of genealogists can be solicited for any area in the United States from the Board for Certification of Genealogists, 1307 New Hampshire Ave., NW, Washington, DC 20036.

Many directories are published annually and have been around for decades. An old edition is a record fixed in time. It allows history to be reconstructed, and in this way it's a kind of original research. I recall one researcher who was trying to establish the year the Ponce de Leon Hotel in St. Augustine, Florida, ceased operating. Many hotels and motels in that area still use the Ponce de Leon name, and it became confusing to sort out who was who. The *Hotel and Motel Redbook*, published annually since 1886, allowed him to trace the hotel's existence to its last listing in 1968.

Without delving into the past (and that includes pursuing old addresses), it's often difficult to pick up the threads of the present. People and businesses move, change names, or do both—and they sometimes do this more than once. It may be difficult to trace them without starting from the beginning.

The starting date of any continuously published directory or magazine can be determined by checking a set of reference books called *Union List of Serials* and its recent volumes called *New Serial Titles*. A library's online computer catalog can also provide this information in the case of a recent serial.

Since libraries usually keep only the most current volume of a directory in their reference department, old reference books can be checked out or copies borrowed through interlibrary loan.

Carefully check your local libraries. The old editions you need may be there; but because of overcrowding, excess volumes are often relegated to the basement for storage. Some complete runs of reference books presently coming out in microform may be kept in yet another section of the library.

ADDRESS SOURCES IN MICROFORM

Phonefiche is, of course, the most prominent address-finding tool currently in microform. But there are also reference books in microform which might prove useful. Granted, entire reference book runs are not rushing into microform as quickly as other categories of material, such as magazines and books, but the list is growing. Old and new business address sources in microform have been included throughout this book.

Two business-related sources not mentioned in other chapters are listed below.

1. *Colt Microfiche Library of the 50 State Industrial Directories.* Colt Microfiche Corporation. Annual. This set is a compilation of the major industrial directories published for each state. As a collection, it lists almost twice the number of manufacturers as found in the *Thomas Register of American Manufacturers.* Each printed directory is also sold individually. But this microfiche set offers all the state's directories at the cost of just a few individual subscriptions, and it includes single directories that many libraries might not buy because of the cost.

2. *Dun's Account Identification Service.* Dun & Bradstreet, Inc. Annual. *DAIS* lists more than four million businesses, many of which are too small to appear in many of the commonly used business directories. There is no single print counterpart to *DAIS.* It assembles company names and addresses that appear in many different sources.

Perhaps the solution to all our address questions will be an all-in-one nationwide telephone book accessible through our home information centers. The idea isn't so farfetched. An on-line Yellow Pages is already operating.

―――――――――――― *CHAPTER SUMMARY* ――――――――――――

I. Looking for addresses is a common research task.
   A. Most current biographical directories provide an individual's address, as well as other information about him. (page 291)
   B. Telephone books, especially those for large cities, offer many approaches for finding goods and services through both the Yellow and White Pages. (page 292)
   C. The *Zip Code Directory* includes street addresses of universities, military installations, hospitals, hotels, motels, government buildings, and apartment buildings in major cities. (page 293)
   D. *Directory of Directories* identifies a wide selection of reference sources that list names and addresses of organizations in almost any field. (page 293)
II. Even with a host of directories to search, some addresses may elude you. Here are things to remember in such a case:
   A. You may have to take more than one step to find an address. (page 297)
   B. Don't assume an old directory has current addresses. (page 297)

C.   Check any directory's physical arrangement so you don't miss what's really included. (page 298)

D.   Whenever possible, select a directory offering a specific, rather than a general focus. (page 298)

E.   No directory includes everything or everyone. Check more than one appropriate directory. (page 299)

F.   Some individuals or groups aren't listed anywhere. They may be too new, marginal, short-lived, or temporary. (page 299)

G.   If you've reached a dead-end, try unexpected sources such as magazine articles. (page 300)

H.   Although old directories are not appropriate for current addresses, they may be useful in reconstructing events which could eventually lead you to the right address. To find out when certain directories started publication, check the *Union List of Serials, New Serial Titles,* and a library's catalog. (page 300)

III.   Address sources also exist in microform. *Phonefiche* is the most common. But many reference directories containing addresses are also coming out in microform. Sometimes these microform sets of directories have no single print counterpart. Other packages include far more directories than a library might ordinarily subscribe to were they in print form. (page 301)

Facts & Figures:
LOOKING FOR STATISTICS

There are three kinds of lies: lies, damned lies and statistics.
—Benjamin Disraeli,
Reader's Digest, February, 1949

Americans are bombarded and infatuated with statistics. Whether they cover the stock market, the arts, sports, finances, population trends, politics, health, or socio-economic matters, percentages talk and numbers matter. Important decisions are made on the basis of statistics.

Consider that the data from the federal census is used to determine the distribution of public funds in many arenas of American life. Or that cities can decide to build or repair roads on the basis of how many cars use them. Or that people buy securities based on a company's percentage of profit. Or that a firm determines the price of its product according to demand—the number of people who want it. Numbers quantify, verify, clarify, and even rectify situations all around us.

WHY STATISTICS?

Sooner or later in your research effort, you will need statistics. Maybe you'll use figures to add solid weight to an argument (the growth rate of professional football salaries over the last 25 years is . . .). Or you may add a statistic to your speech for dramatic impact (the ratio of men to women in Alaska is . . .). Perhaps you'll need some quantitative input to help describe a societal trend (the percentage of today's high school seniors attending college immediately after graduation as compared with the number in 1974 is. . .).[1]

You're not alone in your quest for numbers. A random check through a newspaper will reveal just how many articles depend on statistics to make their point. (These headlines appeared in *The San Diego Union*.)

"Prison Population Up 4 Percent." (In 1980 the prison population in-

---

[1]Be aware that if you're getting these figures from interviewees who quote statistics from memory, it's best to verify them in print sources before you use them.

creased by 4 percent from 1979, according to a 1981 issue of *Corrections* magazine.)

"Fewer Women Smoking." (The percentage of American women who smoked in 1980 dropped below 29 percent, the lowest level in 15 years, according to a study conducted by the National Center for Health Statistics.)

"Preview Surgery." (Of 129 patients scheduled for surgery in a study at the University of Rochester Medical Center, 25 percent showed reduced anxiety when surgery procedures were explained to them beforehand; this compared with 11 percent of the same number of patients who did not receive explanations.)

Whether you need them to settle a bet or to document your dissertation, finding statistics is as much a part of the research process as knowing how to use a periodical index.

USING STATISTICS

Equally important is the way you use numbers. Statistics can be powerful weapons. They can confuse, sensationalize, minimize, or overstate a case. The variables in how, when, why, where, and by whom statistics are generated suggest that the numbers themselves don't necessarily reflect the obvious.

You may be intrigued with the results of a survey, for example, but the survey could have been biased from the start. You could interview people in the street, and in turn, not properly represent people who stay home. If a person from an ethnic minority interviews people from the same minority, he might get different responses than would an interviewer who asked the same questions, but happened not to be a member of the same group.

How you use and interpret numbers often depends on your information needs. Volumes can be written on how wrong statistics can be and how wrongly they can be applied. Darrell Huff's book, *How to Lie with Statistics* (Norton, 1954), is as relevant today as it was years ago. You can use numbers to state something negatively or positively, as in "the glass is half empty" versus "the glass is half full"; or "more than three-fourths of all American farms have electricity" versus "one-fourth of all American farms do not have electricity." Are these statistics really the same?

Indeed, judgment enters into the use of statistics in research. Knowing where the numbers come from and how they are collected and interpreted gives you some clues as to the credence you can place in whatever stats you find. Locating them is easier if you have some idea where these numbers come from. Most statistics emanate from academic, industrial or private, and government research.

ACADEMIC RESEARCH

Academic or scholarly research covers not just the sciences but the humanities as well. Many scholarly studies look at the human or behavioral side of statistics: the degree of assertiveness in professional women, the sex habits of rural teens, the effect of TV viewing on violent behavior. Studies like these invariably set up laboratory models, study case histories over a predetermined period of time, or poll people via questionnaires. Numbers result, and the social scientists draw their conclusions from them.

Academic research is important. Scientists (astronomers, chemists, etc.) who are employed by universities may, in fact, spend as much time in research as they do in the classroom. Besides advancing knowledge, the positive results of research—a cure for warts or a revolutionary new heart treatment, for example—attract income, grants, and honors to the institution.

Academic research and the resulting statistics are published in a thesis or dissertation, as a scholarly journal article, or as a book instead of a statistical directory. Occasionally, studies end up as unpublished papers with a limited number of copies available. Sometimes they're read at such professional meetings as the annual conference of the American Psychological Association or the National Association of Social Workers. Papers which are eventually published may appear in conference proceedings, many of which are collected by large libraries.

INDUSTRY, CORPORATION, AND ORGANIZATION RESEARCH

Research sponsored by corporations, organizations, or industry groups usually results in hard data: the number of hospital beds in Kentucky, the number of Catholics in the United States, the percentage of increase in the use of nonprescription drugs in a decade. The data may be collected to provide public information about a particular industry and to enhance its image. It may also be self serving.

Most industry and organization statistics are eventually published in the group's magazine, newsletter, or directory.

Q. A friend maintains that most Americans can afford to buy a $10,000 treasury bill, but I say the average American has far less than this in savings. What is the average amount in an American savings account?

A. The annual *Savings and Loan Fact Book* includes a section on savings accounts statistics. It says that in 1976, there was $336 billion in 750,622 savings accounts with the average account containing $4,800. (Thirty-two percent are passbook accounts and 68 percent are certificates and special accounts taking advantage of higher interest rates.) According to an Associated Press article, the average American worker in 1976 made $13,847 but ended the year $500 in debt.

Books written by investment advisors suggest saving 5 to 10 percent of your gross annual income, which would mean $750 to $1,500 a year on a $15,000 income. Treasury bills can be purchased in minimum amounts of $5,000, but books on investment acknowledge that they are out of the reach of many people.

GOVERNMENT RESEARCH: FEDERAL, STATE, LOCAL

The federal government could not function without statistics. It could not apportion funds or determine the number of representatives allotted per state without some reference to numbers. As the nation's largest publisher fulfilling its appointed role, the various agencies, departments, and bureaus of the government issue countless statistical reports in their areas of concern.

State, county, and city governments likewise issue statistics. You can find figures on your state's rate of interracial adoption, as well as its number of archaeological sites, endangered species, and race horses. You can learn of the dollars spent on health care, the amount of state employee investment funds, and the revenues of a particular industry.

On the local level, government statistics can give you the number of historic buildings in the city or the amount of expenditures for public libraries. You may wish to see a study on noise abatement, residential parking needs, or crime. Such local government documents and reports contain numerous statistics. Like their federal counterparts, many regional and state documents are kept in large local libraries, usually in the documents department.

FINDING STATISTICS

There are countless titles of statistical directories in print—enough to fill a book. In the past few years, however, three new indexes have come along which do for the hundreds of statistical directories what bibliographical master indexes do for countless biographical directories. They index them jointly.

American Statistics Index (*ASI*), *Index to International Statistics* (*IIS*), and *Statistical Reference Index* (*SRI*) are published by Congressional Information Service, Inc. (CIS) in Washington, DC. Together, these sources index more than 3,000 statistical directories, and numerous selected articles and reports containing charts or tables. The publications indexed are issued by federal and state agencies, commercial publishers, and international intergovernmental organizations.

Despite the many statistical publications that exist, only a small portion of them are available in libraries. This fact underscores the importance of *ASI*, *SRI*, and *IIS* for researchers. The indexes themselves are in print format; the full text of all the publications and articles they index comes in separate microform collections.[2] All the indexes are issued monthly and cumulate into annual volumes.

1. *American Statistics Index (ASI)*. 1974-date. *ASI* is the key to federal and state government-published statistics whether they're buried in articles and reports or issued in statistical directories, such as *Activities of the U.S. Army Corp. of Engineers in Saudi Arabia*, *FBI Annual Report*, or *Ground Water Data for Michigan*.

2. *Index to International Statistics (IIS)*. 1983-date. *IIS* leads you to statistics from the publications of more than three-and-a-half dozen United Nations agencies and commissions and dozens of other international, intergovernmental organizations: the International Wheat Council, the International Monetary Fund, the World Bank Group, the European Community, the International Labor Organization, and many others. These groups issue such publications as *Main Economic Indicators*, *Yearbook of World Energy Statistics*, *Balance of Payments Statistics*, *World Employment Program Studies*, and *World Bank Atlas*.

3. *Statistical Reference Index (SRI)*. 1980-date. *SRI* covers statistical publications offered by commercial publishers (*Business Week*, issued by McGraw-Hill); associations (*Traffic Safety*, published by the National Safety Council); business or commercial organizations (*International Finance*, issued by the Chase Manhattan Bank); university research centers (*Employee Ownership*, offered by the Institute for Social Research at the University of Michigan); and some state agencies (*Texas Vital Statistics*, issued by the Texas Department of Health).

All three sources are arranged in similar fashion. Each comes with an index volume and a companion abstract volume. First, check the index volume by year under the subject you need. When you find an item you want to examine more closely, copy its item number (e.g. U4743-2.1) and check it by that number in the companion abstract volume. This will give you a summary of the article or chart and the title of the publication in which the information originally ran. You can then borrow the item in print or in microform from the library and read it in full. If your library only subscribes to the print indexes, borrow through interlibrary loan the ac-

[2]As with the many index/microform sets mentioned in Chapter 12, libraries may own the print indexes but not the microform sets. Identifying items to borrow through interlibrary loan, however, is facilitated by the indexes.

tual article or report the index identifies. (First check to see if the library owns it in hard copy.)

The sample entry below comes from the 1979 edition of *ASI*.
STRATEGIC ARMS LIMITATION TALKS (SALT)

SALT II basic provisions, limitations on U.S. and Soviet nuclear weapons and delivery systems, 1979-1985, 7008-13.

The abstract volume under item 7008-13 states:

Report summarizing the major provisions of the SALT II agreement to limit the number and type of nuclear weapons and delivery systems allowed the U.S. and Soviet Union and provides verifications of compliance measures.

The entry also gives the Sudocs call number of the 12-page Department of State report—S 1.71:311.

These rich index resources are easy to use once you're comfortable with their format. Toward that end, I submit the following observations which may help you use and understand them even further:

■ Despite the fact that the three print indexes and microfilm collections cover entirely different publications, the subjects they cover are similar. For example, the subjects below from *SRI* also appear in *ASI* and, in many cases, in *IIS* which covers them from an international perspective.

MATERNITY (see also birth defects, birthweight, family planning, fertility, fetal deaths, illegitimacy, teenage pregnancy)	MILITARY WEAPONS
	MINIMUM WAGE
	MISSILES AND ROCKETS
	MONEY SUPPLY
MEDICAL COSTS	MOONLIGHTING
MEDICAL EDUCATION	MOTION PICTURES
MEDICAL ETHICS	MOTOR VEHICLE INDUSTRY
MEDICARE	NATIONAL PARK SYSTEM
MENTAL RETARDATION	NEW ORLEANS, LA.
MILITARY CLUBS AND MESSES	NICARAGUA
MILITARY PENSION	

Each of the indexes contains many entries under cities, states, and countries. Following are three sample entries and the headings under which they occur in *SRI*, 1981. (Since the indexes provide multiple approaches, there are many subject terms to choose from that will lead to the statistics you need.)

DELAWARE

Traffic accidents and fatalities, by type of vehicle and circumstances, with traffic arrest data, 1979-80 and trends, annual rpt., S1435-1.

[This entry leads to a 61-page publication called *Annual and Statistical Analysis, Delaware State Police Traffic Section* issued by the Delaware Dept. of Public Safety.]

LITTLE ROCK, ARK.

Creditors collection practices for delinquent debts, and consumer views, 1978-79 survey, U4370-1.15.

[This entry leads to a 61-page report called *Costs and Benefits of Restrictions on Creditors' Remedies*. It's part of a series issued by the Credit Research Center of Purdue University.]

NEW YORK CITY

Abortion rates for United States, NYC and 11 foreign countries, 1972, article, A5160-1.205.

[This entry leads to a 7-page article in a bimonthly periodical called *Family Planning Perspectives* issued by the Alan Guttmacher Institute.]

■ *SRI* indexes articles containing statistics from many newsstand and trade magazines with which you may be familiar: *Advertising Age, Aviation Week and Space Technology, Black Enterprise, Broadcasting, Business Week, Forbes, Fortune, Iron Age, Library Journal, Oil & Gas Journal,* and *Publishers Weekly.* Therefore, if you want to relocate a *Publishers Weekly* survey that reported on the types of books people read during the last five years, *SRI* will help you find it.

■ Magazines that report the results of public opinion polls are covered at the end of this chapter, but *SRI*, too, indexes issues of the monthly *Gallup Report.*

■ Though *ASI* (governmental statistics sources) started publication in 1974, *SRI* (commercial statistics sources ⸱iarted in 1980, and *IIS* (international governmental statistics sources) s arted in 1983, statistics for earlier periods are often included in the charts and graphs. Such retrospective elements are specifically referred to in the abstract. For example, a report, *Supermarket Business,* issued by Fieldmark Media, appears in *SRI*, 1981. The abstract, however, says that the report contains three tables showing grocery store sales for single unit firms for 1972 and 1977.

ALTERNATIVES: TWO STATISTICAL INDEXES

What if *ASI, IIS,* and *SRI* are not available in your area, or they don't cover the time period you need? There are some smaller statistics indexes that many libraries own. They will help you find figures in the many popular statistical directories libraries carry.

1. *Encyclopedia of Business Information Sources.* Gale Research Co. 5th ed. 1983. (Issued every 3-5 years.)

Many of the individual statistical publications indexed by the three statistics indexes mentioned earlier are named in this directory of reference sources which covers dictionaries, handbooks, encyclopedias, etc. (See Chapter 8.) Entries are arranged by subject. Some sample headings and related statistics publications follow:

EXHIBITIONS [heading]
    STATISTICS SOURCES
        ANNUAL STATISTICAL REPORT. International Association of Fairs
        and Expositions, 1010 Dixie Highway, Chicago Heights, Illinois
        60411.
GOLD INDUSTRY
    STATISTICS SOURCES
        *ANNUAL REPORT OF THE SECRETARY OF THE TREASURY
        ON STATE FINANCES.* U.S. Treasury Department, U.S. Govern-
        ment Printing Office, Washington, D.C. 20402. Annual.
        MINERALS YEARBOOK. U.S. Bureau of Mines. Available from the
        U.S. Government Printing Office. Washington, DC. 20402. Four
        volumes. Annual.

2. *Statistics Sources (SS)*, edited by Paul Wasserman. (Gale Research
Co.). Issued every 5-7 years.

SS is a small index covering about 150 government and commercially
published statistics publications such as the UN- and UNESCO-issued
statistical abstracts; the *Statistical Abstract of the United States;* several publications of the Food and Agricultural Organization of the UN such as *Trade
Yearbook, Production Yearbook, Annual Fertilizer Review,* and *Animal Health
Yearbook;* and special issues of trade association and professional journals, among others. Most of the publications are issued annually or bian-
nually even though *SS* itself is not issued annually. (*SS* also often lists
more than one source for a statistic.)

Below are sample subjects with the names of the publications in which
the statistics can be found and their sponsoring agencies—as they appear
in *SS.*
    GROSS NATIONAL PRODUCT—HEALTH EXPENDITURES—
    PERCENTAGE OF GNP
        Social Security Bulletin. (Dept. of Health, Education and Welfare, Social
        Security Administration.)
    OBSTETRICAL SERVICES—CHARGES, ETC.
        *Consumer Price Indexes for Selected Items and Groups, Monthly and Annual
        Averages.* (Dept. of Labor, Bureau of Labor Statistics.)
    SPORTS
        The *National Survey of Fishing and Hunting* (Fish and Wildlife Service,
        Dept. of Interior) and the *World Almanac.*

Q. In the coming months I will need information on the construction industry; namely, how many board feet of lumber do we use in the United States annually?

A. By checking a reference book called *Statistics Sources*, under LUMBER AND
ALLIED PRODUCTS, I was referred to a pamphlet series called *Current Industrial Reports* issued by the Department of Commerce's Bureau of the Census. The specific
report entitled *Lumber Production and Mill Stocks* is usually 2-3 years behind, but
these figures may help: Production of lumber in the United States for 1975 was ap-

proximately 32.6 billion board feet, a decrease of 9 percent from 1974. In 1977, the output was 37.8 billion board feet, and in 1978, 38.2 billion board feet. The pamphlet also breaks down production by region and kind of wood (hardwood vs. softwood). The report is available in the government publications section of large libraries.

STATISTICAL YEARBOOKS

The statistics indexes already described refer you to major statistical yearbooks like the *United Nations Statistical Yearbook*, which consists solely of tables. The following is a list of this and other major statistical yearbooks with tips on how you might use them to gather recent and old data about various states and countries, especially if no statistical index is handy.

1. *European Historical Statistics, 1750-1975*, by B.R. Mitchell. 2nd rev. ed. Facts on File. 1980.

Most countries issue an official statistical yearbook. Data in *EHS* are compiled from the yearbooks of approximately two dozen countries covering dozens of subjects over a 225-year period. Sample topics on which data are reported are climate (e.g., mean temperature in January and July in major European cities); population (immigration figures); labor (rate of unemployment in various industries); agriculture (vineyard output); industry and trade (motor vehicle production); transportation (amount of freight traffic on the railways); finance (cost of living indexes); etc.

2. *Historical Abstracts of the U.S.: Colonial Times to 1970*. 2 volumes. U.S. Dept of Commerce, Bureau of the Census. 1975.

Sample charts give such statistics as total population by race, sex, and age (1900-1970); the number of immigrants who came to the United States by country (1820-1970); the size of the labor force by age and sex (1890-1970); the gross national product (1909-1970); the average annual earnings per full-time employee by industry (1900-1970)—and much more.

3. *Statistical Abstract of the United States*. U.S. Dept. of Commerce, Bureau of the Census. 1878-date. Annual.

Reports figures on a variety of subjects for an average of two decades. Included are statistics on population breakdown by age, race, and sex; national defense (the size of the military forces, pay rates, the number of people receiving veterans' benefits); energy (the number of nuclear power plants and their capacity); finance (characteristics of stock owners by sex, age, education, income, population of place of residence); recreation (the number of people who use national parks and public lands for sightseeing, riding off-road vehicles, hunting, fishing, camping, etc.).

4. *Statistical Yearbook.* UNESCO, Paris. 1963-date. Annual.

Reports statistics for more than 200 countries in the fields of education (percentage of repeaters by grade); science and technology (the number of scientists and engineers engaged by specific field); publishing (number of new books issued yearly); film (number of long films imported); cinema (number of theaters and seating capacity); broadcasting (number of radios and televisions per 1,000 people); and other cultural areas.

5. *Statistical Yearbook.* United Nations, Dept. of International Economic and Social Affairs, Statistical Office. 1948-date. Annual.

This publication covers statistics on agriculture (production figures on cocoa beans, milk, soybeans, and other products); mining and quarrying (gold production); manufacturing (production rates of tires, beer, cigarettes, wool yarn, etc.); construction (rate of home building); energy (consumption of gas, electricity, and water); health (number of hospitals and personnel); finance (the amount of gold reserves); etc., for over 125 countries. If you were researching an article, report, or book on food or cooking, you might want to know which country is the world's highest producer of soybeans. This volume could tell you. (It's the United States, followed by Brazil and then China.)

OTHER STATISTICS SOURCES

In addition to these specific statistical sources, there are several general references which you might check in your numbers search.

1. General almanacs.

Most of the charts in general almanacs derive from other sources. For example, a chart showing the apportionment of the budget dollar indicates that it originally came from the U.S. Office of Management and Budget. The chart, FEDERAL GRANTS TO STATES, names its source as Tax Foundation, Inc. Other charts and their sources included in recent general almanacs are these:

PER CAPITA PROPERTY TAX COLLECTIONS. (Bureau of the Census and the Tax Foundation, Inc.)

GOLD PRODUCTION. (U.S. Bureau of Mines)

COMPANIES WITH THE LARGEST NUMBER OF COMMON STOCK-HOLDERS. (New York Stock Exchange)

U.S. CORPORATION PROFITS. (U.S. Dept. of Commerce, Bureau of Economic Analysis)

MONEY DEPRECIATION: ANNUAL RATES. (Citibank)

ESTIMATED U.S. EDUCATION EXPENDITURES. (National Center for Education Statistics)

UFO. (Center for UFO Studies)

The drawback here comes in trying to track down the original publication which reported the statistics. Generally, only the issuing agency is given. It's best to check an index to statistics for data on a subject. You may also find the title of the specific publication the almanac chart mentions.

2. Individual statistical yearbooks for each country.

These yearbooks offer statistics similar to those found in UN-sponsored yearbooks, and much international data are available in those publications. The national statistical yearbooks, however, also offer some unique data. For example, the *Pakistan Statistical Yearbook* breaks down figures by region, while those reported in the UN yearbooks cover the country as a whole. Therefore, you may have to go to the official national publication if you need the size of the literate population by specific urban/rural area, or the prices of that country's agricultural products which are not all specified in the broader statistical yearbooks.

Some libraries carry the individual statistical yearbooks for major countries issued by their government's central statistical bureaus. These and other statistical publications can be identified through one of Joan Harvey's bibliographies: *Statistics/Europe, Statistics/Asia and Australia, Statistics/Africa,* and *Statistics/America (North, Central and South),* or through a library's catalog under the name of the country followed by the term STATISTICS.

The major statistical publications of approximately 75 Third World countries are well represented in a microfiche collection called *Current National Statistical Compendium.* With coverage beginning in the late 1970s, this set comes with a printed checklist and covers nations from Fiji to Botswana.

3. Individual statistical yearbooks for each state.

Large libraries own a selection of annual statistical directories for major and/or nearby states. *Florida Statistical Abstract* and *Statistical Abstract of Louisiana* are two such publications. Much of the information they contain, such as number of miles of highway, number of people with motor vehicle registrations, number of accidents or abortions, figures on school enrollment, etc., is also found in the *Statistical Abstract of the United States* (Item #3). However, like the national statistical yearbooks described above, the state yearbooks may include many more specific categories of information. These may cover the enrollment of colleges in the state, the amount of farm acreage devoted to tree fruit crops, or the breakdown and distribution of various ethnic groups by county.

4. Trade and professional association reports.

Many associations keep statistics about their services or products. Large groups issue their own statistical publications and many are covered in statistics indexes like *ASI* and *SRI.*

Contact the organizations directly for information about statistical reports they make public but may not publish. Association addresses appear in the *Encyclopedia of Associations* and *National Trade and Professional Associations of the United States and Canada.* (*EA* is easier to check since *NTPA* uses broad subject headings in its index.)

Q. I am writing a book on the psychological effects of parental pressure on children in organized recreation and sports such as Little League and dance classes. Publishers' responses to my manuscript are that it's an interesting topic and well written, but there's no market for it. I believe they're wrong, but I need statistics to back up my claim. Where can I find statistics that show the number of children who participate in these activities so I can prove that there is a large potential market for a book on this subject?

A. I've checked several indexes to statistics and don't find anything relevant. These figures may be available from organizations of teachers, coaches, or counselors. The *Encyclopedia of Associations* shows a National Council of Dance Teacher Organizations (107-43 106th St., Ozone Park, NY 11417) for example, which may issue statistics. Certain data from *EA* itself, are revealing. For example, the entry for a group called Little League Baseball (Box 3486, Williamsport, PA 17701) shows that it has been in existence for about half a century (founded in 1939). The group organizes 14,000 programs for children 6-18 in every state, and it has 2,500,000 members.

STATISTICS IN DISSERTATIONS

Dissertations offer an intensive, analytical look at a subject or a small segment of it. They are usually a culmination of several years' work during which a Ph.D. candidate conducted many tests, surveys, polls, etc. (some of which appeared as articles in scholarly journals). A dissertation offers his observations and results in a completed form—usually with many statistics to support his conclusions.

Dissertation titles are straightforward and specific. They sound more like the summary of the work rather than its title, e.g., "The Bearing of Certain Aspects of the Mother-Son Relationship Upon the Son's Tendency Toward Narcotics Addiction."

Many periodical indexes, such as *Psychological Abstracts* and *Abstracts for Social Workers*, mention dissertations in addition to articles. They are also listed in an index of their own—*Dissertation Abstracts International (DAI)*, published by University Microfilms International.

DAI is an annual list (1861-present) of dissertations written at approximately 500 participating American and foreign colleges and universities. To find a dissertation by subject, check the key-word index.[3]

There are approaches to a dissertation under every word in the title (except for small words such as pronouns, conjunctions, etc.). Below is a sample entry from *DAI* (1984):

---

[3]The cumulative index set covering 1861-1972 is entitled *Comprehensive Dissertation Index, 1861-1972*. It comes both in a hardcopy set and in microform. After 1972, you must check the indexes in each annual *DAI*. If your library owns them, use the five-year cumulative indexes.

WHEAT
> An econometric analysis of potential price variability in the world
> wheat market. (Economics, agricultural) Schwartz, Nancy Eileen.
> p.2839-A.

The page number (2839) of the volume marked Part A gives a brief summary of the dissertation plus an order number. (Part A covers humanities and social sciences; Part B covers sciences and engineering.)

You can buy most dissertations listed in either a print version or in microfiche. Libraries and individuals may buy them for about $20 each (slightly less for microfiche), regardless of dissertation length. Many academic libraries buy some, but the number published annually is far too great to permit large-scale purchase. If you've identified a dissertation you'd like to examine, look it up in the library's catalog. If your library doesn't own it, borrow it on interlibrary loan.

HIDDEN STATISTICS

Though the number of statistics-finding tools is adequate for most of your needs, don't expect to find all statistics—especially results of behavior or attitude studies—neatly arranged in charts and tables in statistical handbooks. In many cases, the figures are buried within the text of a book, report, document, or article and may not be covered by a statistical index at all. In such cases, you'll need a different approach to find them.

I once needed to know the percentage of affairs that resulted in the breakup of a marriage. Since no statistical index mentioned charts giving this kind of data, I checked a periodical index to scholarly magazines hoping to find an article on the subject. I found several under the topic INFIDELITY in *Social Sciences Index*. I scanned three pertinent articles and found the figure I needed.

Books often help also, particularly those written by specialists. By checking *Subject Guide to Books in Print* under ADULTERY and MARRIAGE, I discovered a few relevant titles. One by psychologist Herbert Strean was entitled *Infidelity*, in which he quoted statistics based on actual case histories.

Some reference books and directories, though not specifically statistics sources, often include charts and other numerical data. The *Yearbook of American and Canadian Churches*, for example, includes figures on the amount of the seasonal fluctuation in church attendance; the effects of inflation on church donations; the number of priests, deacons, brothers, and sisters in the United States, etc. The *Europa Yearbook*, arranged alphabetically by country, includes charts that give national figures for the amount of money in national bank reserves, cost of living indexes, money supply, number of telephones, amount of livestock, etc. The *Yearbook of Higher Education* has charts giving selected characteristics of first-year college students: statistics on students' average grades in high school, parents' education and income level, religion, political orientation, source of college financial support, etc.

Q. I want to gather information on police officers' salaries all over the country. Are such statistics available?

A. In a book called *Municipal Yearbook*, check the chapter called "Public Services: Police, Fire and Refuse Departments." It lists figures for salaries, size of departments, expenditures, and city contributions to retirement and insurance, among other data. Keep in mind that this is an annual publication, and salaries can change in midyear.

According to *Statistical Reference Index* (1981), another source of salary figures is published by the Fraternal Order of Police (G-3136 W. Pasadena Ave., Flint, MI 48504). The data you need appear in the FOPs annual publication, *Survey of Salaries and Working Conditions of the Police Departments in the U.S.* The 30-page report sells for $8.50, or you can borrow it through the library's interlibrary loan service. All material indexed by *SRI* is available in a corresponding microform collection.

PUBLIC OPINION POLLS

Running a close second to our fascination with other people's lives is our fascination with what they think. Opinion polls may not represent hard, undisputed figures, or the results of a longitudinal study, but they often influence our actions as much as if they did.

As you conduct your information search, you may find it useful to contrast people's beliefs and opinions with the "facts" in your research. Perhaps you want to know the number of people (in a representative sampling) who did not vote in the last presidential election and why not, or the number of people who believe credit cards promote overspending, or the number of people who believe in heaven and hell.

Though not all public opinion surveys are necessarily conducted with scientific precision, their results are usually computed according to any of several standard categories: sex, race, age, education and income level, religion, political party, city size, and region of the country. The results of the polls often run in newspapers and magazines, but the publications below preserve the studies permanently.

1. *Gallup International Public Opinion Polls, France: 1939, 1944-75.* 2 volumes. Greenwood Press. 1976. *Gallup International Public Opinion Polls, Great Britain: 1937-75.* 2 volumes. Greenwood Press. 1976.

These polls are arranged chronologically by date. An index provides a subject approach. Polls have been taken in France on attitudes toward priests, the perceived role of the Socialist Party, South America as a choice for emigration, and the most admired people. In Britain, questions have been asked concerning law enforcement as a career for your son, and the personal effects of petrol rations.

2. *The Gallup Poll: Public Opinion.* Scholarly Resources, Inc. 1935-date.

This set compiles into annual volumes all the public opinion polls published by the Gallup organization since it was founded in 1935. Polls are arranged chronologically by date, but you can find specific ones through the subject index. Some early topics cover opinions of Prohibition, America's drinking habits, the degree to which Americans supported England during World War II, the attitude toward women in politics, opposition to the 1938 Olympic Games, etc. Any project you have that is set during the 1930s might benefit from a definitive statement reflecting the country's attitude about "sending our boys to war"—and you won't have to wade through old newspapers and magazines to deduce it.

3. *The Gallup Report.* The Gallup Poll. 1965-date. Monthly.

Many issues of *GR* are devoted to a single topic such as Religion in America, 1982; but normally each issue features from two to ten different polls covering a wide range of subjects: nuclear disarmament, the president's economic package, legalizing marijuana, the death penalty, a constitutional amendment for or against abortion, support of prayer in the public schools, etc. The subject index helps you find polls on a particular topic. *GR* is also indexed by *Statistical Reference Index* (the index that covers commercially published statistics sources).

Q. I would like the latest poll showing the number of Americans who believe in God.

A. The *Gallup Report*, a magazine issued by the Gallup Poll organization, ran the findings of an extensive poll in their June/July 1982 issue. The answers were broken down by sex, race, education, geographical area, age, income, occupation, city size, marital status, etc., as well as average totals.

The poll covered such issues as the belief in the divinity of Christ (85 percent of the people questioned said they believed in this); the number who take personal comfort from religion (78 percent); the number who put their religious beliefs into practice (80 percent); the number who believe God loves them (89 percent); and those who say religion is the most important influence in their lives (69 percent).

Check the magazine for more specifics on this poll and later ones on the subject. *GR* should be in large libraries, or write the Gallup Organization, Box 628, Princeton, NJ 08540.

---

4. *Index to International Public Opinion,* prepared by Survey Research Consultants International, Inc. Greenwood Press. 1978-date.

This index covers by country a variety of international issues, such as: Do you oppose or support the separation of Quebec from the rest of Canada?; How many hours per day do you spend on leisure time? (asked of Czechs and Rumanians); Do you view yourself as politically left or right? (asked in 11 European countries). The publication includes a subject index.

ODDS 'N' ENDS

The following books pull together comparative and other quantitative data from a variety of sources. Though they are designed for popular reading, they're also reference books. Each was issued as a single volume rather than as part of an ongoing series. As these books get older, their historical value increases, because the information they contain continues to reflect the periods they cover.

1. *The Book of American Rankings: Social, Economic and Political Rankings*, edited by Clark Judge. Facts on File. 1979. 2d ed., 1984.

Arranged geographically, this book will tell you about America's habits and trends through such statistics as where in the country car pooling is highest, who uses mass transit, how much money is spent on media campaigning in presidential elections, how many people in the United States belong to a union, how many work stoppages occur annually, and what was the female unemployment rate for a certain year. Did you know, for instance, that beer consumption in the United States is highest in Nevada (44.27 gallons per capita), followed by New Hampshire (44.04 gpc)? You can draw a different picture of the population by knowing the parts of the country where the circulation of certain magazines—*Reader's Digest, Rolling Stone, Smithsonian, Stereo Review, Psychology Today*—is highest and lowest. The book's statistical charts may include coverage from one to ten years; a subject index is included.

2. *Book of World Rankings*, edited by George Kurian. Facts on File. 1979.

This volume compares statistics in broad topics (climate, vital statistics, religion, political leanings, finance, health, etc.) by country. For example, the chapter on housing includes such charts as NEW HOUSES BUILT PER 1,000 INHABITANTS (ranks 57 countries from 1971 to 1973); HOUSEHOLDS OWNING THEIR DWELLINGS (ranks 115 countries in 1973); and DWELLINGS WITH ELECTRIC LIGHTS (ranks 111 countries from 1970 to 1976).

Q. How does the United States rank among countries giving foreign aid? A recent newspaper article said that although most Americans support foreign aid, the United States ranks 14th out of 17 nations giving developmental assistance.

A. *The Book of World Rankings* says that 17 developed nations, all members of the Development Assistance Committee of the Organization for Economic Cooperation and Development, as well as five nonmember nations, give aid to developing countries.

Development assistance, computed as a percentage of Gross National Product, made the United States 12th in 1976, donating 2.4 percent of its GNP in aid.

In dollars, however, the United States is highest. The Netherlands ranks first in percentage, with 4.9 percent of its GNP going toward aid. The other countries with descending percentages after the Netherlands are Belgium, Switzerland, France, Canada, Sweden, the United Kingdom, Norway, Denmark, Japan, West Germany, the United States, Italy, Australia, Austria, New Zealand, and Finland.

3. *Comparisons: of Distance, Size, Area, Volume, Mass, Weight, Density, Energy, Temperature, Time, Speed and Number Throughout the Universe,* by the Diagram Group. St. Martin's Press. 1980.

This book is a treasury of comparisons shown largely through illustrations. You'll see the size differences in the playing fields or arenas used in boxing, football, baseball, tennis, and other sports; the compared weights of different animals, and their gestation and incubation periods; the sizes and weights of various aircraft from the single engine propeller models to supersonic airliners. Perhaps you'd like to compare the energy release for volcanoes, earthquakes, atomic bombs, and hydrogen bombs. (The H-bomb tested at Novaya Zemlya in October 1961 was 3,000 times as powerful as the A-bomb dropped on Hiroshima in August 1945.)

All fields—from microorganisms to astronomy—are covered, and a subject index is included.

4. *The Complete Book of American Surveys,* edited by Craig Norback. New American Library. 1980.

This paperback has no subject index, so you must use the table of contents. The book is arranged by a question followed by Norback's narrative summary of the results of various polls that ran in magazines and newspapers sponsored by associations, the government, and professional polling institutes like Gallup and Harris. It profiles American attitudes on health, politics, morality, family life, etc. Sample questions are: What have you (asked of women) given up because of inflation? How much money do you spend for dental care each year? Are you in debt? Do you feel that a terminally ill person has the "right to die"?

5. *The World Books of Odds,* by David Neft. Grosset & Dunlap. 1978.

Have you ever wanted to know the odds against an actress, actor, film, or director being nominated for an Academy Award? How about the odds against a woman becoming pregnant using one of several popular birth control methods or devices; the odds against being dealt a royal flush in poker; the odds of a marriage lasting, according to education and age; the odds of dying of lung cancer according to age, sex, and country;

the odds of a baseball rookie ever playing in the major leagues?

There is no subject index, but the book includes a detailed table of contents. It shows such categories as Games and Gambling (auction pinochle, backgammon, blackjack, state lotteries, etc.), Accidents and War Deaths, Sports, Sex and Pregnancy, Health, Wealth, etc.

STATISTICS BY COMPUTER

Aside from the variety of print material that yields statistics, you can also get them by computer. The three major statistics indexes, *SRI*, *ASI*, and *IIS*, as well as many other statistical data bases, are available on-line through the same computer search services that scan magazine indexes. Search services can also extract a number of statistics found within the text of newspapers such as *The New York Times*. But a more structured search using any of the directories and indexes described in this chapter works as well—and at this time, is cheaper.

Statistics are a fact of life in a society where quantifying statements is practically an obsession. For good or bad, we are interested in how many of us are going to Europe next summer, how many hours of television our preschoolers watch, and what's happened to the Consumer Price Index since last fall. This chapter should give you some idea where the media, writers, and speechmakers get some of their "fancy figures." Now you know where to look for some numbers of your own.

CHAPTER SUMMARY

I. Statistics emanate from research conducted at universities and colleges, in industry and private organizations, and in government. Statistics and other numerical data are published in articles, books, reports, dissertations, and statistical yearbooks and directories. (page 306)

II. There are many statistics-finding tools in large libraries.

   A. Three monthly indexes help you find statistics in most publications: *American Statistics Index* (covers federal and state governmental statistics); *Statistics Reference Index* (covers statistics in articles, as well as those issued by associations, university research centers, and some state agencies); *Index to International Statistics* (includes statistics from over 40 UN agencies and intergovernmental organizations). Each index comes with a full set of all the publications it indexes in a microform collection. (page 308)

      B.   If your library doesn't own these indexes, try *Encyclopedia of Business Information Sources* or *Statistics Sources*. (page 311)

III. Most large libraries own a variety of statistical yearbooks and other resources which provide researchers with both historical and current data.

      A.   General almanacs which contain many charts and figures include the sources of their statistical information to guide you to more on that subject. (page 314)

      B.   Statistical yearbooks for individual countries and states provide specific information not always available in more general directories. (page 313)

      C.   Specific professional and trade associations issue statistical reports. (page 315)

      D.   Dissertations are frequently filled with statistical information. Use *Dissertation Abstracts International* to identify these works. (page 316)

      E.   Many statistics are "hidden." They don't appear in charts and tables, but instead are buried in the texts of articles, books, and other documents. (page 317)

IV. Public opinion polls may also help in your research.

      A.   Recent and older Gallup polls taken here and abroad are published in a series of Gallup publications, including the monthly *Gallup Report*. (page 318)

      B.   Some reference books present numerical data for popular reading: *Book of American Rankings*, *The World Book of Odds*, etc. (page 320)

V. You can also search for statistics by computer. Besides *ASI, IIS*, and *SRI*, many other statistical data bases are on-line. Check on-line search services that have access to the data bases with the figures you need. (page 322)

18

Getting It Firsthand:
LOOKING FOR
ORIGINAL MATERIAL

History is an account, mostly false, of events, mostly unimportant,
which are brought about by rulers, mostly knaves, and soldiers, mostly fools.
—Ambrose Bierce

If you're determined to get to the roots of your subject, this chapter will tell you how to do it. Sometimes no amount of periodical index or on-line searching can give you the conclusive information you need. Perhaps recently published, secondary sources don't go back far enough or deep enough to give you the insight you need about a person, an event, or an era.

So, you set out to record your own experiences and observations—you do original research—because you decide not to depend on the information that has already been collected in published books, magazines, and directories. Original research means getting to the bottom of a subject; it means studying unpublished material such as correspondence, written reports, and personal notes. It means going back to the source. This is a critical step in research because it's often the only way you can reconstruct facts that have become distorted with age and handling. Original research is perhaps one of the most rewarding kinds of information gathering.

Jackson Benson's research experience is typical of one who searched through original material looking for the truth. He wrote a book on John Steinbeck (*The True Adventures of John Steinbeck, Writer: A Biography*. Viking Press, 1984) which shattered some myths tenaciously held and reverently passed on by a number of publications including encyclopedias. One of these accepted facts was that Steinbeck had visited Oklahoma to research *The Grapes of Wrath*. In truth, Benson's probing through primary material determined that Steinbeck never visited that state at all—regardless of the "facts" in print for decades.

In a different kind of search in the 1930s, John Carter and Graham Pollard, two young rare-book dealers in London, suspected that certain editions of Tennyson, Kipling, Swinburne, Elizabeth Barrett Browning, and other collectible authors were forgeries. Their original research into primary material pointed a finger toward Thomas Wise, a respected British book collector, dealer, and bibliophile. To question an august figure such as Wise (even his name defies negative thoughts) would require rare nerve and ironclad evidence.

Carter and Pollard let the facts speak for themselves. Through original research, they not only analyzed ink, type, and paper samples, they also traced the manufacturers of each, proving conclusively that the rare editions could not have been published in the early 1800s as their dates implied.

In his book, *Scholar Adventurers* (Macmillan, 1950), Richard Altick acknowledges one important point about literary figures that applies to original research in general. "There is no major . . . figure whose biography has been innocent of falsehoods and half-truths, placed there by an early memoirist and then uncritically repeated from writer to writer—and usually embroidered in the transmission—until at last they are disproved by the researcher."

Original research is the key to those truths.

Q. My husband says that when he was in high school in the late 1930s Albert Einstein was visiting small towns across the United States. He swears that Einstein visited his high school in Oklahoma City. We've checked biographies of Einstein and cannot find this information. Can you offer any other suggestions, so he can regain his credibility with the family?

A. According to entries in *The New York Times Index* for the 1935-1940 period and *Encyclopedia Americana*, Einstein, born in 1879, won the Nobel Prize in physics in 1921. In the 1920s and 1930s, he accepted numerous invitations to lecture in this country. He was visiting California in 1933 when Hitler came to power, and he did not return to Germany. In 1941 he was granted a permanent position at Princeton University, where he remained until his death in 1955.

It's not inconceivable from these brief facts that Einstein could have lectured in Oklahoma. Write to the high school your husband attended. Many schools keep records and scrapbooks of memorable events. (Addresses for high schools are in *Patterson's American Education*, or the phone book in the library.) Newsworthy events are also reported in the local newspaper, and you might easily verify this one by writing to the Metropolitan Library System of Oklahoma County, 131 Dean A. McGee Ave., Oklahoma City, OK 73102.

PUBLIC RECORDS

One place to look for primary information is in public records. You'd be amazed at the kinds and amounts of information that is stored—and available—on just about everyone.

During our lives we sign dozens, even hundreds, of certificates, applications, and other forms which result in a huge body of public and private records. The process starts at birth with a certificate; it continues if we marry or divorce, join a church, apply for a driver's license or even a pet license, buy property, register to vote, start a business, enter a hospital, apply for a social security card, join a professional or trade association, enlist in the military, buy insurance, subscribe to a magazine, apply for credit, file a lawsuit, join a union, get arrested, attend college, and on and on. People, especially today, leave a trail of movements in the process of merely living.

These records may provide clues to a person's wealth by the property he owned (according to property tax receipts and land deeds); they may show when and how often he traveled abroad (from passport or visa applications); they may indicate what schools he attended (by enrollment records). Public records often fill in blanks with information you can't find anywhere else: someone's full or real name, the date he attended a conference (to prove he couldn't have been somewhere else at the time), confirmation of someone's financial standing in 1944, the facts surrounding the little-known death of an infant.

Keep in mind that even public records contain errors, misspellings, and misrepresentations. They were recorded by human beings, after all. Use them with caution, and if possible, cross-check data against other material. Many of us share the story of how our surname was shortened or changed because a clerk at Ellis Island couldn't understand our immigrant ancestor's accent.

Public records exist in great numbers, but the older they are, the harder it may be to find them. And they may no longer be with the agency that originally collected them. Eventually, the records (such as military records) gathered by federal agencies wind up in the National Archives. Within a state, they may be microfilmed and sent to a central department in a county seat or state capital. This makes the process of tracing them slightly more involved since different states may follow different procedures. It takes persistence, but getting copies of public records is not impossible.

Genealogy books such as *Genealogical Research: Methods and Resources* (two vols.), edited by Milton Rubincam; *The Researcher's Guide to American Genealogy*, by Val D. Greenwood; and *How to Find Your Family Roots*, by Timothy Beard are useful for more detailed descriptions and locations of various state records. The kinds of public records available are, therefore, only briefly described here.

1. Census Records (State and Federal)

With each 10-year census, the census becomes longer and more detailed. Therefore, the amount of information available about us increases. However, only censuses over 75 years old are open to public inspection. Check the National Archives' *Federal Population Censuses 1790-1890* for order forms and a list of available rolls. The Bureau of the Census catalog, 1982-1983, published by the Government Printing Office, gives citations, abstracts, prices, and ordering information for all census pamphlets, books, data base files, maps, and other census products issued between January 1980 and March 1983. (It's not always necessary, however, to borrow census rolls on microfilm from a genealogy library or regional branch of the National Archives. Your library's interlibrary loan service may be able to get them for you.)

A genealogy book will tell you how much and what kind of information each census contains. In the early years, the census gathered far less data than it does now. It originally started as a means of apportioning taxes and determining legislative representation. Over the years it developed into a tool for social planning and, accordingly, has grown in the number of questions it asks. The first census in 1790 counted only heads of households. By 1850, every individual in a household was named and identified by age, sex, color, and birthplace. Successive censuses included more and more data—from the number of rooms in a house to the owner's occupation.

In addition to the national census, many states in the early days took their own censuses for a number of reasons (one was to declare eligibility for statehood). You can identify available state censuses and the dates they cover by checking *State Censuses: An Annotated Bibliography of Censuses of Population Taken After the Year 1790 by States and Territories of the United States*, prepared by Henry Dubester (Burt Franklin, 1969). The book should be available in large libraries.

2. Church or Synagogue Records
The records of religious groups vary considerably and often depend on the person who keeps them. Church records can include dates of baptism, confirmation, marriage, burial, conversion, and other church-related activities along with dates, names of relatives, witnesses, etc.

3. Divorce Records
Divorce records are issued in most states. Write for them by checking the appropriate address in the government pamphlet, *Where to Write for Divorce Records, United States and Outlying Areas*, available in a library. Divorce documents contain the names and ages of dependent children, date and place of divorce, grounds, settlement, and other facts pertaining to a couple's situation at that time

4. Education Records
Records with varying amounts of information are kept by private schools, church schools, colleges, and universities. From these records you may be able to determine a person's home address at the time of his enrollment, his religion and financial status, as well as siblings' and parents' names.

Q. In trying to document some of the dates and facts in the family genealogy, we have hit a blank wall where my husband's great-grandmother is concerned. We only know her name (enclosed—I'm not positive of the spelling of her last name). Family stories have it that she was the first woman in Kentucky to graduate from college. Can you help me verify this? She must have been born somewhere around 1840, so she would have graduated about 1862.

A. It would help to establish some facts of history first. For example, the *College Blue Book* identifies colleges by state and the date of their foundation. Out of a list of several dozen for Kentucky, less than a dozen existed as far back as the 1860s. You may be able to reduce this list further, because several are run by different church denominations. You can then send a letter to each of the colleges remaining to see if they show a student with her name in their archival records (often kept in the special collections department of the campus library). (The *College Blue Book*, of course, will not mention colleges that existed at that time but are no longer operating. Check earlier editions for those.)

The Kentucky census for the middle 1800s should also be easy to get on microfilm. Check the public library for information on how to order them. Bibliographies of genealogy books and directories indicate that most of the specialized material you need is either in a large genealogy library or in sources in the state of Kentucky. One useful bibliography to check which lists Kentucky genealogy references is Nettie Yantis-Schreiner's *Genealogical and Local History Books in Print*.

5. *Land Records*

Also on file in county courthouses are a variety of documents that cover different land transactions. They may be deeds of sale, mortgage papers, leases, etc. They mention names, financial information, occupations, dates, and other "original" information. (Be aware that they can also blanket the facts—with business or other cover-up names to discourage the curious.)

Q. How do I check on records pertaining to an old farm in Alexandria, Virginia? I believe it was next to General Lee's home.

A. Nineteenth- and 20th-century land records are usually on file in the county where the land was registered. In Virginia, however, according to Val Greenwood's *The Researcher's Guide to American Genealogy*, many cities that incorporated, established their own courts and government separate from the counties where they were located. For Alexandria land records, contact the Circuit Court, 130 N. Fairfax St., Alexandria, VA 22314.

6. *Military Records*

Military service started in this country with the arrival of the settlers. Though many of the early records were destroyed by fire (one which occurred on November 8, 1800 destroyed the archives of the U.S. War Department), many others exist on file in the National Archives. The records for the different wars are in varying degrees of completeness and helpfulness. Depending on the particular military records you need, consult genealogy guides to direct you to them.

7. *Miscellaneous Federal Records (Pension Records, Courts-Martial, Passport Requests, etc.)*

Federal actions and applications of various types are on file in the appropriate departments and agencies of the government. Older records are sent to the National Archives, and some are in regional courthouses. The genealogical books mentioned in this chapter will help you find them.

8. *Naturalization Records*

Immigrants who sought naturalization have applications on file with the Department of Naturalization or "any common law court of record." They often show the person's place and date of birth, plus the port and date of his entry into this country. Since they usually show the person's address at the time of application, they are also a clue to which census records to pursue and the location of other regional records.

Naturalization records are scattered in federal, state, and regional courts.

9. *Probate Records*

Wills on file in county courthouses are public records and sometimes reveal a great deal of personal information. Through clues in the text of a will you can verify, discover, or infer the person's occupation, religion, financial status, friends and/or heirs, resentments, etc. Since certain property and assets can be passed on in ways other than through a will, however (joint ownership is one way), much information may not appear in this kind of document.

10. *Records of Social and Fraternal Organizations*

Long-standing groups may keep scrapbooks and other records of social and charitable events with names of participants, officers, and applications for memberships. You may be able to contact the main headquarters of a nationwide group for this information.

11. *Tax Records*

Property and real estate taxes are two categories of taxation which generate records. Such records not only help track a person's movements, they may also establish the size of his holdings. These are usually found in a county courthouse.

12. *Vital Records*

These cover births, deaths, and marriages, yielding such information as names of parents, mothers' maiden names, date and place of a person's birth, marriage, death, etc. Check the following government pamphlets in the library for addresses, copy fees, and dates of records covered: *Where to Write for Birth and Death Records; Where to Write for Marriage Records; Where to Write for Births and Deaths of U.S. Citizens Who Were Born or Died Outside of the United States;* and *Birth Certificates for Alien Children Adopted by U.S. Citizens.*

Before official record keeping began (it varies in different states), births were recorded (when they were recorded) in church records which may also be accessible.

There is almost no end to the kinds of records you might tap for "original" information, depending on how far you wish to pursue a search. The best way to think about what might exist in public records is to think about the many forms and registers you yourself have filled out or signed. They're on file somewhere. All that remains is to trace their location with the help of directories that give addresses.

ORIGINAL MATERIAL IN MICROFORM

Public records are fine for gleaning clues and picking up "quick" facts about someone or something. But if your research requires in-depth information, you'll have to dig a lot deeper for answers. Once again, microform gives you access to a variety of original material.

Now that microform publishers have filmed and are filming much "basic" material—books, magazines, and newspapers—there seems no reason to stop there. Micropublishers today are also filming special collections and personal and organization papers. These consist largely of unpublished or ephemeral material such as correspondence, notebooks, posters, pamphlets, etc. These kinds of materials reveal the background of significant events in American history (from new educational theories to labor movements) whose stories might not yet be told in books. These original snatches of life are a researcher's delight.

Many of these collections in their original form have been donated to large libraries, but they're inaccessible to most of us unless we travel to them. As the number of collections in microform increases, however, the information becomes available on a broader scale. So much original material is being converted to microform and sold to large libraries that it's almost impossible to capture its scope here. The list below reflects a very small but diverse selection. You can find many other collections by checking micropublishers' catalogs. (See page 261).

Special Collections

1. *American Indian Correspondence: The Presbyterian Historical Society*

[Philadelphia] *Collection of Missionaries' Letters, 1833-1893*. Greenwood Press.

Anglo-Saxon law and the white man's religion resulted in a drastic change for many Indian tribes in the 19th century. This collection includes 13,422 unpublished letters describing 60 years of missionary influence on 39 tribes between 1833 and 1893. Students of women's history will also find the letters valuable for the missionaries' concept of the ideal Christian woman which was imposed on Indian women. The set comes with a printed user's guide of the same name.

2. *Presidential Election Campaign Documents, 1868-1900*. University Microfilms International.

The original collection, housed at Dartmouth College Library in New Hampshire, consists of hard-to-find campaign pamphlets, speeches, and miscellaneous printed matter issued by major and minor political parties between 1868 and 1900. The collection spans nine administrations and covers important political issues of the period, as well as the points addressed to ethnic groups and minorities, and electoral strategies. It also reveals the structure and content of many 19th-century political speeches. There is no printed guide to this collection, but a table of contents is included at the beginning of each reel of microfilm.

3. *Slavery and Anti-Slavery Pamphlets*. University Microfilms International.

In Lincoln's day, the controversy surrounding slavery was intense. Much literature issued at the time appeared in pamphlets; most of it has disappeared. Some items, however, are buried in hard-to-find, mid-19th-century reports, published legal opinions, and convention proceedings. These are reproduced in this microform set through which you can explore the Civil War and its causes, establish the nation's mood at the time, and trace part of the history of slavery.

The microform set duplicates the personal libraries of Salmon P. Chase (1808-1873), chief justice and member of Lincoln's cabinet, and New Hampshire Senator John Hale (1806-1873). The printed guide that accompanies it is entitled *Slavery and Anti-Slavery Pamphlets, an Index to the Microfilm Collection*, edited by Trudy Heath. (University Microfilms International.)

Organization Papers

The microform organization papers listed below are all published by Microfilming Corp. of America, and they all come with printed guides. Some sets are updated annually as some of the organizations are still active. Each collection offers original material which you can use to reconstruct significant events and legislation influenced by these groups.

The collections also include, in some cases, lengthy correspondence extending for many years, even decades, and written by people whose names are now well known in history. If you're writing a biography, check for the existence of the collected papers of an organization with which your subject was associated. You may uncover a gold mine of personal material and references.

1. *American Association for Labor Legislation, 1905-1943.*

The AALL, an arm of the American Economic Association, was formed in 1905 to study U.S. labor conditions and related legislation. The group was responsible for major changes in laws governing workmen's compensation, occupational health and safety, and child labor. The microform set includes voluminous correspondence from such labor reform figures as Louis Brandeis, Samuel Gompers, Fiorello La Guardia, Jane Addams, Ida Tarbell, Franklin D. Roosevelt, and Walter Lippmann. The original collection is housed at Cornell University.

2. *The American Civil Liberties Union Records and Publications, 1917-1978.*

This microform collection documents the development of now famous civil liberties issues and court cases as far back as Sacco and Vanzetti and the Scopes "Monkey" trial and as recent as the American Nazi Party and George Wallace. It includes minutes of the Board of Directors, conference papers, policy guides, organization manuals, the group's constitution and bylaws, legal briefs, pamphlets, and leaflets. The material comes from ACLU's personal archives.

3. *The Hopedale Community Collection, 1821-1938.*

The records in this microform collection document the growth of the 32-member Hopedale Community, founded in Mendon, Massachusetts, by a Universalist minister as an experiment in communal living. By 1855, it had grown into a village of 600 acres with 300 members, schools, shops, and mills. By 1867, it disbanded and merged with a nearby town. The filmed materials come from the collections of various libraries.

4. *The Indian Rights Association Papers, 1864-1973.*

This microform collection consists of the papers of the first major group to support Indian rights and causes. It was formed in Philadelphia by white reformers and churchmen, and for years it was the only effective group the Indians could turn to for support.

The IRA was responsible for the passage of the Dawes Land-in-Severalty Act of 1887 which established U.S. policy toward the Indians. The print collection is housed at the Historical Society of Pennsylvania in Philadelphia.

5. *National Woman's Party Papers, 1913-1974.*

The correspondence, minutes, legal papers, financial records, photographs, and printed materials in this microform collection document the background of women's issues in this country such as equal voting rights, birth control, labor laws, and the legal status of women. The Library of Congress owns the original collection.

6. *Records of the Committee on Fair Employment Practice, 1941-1946.*
The FEPC, established by Presidential Executive Order, was formed to eliminate employment discrimination based on race, creed, color, or national origin in the wartime national defense economy. The committee investigated over 14,000 discrimination complaints in five years; the collection consists of correspondence, personal case records, studies and reports, minutes of meetings, and memos. This collection documents one segment of the struggle for racial equality. The National Archives owns the original material.

7. *Students for a Democratic Society Papers, 1958-1970.*
Records kept by the most important radical student movement in U.S. history enable you to study student violence in the 1960s, campus unrest, the Vietnam peace movement, and other specific protest marches, sit-ins, etc. It includes correspondence from such participants as Rennie Davis, Bernadine Dohrn, Al Haber, and Tom Hayden. The original records belong to the State Historical Society of Wisconsin in Madison.

Personal Papers

By examining the personal papers of individuals who have influenced history and social events, we have a better understanding of those events as well as the individuals themselves. The collections of their papers vary in size and consist of miscellaneous correspondence, notebooks, legal papers, journals, etc. The collections below have been microfilmed by Microfilming Corporation of America.
1. *The Papers of Aaron Burr, 1756-1836.* (A controversial political figure in American history)
2. *The Papers of George Washington Carver, 1864-1943.* (A noted scientist and black American)
3. *The Papers of Betty Gannett, 1929-1970.* (A controversial Marxist and teacher)
4. *The Collis P. Huntington Papers, 1856-1901.* (A noted entrepreneur)
5. *The Papers of Robert M. La Follette, 1876-1924.* (A leading figure in the Progressive Movement)
6. *The Papers of John L. Lewis, 1879-1969.* (A prominent labor leader)

HOW TO FIND ORIGINAL MATERIAL

I've already mentioned several print directories and indexes that will help you locate original material in libraries and archives around the country: *The National Union Catalog of Manuscript Collections* and *Subject Collections,* for example. (See pages 283-85.) There are countless other directories to use, many of which locate esoteric material such as Buddhist manuscripts or ephemeral items such as individual maps and diaries. You'll find these directories by checking *SGBIP,* or the library's catalog under the headings ARCHIVES and MANUSCRIPTS. Your search will identify such publications as:

Manuscripts Relating to Commonwealth Caribbean Countries in United States and Canadian Repositories, by K. E. Ingram. St. Lawrence, Barbados: Caribbean Universities Press, 1975.

This guide is arranged geographically by state, then by city. It lists museums, libraries, and historical societies that own items or collections relating to the Caribbean area. For example, The Dupont Wintherthur Museum in Wilmington, Delaware, owns sailing orders from William Plumsted, part owner of the ship *Tryal,* to Captain Samuel Bicknell, dated Barbados, 1730. The Maryland Historical Society in Baltimore owns an account book for mess supplies ordered in December 1888 on the U.S.S. *Constellation.* This guide also lists the locations of many hand-drawn maps.

Don't forget that countless historical societies and special libraries in individual communities collect original material about their own regions. For addresses, consult the *Directory of Historical Societies and Agencies in the United States and Canada* and *Directory of Special Libraries and Information Centers.*

Q. I wonder if you could check out this old family story. The Barnum and Bailey circus went broke in Carson City, Nevada, between 1875 and 1890. During this time, the circus had rented my great-great-uncle's pasture, and because they couldn't pay the rent they gave him a camel and a coach instead.

We have searched the local library for a history of the circus to no avail. We are writing a genealogy for our grandchildren and hope to make it as interesting as possible, not just a list of names and dates but anecdotes, too.

A. There are many biographies of P. T. Barnum, including his autobiography, which do not give the kind of precise detail you need. They do confirm that the B&B circus traveled across country by rail for the first time in the 1880s and suffered periodic financial ups and downs as well as occasional outright ruination by fire.

For confirmation of the Carson City debacle, check with the Ringling Museum of the Circus, Box 1838, Sarasota, FL 33578. (Ringling Bros. bought out B & B in 1907 when Bailey died.) The museum collection includes route books, press clippings, financial accounts, programs, posters, and articles. You might also want to check with the Ormsby Public Library, 900 N. Roop St., Carson City, NV 89701 or the Nevada State Library, 401 N. Carson St., Carson City, NV 89710.

Members of Congress: A Checklist of Their Papers in the Manuscript Division, Library of Congress, compiled by John L. McDonough. Government Printing Office, 1980.

You'll find eminent names in this list: Elihu Root, Daniel Patrick Moynihan, Horace Mann, and Thomas Jefferson. The guide, arranged alphabetically by name, includes the years during which each person served in Congress and the location of his papers.

Philippine-American Relations: A Guide to Manuscript Sources in the United States, compiled by Shiro Saito. Greenwood Press. 1982.

This lists small collections of material that once belonged largely to military officers and politicians. It includes single items such as a diary or several boxes of miscellaneous papers held by libraries, museums, and historical societies nationwide. The guide is arranged alphabetically by the name of the collection or donor and includes a subject index.

Some special collections of original material have been reprinted in book form rather than in microform. The few in print occupy a great deal of shelf space: the 25-volume *Facsimiles of Manuscripts in European Archives Relating to America, 1773-1783,* for example. But they do exist in large libraries. And since they're in print, they can be checked out.

The sample sets below are photographic reproductions of a variety of material: letters, published reports, old government documents, etc. (The number of special collections in microform, however, is still greater than the number of those in the print format.)

1. *American Diplomatic and Public Papers: The United States and China.* Series 1, 1842-1860, 21 volumes. Series 2, 1861-1893, 18 volumes. Series 3, 1894-1905, 14 volumes. Scholarly Resources, 1973-81.

These sets include reproductions of actual diplomatic correspondence, Congressional and other government documents both written and printed: correspondence of American commissioners and ministers to China, for example, presidential messages, reports and dispatches sent to Congress, treaties, agreements, acts of Congress, etc.

One chapter on the Kearny Mission, in Series 1, is divided into three sections: 1) The opium trade; 2) Protection of Americans and claims for injuries at Canton; 3) Efforts to secure American commercial rights and privileges. If you're looking for information on the immigration of the Chinese to the United States and California in the 1850s, you'll find reproductions of original documents that record the growing trade in coolies, their revolts, and much more.

2. *American Indian Ethnohistory.* 118 volumes. Garland, 1974.

The reports and unpublished papers in this set were selected from scores of unindexed files largely in the Indian Claims Commission records in the National Archives. They concentrate on over 30 American Indian groups. The five-volume report on the Paiute Indians, for example, covers their total culture—social organization, habitat, agriculture, hunting, language, marriage patterns, etc., as recorded by the Indian Claims Commission documents.

3. *Blacks in the U.S. Armed Forces: Basic Documents*, edited by Morris J. MacGregor & Bernard C. Nalty. 13 volumes. Scholarly Resources, 1977.

Papers from state and federal governments and other sources cover from 1639 to the mid-1970s. Sample documents included are a 30-page, 1940s report disclosing the results of a NAACP investigation into the problems of black servicemen in Germany; a proclamation issued by General Thomas W. Sherman, October, 1861 at Port Royal, South Carolina, in which he says he will not disturb the institution of slavery in territory conquered by Union forces under his command; and a memo from Truman K. Gibson, Jr. for Assistant Secretary McCly, August 8, 1945, in which he reviews the development of the Army's racial policy and warns against unquestioningly accepting certain premises in the study under discussion.

Since the above sets are in print, you'll easily find them when shelf browsing. You will also find several when you check *SGBIP* under the appropriate subject. They are usually easy to identify because of their large number of volumes, and sometimes by giveaway words in their titles or subtitles (e.g. basic documents, public papers).

USING SECONDARY MATERIAL IN ORIGINAL RESEARCH

Once a book or article researched from original material is published, it becomes a (secondary) resource. It's imbued with the author's interpretations and any inconsistencies or errors he has picked up along the way.

The term "secondary" appears cut-and-dried, but it isn't. Many printed (secondary) resources are useful, if not essential, to original research. There may be no other way to trace a fact or an address except to use an old directory or magazine article to help you reconnect the strands of your story. Even genealogical research, which is almost entirely "original" since it is compiled from family stories and public records, relies on printed resources—obituary notices in newspapers and entries in old biographical directories, for example.

Not all secondary sources are equal. A book published right after the Chicago World's Fair of 1893 by someone who was there will undoubtedly reflect the mood, emotion, and the facts of the occasion more accurately than books researched from materials published 50 years later. Each successive generation of printed material multiplies old and transmits new errors. The further an author gets from an original event, the less his published material may adequately reflect it.

Researchers recognize this distinction and sometimes use the expression "tertiary resources" to describe published material that is further removed from a particular event than another. But trying to label each generation of writing in proper numerical sequence is self-defeating, if not confusing. The point to remember is that many materials published close to an event or period that you're studying are useful resources in original research. They are still secondary sources, but they may have a place in your original research.

Q. I am researching automobile travel in the 1920s covering the areas from Kentucky to Florida and from Kentucky to Montana. Before the numbering system arose, U.S. highways were identified by a system of colored bands painted on telephone poles. Different combinations of colors designated different highways, many of which at that time were named rather than numbered. (Trouble arose when the plethora of names caused confusion.) I understand the Dixie Highway had a certain combination of colors which a motorist could use in driving from Chicago to Florida.

I'm interested in learning more about this system of colored bands. How did it originate and what were the colors for the Dixie Highway of the Middle West?

A. According to *Historic American Roads*, by Albert Rose (1953), the adoption of uniform signs throughout the country started in 1925 to end the chaos caused by the different systems in each state. A committee of federal and state highway officials was appointed to do the job. Among other things, they assigned odd numbers to north-south highways and even numbers to east-west highways.

There are an amazing number of books on the history of roads and highways, and you might be able to get information about the color system from following up on references in the footnotes of these books. *The Road and the Car in American Life*, by John Rae (1971), is one such book. In another book, I found reference to an article "The Highway Movement, 1916-1935," which appeared in the January 1946 issue of the *American Historical Review*. Information on specific state highway policies might be available from the Department of Transportation in the individual states. Their addresses are in the *National Directory of State Agencies*, found in a large library.

REPRINT BOOKS

As I've already mentioned, the availability of books in reprint editions gives researchers access to the many old books owned by distant libraries. . The originals are fragile and scarce, and therefore not frequently loaned through interlibrary loan; but the reprints are available for your research. These secondary sources may be as "original" as anything you can find on your subject. Many, like the titles below, are listed in *Subject Guide to Books in Print* as reprints.

INDUSTRIAL SURVEYS

Kent, William. *Investigating an Industry*. 1975. Reprint of the 1913 ed. Hive Pub.

OCCULT SCIENCES
Mackey, Samson A. *Mythological Astronomy of the Ancients Demonstrated*. 1973. Reprint of the 1822 ed. Wizards.
STOCK - EXCHANGE
Van Antwerp, William C. *The Stock Market from Within*. 1975. Reprint of the 1913 ed. Arno.

Q. My paternal grandfather served in the U.S. Cavalry in the 1860s and again from 1886 to 1889. I'd like to get a sense of that era from the cavalry viewpoint, but haven't been able to find anything. Any suggestions?

A. Among the several books on the cavalry that are currently in print according to *Subject Guide to Books in Print*, one is a reprint of a book originally published in 1888 entitled *15 Years as a Cavalryman*, by H.H. McConnell (Arno Press). You should be able to get a copy from a bookstore, the publisher, or a library.

Reprints eventually go out of print once the run sells out; but large libraries, academic libraries in particular, own many. It is not inconceivable, therefore, to find a great many "old" books on their shelves. (Your local library may also own many originals which they bought long ago or which they currently buy from out-of-print book dealers.) In addition to using *SGBIP,* you can find relevant titles covering many subjects and periods through *Cumulative Book Index (CBI)* (see page 277), and subject bibliographies.

Q. I recently bought an old electromechanical phonograph made by Capehart Automatic Phonograph Corp. in 1928. It needs much repair. Do you know where I might be able to find instructions on how to repair it?

A. The *Standard & Poor Register of Corporations, Directors and Executives* shows a Capehart Corp. at 770 Lexington Ave., New York, NY 10021 that now makes stereos. If they can't help, the 1936 volume of *Index to Handicrafts* gives some possibilities under PHONOGRAPH. First is a chapter on phonograph repairing in a 1935 book, *You Can Fix It*, written by John Wells. Another is an article called "Electric Gramophone Motor to Run on a.c. Supply," in the July 26, 1929 issue of *Model Engineer and Light Machinery Review*. Finally, in *Cumulative Book Index* (1928-32 volume), there's a book called *Gramophone Adjustments and Repairs* published in 1929 by Marshall, Percival. You can borrow all of these through the interlibrary loan service at the library.

USING OLD REFERENCE PUBLICATIONS

Since the perspective from publications issued in another time may differ from present-day interpretations, you can use reference books of another period to connect loose ends, make more accurate deductions, or confirm facts. [1] It might be possible, for example, to verify Paul Revere's address by checking the *Boston City Directory* for 1776. While a recently published book may refer to direct flights in 1933 between Miami, Florida, and Veracruz, Mexico, the *Official Guide of the Airways*, published annually since 1929, will confirm that possibility. The *Official Railways Guide*, published since 1868, might prove how long it took a train to get from New York to Washington, DC, in 1935.

When annually published reference books cease publication or a new edition comes out, the dated copy is no longer useful for current information, so it may be discarded in small libraries. In large libraries, it's usually transferred to the stacks to make room for the new edition. Old directories in complete runs from volume one to the present are also coming out in microform in increasing numbers.

To determine when a directory started publication, simply check the library's catalog. (The catalog may also show which editions the library owns.) Or, check a general reference book called *Union List of Serials (ULS)*, covering pre-1950 serials (directories, magazines, and other continuously published items, except newspapers), or *New Serial Titles (NST)* covering those serials in print from 1950 to the present.

If for your novel you'd like to know typical hotel rates in Indianapolis in 1935 or the name of a public school which no longer exists there, consult *ULS*. It will tell you that the *Hotel & Motel Redbook* began publishing in 1868, and that *Patterson's American Education* began in 1904. So, you know you can use these references to check for the information you need.

(A word of caution: looking on the library shelves for directories can be misleading, because some parts of a series or set may be kept in another location or be checked out. Performing math magic (e.g., if the 10th edition was published in 1950, the first edition must have been published in 1941) can also be inaccurate, since reference books may suspend publication for several years and then resume, thereby throwing off your calculations in matching years and volume numbers precisely.)

HOW ACCURATE IS ORIGINAL AND PUBLISHED MATERIAL?

Researching from original materials, whether they are public records, personal papers, or even the "secondary" materials published a hundred years ago, is a different game from gathering your facts from up-to-date, recently published resources. But no matter how old or new the resources you use in original research, you'll always be faced with a variety of chal-

---

[1]For information about old almanacs, yearbooks, encyclopedias, newspapers, documents, out-of-print books on microfilm and in hard copy, etc., check the appropriate chapters in this book.

lenges related to the material itself. Indeed, all material contains some biases, errors, and inaccuracies. To some extent, print material—old city directories or phone books, old catalogs and newspapers—is used to bridge gaps in original research. But even directories are not exempt from flaws.

Some errors are easy to spot, some are not. For example, the 1983 *International Motion Picture Almanac* lists the address of *The San Diego Union* as 940 Third Ave., San Diego—a location it vacated in the early 1970s. That error was easy for me to spot, though it would not necessarily be obvious to others.

Errors creep into original research for any number of reasons. People who are being interviewed may speak faster than an interviewer can take notes. And if the interviewee wants to hide embarrassing moments out of his past, he can easily do so by not mentioning them, or by somehow reslanting them for the benefit of the interview. As a result, many errors and inconsistencies sneak into a finished product and are subsequently passed along by other researchers.

And what about the types of printed material that make a correct interpretation of the "facts" very difficult? Gossipy movie magazines, supermarket tabloids, and politically radical publications are seen by many as being emotionally charged and sensational (depending, of course, on your point of view). As time passes, it becomes harder to accurately judge and interpret their message.

The media (newspapers and broadcasting) have long been accused of slanted news reporting. Less-than-objective attitudes and sources with half-the-story may be part of the problem. Short deadlines is another factor that contributes to mistakes and inaccuracies in print and on the air. Nevertheless, the news, once set in print or on film, is a permanent record for future researchers—to accept or question as they see fit.

CONFIRMING/RESOLVING INACCURACIES

If both print and primary material are subject to factual and interpretive errors and biases, how can we interpret them correctly? As a researcher, one of the things you do is compare the data you've collected so far with new information. In the process, you often discover that certain facts don't match. If Thomas Edison was supposed to have been on the West Coast in the 1890s, something is obviously wrong if another source says he was on the East Coast at that time. To resolve the inconsistency, you have to research further until you break out of the impasse.

Before you interpret the material you've collected, you may also have to study the background of a period or event to understand the attitudes that prevailed at the time. For example, today you might quickly notice subtle prejudices and propaganda in a 1941 issue of *Life* magazine which illustrated (through patriotic slogans and inflammatory headlines) the war enemy as ugly and mean-looking. But readers of that age may not have so easily detected these biases. If you study the nation's mood during the prewar era, you can understand what gave rise to—and perhaps tolerance for—such prejudices.

To comprehend Salem witchcraft, you should first study the hysteria that reigned during the period. To understand Shakespeare, the man, and his drama, you must first know something of the Puritan ethic that waged war against drama in the 16th century. To determine why unmarried mothers relinquished babies in 1940, it helps to understand the social climate and pressures that prevailed at that time. Only after we know about the era in which an event took place can we accept, for instance, that during his lifetime, Abraham Lincoln was one of the most hated Presidents who ever lived.

Just how much fact checking, analysis, and getting-to-the-bottom-of-a-subject can you reasonably accomplish without hampering your efforts to complete the work at hand? Consider that large publishers today are faced with having to recall and stop the presses for books whose facts have been challenged by someone involved. You can follow the dialogue in newspapers and in *Publishers Weekly* magazine, but many questions remain unanswered. Who—author or publisher—is responsible for checking facts? How many facts must be checked? Whom do you believe, and when does the checking stop? Where should you, as an information seeker, draw the line and accept something as the truth?

A creditable piece of work, whether it's a book, article, report, family history, or letter, must be based on sound facts and research. Conclusions demand proof. Assumption, unfounded deductions, and guessing are unacceptable. And publishers maintain that the job rests with the author.

Whatever your particular research purpose, there are degrees of checking you can do. And there are choices you have to make. You can draw from a hazy memory (yours or someone else's), or you can try to verify a point from two or three different sources (whether or not it turns out to be correct in the end is not the issue here). You can make something up, or you can call someone who should know. You can put reasonable effort into checking facts, or you can let your effort slide.

Part of the logjam (and ultimate lack of drive) for many of us can be traced to shaky research skills. The task is harder when you don't know where to look. The jobs and the responsibility of getting the facts straight are fraught with risk. And a certain amount of checking is sometimes not done simply because it takes too long to examine every single fact.

Knowing where to look for the primary materials described in this chapter will shed light on your search, and make your job of checking and double checking a lot easier.

Original research means playing detective and piecing together parts of a disjointed puzzle. Besides having to locate your materials somewhat differently from newly published secondary sources, you never quite know what form primary materials will take. Your approach to researching them may also vary. You may not only have to study the era in which the subject of your research took place, but you may also have to struggle with hard-to-read handwriting, old English vocabulary, obsolete spellings, changes in the calendar centuries ago, and many other unique research challenges.

The real satisfaction in doing original research is that you may come upon something that has been overlooked by everyone else. The euphoric feeling that results from this kind of discovery—or its possibility—makes the effort worthwhile.

_____CHAPTER SUMMARY_____

I. Original research is the study of original, unpublished material—correspondence, notebooks, diaries, etc.—that ultimately leads you to new conclusions and/or previously unpublished information. (page 325)

II. Original materials come in many forms and from many sources.

    A. Primary information exists in the vast quantity of public records that contain data on each of us. There are records of birth and death; marriage and divorce; records that show we entered college or the military; information we supplied when we filled out a census form, had a baby, bought property, etc. (page 326)

    B. Much primary information exists in personal and organizational papers and reports. Many collections of the personal papers of well-known and not-so-well-known people and organizations are being reproduced in microform. (page 332)

III. Finding this original material means relying on printed sources.

    A. Micropublishers' catalogs contain information on which materials have been converted to microform. (page 331)

    B. Or you can trace a collection's original location through a directory like the _National Union Catalog of Manuscript Collections_. (page 333)

    C. Primary material can also be identified by subject through _Subject Collections_ or via one of the many directories of manuscript and archival material such as _Philippine-American Relations_. (page 335)

    D. A small selection of personal and organization papers has also been issued in sets of books that many large libraries own. (page 335)

IV. Some secondary sources (that material which was published long ago and close to when an event occurred or a person lived) are useful in original research. These resources bridge information gaps, and report events and attitudes with a perspective unique to that day. (page 337)

    A. Many old books that can give you the benefit of an authentic attitude have been reprinted and are listed in *Subject Guide to Books in Print*. (page 338)

    B. Check previous chapters for tips on how to use old newspapers, directories, almanacs, etc., in original research.

    C. The *Union List of Serials* and *New Serial Titles* are two important reference books to help you determine when a continuously issued publication began. (page 340)

V. Whether information is gathered firsthand or channeled through published sources, it is still subject to errors and biases. There are ways to cross-check many of the inaccuracies.

    A. Compare all data you find and continue searching until judgment tells you when to stop. (page 341)

    B. You may find it useful to study the background of a period to understand the material you find in the context of its own time. (page 341)

19

Says Who?
LOOKING FOR QUOTATIONS

I often quote myself. It adds spice to my conversation.
—George Bernard Shaw

A nicely turned phrase, maybe a line from a song or poem, captures the essence of a thought. That's one reason we remember selected phrases and inject them into our own writing and conversation. A vivid phrase is like the proverbial picture—it's worth 10,000 words. The more terse it is, in fact, the greater its impact.

> We are drowning in information data and starving for knowledge.
> —JOHN NAISBITT
> at the 13th annual meeting of the
> Association of American Publishers,
> 1983

People have always been intrigued with other people's words; so much so, that these words have been repeated through the ages and often subjected to changes and modernizations. Quotes—other people's words—portray those human qualities and beliefs that transcend time. They show us how little we've changed, for example, in our attitudes toward death, morality, and even raising children.

> By honest means, if you can, but by any means, make money.
> HORACE 65-8 B.C.

> Study the past, if you would divine the future.
> CONFUCIUS, 551-479 B.C.

As a researcher, you look for quotes for any or all of the following reasons: You want to determine who said something or where it came from; you want to get the correct wording, and you recall only a few key words; or you need a quote—any appropriate quote on a particular subject. (This motivated my search for quotes to head the chapters in this book.)

Next to looking for addresses, librarians probably spend more of their time tracking down catchy phrases or verses than anything else. It's often a quote the library patron memorized back in the fourth grade, or something he saw on a greeting card or poster. Though finding tools exist, the search for a specific quotation is often fruitless.

TIPS TO FINDING QUOTES

Finding quotes is like other forms of research—there's a pattern to follow. Whether you're looking for the author, source, or exact wording of a quote, you'll repeatedly use these same few steps. And sometimes you won't find anything. The dozen tips below will help make your search easier and also explain why you sometimes find nothing.

■ A quote can be many things: a line from a song, nursery rhyme, poem, speech, newspaper or magazine article, novel, etc. It can be a title of a book, play, song, speech, or even a slogan. Quotes can also be twisted definitions, puns, parodies, and famous last words.

> And while I am talking to you mothers and fathers, I give you one more assurance. I have said this before and I shall say it again and again and again. Your boys are not going to be sent to any foreign wars.
> FDR, Speech,
> Boston, October 30, 1940

A quote is anything that has been uttered, sung, or penned, and above all, is memorable or catchy.

> Barney Google with his Goo Goo Googly eyes
> Song, by BILLY ROSE AND
> CON CONRAD, 1923

■ General quotation books contain excerpts of all kinds of quotable expressions, and they vary greatly. Some focus on quotes from classical sources; others emphasize modern expressions. Some are subject-oriented (quotes from motion pictures or science), and some are a mixture of all kinds of tidbits from puns to poetry. Some quotation books limit themselves to one- and two-line expressions; others quote at length. Because of these wide differences, checking one or two quotation books is usually inadequate in tracing a quote. Sometimes, in fact, you may not have to check a quotation book at all. It may be best to use a song index rather than a quotation book to verify a line from a song. Other times, you may need to check a book or article as was the case involving the Alcoholics Anonymous motto mentioned in Chapter 5.

Q. When the late Adlai Stevenson was UN Ambassador, he addressed the General Assembly and made a quotable remark concerning the Russians. It came at the beginning of the Cuban Missile Crisis and concerned Russian denials that weapons were being sent to Cuba. I think the statement had something in it regarding "hell freezing over." How might I find the exact source and the context of this statement?

A. As you might imagine, this saying is not original, nor was Stevenson likely the first to say it; therefore, quotation books are not helpful here. But I did find a particular speech of Stevenson's through *Reader's Guide to Periodical Literature*. It's called "Has the U.S.S.R. Missiles in Cuba? debate, October 25, 1962," reprinted in a magazine called *Vital Speeches of the Day,* the November 15, 1962 issue. This expression appeared in that speech.

It happened when Stevenson was questioning Soviet Ambassador Zorin about Russian weapons in Cuba, and Zorin continued to deny it. Stevenson said something about Zorin's talent for obfuscation, distortion, confusing language, and double-talk. As tempers soared, Zorin replied that he was not in an American court subject to the rules of cross-examination, and that Stevenson would have his answer "in due course." Stevenson then responded that he was prepared to wait until hell freezes over.

■ Memories are shaky; we don't always recall a quote correctly. Misplacing one word can make the difference between finding it and not finding it, especially if you're checking the first line or title of a poem rather than a key word in context.

Q. Years ago I was taught a poem that has stayed with me. It begins: "There was a little boy whose name was Jim, His friends were very good to him, They gave him tea and cakes and jam, And slices of delicious ham." The poem continues to tell of naughty Jim who ran away from his governess at the zoo and who was eaten slowly by a lion. How can I find the rest of the poem and the name of the poet?

A. With the first line or title of a poem as a clue, you can use a poetry index such as *Granger's Index to Poetry* to find the author and also to see which book or books contain the poem in full. I almost missed this one because it starts "There was a boy . . ." (omit the word 'little'). It's by Hilaire Belloc and appears in several collections of poetry. One collection is *Beastly Boys and Ghastly Girls,* edited by William Cole.

■ Clues are vital. A title, author, subject, first line, a striking phrase, where and when you heard it—anything—is potentially helpful. Librarians spend much time tracking quotes, and they pick up stray odds and ends that are useful later on. You never know if what you say may turn out to be the missing link.

■ Start with the best known and biggest quotation books (back editions as well as recent editions, if any).

1. *Dictionary of Quotations,* by Bergan Evans. Delacorte Press. 1968. (2,029 pages.) *DQ* is arranged alphabetically by subject and includes keyword and author indexes. It contains a combination of popular, contemporary, and classical quotations.

2. *Familiar Quotations,* by John Bartlett. 15th edition. Little, Brown. 1980. (1,540 pages.) Bartlett's is arranged chronologically by the birth date

of the person quoted (Cecil Day Lewis, 1904-72; Pablo Nerudo, 1904-73; J. Robert Oppenheimer, 1904-67). You must use the subject/key-word index to trace a quote to its source in this book.

3. *Home Book of Quotations,* by Burton Stevenson. 10th ed. Dodd, Mead. 1967. (2,816 pages.) *HBQ* is arranged alphabetically by subject: HEART, HEAVEN, HELEN OF TROY, HELL, HELP, HERACLITUS, HERESY, HERMIT. It also includes key-word and author indexes. It's best to start with the key-word index first.

Sources quoted are heavily classical and historical: Ralph Waldo Emerson, Samuel Johnson, Nicholas I (Emperor of Russia), Benjamin Disraeli, Lord Byron, Alfred Lord Tennyson, and Sir Isaac Newton.

■ Hundreds of quotation books are in print, and you may want to find something more specialized than the three mentioned above. See *Subject Guide to Books in Print* under the term QUOTATIONS for titles of other quotation books. You'll also find "see also" references leading you to close relatives—books on maxims, proverbs, etc.—under which even more titles are listed. For example, *The Book of Rock Quotes* would be best to check for a possible rock song lyric. If the quote were not there, you would understandably try other music quotation books or a general quotation book. The lyrics would undoubtedly not appear in a book such as *Feminist Quotations.*

Q. I am interested in a book that would give the meaning of old Latin sayings like "E Pluribus Unum," "Ora et Lavora," "Veni, Vidi, Vici," etc. I cannot find anything in bookstores. Do you know of any books on the subject?

A. I found a book of Latin sayings entitled, *Beautiful Thoughts from Latin Authors,* by C.T. Ramage, which should explain a great many. Books of classical quotations and the standard Bartlett's *Familiar Quotations* also include a selection of Latin quotes.

■ Not every large library keeps all its quotation books in the reference section. Many are on open shelves and can be checked out. The librarians' judgment determines which ones are chosen to circulate.

■ Ask a librarian's help, especially if you're researching in a large library. Since quotation questions are common, many libraries are prepared with in-house files and other aids and tricks (as well as the librarians' experience) to make the job easier. The Los Angeles Public Library, for example, has a card file jointly indexing all editions of Bartlett's *Familiar Quotations.* (Each edition of Bartlett's, published at about 10-year intervals, changes as much as 25 percent. The first edition was published in 1855; later editions are quite different from the original.)

■ If you have a reputed author or a first line or title of a poem, check a poetry index or the author's collected works before trying a quotation book. Popular poetry indexes are *Granger's Index to Poetry* and *Chicorel Index to Poetry*.

Check the library's catalog under the author's name to find his collected works. The collected work often includes a key-word index to help you find that particular poem more quickly.

Q. Can you help me identify a poem I once heard? I only recall "Ships that pass in the night and speak each other in passing."

A. *Granger's Index to Poetry* shows two poems that begin, "Ships that pass in the night." Yours comes from Longfellow's "Tales of a Wayside Inn." It goes: "Ships that pass in the night and speak each other in passing. Only a signal shown and a distant voice in the darkness. So on the ocean of life we pass and speak one another, Only a look and a voice, then darkness again and a silence." One anthology in which the poem appears is *The Eternal Sea: An Anthology of Sea Poetry*, edited by W.M. Williamson.

■ Shakespeare and the Bible are prolific sources of memorable sayings, but quotation books include only a small selection from each of them. Don't overlook concordances (word-by-word dictionaries) to Shakespeare and the Bible. Large libraries should have some, such as *Walker's Comprehensive Bible Concordance*, by J.B.R. Walker (Kregel Publications) or the eight-volume *Complete and Systematic Concordance to the Works of Shakespeare*, by Marvin Spevack (Georg Olms Verlagsbuchhandlung, Hildesheim, Germany).

■ Quotes may change several times as they filter down through the ages, and you may actually find them in different forms in different quotation books. This is part of their history.

Q. I recently saw this saying in a writer's newsletter: "Say nothing, do nothing, be nothing." Can you tell me who said it?

A. I've checked about a dozen quotation books and only find one reference that's close, though not exactly the same. It's this line from Shakespeare (*All's Well That Ends Well*, ii, 4,25). "To say nothing, to do nothing, to know nothing, and to have nothing." Yours could be a shortened version derived from it.

■ A less than 50 percent success rate in tracing quotes is normal. Not everything "quotable" has been recorded. Also, quotation books say that their goal is to record memorable sayings, yet they confess that they cannot define what "memorable" is. Furthermore, no book is comprehensive; nor is every quote featured in every quotation book. Some quotes are even incorrectly attributed.

You'll struggle with many familiar quotes without success. You'll swear that everyone has heard them, recognizes them, and uses them, and you'll *still* be unable to trace them. Catchy thoughts such as "killing the messenger," "there's no such thing as a free lunch," "the only thing necessary for the triumph of evil is for good men to do nothing" have been tossed around by generations of librarians and researchers. To date, I know of no one who has yet traced them successfully.

I (and librarians all over the country) would be thrilled to have someone write and say they have the correct attributions. The three quotes above, however, have been scrutinized, discussed, and searched intensively. *RQ*, a magazine for librarians (*RQ* stands for "reference quarterly"), includes a column in which librarians request help on difficult questions they've been asked. Librarians nationwide have been working on these quotes for years with no luck.

In the Fall 1982 issue of *RQ*, one librarian noted that "the only thing necessary for the triumph of evil . . . " has been attributed, according to the 14th edition of Bartlett's, to Edmund Burke in a letter to William Smith. But *The Great Quotations*, edited by George Seldes, attributes it to Burke in a letter to Thomas Mercer, whereas books on the correspondence of Burke don't mention the quote at all. Subsequent issues of *RQ* have continued the discussion. One librarian referred to the same quote as scrutinized, discussed, and searched 20 years earlier! She said that all the standard sources attributing it to Burke were incorrect. The challenge was also picked up by William Safire of *The New York Times* with no enlightenment from him. And so far, Burkian scholars have been notably silent.

HOW TO LOOK UP A QUOTE

Most quotation books have key-word indexes, some of which occupy half the book. If you want to verify a quote's accuracy or its speaker, check the index first.

The next question is, which key word in the quote should you check? The following example sheds light on the problem.

A reader of my newspaper column once wrote me this question: "Last spring when I was on a cruise, a prize was offered to anyone who could identify the person who originally said, 'Go west, young man, go west.' We were told it wasn't Horace Greeley. Can you tell me who said it?"

By checking the quotation books in tip #5, I discovered that it was actually said by John L. Soule in *The Terre Haute Express* in 1851. A footnote added that Greeley had later quoted Soule's expression in an editorial in *The New York Tribune*, and despite Greeley's persistent denials, the saying has been attributed to him ever since.

The index in Bartlett's *Familiar Quotations* lists the saying under four key words:

GO
  G. west, young man
MAN
  Go west, young m.
WEST
  Go w., young man
YOUNG
  Go west, y. man

The index in Stevenson's book lists the saying under only one key word: WEST. There are no other approaches.

The index in Evans' book lists the saying under two key words: GO and WEST. There are no approaches under the words YOUNG or MAN.

To answer then, "which key word in a quotation should I check?" I'd say, "as many as possible."

The easiest and most enjoyable way to deal with quotes is to look them up by subject. Some of the quotes I've chosen to head the chapters in this book came from *Reader's Digest Treasury of Modern Quotations*, compiled by the editors of *Reader's Digest* and *Quotable Quotations Book*, compiled by Alex Lewis. I like their pithy definitions and sayings.

> A celebrity is a person who works hard all his life to become well known, then wears dark glasses to avoid being recognized.
> FRED ALLEN,
> quoted in *Paris After Dark*.

Recommended Quotation Books

I had considered making a list of quotation books, but because they're so uneven and because every researcher's needs are unique, I refer you to the recommended steps in the Tips section of this chapter.

Don't feel overwhelmed with the huge number of quotation books that exist. Consider them as potential resources, but recognize that none is comprehensive and many won't be pertinent to all your needs each time you check a quote in them. The following quotation books will suggest the scope and variety available. (Each of these volumes has either a key-word index or a subject index.)

1. *Harvest of a Quiet Eye: A Selection of Scientific Quotations*, by Alan Mackay. London: Institute of Physics. 1977. (Quotes of well-known men, both fictitious and real, that relate to science.)

> I fear that the spinning wheel is not stronger than the machine.
> NEHRU, trying unsuccessfully
> to promote village industry over
> industrialization in India

> From a drop of water, a logician could infer the possibility of an Atlantic or a Niagara without having seen or heard of one or the other.
> SHERLOCK HOLMES, *A Study in Scarlet*,
> by Sir Arthur Conan Doyle

2. *Manual of Forensic Quotations: A Compilation of Great Thoughts of Leading Members of the Bar, in Famous and Important Criminal and Civil Trials,* by Leon Mead and F. Newell Gilbert. J.F. Taylor and Co. 1903. Reprinted by Gale Research Co. 1968.

> The more horrid and atrocious the nature of any crime charged upon any man is, the more clear and invincible should be the evidence upon which he is convicted.
>
> JOHN P. CURRAN, Trial of the Dublin
> Defenders, Dec. 22, 1795

> A king has a greater right in the goods of his subjects for the public advantage than the proprietors themselves. And when the exigency of the State requires a supply, every man is more obliged to contribute toward it than to satisfy his creditors. The sovereign may discharge a debtor from the obligation of paying, either for a certain time or forever.
>
> PATRICK HENRY, Argument on the right
> of a state, during the Revolution, to
> confiscate British debts, Richmond, Va.,
> November, 1791

3. *The Movie Quote Book,* by Harry Haun. Lippincott & Crowell. 1980. (Contains bits of dialogue from movies.)

> I'm on my way to town to become a country music singer or star.
>
> BARBARA HARRIS, heading for Nashville
> in Robert Altman's *Nashville*

> Darling, you poor fool, don't you know I'm in love with you?
> BETTE DAVIS TO GEORGE BRENT
> in Edmund Goulding's *Dark Victory*

4. *The Quotable Woman, 1800-1975,* compiled by Elaine Partnow. Corwin Books. 1977. (Clips from the works of women writers.)

> All things ready with a will, April's coming up the hill.
> MARY MAPES DODGE (1838?-1905)
> Vulgarity is, in reality, nothing but a modern, chic, pert descendant of the goddess Dullness.
> DAME EDITH SITWELL (1887-1964)
> *Taken Care of,* Chapter 19

Though you are constantly warned against using trite expressions in original work (you can lead a horse to water, but you can't make him drink), borrowing someone else's words, naming the source, placing the quote strategically—and not overdoing it—can give your work a lift.

> You can lead a horse to water, but if you can get him to float on his back, you've got something.
> CONRAD SCHNEIKER
> University of Arizona, 1974

———————————— *CHAPTER SUMMARY* ————————————

I. Quotations capture a thought in a unique way. There's a pattern to looking for and finding quotes—you look for them by subject; to determine who said them when; or to verify their wording. (page 346)

II. Use these tips for finding quotes you need.

    A. Remember that a quote can be any kind of expression (song, headline, etc.), as long as it's catchy and likely to be remembered. (page 346)

    B. Because quotation books are so different in what they include, always check more than one. (page 346)

    C. The exact wording of a quote may matter, especially if it's part of a poem. Indexes you need to trace poems organize them by title and/or first line. (page 347)

    D. Consider all the clues you have about a quotation even if the information seems irrelevant to you. (page 347)

    E. Start your search with large general books which contain quotes; some are Bartlett's *Familiar Quotations* and *Home Book of Quotations*. (page 347)

    F. *Subject Guide to Books in Print* lists many unique and specialized quotation books. (page 348)

    G. Some quotation books are in the reference section of libraries; others may circulate. (page 348)

    H. Ask for a librarian's help if you're stuck. Librarians handle many quotation questions and may have research aids to make the search easier. (page 348)

    I. Quotation books don't include everything that's been quoted. You may have to use other books (indexes, an author's collected works, etc.) to trace a quote. (page 348)

    J. Though Shakespeare and the Bible are heavily quoted, they are not greatly represented in quotation books. Check concordances for sources of quotes from them. (page 349)

    K. Quotes may be worded differently as they are passed down from one century to another. (page 349)

    L. Don't be alarmed if your success rate for tracing quotes is less than 50 percent. (page 349)

III. When tracking the source of a quote, check it by as many keywords as possible. (page 350)

IV. No single quotation book will do in *every* case. Compilers agree that deciding what's memorable—and what should be included—is not an easy task.

20

When Words Are Not Enough:
LOOKING FOR
PICTURES

You furnish the pictures and I'll furnish the war.
—William Randolph Hearst

Few of us can deny the impact, personal value, and pleasure of pictures. They're nostalgia, art, education, even decoration. We take snapshots to help us recall stages in our lives and places we've visited. We cut out cartoons and collect pictures; we save greeting cards because of the images they capture. Pictures help us envision times before our own and places and things we've never seen. Without them, none of us but a select group would know the sight of the earth from an Apollo spacecraft or an amoeba magnified several hundred times.

Aside from their personal value, why are pictures important to researchers? Just like the source of a quotation or a statistic from an almanac, pictures answer questions, validate hunches, even settle arguments. You may need them for a variety of reasons: to explain an exhibit, illustrate a brochure, or add documentation to a book or article you are writing. (Illustrations and photographs add life to a printed page; in fact, books and articles on some topics—antiques or Western art, for example—are often more meaningful for the illustrations they contain. Brochures, too, are more likely to be read if they're highlighted with head-turning pictures and captions.)

Perhaps you need a picture to support a theory, or just to satisfy a curiosity whether it's the latest skyjacking, a World War II Japanese POW camp, a street market in Damascus, a wedding ceremony in Bali, an early-20th-century typewriter, a beached whale, or a rock concert. Pictures come in a variety of formats. They can be reproductions of paintings, sculptures, lithographed cartoons, magazine covers, song sheets, pages from an old newspaper, old stock certificates, posters, or wood engravings.

Whether or not it's visible to the naked eye, someone has probably captured it in film or art. Indeed, images of almost anything from ancient times up to the past 24 hours are collected by somebody, somewhere. Where to look for them in order to buy, borrow, or lease them is the subject of this chapter.

HOW TO GET PICTURES

You have two major choices for getting pictures you need. The first is to order them from an individual, organization, company, historical society, museum, library, government agency, tourist board, or other agency that collects them.

For example, the main library building at the University of California-San Diego has won many architectural awards (many people say the diamond-shaped building looks "outer spacey"), and pictures of it grace the pages of many books. Campus visitors frequently want their own frameable, enlarged copy. In response to endless requests, the university (like many organizations and institutions) offers prints for sale at a reasonable price.

The second option you have is to travel to the place where the original photographs or pictures are stored and riffle through archives or private files which may or may not be cataloged and organized. (More on this later.)

A third option, of course, is to take your own photos, which is not always a viable choice. And even if you could take that coveted photo, you still might not be able to use it, depending on your purpose. For example, if you wanted to reproduce your photo of the Hope Diamond, or even photograph it at all, you may need to get permission.

Often, researchers in search of pictures opt for choice one or two.

Look at a recent book or magazine and notice the sources of the photographs and illustrations used (the Smithsonian Institution, the Bettman Archives, etc.). There's nothing to stop you from using the same pictures in your research project as long as they're available for reproducing. (If originality is your goal and you plan to reproduce the picture in a widely circulated publication, keep in mind that the easiest picture to get may already have been seen in countless other publications.)

To find out about reproduction rights, photocopy the picture from the book or article in which you saw it (for identification purposes); get the source's address from an appropriate directory; forward the photocopy; and request information about ordering prints. Pictures may also be ordered through catalogs published by some lenders themselves.

To get images that haven't been seen over and over in other publications, you may have to dig through archives, private files, and other sources of original research. This sometimes means travel, more time, and more money.

HAVE A PLAN

Whether you conduct your picture research through the mail or in the flesh, your hunt will be considerably faster and cheaper if you target your efforts carefully. The list below tells you who collects photographs, pictures, postcards, and other images for reproduction. In addition, check MISCELLANEOUS SOURCES on page 365 for directories which identify other picture sources.

Public Institutions
Libraries, Museums, Historical Societies

You already know that many large libraries, museums, and historical societies own collections of miscellaneous materials grouped by subject, and that these caches often include photographs and other pictorial material. These organizations may also own collections of the work of well-known artists and photographers, many of which may be reproduced with permission. You can find many of these varied collections through the directories below.

1. *Contemporary Photographers*. St. Martin's Press. 1983.

It's not uncommon in books published today to feature the work of present-day artists. *The Women We Wanted to Look Like*, by Brigid Keenan (St. Martin's Press, 1977), is one example of a heavily illustrated book that uses pictures of famous women taken by well-known contemporary photographers rather than pictures leased from stock photo agencies (agencies that lease pictures regardless of who took them).

Contemporary Photographers is a who's who of internationally known photographers. It will lead you to museums and libraries that own their work. It also lists exhibitions in which their work was shown, printed exhibition catalogs, and published books and articles by and about them. See also *Index to American Photographic Collections*, page 358.

2. *Directory of Special Libraries and Information Centers*. 5 volumes. Gale Research Co. Issued every two years with supplements.

This set is an alphabetical arrangement of art, media, company, museum, society, hospital, law, and other special libraries. Included are such picture sources as the Brown and Williamson Tobacco Corp. library; the Discovery Hall Museum (owns photographs documenting local and industrial history of the South Bend, Indiana area); the American Cancer Society library; and the Antique Automobile Club of America library. Since the purpose of this reference book is not specifically to trace picture collections, entries are not uniform concerning a library's pictorial holdings. Many libraries listed may actually own little or no pictorial material. Other libraries own pictures, but that fact may not be mentioned in the entry.

Since many special libraries own picture material, you may want to contact one of those listed. Also check the subject index. It includes both broad and specific topics such as MARIMBA, KARL MARX, PHILOSOPHY, SOCIAL INTERACTION, STEAMBOATS, WYOMING. Fifty-four stock photo agencies with their addresses and a brief description of the fields in which they collect are also listed. You'll find them by checking under the subject heading, PICTURES; additional approaches are by specific subject.

The geographic index can help you identify organizations, companies, and libraries in your own region that have special collections. Check under the name of your city or town.

3. *Guide to the Special Collections of Prints and Photographs in the Library of Congress*, compiled by Paul Vanderbilt. Library of Congress. 1955.

This resource lists 802 individual collections in the Prints and Photographic Division of the Library of Congress as of 1955. (No revised edition has been published.) The guide is arranged alphabetically by collection name such as the Yovin Collection (11 glass plate negatives of costumed figures in Tunis and Marseilles, 1885-87) and the Royal Navy of Great Britain Collection (official British photographs of vessels, minesweepers, convoys, etc. covering 1939-1945, ca. 200 photo prints). Consult the subject index first.

4. *Index to American Photographic Collections*, compiled at the International Museum of Photography at George Eastman House, edited by James McQuaid. G.K. Hall & Co. 1982.

This reference lists 458 private and public collections of photographs (taken by some 19,000 19th- and 20th-century photographers) which are owned by historical societies, galleries, museums, libraries, government agencies, universities, etc., throughout the country. The index mentions collections of photographs by subject—the Harry S Truman Library in Independence, Missouri, for example, contains 71,000 photographs; the Liberty Memorial Museum of Kansas City owns 1,600 World War I photographs.

The book also includes a photographer index listing all the collections that hold a particular photographer's work. In many cases, an itemized list of exactly what each collection contains is available from the organization itself. Check the index's chapter called "How to Use This Index" for further information on using these collections and tips on getting prints from them.

5. *Index to Reproductions of American Paintings*, by Isabel Stevenson Monro and Kate M. Monro. H. W. Wilson. 1948. Supplement. 1964.

Photographs are not the only illustrations that are useful in a project. *Kings, Rulers and Statesmen*, compiled by Edward Egan, Constance Hintz, and L. F. Wise is one book that uses drawings, paintings, engravings, busts, and other artistic representations rather than photographs to illustrate, in this case, rulers who lived before the invention of the camera in the 1830s.

IRAP is one of several guides that will help you locate art work in museums from which you can order poster-type prints or photographs, whether you want to reproduce them in a published work or hang them on your wall. Besides naming the museum that owns the original work, *IRAP* lists paintings by artist, title, and subject.

For a preview look at any painting mentioned in the index, *IRAP* identifies 1,200 books that have published illustrations of the works. This may be helpful. Whether you want an artistic representation of Pocahontas, a battle scene from the American Revolution, or ice cream cones, you may want to see the picture before you order it. For intangibles like facial expressions, it is critical.

6. *Index to Reproductions of American Paintings,* by Lyn Wall Smith and Nancy Dustin Wall Moure. Scarecrow Press. 1977.

This index lists by artist, title, and subject thousands of American paintings owned by U.S. museums. It also names more than 400 books with illustrations of the paintings.

7. *Index to Reproductions of European Paintings,* by Isabel Stevenson Monro and Kate M. Monro. H.W. Wilson, 1959.

This list of European paintings is arranged by artist, subject, and title of work. The index also gives the name of the foreign or American museum that owns the original painting, and 328 books commonly found in art libraries, which illustrate them.

8. *Official Museum Directory.* American Associaton of Museums. 1973-date. Annual.

This directory covers general and special museums such as art, history, and science museums, as well as art centers, historic houses and sites, historical societies, aquariums, arboretums, botanical gardens, herbariums, planetariums, zoos, wildlife refuges, and national parks—most of which sell photographs relating to their subject specialty. Some institutions listed are the American Bible Society in New York City; the Barbed Wire Museum in LaCrosse, Kansas; the Alling Coverlet Museum in Palmyra, New York; the Abrams Planetarium at Michigan State University; the Shaker Museum in Poland Spring, Maine; and the American Museum of Immigration in the Statue of Liberty in New York City.

Since this directory is arranged geographically by state, then by city, check your region to see what photographic material local groups may own. Also check the broad subject index in the back.

9. *Sculpture Index,* by Jane Clapp. 4 volumes. Scarecrow Press. 1970.

This is an artist, subject, and title index to photographs of sculptures in several thousand American and foreign museums. It also lists more than 925 books which reproduce pictures of them.

10. *Subject Collections,* by Lee Ash. R.R. Bowker & Co. Published approximately every five-seven years.

This excellent source lists by subject special collections in public, company, university, museum, historical society, and other special libraries. Most of these collections own some pictorial material, although entries are not detailed nor are they standardized. For example, the entry for the Isadora Duncan collection in the New York Public Library's dance collection mentions that it contains over 200 original photographs, original drawings, scrapbooks, programs, and posters; whereas the collection of radio programs in the Broadcast Pioneers Library in Washington, DC says it owns "4,000 pictures." The El Paso Public Library has photographs in its Mexican Revolution of 1910 collection, but the entry doesn't say how many. Even with these inconsistencies, *Subject Collections* will help you trace an immediate source of specific pictorial material in a public or private institution on anything from Rough Riders to roofing.

Public Relations Departments
Corporations, Manufacturers, Zoos, Banks, Hospitals, Universities and Other Large Organizations

Many organizations keep records of their activities through in-house archives or libraries. They collect photos of their product or service, the grounds, building or buildings owned by the group, their officers, and employees at work. Such photo collections are often available free or at low cost to researchers.

Check your local Yellow Pages for addresses of groups in your area, or consult the *Directory of Directories* for an appropriate directory of banks, colleges, manufacturers, etc.

The types of photographic material that might be available are as varied as the kinds of groups and their activities or products. If you're trying to locate pictures of specific products—eggs, boats, cookware, aircraft, draperies—try firms that make, sell, or deal in them. An optical manufacturer or supplier listed in the *Blue Book of Optometrists* or the *Thomas Register of American Manufacturers* may have photographs relating to eye care. A shipping firm listed in a directory such as *Worldwide Shipping Guide* will likely own photographs of ships and shipping activity. These and other directories are listed in the *Directory of Directories*.

If you need a picture of a place—perhaps a Las Vegas hotel or Boston's Massachusetts General Hospital—you should be able to get it from their public relations office. You'll find their addresses in their city phone book, under the special listings for hotels and hospitals in the *Zip Code Directory*, or from a directory of hotels and hospitals listed in *DOD*.

Even auction houses offer pictures. Sotheby's, for example, takes photographs of sale items—lamps, cigarette cards, Dutch tiles, military collectibles, old scientific instruments, primitive money, etc.—for its various catalogs. These photos may be available to researchers. (*The Auction Companion* by Daniel and Katherine Leab [Harper & Row, 1981] lists the specialties and addresses of 494 large auction houses worldwide, 130 of which are in the United States.)

To stimulate your thinking about where else to get the pictures you need, consider these directories listed in *DOD: Directory of Black Fashion Specialists, Directory of Miniatures and Dolls, Calendar of Folk Festivals and Related Events, Vintage Auto Almanac, Big Book of Halls of Fame in the United States and Canada—Sports,* and *Green Book of Home Improvement Contractors.*

Societies, Associations, Clubs

Many societies (professional, trade, hobby) own or have access to a collection of visual material relating to their interests and activities— UFOs, model trains, Basenji dogs, or whatever. Their collection may turn out to be nothing more than home photographs taken by an officer of the group. Or it may include a full range of picture material in a carefully kept, well-cataloged archive.

Approach societies, associations, and clubs (especially the smaller ones), as picture sources only when you have a great deal of time to gather your photos. Many groups may be ill equipped to fill requests. Perhaps they have no staff to handle them, or their photographs may not be good enough to reproduce. It always pays to shop around if you're looking for just the right photo at the right price.

1. *Encyclopedia of Associations.* Gale Research Co. Annual.

If you're looking for an organization, this is the voluminous resource to use. It lists some 17,000 associations, many of which make photos available. Examine the entries carefully for clues on the extent of pictorial material. As with some other directories, *EA's* primary function is not to point out the existence of picture collections. Therefore, mention of photograph availability is not consistent: The entry for the Bostonian Society tells you the group owns a picture collection of antiques connected with Boston history; other entries may say nothing about pictures. Sometimes you might assume that groups have pictorial resources. Action for Children's Television may own a picture collection simply because it's big (15,000 members nationwide), has a central headquarters, and issues its own magazine. Yet no mention is made of pictures in ACTs entry. The listing for the National Theatre of the Deaf doesn't specifically mention pictorial material either, but the group could well have photographs since you'd *expect* that a theater group would. Save time and disappointment by contacting the organization directly *before* you make a request for photographs.

Some groups don't have a staff or a central headquarters, and this might make your picture research difficult. The Whooping Crane Conservation Association, for example, consists of 500 naturalists, ornithologists, and aviculturists scattered nationwide. Individual group members have their own photographs, but getting them could be tedious and even unreliable. It might be faster to use a commercial source such as a stock photo agency that specializes in animal pictures, unless the picture you want just isn't available anywhere else, or you have lots of time and little money.

Tourist Boards, Chambers of Commerce, Embassies

Most cities, states, and countries maintain chambers of commerce, tourist divisions, and consulates to encourage tourism and attract business. Many foreign tourist boards have offices in major American cities. They are usually pleased and even anxious to supply photos (often free), because published pictures of their areas represent free publicity if they're to be published in a book, article, or brochure. The shortcoming of publicity photos is, of course, that they're cosmetic and show nothing negative.

Chambers of commerce, consulates, and tourist boards are listed in the following:

1. *Encyclopedia of Associations*. Gale Research Co. Annual.

2. *Foreign Consular Offices in the United States*. Government Printing Office. Annual.

Arranges in geographical order the name of the foreign consul and the address of the consulate in the United States. Among its listings, *EA* includes about 100 American chambers of commerce in foreign countries and foreign chambers of commerce in the United States.

3. *1,001 Sources for Free Travel Information*. Travel Information Bureau. 1978.

A geographical list of 1,200 travel information sources, including tourist information bureaus, embassies, consulates, UN missions, airlines, railroads, chambers of commerce, state development offices, hotel chains, and other sources of travel information in foreign countries and the United States.

4. *World Wide Chamber of Commerce Directory*. Johnson Publishing Co. Annual.

This volume lists chamber of commerce contacts in approximately 7,750 American cities and towns and in 275 foreign countries.

Press Agencies and Newspapers

Pictures of current events appear in newspapers and news magazines like *Time* and *Newsweek*. Local newspapers illustrate local news. Press agencies such as United Press International and news magazine correspondents cover the national and international scene with words and pictures. These agencies and publishers often sell their photographs for reproduction. Addresses of newspapers and press agencies can be found in the following:

1. *Ayer Directory of Publications*. Ayer Press. Annual.

2. *Editor & Publisher International Year Book.* Editor & Publisher, Inc. 1920-date. Annual.

3. *News Bureaus in the U.S.* Public Relations Publishing Co. Biennial, odd years.

4. *Working Press of the Nation.* National Research Bureau. Annual.

Government Agencies

Many city, state, and federal agencies that oversee transportation, labor, health, environment, and other services have collections of photographs documenting their activities. For example, the New York City Department of Sanitation has more than 35,000 items in its department archives—photographs of refuse collection, street cleaning, waste disposal, landfills, snow removal since 1900, etc. The Nebraska Game and Parks Commission has some 50,000 items portraying Nebraska out-of-doors: hunting and sports, flora and fauna, scenic views, points of interest, to name a few.

The federal government is a rich and varied source of pictorial wealth representing every imaginable subject. The Center for Polar Archives, for example, has records of the activities of all branches of the military, the Weather Bureau, and other government agencies in the Polar region in the 1940s and 1950s; the U.S. Customs Service owns more than 2,000 photos recording border inspection and detection of smuggled goods, training of inspectors, and other activities of agents and patrols; the Drug Enforcement Administration has over 25,000 photos covering subjects such as drug trafficking, preventive programs, and the counterculture of the 1960s and 1970s.

1.*Free Stock Photography Directory.* Infosource Business Publications. 1979.

This directory lists over 260 federal, state, and local government offices, and some corporations, which offer free photos for commercial use. A geographical and a subject index are included.

2. *Pictorial Resources in the Washington DC Area*, compiled by Shirley L. Green. Library of Congress. 1976.

This work describes the general picture resources of government agencies and other government-affiliated organizations such as the Library of Congress and the Smithsonian Institution. (Entries for these two organizations are brief compared to their varied and huge holdings. Both of them own enough pictorial material to occupy a book in themselves— for example, *Guide to the Special Collections of Pictures and Photographs in the Library of Congress,* by Paul Vanderbilt, on page 358.)

This directory also lists private and international organizations in the District of Columbia that own picture collections. Groups such as the Inter American Development Bank, the Food and Agricultural Organization of the United Nations, the Southern Railway Co., and the Textile Museum are represented.

Stock Photo Agencies

Stock photo agencies are commercial firms that buy photographs from many photographers or sources. They often specialize in certain subjects, and as a result, they can offer comprehensive picture coverage in that field. AlaskaPhoto in Anchorage, for example, has more than 150,000 photos taken in Alaska and Northwestern Canada covering the wildlife, industry, towns, and people. Culver Pictures in New York City incorporates a broader spectrum of topics with its collection of nine million photos—movie stills, images of history and inventions, photos of science, sports, and theater. There are about 150 stock photo agencies nationwide, located mostly in big cities. Their photos may be leased for any price upwards of $10. Stock photo directories include the following:

1. *Art in Life,* by Jane Clapp. Scarecrow Press. 1959. Supplement. 1965.

This is a subject index to the pictures that appeared in *Life Magazine* between 1936 and 1963. Most pictures are owned by the magazine, and many are available for lease from Time Inc.'s Life Picture Service in New York City.

2. *Illustration Index,* compiled by Marsha C. Appel. 4th ed. Scarecrow Press. 1980.

This resource indexes the illustrations that have appeared in *American Heritage, Ebony, Holiday, National Geographic, National Wildlife, Natural History, Smithsonian,* and *Sports Illustrated* between 1972 and 1976. Reproduction rights for many of the staff-taken pictures are available for lease through the magazines listed.

3. *Illustration Index,* compiled by Roger Greer. 3rd ed. Scarecrow Press. 1973.

This edition indexes pictures from *American Heritage, Ebony, Grade Teacher, Hobbies, Holiday, Instructor, Life, Look, National Geographic, School Arts, Sports Illustrated,* and *Travel* between 1963 and 1971, and two books: *America's Wonderlands: The Scenic National Parks and Monuments of the United States,* by the Editors of National Geographic Society, and *History of Rocketry and Space Travel,* by Wernher von Braun and Frederick Ordway.

4. *Illustration Index,* compiled by Lucile Vance and Esther M. Tracey. 2nd ed. Scarecrow Press. 1966.

Pictures are indexed by subject from *American Heritage, Grade Teacher, Hobbies, Holiday, Ideals Magazine, Instructor, Life, Look, National Geographic, Nation's Heritage, Sports Illustrated, Theater Arts,* and *Travel* between 1950 and 1963, and 10 books.

5. *Illustration Index,* compiled by Lucile Vance. 1st ed. Scarecrow Press. 1957.

Pictures are indexed from *American Heritage, Grade Teacher, Hobbies, Holiday, Ideals Magazine, Instructor, Life, Look, National Geographic, Nation's Heritage, School Arts, Sports Illustrated, Theater Arts,* and *Travel* between approximatley 1950 and 1956, and six books. (The editions of *Illustration Index* are especially useful if you don't need a copy of the picture, but just want to see it. If you're wondering what a birthday card in 1900 looked like, you could skim books on greeting cards. But if you checked *Illustration Index*, you might find reference to a publication that has a representative picture of a turn-of-the-century birthday greeting card.)

Q. I'd like to see pictures of present-day police officers' uniforms from various European countries. What is the best way to do this?

A. Check *Subject Guide to Books in Print* under UNIFORMS. There happens to be one book in print, with illustrations, called *Uniforms of the World's Police*, by James Cramer. It was published in 1968.

Also try *Illustration Index*. Its four editions index pictures since 1950 in about three dozen magazines and books. There are several listings in recent editions under POLICE, followed by the name of the country. The entries will lead you to pictures in magazines such as *National Geographic, Life,* and *Smithsonian*.

---

6. *Literary Market Place*. R.R. Bowker & Co. Annual.

Among its countless chapters of information for people in the book business, this resource also lists about 100 stock photo agencies in one chapter and approximately 140 photographers in another. These lists are alphabetical with no separate subject access, so each entry must be examined for the subject you need.

7. *Photographer's Market: Where to Sell Your Photographs*. Writer's Digest Books. Annual.

This is primarily a market guide telling photographers where to sell their work. One chapter alphabetically lists 110 stock photo agencies as possible buyers of their photographs. These agencies are the same ones that lease photos to book, calendar, and encyclopedia publishers; advertising agencies; and individuals. As with *LMP* above, entries must be checked individually to match their subject specialties with your needs.

Miscellaneous Sources

Many directories list a variety of categories encompassing all or several of the picture sources already mentioned. The resources which follow represent a potpourri of these and other picture-finding tools.

1. Hart Picture Archives Series. Hart Publishing Co.

This is a series of over a dozen and a half books that reproduces artwork (cartoons, drawings, sketches, and engravings) from out-of-print books and magazines in the public domain. These pictures can be reproduced without fees or permission. The books state that the artwork is ready to be reproduced, and they give instructions on how to do it. The subject scope is varied. Some volumes in the series are *European Designs; Oriental Designs; Ships, Seas, and Sailors; Holidays; Borders and Frames; The Animal Kingdom; Humor, Wit, and Fantasy; Jewelry; Chairs; Weather; Dining and Drinking; Faces; Weapons and Armor; Jars, Bowls, and Vases;* and *Merchandise.* Each volume has a subject index.

Some of the old publications from which sources were drawn include *Works of Rabelais; Picture Book of the Graphic Arts, 1500-1800; Collected Drawings of Aubrey Beardsley;* an early edition of *Gulliver's Travels;* and some century-old issues of *Harper's New Monthly Magazine.*

2. *Picture Sources,* by Ann Novotny 3ᵤ ed. Special Libraries Association. 1975.

This book lists picture collections in public libraries, state agencies, museums, universities, newspapers, and stock photo agencies such as the Bettmann Archives. The book is arranged by broad subject category (e.g., TRANSPORTATION), then alphabetically by agency. It also includes a subject section (MILITARY HISTORY, HEALTH, etc.) which refers you to the collection with pictures on that subject.

3. *Stock Photo and Assignment Source Book: Where to Find Photographs Instantly,* edited by Fred W. McDarrah. R.R. Bowker & Co. 1977.

This volume covers a wide variety of sources: museums, societies, historic sites, television stations, newspapers, government, motion picture studios, companies, special libraries, and stock photo agencies. Check its extensive subject index to help you find the right source for the pictures you want.

Q. Where can I see a picture of Peter and Jane Fonda's mother?

A. Frances Seymour Brokaw, 1907-1950, appeared in pictures with her family in the July 1948 issue of *House Beautiful* (traced through *Biography Index*). You can see it in a large library. The pictures aren't very clear, but until one of the Fondas writes an autobiography, we aren't likely to find any outside the family album, or those which may appear randomly in books. According to Jane Fonda's unauthorized biography, Thomas Kiernan's *Jane,* which has no photographs, movie magazines of the period ran picture stories on Brokaw after her suicide. Many such magazines are owned by the library of the Academy of Motion Picture Arts and Sciences in Beverly Hills (which also has an in-house index to them). You might also try shops such as Larry Edmunds Bookshop in Hollywood which deals in movie magazines. If you want to pursue it further, check with a stock photo agency that specializes in pictures of notable people (New York Times Pictures is one), listed in *Stock Photo and Assignment Source Book.*

4. *Subject Guide to Books in Print.* R.R. Bowker Co. Annual.

SGBIP can help you find illustrated books on any subject. If you're looking for pictures in the general area of astronomy, check that subject for books on the topic.

If the book is not more than about 25 years old, it should credit the source of its pictures (perhaps the pictures in that book on astronomy came from NASA, the Hayden Planetarium in New York City, and the Griffith Observatory in Los Angeles). A book on European peasant fashion of the 16th century may name specific museums and costume collections as its sources. A book on a little-known but colorful historical character may name as its picture source a special collection of original material buried within a university library. Relevant directories will help you find the addresses of the libraries, museums, and companies mentioned.

The following list names just a few of the thousands of subject books that will, in the credit lines of the photos they feature, lead you to sources of pictures or art. (Most, but not all of the *SGBIP* entries, include the abbreviation for illustrations in the annotation.)

ACROBATS AND ACROBATISM
> Meyer, Charles R. *How to Be an Acrobat.* (Illus.) 1978. McKay

BUTTERFLIES
> Harris, Lucien, Jr. *Butterflies of Georgia* (Illus.) 1975. University of Oklahoma Press.

CLEVELAND MUSEUM OF ART
> Cleveland Museum of Art. *Handbook of the Cleveland Museum of Art.* 1976. Indiana University Press.

DRAWINGS, FRENCH
> Hattis, Phyllis. *Four Centuries of French Drawings in the Fine Arts Museums of San Francisco.* 1978. Fine Arts Museum.

PAINTINGS, JAPANESE
> Shimizu, Yoshiaki, & Wheelwright, Carolyn, eds. *Japanese Ink Paintings from American Collections: The Muromachi Period.* 1976. Princeton University Press.

SCULPTURE—AFRICA
> *Yoruba Sculpture in Los Angeles Collections.* 1969. Galleries of the Claremont Colleges.

5. *Ulrich's International Periodicals Directory.* R.R. Bowker Co. Annual.

Ulrich's helps you identify magazines with a specific subject orientation through its subject category arrangement. In the category called SPORTS AND GAMES—BALL GAMES, for example, you'll find *Tennis Magazine.* Under SPORTS AND GAMES—BICYCLES AND MOTORCYCLES, you'll find *Motorcyclist.* Back copies in the library can help you check pictures and picture credits; if photos were taken by the magazine staff, they may be available from the magazine.

6. *World Photography Sources,* edited by David N. Bradshaw. Directories. 1982.

This is a collection of varied picture sources worldwide: foreign embassies in the United States, museums, libraries, stock photo agencies, movie studios, tourist bureaus, press agencies, individual photographers, etc. It's not as comprehensive as other sources, and some of its entries are not annotated, but it's one of the few directories that list picture sources abroad.

7. *Writer's Resource Guide*, edited by Bernadine Clark. 2nd ed. Writer's Digest. 1983.

This directory lists associations, museums, organizations, companies, and special interest groups that provide information, and often pictures, for researchers. The book is divided into 30 subject sections, such as The Arts, Business, Health and Medicine, House and Home, Products and Services, Sports, Tourism and Travel, and Transportation. Each entry is annotated with the particular services offered and their collection features.

Picture Catalogs in Microform

Many collections of photographs have been reproduced in microform primarily for use by art scholars. However, they also function as catalogs of photographs owned by particular collections. You can, therefore, scan the pictures a collection owns before ordering them. (Prints can be ordered from most of them.)

The catalogs below are about half of those which have been filmed to date. They are listed in the pages of *Microform Review*. (See Chapter 14.)

1. *Ancient Roman Architecture*. This microfilm collection reproduces 14,000 photos from the archive of the Fototeca Unione in the American Academy of Rome in Italy.

2. *Architecture of Washington, D.C.*, edited by Bates Lowry. Dunlap Society. This collection of visual materials is of a selective group of major buildings in Washington, DC. Photographs cover from early sketches of the buildings in the planning stages up to the present.

3. *Christie's Pictorial Archive*. Mindata, Ltd., London. 1980. One thousand two hundred nine fiches cover thousands of photographs of sale goods from the 1890s to 1979 that have been pictured in Christie's auction catalogs. Most pictures date from 1945 when Christie's catalogs became quite elaborate.

4. *Dorothea Lange: Farm Security Administrator Photographs, 1935-39*. Texte-Fiche Press. 1980. Thirteen hundred photos by Lange show the dispossessed farmers of the Depression; these were selected from her works in the Library of Congress.

5. *The International Archives of Photography*. Macmillan Publishing Co. This microfiche series will make available the complete photographic work of master photographers. The first microform set features 486 pho-

tos of Jacob Riis showing the slum life of the New York immigrant.

6. *A Photographic Record of the Principal Items in the Collection of the Victoria & Albert Museum, London*. Mindata, Ltd., London. 1977. This is a pictorial guide to over 40,000 decorative art objects (furniture, sculpture, ceramics, textiles, etc.) from the museum's permanent collection. The reproductions are from the museum's own photograph library.

7. *An X-Ray Atlas of the Royal Mummies*, edited by James E. Harris and Edward F. Wente. University of Chicago Press. 1980. This catalog consists of a 403-page book and 5 microfiches showing 103 plates of the interior of the Tomb of On Inhapy and x-rayed mummies.

YOUR OWN BACKYARD

The above sources should help you locate just about any picture you need; but in the interest of time, start your picture search close to home. You'll find that with a little ingenuity, local sources can often provide at least some of the pictures you need. The best part of starting close to home is that you can see the photos before ordering prints. Seeing them can make a difference.

Pictures from historical societies, for example, may not be identifiable by a particular geographical region, which means you might be able to use them for general historical images. They can represent fashions or furniture of another period, a horse and buggy, a trolley car, an Indian reservation, daguerreotypes, posters, or old greeting cards.

Large newspapers in your area will have staff photos of well-known celebrities or political figures who have been the subject of articles in their newspaper. Photos of local scenes, buildings, crowds, landscapes, riots, fires, traffic accidents, snowstorms, weather damage, etc., that have appeared in the newspaper, are normally for sale. Since they've only been seen locally, they're potentially useful in other projects.

A natural history museum in town may be able to furnish pictures of flowers and insects indigenous to the area. Local banks may keep pictorial histories of growth and development, not only of their own institution but of others in town.

Don't forget large companies, manufacturers, hospitals, theater or dance companies, restaurants, museums, schools, blood banks, and zoos. Use your Yellow Pages. There may be a wealth of pictures within your city or county limits.

There may be a directory of picture sources or outlets in the area. Sometimes it is a mimeographed pamphlet compiled by the local public library, and it may be available free or at nominal cost. There's one such directory for picture sources in the Los Angeles area; it was compiled by the staff of the Los Angeles Public Library.

Also check the geographic section of directories already mentioned: the *Directory of Special Libraries and Information Centers*, the *Official Museum Directory*, and the *Stock Photo and Assignment Source Book*. There are probably picture agencies and photographers in your area that you haven't yet discovered.

Stick-to-Itiveness

Whether your picture source is right in your own zip code area or halfway around the world, you should know some basic guidelines for finding, getting, and using the print you want. Perhaps the most basic guideline in picture research is perseverance.

The way pictures are organized in many public institutions is often a problem that impairs both quick service and finding images in the first place. Photos, artwork, and other pictorial material are often parts of individual collections of manuscripts, books, and papers. They are not often separated into picture collections for easy access by picture researchers. Even if the library, museum, or other organization does have separate collections of pictures, the images may not be cataloged.

There are some nine million prints, negatives, slides, and photographs in the Prints and Photographic Division of the Library of Congress. According to the curator, the collection is largely uncataloged because of its immense size; it is little used because it's not cataloged. (Imagine trying to uncover a photo of the Sioux Indians in 1865 under those conditions!)

The Library of Congress also owns pictorial materials in the form of old securities, documents, calendars, post cards, advertisements, etc., as well as other photographs in its dozens of other divisions: music, rare books, astronomy, etc. The harder it is to identify specifically what you want (sometimes you don't *know* what you want until you see something that strikes you "just right"), the less likely it is that you can get it by mail. Most people don't like to buy pictures, or anything, sight unseen.

Guidebooks to archives and manuscript collections can be helpful, although some are better in describing their picture contents than others. (Check the suggestions in Chapter 18 for finding these guides.) Maybe you're looking for some early-20th-century photos of Niagara Falls; and the special libraries and historical societies you've checked have many pictures, but these groups are not equipped to help you by mail. You check the *Guide to Manuscript Collections in the National Museum of History and Technology* (part of the Smithsonian Institution), and you notice an entry in it called "The Niagara Falls Power Company Records, ca. 1890-1919." The annotation says that this small collection consists of "printed records and photographs." Without further specific information, you could refer to that collection and take a chance on ordering some prints sight unseen. (If the photos are accessible in this collection and there aren't many of them, the staff may photocopy the pictures to help you make a decision.)

What if you wanted to find a copy of the first photograph ever taken of the moon? You'd probably never find it unless you already knew it was part of "The Draper Family Collection, ca. 1835-1908" in the National Museum of History and Technology. And you would discover it only with persistence, because this particular collection of Draper material (Draper was a 19th-century chemist and photography pioneer who took the first picture of the moon in 1839) is not listed in two major conventional directories of special collections: *The National Union Catalog of Manuscript Collections* and *Subject Collections*.

This is part of the detective work you must be prepared to do to track down specific photos; and this is where sheer determination comes in handy. Getting photographs from many public institutions means one of two things: either you must provide precise descriptions of what you want (from published guidebooks, if they exist) in order for the staff to be able to send you what you want; or you'll have to dig it out yourself. (This is another reason why starting close to home is usually best.)

SERVICE AND FEES

Pictures are collected by both public and commercial agencies with differing motives for lending you their material. Therefore, the level and speed of their service varies. It usually depends on the stake the lender has in the use of the photo. Stock photo agencies, newspapers, some zoos, and others are profit-making organizations, and they generally provide the quickest service. Chambers of commerce, tourist boards, and manufacturers also usually respond quickly to picture requests, because your use of their photo represents free public exposure (their pictures are usually free, too).

On the other hand, public agencies such as libraries, museums, and historical societies exist primarily to collect and preserve unique material. They may not be set up to provide prints quickly or at all. And if a negative (from which copies are made) doesn't exist, it will take more time to have one made. Making prints available to the public is a secondary chore for public institutions. The cost of their prints is often lower than those from commercial sources, but their service is usually slower.

The ultimate use of a picture usually determines the fee charged. If it's used in an article, the fee may be lower than if it's used in a book. If the book is to have a high first-print run, the cost may be more than that for a low first-print run. A stock photo agency may charge an average of $10 to $30 per onetime use of a picture, but a museum or library may charge less than half that amount.

If fast service is your major concern, approach a commercial source first. In cases where pictures are available only from public sources like libraries and museums, you may have no choice but to be patient.

COPYRIGHT AND PERMISSION

Organizations that lease their photographs state the conditions under which the photo can and cannot be used. Permission to reproduce a photo is usually part of your leasing agreement. For example, a picture may be limited to use in books and articles but not in advertising. The lender will usually specify also that you not make your own copy for reuse after you return the print, because you bought the right to use the image only once (onetime rights). There are usually no "use" restrictions if you buy a photographic print as a gift or souvenir photo for personal enjoyment.

If you take your own photographs and intend to sell them, the issue of copyright becomes crucial. A book on the subject—one like *Photography: What's the Law?* by Robert M. Cavallo and Stuart Kahan (Crown Publishers, Inc.)—should be part of your personal library. You must know, for example, that although you may be able to take your own photograph of a famous work of art, you may not be able to reproduce it in a publication without permission of the artist or institution that owns the work. The photograph is yours, but the right to reproduce it publicly may not be. The book also covers rules on publishing photographs of public versus private figures. For public figures you usually don't need a model release (depending on how you intend to use the picture). But for private citizens, a model release is advisable.

A book on the legal aspects of selling your photos explains the nuances of permissions as they apply to photography. Even if you borrow or lease photos from others and don't intend to sell them, you should be aware of what you can and cannot legally do with a picture in your possession. Check for other books on this subject in *SGBIP* under PHOTOGRAPHY—LAW AND LEGISLATION.

PICTURE RESEARCHERS

If you must have that one particular picture and you can't find it yourself (or a librarian in a public institution can't dig it out for you), you might consider using the services of a professional picture researcher. *Literary Market Place* lists 50 of them nationwide under the category PHOTO RESEARCHERS in the chapter on Editorial Services.

What these researchers offer may depend to a large degree on where they are located. Picture Research, for example, is a company in Bethesda, Maryland, that has access to the vast picture collections in Washington, DC. Location may be something to consider when looking for a commercial service.

Rates are usually computed by the hour plus the picture charges of the institution from which the image comes. Consult individual picture researchers for their rates and specific services.

Though I have highlighted several ways to locate pictures and picture collections in this chapter, finding the picture you need is still not an exact operation. Unlike searching for print material which is constantly becoming easier because of technology, the picture-finding process may improve only slightly. Cataloging or inventorying pictures is as difficult as ever. The numbers of pictures that need cataloging is tremendous.

The best this chapter can do is help you locate more picture collections than you ever knew existed. Beyond that, it's a matter of diligence in sorting through the wealth of images you are likely to find.

CHAPTER SUMMARY

I. Pictures represent a unique kind of information resource. They depict objects, places, and times that we may not have experienced; they verify the details of something from our past; they provide evidence. (page 355)

II. Whatever your reason for needing an image, you can be sure someone has probably photographed, painted, or sketched it. And that visual record likely exists somewhere.

   A. Public institutions (libraries, museums, historical societies, etc.) have various kinds of pictorial material. Several directories listed here will help you locate special subject collections, many of which contain photographs. (page 357)

   B. Public relations offices in corporations, manufacturing companies, banks, hospitals, universities, hotels, auction houses, zoos, etc., are well-equipped picture resources. They keep records, including photographic documentation, of their products and services, their history, physical layout, etc. (page 360)

   C. Societies (professional, trade, and hobby) and associations often maintain archives and may make their pictorial material available to the public. (page 361)

   D. Tourist boards, chambers of commerce, and consulates and embassies may give photos free of charge in exchange for the publicity. Be aware that these kinds of pictures are usually cosmetic since they are intended to show an area in its best light. (page 362)

   E. Press agencies and newspapers offer pictures depicting current events and human interest. Contact these sources directly by checking one of the newspaper directories listed in this section. (page 363)

   F. Government agencies may be able to supply you with the print you need. Many arms of the federal, state, and local government collect extensive materials in their area of responsibility, be it labor or transportation. (page 363)

G. Stock photo agencies are commercial ventures that sell photographs and often specialize in a subject area. Several directories give the names and specialties of stock photo agencies. (page 364)

H. There are many miscellaneous picture sources which are identified in directories that list a combination of all of the above pictorial sources, from public libraries to commercial operations. The *Hart Picture Archives* series and *Subject Guide to Books in Print* are just two excellent all-purpose references. (page 365)

I. More and more picture catalogs are coming out in microform; you can find them listed in *Microform Review*. These cover a variety of sources, from Christie's auctions to some of the better-known picture collections in the Library of Congress. Microform catalogs let you preview the pictures in these collections before you order any. (page 368)

III. Many of the picture sources available nationwide may also be in your own backyard. Hospitals, zoos, planetariums, theater groups, hobby clubs, and museums in your area are logical places to begin. Your local library may even have a handy list of the area's photo or picture sources. (page 369)

IV. No matter where you look or what you eventually find, there are some things about looking for and using pictures that you should know.

A. Patience is a must. Many museums and associations collect pictures primarily to preserve them, not to lease or sell them for reproduction purposes.

B. Unless you always take your own pictures and you never need a "historical" shot, you will likely buy and/or lease photos for your research project. The kind of service you get from various lenders depends on their motives for lending.

1. Stock photo agencies lease their photos for profit. Their service is usually faster than that of public institutions.

2. Prices that public, nonprofit groups charge are usually cheaper than stock photo agencies (including some newspapers and zoos)—but their service is also slower. (page 371)

C. When you lease a photo, permission and copyright matters regarding it are covered in your leasing agreement. If you take your own photos and plan to sell and/or reproduce them on a mass scale or for advertising purposes, you must know more about copyright and permissions. One of the books on the subject will give you this information. (page 372)

V. If you do not have the time—or patience—to search for your own pictures, you may want to consider the services of a professional picture researcher. (page 372)

21

It's the Law:
LOOKING FOR LEGAL INFORMATION

*Litigation is a machine which you go into as a pig
and come out as a sausage.*
—Ambrose Bierce

The reasons we need legal advice are many and varied, simple and complex. Whatever the circumstances, we want answers to our legal questions. And because we often consider information about the law to be a "trade secret" reserved only for those with a law degree, most of us believe the cost of getting answers is prohibitive.

Actually, insights or even answers to some legal questions *are* available without paying money or contacting a lawyer. (In most cases, you will still consult an attorney if you plan to take any kind of action, but you can use his expertise more effectively if you do some searching on your own first.) You can get some basic legal information for yourself if you know where and how to look. And if you know *that*, you might not postpone getting answers.

Suppose your next-door neighbor backs his car out of his driveway, and it stalls broadside in the middle of the street. Since the street is a dead end, your neighbor doesn't feel rushed to move it. But it's dark, and your spouse, arriving home at that moment, fails to see the car and hits it in this poorly lit section of the street. Who's to blame?

What about your rich Aunt Martha who recently died? Her closest living relatives are two sisters and a dozen nieces and nephews of whom you are one. You and your relatives learn that Aunt Martha has left her fortune to two of your cousins. The rest of you wonder if you have any rights in the matter. If so, you want to pursue it. How can you find out more about your options *before* approaching a lawyer?

Questions like these come up every day. Unless the situation is extreme, we often let it drop. But we still wonder, and may for a long time—without getting answers.

WHY YOU SHOULD KNOW THE LAW

The steps of legal research are similar to other kinds of research in one way: You must use prescribed reference books and learn their unique formats, abbreviations, codes, tricks, and traps. This chapter introduces you to legal reference books, codes and statutes, and some of the methods lawyers use to gather information when they tackle a legal problem.

My goal is not to teach you how to be your own attorney. I'm not qualified to do that. Some knowledge of legal research, though, can help you decide when you might need an attorney, as well as maintain some control when you do use one. If you want to act as your own lawyer, time and experience are indispensable. A professional who offers you both is worth having. But you can greatly affect the rates you pay for an attorney's time when the costs are computed by the hour. And that's another benefit to knowing something about legal research: It can save you money.

One lawyer told me that many people ask his advice on matters that don't even require a professional's service. At high hourly rates, he winds up explaining basic matters they can easily get from a book. (Would you rather have a lawyer explain the principles of making a will at $100 an hour or would you prefer to buy a $15 book that explains the subject before a lawyer even enters the picture?)

If you plan to do some information seeking in the legal literature, be prepared for possible resistance. The lay public doing legal research is often viewed with mixed emotions by attorneys. The self-help law movement is partly responsible for their skepticism, since it opened territory previously understood and used only by legal professionals.

I have experienced resistance firsthand. I was researching a question for my "Reference Librarian" column, and one lawyer told me I was practicing law without a license. (Not all attorneys react this way, of course.) I believe there's a vast area of gray between practicing law, with or without a license, and being informed.

Knowing your rights and obligations certainly violates no legal code; in fact, it's our duty to know the law and how it affects us. We're told that our ignorance of the law is no excuse for breaking it. Our personal fates are too important to be left entirely to others or to chance. We must share in the knowledge that enables us to assume responsibility for our lives.

So, in the interest of being informed, the following steps are presented, to help you get some answers on your own.

Background for a Search

A lawyer with a good memory is blessed, but no one can possibly know or remember everything about every area of the law. Most attorneys today focus on one or two specialties: estate planning, personal injury, bankruptcy, etc. Since attorneys cover the same ground repeatedly, they become familiar with the steps you are about to learn. Regardless of their expertise and training, however, they always do this basic research before starting a new case. What do they research, and what are they looking for?

Attorneys look for two things in their preliminary research: 1) court cases that suggest precedents to use (secondary sources) and 2) the state or federal law (statutes) governing the situation in question (primary sources). Precedents and court interpretations of the statutes are important, because they are as much a part of the law as the statutes themselves.

Summaries of court cases are published in sets of books called law digests and state reports or reporters, as well as other legal reference books. Law textbooks and legal dictionaries quote from or refer to specific court cases, so you can read them in more detail. To find the pertinent legal material, you must use the right kind of library: a law school or county law library. Many of these are open for public use. A public library with a random or incomplete selection of legal books will not do.

Using Secondary Sources

To help establish a likely procedure that you would follow in your search, let's use a hypothetical case. You're driving through an alley, and as you enter the street, you collide with another car in traffic. You claim the sun blinded you. Should you be held responsible? The beginning research steps that follow establish a general background of information for any question you may have.

1. Check trade books or legal texts on the subject.

Your legal question might easily be answered by checking a self-help or popular legal guide. The philosophy behind many legal concepts like child support are consistent throughout the country. However, there may be some variables from state to state—the number of witnesses required for a will, or the grounds on which a person may file for divorce, for example. Therefore, it's possible to answer some questions from general books and perhaps resolve your particular dilemma without going any further.

If there is no good popular book on the subject, use a legal textbook (also called a hornbook). They're easy to find in law libraries, law school libraries, and law bookstores.

Q. Can you help me obtain information concerning property about to be foreclosed? The information must be up-to-date, with points on how to proceed, what legal documents are needed, etc. I have checked the library and their books are not current.

A. To get basic background on the philosophy of foreclosure, try a law text such as *California Real Estate Law: Text and Cases*, by Theodore Gordon, or one of the general books on foreclosure you might have seen in the library. Many law texts include sample legal forms that you might find useful, too. (The wording on foreclosure forms applies to general foreclosure matters.) They're usually sold in a stationery or law bookstore.

To get the most current application of foreclosure laws in the state check the codes in a law library. In California, there are three sets published by the state and two commercial publishers, Deerings and West. If you use *West's Annotated California Codes*, for example, search the general index volume and pocket update under FORECLOSURE. You'll find many subdivisions of the topic, as well as cross references to related topics. One subtopic, for instance, is called "Reassessment on Public Property." Next to this it says GOV 59507 et seq. GOV stands for the volume of the codes entitled "Government." Item 59507 (et seq.—"and that which follows") will tell you what the law says about foreclosure as it relates to reassessment on public property.[1]

Take the case of Aunt Martha's will. It's easy to determine from a general book on wills (*Who Gets It When You Go*, by David Larsen, for instance) that when someone dies *without* a will, the relatives who inherit his or her estate follow a certain order. In Aunt Martha's case, if she had no living parents, husband, or children, her living siblings (in this case her two sisters), would inherit her estate equally, regardless of their personal wealth or Aunt Martha's feelings toward them. If Aunt Martha had a will, however, she'd be able to leave her possessions to whomever she pleased, especially since no laws concerning community property apply in her case. By reading a popular book on the subject, you would also learn that she could have added a section to her will disinheriting anyone who challenged the will.

If these were your only questions, there would be no need to proceed further unless you wanted to verify the situation with an attorney. (Remember, with your prior homework, your fees would likely be lower, because you'd arrive prepared.) If your questions weren't answered by the popular books you checked, you'd continue with the subsequent steps.[2]

In our hypothetical case of an auto collision, neither a popular book nor a textbook treating this specific problem seems to be currently available under the subject TRAFFIC ACCIDENTS in *Law Books in Print* and *SGBIP*. For the last word, ask a law librarian or check with a law bookstore. If your library does own some of the books from *Law Books in Print* or *SGBIP* that you want to double check (the more specifically they cover

---

[1]Remember to check each numbered item in the pocket parts (see page 382) as well as in the main body of the codes. This will give you updates to the law as they are made by the legislature.

[2]Like you, I've tried reading books on estate planning and wills, and my eyes glazed over. One way to learn material like this and have it stick is not to read an entire book while trying to memorize lots of concepts that don't pertain to your situation right now. Instead, use the book as a reference text and just look for the answers to your specific questions.

cases like yours, the better), you can do that quickly, then move on to the following steps.

2. Check a legal summary.

Some laws can be easily charted state by state. Some of these variations by state may be the age at which a woman does not need adult consent to marry; the age at which a person is eligible to drink or drive; the amount of major auto accident compensation awards; and the rate of personal, corporate, and excise taxes. You can quickly check variations in laws for different states by checking such legal summaries as the *American Jurisprudence Desk Book, Law-in-a-Nutshell, Gilbert's Law Summaries, Smith's Reviews,* or the *American Legal Almanac: Law in All States.*

Q. *Good Housekeeping* magazine reports that a will made in one state may not be valid in another. Also, if it is valid, it may be costly to probate and subject an estate to taxes from both states. Can you give me more information?

A. Popular books on wills and estate planning say that state statutes differ on certain fine points of making a will. Some states require two witnesses; some require three. Some states specify certain ages for witnesses; some prohibit persons with criminal records from being witnesses. You can find out some of these variables by checking a legal summary such as the *American Jurisprudence Desk Book,* or the published statutes for the states in question at the county law library.

If a person has left property in another state, taxes may have to be paid on it. Tax credit may not be given in the state where the person died. Lawyers advise making a new will or having the old one reviewed to avoid problems that result from having moved to a state where the laws may be different.

---

3. Check a legal phrase book.

No matter what the subject, you must know the jargon. As you begin skimming legal texts, you'll soon realize that knowing "the language" is especially important for understanding legal matters. Don't ignore it. Lawyers are notorious hairsplitters. An alley may be described in many different ways, and it's often necessary to define even those terms you think you already know.

The most useful resource to check is the 50-plus-volume set called *Words and Phrases.* It will describe the precise kind of alley involved in other incidents. For example, the alley your accident occurred in may have been a narrow passageway between apartment houses designed for public use. Perhaps your opponent will argue that this passageway was not an alley for public use. A reference like *Words and Phrases* quotes various descriptions from other court cases involving alleys. It can help you be precise, especially since it refers to other court cases and names the books in which they are published so you may read them for specifics.

In the beginning phase of our hypothetical alley collision case, you might want to check all relevant terms: AUTOMOBILE or MOTOR VEHICLE, ALLEY, TRAFFIC, and COLLISION.

Besides knowing legal terminology, you'll need to know how to read legal citations in the reference books and indexes you'll use.

A case citation in a legal book doesn't look like an article citation in a periodical index, but it gives the same information. For example, you may find a citation that looks like this: (Williams v Wachovia Bank & Trust Co.) 292 *NC* 416, 233 *SE2d* 589. This means that the case involved a person whose last name is Williams who opposed the Wachovia Bank & Trust Co. (In most cases, the plaintiff's name comes first.) The major points and summary of the case were published in volume 292 of the publication entitled *North Carolina Codes* on page 416. Another copy of this case ran in volume 233 of the published set of codes called *Southeastern Reporter*, 2nd edition, page 589.[3] The abbreviations for the published codes (e.g., *NC* and *SE2d*) are spelled out in the book's key.

Another feature of law publications is that they are kept up to date with supplements called pocket parts. These are simply copies of the latest laws and changes to existing laws. They are issued in pamphlets and sent to subscribers who then slip them into an envelope or "pocket" attached to the inside back cover of the law book. Always check for pocket parts in the legal book you're using, in case the particular law you're checking has recently been changed in some way. The changes will eventually be incorporated into the new edition of the codes when they're reprinted, but until they are, pocket parts are needed.

Q. I would appreciate receiving a copy of the Natural Death Act and other information relating to the right to die.

A. The Natural Death Act gives adults the right to control decisions relating to their own medical care, including the decision to have life-sustaining procedures withheld or withdrawn in cases of a terminal condition. The Act covers five pages in the Health and Safety volume of the California Codes and is easy to read.

Since it is fairly recent legislation, look for it in the pocket supplement rather than in the main body of the codes.

Now that you're aware of the most characteristic features of legal reference books, you're ready to take a look at some of them as they specifically relate to your auto collision case.

4. Check legal encyclopedias (U.S. and state encyclopedias).

A legal encyclopedia, often one of the first publications a lawyer con-

---

[3]*SE* is a commercially published set of codes incorporating cases from supreme and intermediate appellate courts in Georgia, North Carolina, South Carolina, Virginia, and West Virginia.

sults, gives a general look at the matter in question with references to specific cases that occurred in other states.

Two U.S. encyclopedias are *American Jurisprudence 2 (AmJur)*, issued by Lawyers Co-operative Publishing Co., and *Corpus Juris 2*, issued by American Law Book Co. [2 = 2nd edition in both cases]. Both references discuss every area of the law. The encyclopedias are arranged by subject matter and must be accessed through their detailed subject indexes. Use the most recent edition. In this example, I'll use *AmJur 2* and start with the term ALLEY.

There is nothing helpful in the articles here. But the section starting with the term AUTOMOBILE leads to something useful:
AUTOMOBILES AND HIGHWAY TRAFFIC
Anticipating presence or conduct of others
Auto §§ 355, 356, 412[4]

'Auto' refers to the volume called "Automobiles and Highway Traffic." When you check paragraphs 355 and 356 in that volume, you find that they're irrelevant to your case. On the other hand, Paragraph 414 heads a chapter of eight paragraphs called "General Duty of Care in Operation of Vehicle." This is the section to check carefully.[5]

Paragraph 416 ("Duty to anticipate presence of others; lookout") specifically states that a driver may not assume that the road is clear of others. He must be vigilant of and anticipate the possible presence of others.

Apropos of your claim that the sun blinded you, another part of this section is even more pertinent. It says that if a driver's view of an intersection is obstructed when the presence of another may be reasonably anticipated, extra caution is required.

Throughout the section there are summaries of collision cases each of which contributes an added wrinkle. Read in full any of those cases that include the fine points of your situation. A single differing factor—identifying the particular "obstruction" that blocked your view, for example—may change the complexion of your case. What if your view was blocked because you sneezed? Or, a child on the sidewalk threw a ball, hit your car, and distracted or frightened you? What would the legal implications be if the driver of the car on the thoroughfare saw you emerging from the alley and in swerving to avoid you, hit another car before you hit him?

Keep looking for cases that include features similar to yours and read their summaries. The closer another case comes to yours, the more likely it is that you can use it as a precedent (unless, of course, it disproves your point).

A paragraph (with a case reference) in this section of *AmJur* relates to a child throwing a ball and frightening the driver of the car that caused the

---

[4]The encyclopedia misprints 414 as 412.
[5]Despite impressions to the contrary, the legal statutes, casebooks, digests, legal encyclopedias, and other reference books are not hard to read or understand. They sometimes use stilted language or are repetitious, but their purpose is to guarantee that the matter at hand is not ambiguous and is as clearly understood as possible.

accident. It says that the presence of small children on or near a street is a danger signal to a motorist, and he must bear in mind that children have less capacity to avoid danger than adults. Therefore, the motorist must exercise more care than normal. (The case referred to is Williams v. Wachovia Bank & Trust Co., 292 *NC* 416, 233 *SE*2d 589. See page 382 to interpret the abbreviations.)

Of course we have no idea according to the paragraph above how old a "child" is; how much responsibility for his own safety he's supposed to have at his age; or how the driver of the car is supposed to make that judgment on the spot. This is where an actual case can bog down a novice researcher. It's where F. Lee Bailey-type experience and skill can help an attorney turn the case in a direction you hadn't dreamed it could go.

At this point, before you've even checked the legal codes (laws) of your state, you can start to draw a picture of your rights and obligations as a motorist. It seems your collision case is weak unless you can prove negligence or contributory negligence by the other driver, or perhaps by the owner of the property through which the alley passes. Otherwise, the right of way belonged to the other driver, and you are responsible for the accident. If you see an attorney now, you'll be prepared to answer questions he or she might ask. And you'll be aware of some possible implications of pursuing the case.

To continue the search through legal encyclopedias, we'll leave the U.S. legal encyclopedia and check the one for your state (most states have one) such as *California Jurisprudence, Florida Jurisprudence, New York Jurisprudence, Texas Jurisprudence,* and *Ohio Jurisprudence* all published by Bancroft-Whitney Co.

Check the most recent edition of your state's legal encyclopedia. In pursuing the auto collision case, I'll use *California Jurisprudence (CalJur)* and start with the general index. One thing you'll notice as you use different legal reference books, and particularly their indexes, is that they say the same thing using different symbols and words. For example, some legal books print cross references (e.g., ALLEYS see HIGHWAYS AND STREETS) like this:

Alleys
Highways and Streets (this index)

Other legal books may do it this way:
Alleys
Streets and Alleys, generally, this index

When you check ALLEYS in *CalJur,* you're referred to HIGHWAYS AND STREETS. There is nothing pertinent to your auto case in the subheadings under that term. By trying one of the cross-references it suggests (AUTOMOBILES AND HIGHWAY TRAFFIC), you'll find several pages of subtopics in alphabetical order. You must scan them to find the subtopic that covers your circumstance. As with many indexes in legal reference books, there are several possible terms under a major heading that will lead you to

what you're looking for. One of them in this case is:
AUTOMOBILES AND HIGHWAY TRAFFIC
Alleys
entering highway from, right of way, Auto § 247.

According to the abbreviation key, Auto § 247 refers to the volume in *CalJur* called "Automobiles and Highway Traffic." Within that volume, you'll check Paragraph 247.

The information in Paragraph 247 briefly states that the driver entering the highway must yield the right of way to cars that are within a *reasonable* distance. The driver on the highway is not entitled to an absolute right-of-way over approaching vehicles.

Since you're looking for a precedent, don't forget to check the rest of the section for specific cases to match with yours.

5. Check American Law Reports.

Published by Bancroft-Whitney, *ALR* is a set of general reference books with articles that discuss particular areas of case law. The focus of each article is a recent case that addresses a broad legal issue such as the visitation rights of a father of an illegitimate child. The article also discusses other cases involving the same issue.

It's possible that *ALR* may not cover cases or subjects you're looking for. (Search *ALR* the same way you've searched the previous publications discussed, starting with the general index.) In this case, there hasn't been anything written that pertains specifically to your auto case, so you can move on to the next step.

6. Check other case digests.

By now you must be amazed, as I am, that the same thing can be said in so many different ways. Each time it's restated, an even newer facet of the situation emerges. If your exact question hasn't been answered by any of the previous publications you've checked (or if you want to be absolutely thorough), go beyond the state and regional court case reports and check those covering federal and Supreme Court cases. Also check the national digest that prints summaries of cases from the different state reporters.

West Publishing Co. issues *Federal Practice Digest* (for federal cases), *Supreme Court Digest* (for Supreme Court cases) and *American Digest*, a collection of summaries contained in state digests. *AD* is issued every 10 years in publications called *Decennials;* between the decades, the publication is called *General Digest.*

A section of the *Ninth Decennial Digest*, which covers cases from 1976-1981, refers to one that bears directly on your collision accident. It's found in Paragraph 167, "Entering or leaving private premises or alleys." The case occurred in Illinois in 1980. The summary says that a driver who was entering a highway from a driveway and who was partially blinded by the sun had a duty to avoid inflicting injury on anyone who might be using the street. The case, Hartigan v. Robertson, was published in three different reporters and can be read in any of them for more details. (Case citations are 42 *Ill. Dec.* 751;[6] 409 *N.E.* 2d 366;[7] and 87 *Ill. App.* 3d 732.[8])

7. Check treatises and monographs.

Legal experts who study a special field of law may write a book (treatise) on it. Some examples are *Collier on Bankruptcy, American Law of Zoning,* and *Immigration Law and Procedure.* A book that studies one segment of that field is called a monograph. Monographs include references to specific cases; they're useful for getting an overview of a broad situation and delving into the topic in depth. Treatises and monographs are included in *Law Books in Print.* A law librarian may be able to suggest other titles appropriate for your research.

8. Check legal periodicals.

Articles in legal magazines that you'd find through such indexes as *Legal Periodicals Index* and *Current Law Index* discuss practical legal problems. For example, family attorneys sometimes have difficulty dividing a man's pension in divorce cases. Although pensions are community property (in community property states[9]), many women claim they are not getting their fair share.

Articles in law journals discuss such issues which are not clear-cut. Reading about these practical legal concerns may help you understand some of the problems lawyers face. In the pension example, an article in the *California State Bar Journal* (November 1980) entitled, "Dividing pensions on marital dissolution," by attorney Barbara DiFranza and actuary Donald Parkyn, says it is far more difficult to divide future assets such as pensions than to divide tangible assets such as the family home. The article details some of the difficulties in computing an amount based on events that have not yet happened, as would be the case of a man who is not yet retired.

Other legal articles may cover such things as the landlord's dilemma and concerns in forfeiting a lease, the rules of liability in water-damage cases, and consumer problems with solar equipment warranties. One of these may be just what you need to gain a better understanding of a personal matter.

In regard to the auto case, however, there is nothing pertinent.

9. Check formbooks and practice manuals.

Many legal procedures are repetitive and routine. The same information is requested each time that situation is handled. Instead of reinventing the wheel, lawyers use forms. And they're used in most every area of

---

[6]Volume 42, page 751 of *Illinois Decisions.*
[7]Volume 409, page 366 of *Northeastern Reporter,* 2d edition.
[8]Volume 87, page 732 of *Illinois Appellate Reporter,* 3rd edition.
[9]A community property state is one in which all property accumulated during a marriage is divided equally between husband and wife in the event of divorce.

law. They might be one of a variety of contracts, rental agreements, or forms for legally changing your name. Marriage licenses and birth certificates are legal forms.

Publications that include the many forms used in different areas of law are called formbooks, and you can find these through *Law Books in Print* and *SGBIP*. Some useful formbooks are:

Encyclopedia of Real Estate Forms, by Jerome S. Gross. Prentice-Hall. 1973.

Bankruptcy Law and Practice, with Forms, by Daniel R. Cowans. 2nd ed. West Publishing Co. 1983.

EEO [Equal Employment Opportunity] *Compliance Manual—Procedures, Forms, Affirmative Action Programs*. Prentice-Hall. 1981.

Sometimes forms are included in other legal reference books and texts as well. In our auto case, we don't need formbooks, at least not in the initial stages of gathering information.

CHECKING THE LAW ITSELF (PRIMARY SOURCES)

One of the steps in your information search is to check the law itself as set forth in your state's codes. (If your question concerns a federal matter such as social security or copyright, you'll want to check the federal statutes.) It may seem that this is the most important step, but it isn't necessarily. Answers to legal questions are seldom, if ever, simple and straightforward. The codes sometimes make them seem that way, until you read them carefully and discover that they may not mention specifics that exist in your particular case. This is one reason that studying pertinent court cases is as important as, and in many situations more important than, checking the wording of the codes. (As mentioned earlier in the chapter, precedents are as much a part of the law as the law, i.e., codes, itself.)

To get a full picture of any legal matter, you need the information you find in both primary *and* secondary sources. Yes, you must know the laws of your state, but individual court cases apply the law and include the unique twists that the codes do not specifically mention. In other words, the codes don't always mean what they seem to mean—until they've been applied in actual court cases.

With this in mind, you should check your state's laws regarding your auto collision question

10. Check the state codes.

The codes of each state look like sets of encyclopedias. In California there are three sets of codes published by different publishers. Two are commercially published (West Publishing Co. and Deering), and the third is issued by the state. Researchers usually prefer the commercially published codes because they give references to cases the state-issued set does not. For purposes of the auto collision case, I'll use *West's Annotated California Codes.*

After checking various terms in the General Index (ALLEYS, STREETS AND ALLEYS, etc.), I found the following:

TRAFFIC RULES AND REGULATIONS
> Right of way, Veh 21800 et seq.
> Alleys, entering or crossing highway from. Veh 28104

In the volume called "Vehicle," section 21800 to the end of the section, it briefly states that a driver about to enter or cross a highway from an alley must yield the right of way to those already on the thoroughfare. As in *CalJur* and *AmJur,* there are specific cases mentioned, so you can examine in greater depth those which are similar to yours. Remember to check the pocket parts.

Besides consulting established law, you may want to check on the progress of pending legislation. Even if nothing relevant to your auto collision case is being discussed, there may be other important legislation affecting you. (Maybe a new state law proposes to give veterans a reduced rate of interest for home mortgages. Surely that would be relevant if you had been in the service and planned to buy a home soon.) To get information on in-progress legislative matters, check the weekly pronouncements sent to law libraries.

Q. I recently read that there was a new state law passed making it easier to probate an estate. It doesn't apply to me now, but it made me wonder where a citizen could get this information if he needed it.

A. Law libraries and the documents sections of large public and academic libraries receive weekly pronouncements of the state legislature. You can locate the text of any bill discussed or passed in the Senate and House by checking the legislative index under "probate" (or any other topic). It will then direct you to the appropriate section of the weekly "history" publication. Several recent developments concerning probate are now pending.

---

11. Check the federal statutes.

Federal laws may enter the picture in the auto collision case if the accident occurred on federal property, involved a federal employee, or in any other way concerned federal jurisdiction. In such situations, you may actually rely more on court cases and precedents than on the federal codes.

The official *United States Codes* covers federal matters such as federal education policies and federal income tax. It comes in a set of encyclopedia-like volumes that cover different areas of federal law. Each topic—called a title—averages two to three volumes. For example, Title 17 covers copyright; Title 35 covers patents; Title 38 covers veterans' benefits; Title 40 covers public buildings, property and works; and Title 50 covers war and national defense. The *U.S. Codes* are issued by the House Judiciary Committee and are printed by the Government Printing Office.

Two editions easier to use are commercially published: the *United States Codes Annotated* (*U.S.C.A.*), issued by West Publishing Co., and the *Federal Code Annotated* (*F.C.A.*), issued by Lawyers Co-operative Publishing Co. They include references to federal court decisions and opinions of the Attorneys General of the United States. The government-published edition does not. Whichever edition you use, approach the set through the general index.

In this situation, no federal law is involved, and we'll assume no other federal involvement exists. (If, for example, you hit a postal truck, you would quickly find out that postal trucks are immune in traffic accident cases. If the accident happened on a military base, you would ask the military police if any variant traffic laws applied on the base, then you would proceed to check other relevant sources as usual.)

Q. I've heard that in community property states, a divorced woman is entitled to one-half of her ex-husband's Social Security after a marriage of at least 10 years and one-half of his federal retirement after a marriage of at least 20 years. Since I've never seen this in print, could you advise whether they are federal laws or court decisions?

A. According to the Social Security Statutes of the *United States Codes*, as of January 1, 1979, the 20-year marriage requirement for a divorcee to collect Social Security benefits was lowered to 10. The information is easier to read in the *Social Security Handbook* issued by the government; it is available in most large libraries. The handbook cumulates all recent changes and highlights questions most asked. (Remember to check the most recent edition. To be absolutely sure of recency, check the pocket parts in the *U.S. Codes*.)

For dividing federal retirement benefits in community property states, the distinction is less clear, and in fact, legislation is in the process of being challenged, especially where military pensions are concerned. Pension rights earned during a marriage are community property, but many variables affect the way a pension is divided.

The California laws on marriage and pension rights appear in Section 5110 of the Civil Code, and they refer to court cases in which the division of the pension has varied according to circumstances of the couples involved. If you read the cases mentioned, match the circumstances of the one that comes closest to yours for some idea of what you might expect. Check a law library for up-to-date information regarding changes in this law.

WHAT YOU GET FROM RESEARCHING THE LAW

The 11 steps (checking through nine secondary sources as well as the laws themselves) outlined above should be more than enough for you to get some understanding of whatever law-related situation you are in. In many cases, only two or three steps may be needed to give you enough background. When you've completed your homework, you will have learned several things. You will have some idea of what might be involved in this particular legal matter. You will begin to see how the law "thinks," that is, how the law assigns responsibility and to whom. (Your own brand of logic doesn't count here, especially since there are many deviations an actual case could take that a layperson would not know about.) Most important, you will be an informed participant rather than a naive bystander in an action that affects you.

Furthermore, you will learn that you can get answers to the many minor legal questions you have—the ones that aren't significant enough to see a lawyer about but which nevertheless need answers. ("Can my neighbors and I block off our street for a block party?"; "Can I set off fireworks in my city?"; "Can I get back the security deposit on my apartment?")

Legal research will test your tenacity and your penchant for detail, precision, nitpicking, and hairsplitting. In fact, it's not the kind of information seeking that everyone enjoys. You'll easily discover that there are many traps in it, especially for the inexperienced researcher. You may even decide to declare a moratorium on legal research and quit with what you've learned here.

On the other hand, maybe you've found your niche and you're inspired to learn more. If so, I recommend, as a start, the Nolo Press self-help law books (in general), and particularly their *Legal Research: How to Find and Understand the Law*, by Stephen Elias. I also suggest that you read it at least three times and practice the steps in it to build your legal research skills. Good luck.

----------------------- *CHAPTER SUMMARY* -----------------------

I.   We may need legal information for many reasons. Although learning about what the law is and how it works is not a substitute for an attorney's special knowledge and expertise, doing some legal research on your own can answer some basic questions and prepare you for talking with an attorney should you decide on some legal action. (page 377)

II. Legal research consists of consulting court cases (secondary sources) and the codes or statutes (primary sources) that apply in these particular court cases. (page 379)

   A.   Your question might easily be answered by reading a general book published for the lay public. If there is no popular book on a legal subject you're researching, check a law text. (page 379)

B. Check a legal summary. If you're looking for a straightforward answer such as what are the grounds for divorce in different states, you're in luck. Many components of various state laws are easily charted in a reference book known as a legal summary. One such book is the *American Jurisprudence Desk Book*. (page 380)

C. Check *Words and Phrases* for various definitions that have been applied to words involved in describing your particular case. You won't always be looking for dictionary-type definitions. You're checking to see how the word has been defined and applied in various court cases. (page 381)

D. Legal encyclopedias (U.S. and state) discuss every area of the law. They refer you to cases that have occurred in your state as well as other states. The legal encyclopedia that covers the U.S. is called *American Jurisprudence (AMJur)*. (page 382)

E. Check *American Law Reports*. This general reference book prints articles that discuss particular areas of case law. Though not every subject is addressed, *ALR* is helpful for additional background material. (page 385)

F. Some of the above steps show you how to use case reports that refer to court cases in state and regional courts. You may also want to check other case digests, such as the *Federal Practice Digest* and *Supreme Court Digest*. (page 385)

G. Check treatises and monographs for certain legal issues. These references discuss one particular area of law in depth. (page 385)

H. Check legal periodicals via their indexes for articles that discuss many thorny issues, in easy-to-read language. These are helpful for gaining further insight into the problems lawyers have with the "gray areas" of those issues. (page 386)

I. Check formbooks and practice manuals, because at some stage in legal work, certain forms must be filed. Formbooks give samples that lawyers use to save time. (page 386)

J. Primary sources in legal research are the law itself. Check the codes for your state to find the exact law governing the issue you're researching. The *U.S. Codes* cover federal matters such as the draft. (page 387)

III. Legal research may not be for everyone. There are many angles in complicated cases that experienced attorneys are best suited to handle. But legal research does have its benefits for laypersons. (page 389)

     A. You can gain insight into a matter that affects you and possibly reduce your attorney's fees at the same time.

     B. You can answer relatively uncomplicated legal questions on your own, and therefore you can act in an informed manner.

22

From the Horse's Mouth:
LOOKING FOR EXPERTS

A question not to be asked is a question not to be answered.
—Robert Southey in *The Doctor*

Sometimes the information you need is not in books, magazines, statutes, microfilm collections, or computer data bases. Maybe your research topic is so new or your project is so specialized that little has been written or recorded about it. That's when the knowledge and expertise of people resources are indispensable.

Even if you've gathered information from print sources, there is still value in seeking out a person or a group that has either done it, studied it, or lived through whatever it is you're researching.

I've cited many examples throughout this book where I've suggested that you write or call out-of-town experts or organizations for information. But contacting them and in turn receiving just the answer you need do not necessarily go hand in hand. If you've ever requested help by phone or mail—and never gotten an answer—you already know that it isn't as easy as dropping a letter in a mailbox or picking up a phone. Communicating effectively in any medium requires skill.

In this chapter, we'll discusss how to request information from faraway experts so that they will be encouraged to respond. This restores some of the control you lose by having to depend on someone in another state or country. No one can guarantee you complete success, of course, but there are many things you can do (or avoid doing) to tap the resources that only people can offer and to greatly enhance the odds of getting the information you need.

FINDING EXPERTS

Experts are individuals with special knowledge—information that you need. They are often easy to spot because of their titles: pediatrician, mayor, chef. And finding them may be as easy as checking your local phone book. Other experts, however, are less visible: an antique telephone collector, a tatting expert, someone who speaks Esperanto. They may be easier to find via the grapevine, through a specific organization or club, a business, a museum, a newspaper, a university, a hospital, or some other affiliation related to their expertise. Many of these "affiliations" may be listed in the Yellow Pages of your hometown phone book, the Manhattan phone directory, or a specialized reference book such as the *Alphabetized Directory of American Journalists* or *Aviation and Space Museums of America* (both of which are listed in the *Directory of Directories*).

Q. In 1966 John Guillermin made a movie called *The Blue Max* with George Peppard. I scoured the library in a futile hunt for information on the Blue Max which, according to the movie, was a medal awarded by the Germans for certain accomplishments. Can you determine if there was such a medal, and if so, why it was called The Blue Max?

A. The movie was based on Jack Hunter's novel, *The Blue Max*. According to the Quartermaster, a local shop dealing in war souvenirs and collectibles, the term was supposedly invented by Hunter, but it was based on an actual medal, Pour le Mérite, which is how it's referred to in the book. The medal dates back to 1665 (when French was Germany's official court language) and was originally known as the Order of Generosity.

The medal was the highest award for military heroism given in Imperial Germany, and was presumably awarded during World War I to German pilots who shot down more than 20 enemy planes. This practice stopped after the war with the end of the German Empire.

One theory says that the name Blue Max derived from references to the blue enamel of the medal and to Max Immelmann, a World War I flying ace.

For further information, the Quartermaster recommends D.G. Nevill's *Medal Ribbons and Orders of Imperial Germany and Austria* from which most of the above information came.

National associations are prolific sources of information, and you can identify them through the *Encyclopedia of Associations* (*EA*), one of the researcher's most popular and useful tools.[1] I've heard of one writer who was doing an article about popcorn and got everything he needed from the Popcorn Institute, a trade association listed in *EA*. Other associations, such as American Society of Mammalogists (a group interested in the conservation of land mammals), Vivisection Investigation League (a group

---

[1]To save days or weeks of waiting, check a large library for the *Associations Reference File* (*ARF*) in microform (published by Gale Research Co.). This set includes the full text of the brochures and other official literature offered by the organizations listed in *EA*. Although *ARF* can quickly help you screen the literature of many groups and save having to wait for a mail response, it still pays to write. The groups often provide information beyond the literature named in *EA*. I once contacted First Sunday, an organization of parents who have lost a child. Included with the literature I received was a reprint article from a pediatrics journal on the psychological impact of a child's death.

that protests cruel laboratory experiments on animals and human beings), Little People of America (an association of adults four feet eleven inches and under), and Houseboat Association of America (an organization of houseboating enthusiasts), will lead you to experts in their unique fields.

Besides *EA*, many of the directories and reference books mentioned in previous chapters are also useful in locating experts. For example, current biographical directories such as *Who's Who in Finance* and *Who's Who in the Wall and Ceiling Industry* can pinpoint experts. And don't forget to check *Directory of Directories*. It can lead you to publications such as *Armwrestling* (groups associated with armwrestling and names of competition promoters) and *American Square Dance—Vacation Issue* (square dance clubs, dancers, and related businesses). With our basic human need to belong, it's not outrageous to assume that there's an organization—and an expert within that group—for any special interest imaginable. And some of them may live right in your own hometown or state. (I've often found that national directories are better at identifying local experts than the Yellow Pages and other local sources.)

How else can you reach experts? If they've already shared some of their knowledge with the public, that could mean they've written a book on bargello needlepoint or penetrating the criminal mind. Many books are written, not by full-time, professional writers, but by experts in a particular discipline. Astronomers like Carl Sagan write books on astronomy; psychologists like Joyce Brothers specialize in human relationships. An author may be just the person to consult as an expert for your project. You can usually contact him by writing in care of his publisher or by checking a biographical directory which may include a more direct address.

If none of these attempts to reach an expert works, you can try writing or calling the National Referral Center (NRC) at the Library of Congress, Washington, DC 20540. (This is especially helpful to researchers in small towns where local research facilities are inadequate for certain kinds of specialized research projects. NRC will refer you directly to one of the 13,000 organizations in its file that deals with your topic, be it the feather industry or vampires.)

WHAT YOU SHOULD KNOW ABOUT EXPERTS

Once you identify an expert or discover that one exists in your specific research interest, the next step is making contact. Before embarking on your quest for the expert's resources, however, assume that people are busy. Getting the information you want may require more than a direct phone call or letter. It may mean going through the "proper channels," via a secretary (or two or three), a preliminary written request, or a scheduled appointment.

On the other hand, you may want to skirt the front office. In his book,

The Craft of Interviewing, John Brady reports how several writers in search of interviews reached their contacts by *avoiding* routine channels. Many skilled researchers believe that the best way to get information is to bypass the bureaucracy. But there are ways to do it and ways not to. Check Brady's book for the countless tips he offers.

Many written requests for information (such as writing to a library in another city to check old newspaper files) are not complex or don't necessarily require reaching one precise person. In such instances, the researcher may use a host of tricks to encourage a response. They range from enclosing return postage and a name label, to suggesting that the respondent use the letter of request on which to make his reply. Some researchers say their secret to getting a response long distance is either to sound breathless and urgent or to flatter the person in some way.

Sometimes these ploys work; sometimes they don't. Not getting an answer, however, often has as much to do with hidden reasons as it does with violating the above suggestions. Your respondent, after all, is human, and whether you hear from him or not could have something to do with his humanity: He is sick the day your letter arrrives; he is going through a divorce and isn't thinking clearly; he has just won the state lottery.

More important than any trick to elicit a response from a particular expert (or group with which he is affiliated) is the overall strategy you use. This strategy (whether it's via phone or letter) should hinge on making it easy for the respondent to reply. Anything that does—from enclosing postage to being courteous—will increase your chances of getting the information you want.

To Write or to Call

Whether you phone or write depends on several things. If the information you need is specialized, you may have few choices of people to contact. Or perhaps you may want to speak only with Ralph Nader, or only with the President's press secretary, and no one else.

Maybe your budget is limited and keeping costs down is a consideration. Though it's often faster to get information by calling long distance, it's also more expensive.

Finally, there's the condition where time is a critical variable, when you need the information for a deadline or a medical emergency. If you have a limited amount of time to get an answer, you may be forced to call rather than take the time to write and wait for a response.

It's not always easy to prejudge the fastest route to an answer, especially when you get cut off during long distance calls, get put on hold longer than you'd like, or find your letter has been returned "Addressee Unknown." Calling may be faster and cheaper in the long run, but you may not know that until your research is over. Experience (and the size of your budget) will determine your course of action.

If You Decide to Call

Telephoning first may have advantages even if you still end up writing. In gathering information for a magazine article I wrote on tracing obsolete securities, I called local stock brokerages to ask their policy in handling such client inquiries. They told me that they used a few reference books in the office for some inquiries; all others were sent to the research department in the Los Angeles or New York office.

Rather than get bogged down in mass mail research, I made some long distance calls. In the end, I was told no information on reference materials they used would be released without a written request. But at the cost of postage and my time, a few brief long distance calls to narrow the field were a bargain. (If your research needs require frequent long distance calls, you may want to consider service from one of the many long distance calling companies whose rates go down as the number of calls you make goes up.)

Then there are the experts who don't return phone calls for whatever reason. It could mean that the person who is too busy to call back with nothing to say, has nothing to say. Or it could mean "no" in answer to your question for assistance. (Some people get so many phone calls and letters that responding even with negative answers is time-consuming. So they respond only to calls from people they *can* help.) But, of course, unless you follow up with another call, you may never know why a particular expert "neglected" to answer your inquiry.

Remember that the purpose of your call is usually more important to you than it is to the other person. So don't opt for the supposed easy and inexpensive route of waiting to be called back. Wait a reasonable period of time (perhaps based on when that person is supposed to respond plus some hours or days), then call again. If a long time passes, you might correctly assume you'll never hear from the person. If you do call again and do reach him, you might acquire needed information and even answers to questions he didn't have time to call *you* to ask, thus making it easier for him to answer your query.

I've been on the receiving end of telephone call situations like these. Since newspapers work on deadlines, my columns must come first. Therefore, I may take as long as two weeks to return a call, and I'm often relieved when someone calls me back first. When you call someone again before he has returned your call, be sure to explain politely that you wanted to be sure and catch him, and avoid any implication that he was remiss in not returning your call promptly. He'll appreciate your understanding and probably be more helpful.

If You Decide to Write

Sometimes an expert or an organization wants your request in writing—often for the simplest of human reasons. I myself prefer a letter to a phone call, for I'm afraid I'll miss something by copying a request by phone. A letter already has the information in it, and it's probably more legible than my notes. It's also less likely to get lost than a scribbled note. Since a letter is easier for me to handle, it encourages my cooperation.

Writing instead of calling may be your chosen option, because you have the luxury of time and want to save the expense of long distance calls. Whatever the reason, your letter requesting information or help should observe some do's and don'ts.

The most basic requirement of a good letter is legibility. Not everyone has the patience or the time to decipher crowded, illegible hieroglyphs. If you don't have access to a typewriter, write or print clearly. *You* may be able to read your own handwriting, but others may not. Letters that can't be read, can't be answered.

Hand in hand with the appearance of your written request go the contents. Keep your sentences brief, but clear. I once received a letter from a woman who never expressed one thought in a complete sentence. It was like walking into a theater in the middle of a play. It made no sense, because it was totally out of context. In the end, I wasn't really sure what she was asking.

Excessively long sentences are often hard to understand, too. In one letter, a woman rambled on and on for so long that she never got to her question. Bob Holt, a San Diego author, follows a rule when he writes: Never make a sentence more than 15 words long. He believes that this restriction forces a writer to think and present his thoughts more clearly. Many of the sentences in this book (such as this one) will show you that I find this rule hard to follow. But his point is clear.

Don't forget about spelling and grammar. Nothing looks worse than a letter that don't have the wrods right. (If that wouldn't make your expert resource fold the letter carefully into a paper airplane and aim it out the window, nothing would.) Make your letter look and sound correct as well as convincing. There are dozens of grammar guides and dictionaries in print. Keep one of each at your elbow.

Not only *how* you ask, but also *how much* you ask is important. Some researchers believe they can comfortably ask as many as 10 questions in one letter and receive a cheerful and prompt reply. Don't count on it. I agree that 10 might be answered *only* if they're personal questions you might ask in an interview and *only* if you've gotten the go-ahead in advance. Otherwise, asking too many questions is a mistake. Some questions take longer to research than others, and your entire request may be held up by those few.

Perhaps a response to your request can't be comfortably handled by a letter. Many busy people don't have the time to write their life stories in 250 words or less, expound on their opinions of euthanasia, or present their professional findings on weight control. In your query, you might offer the expert the option of responding by either phone or letter. The easier it is for him to respond, the more likely it is that he will.

If time is a factor in your research, be sure to mention it. Concluding your letter with "Thank you for your prompt reply" is nice, but it isn't enough—nor is it clear that you need the information in three weeks, otherwise you can't use it at all. If your project has a deadline, it's a courtesy to let the expert know that. Most people, even if they're busy, would rather know you have a deadline than take their valuable time to provide you information that won't be used.

Another aspect of the time factor is to start far enough in advance to meet your deadline. When my nonwriter friends ask me how long one of my articles takes (because they don't think I spend much time on them), I usually respond with something like, "Well, it takes me xx minutes to gather the names of the people to call, xx minutes to call them, another xx minutes to call them back because they're never there the first time, another xx minutes for us to finally connect," etc. You get the picture.

There are several Murphy's Laws operating simultaneously in finding and communicating with others. One of them is "Everything takes twice as long as you think." If you've written one article or report or served on one committee, you'll know that the completion of projects is seldom smooth. You soon develop a sense of starting far enough in advance to allow for everything to go wrong and for you to still finish on time. (Then again, you can't start too soon. Especially where contacting people is concerned, you'll find it helpful if not necessary to recontact them at some later point so they don't forget.) No two information-gathering projects you undertake will require the same amount of time. Common sense and experience should be your guides in planning a timetable.

It's a given that in order to answer your request, an expert must have received it. If you're writing to someone in care of a large organization or business, it's essential to include his name or at least the correct department or subdivision on the envelope. Large organizations receive their mail through a central mail room where clerks sort and distribute it. Letters addressed to the organization in general must be opened and screened once more before they get to the right person—*if* they get to the right person. (You're leaving it up to a mail clerk or secretary to decide.) Horror stories abound about correspondence that's been missing for months and later turns up behind the postage meter or in the wrong person's in-basket. A name on the envelope, or at least the title of the person (General Manager, Project Director, Managing Editor, etc.) who should know the answer to your question, is one more way to minimize delays and disappointment.

My favorite timesaver is not to mention a person's name on the envelope but instead to mention the purpose of the query, whenever possible, in the lower left corner of the envelope. For example: "RE: request for a birth certificate copy" or "CONTENTS: proposal and outline for a young adult nonfiction science book." This usually gets it to the right department and even to the appropriate person just as quickly as the name of a specific person who, in some cases, no longer even holds that job.

One more thing about mail requests for information. Double check the address. Sound silly? It's not. Many reference books are outdated the moment they're published. Since this applies to the telephone book as well, I usually verify an address from another source against it. Nothing is more frustrating than the time wasted from a returned or forwarded letter—especially when you're in a hurry for a reply. One of the reporters on my newspaper who sells paperback fiction on the side, recently told me that he uses a three-year-old copy of *Writer's Market* for publishers' addresses—and about a fourth of his manuscripts come back stamped "Addressee unknown." Publishers move, merge, or go out of business regularly.

Besides double-checking references, be sure you're copying the correct address. Transposing numbers is not uncommon. And unless there's a sleuthing letter carrier at the other end, your mail may not get delivered to the right place. I often get Dear Abby's mail with my P.O. box number on the envelope because our columns are next to one another in *The San Diego Union*. (None of those letters are in this book.)

A similar problem involves newspaper mail clerks who put letters addressed to syndicated columnist David Horowitz in my box—even though, to my knowledge, we're not the same person. Letters frequently come to me with many strange addresses on them, including that of the San Diego Public Library. The dates of the letters indicate they've been bouncing around for a long time—maybe too long for my answers to be of any use.

NO MATTER WHAT YOU'RE ASKING WHEN

1.Know what you want.

Many researchers ask broad or general questions, because they don't really know what they want, or they don't have a grasp of their subject. (Remember, one of the basic rules for getting research help is to avoid asking broad or general questions.)

I recall one man asking me an open-ended question ("Do you have any information on . . . ?") that required a reassembly of his entire family tree. His approach was incorrect, because if he'd had any idea how to do genealogical research, he would have realized that his query was not a simple—or single—question. He was wasting precious time asking impossible-to-answer questions when he should have first learned the rudiments of genealogy.

2. Do your homework.

If you've really focused your search and you know what information you need, doing your homework will come naturally. It often means doing some background reading or asking preliminary questions. Don't waste a professional's time or risk incurring his annoyance or lack of cooperation by asking basics you can learn from a text, encyclopedia, or a person nearby. He'll appreciate your initiative and your respect for his time. Nothing is less flattering and more likely to start you off on the wrong foot. A doctor or lawyer with appointments scheduled three deep doesn't have a spare moment to explain the fundamentals of blood cells or workmen's compensation, things you should know before you call.

Sometimes an expert doesn't have certain specifics such as a date, the name of a person, organization, or book, or perhaps a statistic even though he seems certain. If he can't recall precisely, verify it elsewhere.

Q. Since coming west from the central time zone I've been wondering why prime time television programs run in the Pacific time zone at the same time as those on the East coast. The schedules used in the central and mountain time zones are different and more convenient for most people.

I have written the historian-archivist for each of the networks asking when the practice started and why it is maintained today even though taping is commonplace. I also contacted the National Association of Broadcasters. None of these people knew the answer.

Can you tell me who originated the practice of treating the two coastal zones the same way? Also, why do you suppose, when taping shows came into widespread use, live programs became the exception rather than the rule?

A. *TV Facts*, by Cobbett Steinberg, answers how the networks decide what shows to air and when to schedule them. Programming executives try to psyche out audiences in different parts of the country by studying their life-styles and habits. Based on these profiles, they select the programs and viewing times that fit the majority of viewers in that time zone.

Bob Shanks, author of *Cool Fire*, a history of television broadcasting, explains that taping allows more flexibility for local programming decisions. A live two-hour special beginning at 8 p.m. on the East coast would run from 5 p.m. to 7 p.m. on the West coast. Taping, which gives TV stars the chance to goof and reshoot a scene, helps avoid awkward scheduling.

---

3. Start close to home.

One way to save time and money is to thoroughly check local sources first. Do you really need to write to London, or call long distance for that information?

In my newspaper column, I often get questions from out-of-state visitors who take our city's newspaper home with them. A man from Indianapolis wrote me for information about scrimshaw (carvings on whale bone or ivory). A woman wrote me from Houston to ask for the address of a company I had mentioned in a column she had since lost. Both of these questions could have been quickly and easily answered by their local libraries instead of being diverted long distance to me and waiting several weeks for a reply.

4. Learn how to ask for information.

Follow the general instructions in Chapter 6 on how to ask a question. Tell the person what you're doing and why. It not only opens possibilities for help in ways you're not aware of, it's also common courtesy in any request for a favor. If you received a question by mail flatly asking "What's your annual salary?" how would you respond? Yet, as part of a sensible interview with a clear and important purpose, the question may not be unreasonable.

Avoid general questions such as "Please send information on dyslexia." What exactly is it about dyslexia that you want to know? Organizations that deal with it? Books or articles on the subject? A definition of it? The names of specialists studying it? What do you want to know precisely and why? Without knowing your particular need, your expert would have to answer *all* those questions. Since that would take too long (especially if you want a written response), you might get no response at all.

In addition, vague requests raise more questions than answers. The person handling your request doesn't have time to become your pen pal to find out exactly what you're after. (This is where an initial phone call can often clarify the procedure, so your letter includes the exact information needed.)

Be specific. Don't say "recently" if you mean 10 years ago. A clerk searching years of file drawers to get your answer has a formidable challenge ahead of him. Unless you can pinpoint the exact bit of information you need, your expert (or that clerk in a large organization) may have to search through countless handwritten files to get your answer. He may even be inclined not to answer your request.

5. Be aware of the tone of your request.

It may seem obvious that politeness counts, but you'd be surprised at some letters I receive, whose writers sound curt, demanding, or exasperated. The same thing goes for phone callers who assume you were waiting for their call all morning. The old saw about catching flies with honey instead of vinegar still works. On the premise that everyone has feelings, you may assume that nasty letters get buried more easily than nice ones. And argumentative phone callers are simply begging to be put on hold for 20 minutes or transferred to maintenance. Be positive and nonthreatening, not negative and attacking. You'll be delighted to learn that your tone can keep the doors to cooperation wide open. And even if the expert can't help you now, you never know when you may need a favor from him another time.

Ferd Nauheim's *Letter Perfect: How To Write Business Letters That Work* (Van Nostrand Reinhold, 1982) is an excellent resource on the art of positive letter-writing to get results (and not just for business purposes). The same psychology and planning goes into making a successful phone call. Check the books (by Brady, Walters, and Garner) mentioned on page 286 for tips on interviewing people and starting and maintaining a conversation.

6. Ask about costs involved in filling your information request.

Whether you write or call for information, you may have to pay for photocopying or other services. An expert may not charge you for a reprint of his article, but some organizations have to charge to cover the costs they incur from multiple requests. Most organizations will not fill orders without first notifying you of the costs, but occasionally a new clerk may fill the order and enclose a bill with it. Many researchers ask up front what costs their query will incur with instructions to fill it unless it exceeds a certain amount. This can help save an additional letter and some time.

Enclose a self-addressed, stamped envelope. Groups listed in the *Encyclopedia of Associations* request it, but the statement is buried on the last page of each chapter, and it's easy to miss. Whether or not the organization is large and can afford to accommodate you free of charge is not the point. It's one of those little things that make it easier for a busy individual within the organization to respond, and I believe it should be done from that standpoint.

7. If you follow up on an unanswered mail or phone request, mention the date and topic of the original query.

A gentleman once wrote asking me to respond to his first letter. Unfortunately, I didn't have his first letter, and since he didn't repeat the original request, I couldn't respond favorably to his second letter either. People in companies or organizations handle many requests every day. They don't recall every question they've answered in the past two months, nor do they always have time to rummage through back files to dig out the original (if they have it in the first place). Again, it's one of those efforts on your part that make it easier for the person to respond.

8. Say thanks.

There's no better way to make a friend and ally than by showing appreciation for a person's efforts, especially when he used his special expertise or time to answer your question. Besides, you never know when you may need help from that same source again.

Expert information is not always as easy to locate as the reference books on your library shelf. But the effort to find a human resource for your information search is well worth the extra effort. Such an expert may be able to give you information not yet recorded in print sources. He may give you personal insights into a subject, trend, or activity with which he has genuine affinity. The key to getting this kind of information from an expert is in the asking.

If you've ever wondered why a letter you wrote or a call you made has not been answered, the tips and anecdotes in this chapter should help you understand why—and tell you what you can do about reversing the situation.

——————— *CHAPTER SUMMARY* ———————

I. People are the expert resources that give researchers the personal view, the enlightened response, or the insightful comment on a subject in which they have special expertise or understanding. (page 393)

II. Before you consult an expert, you must find him. Some experts are easy to find in drug clinics, coroners' offices, and legal aid centers. You might also try a national association, a directory such as the *Directory of Directories,* an author/expert, or the National Referral Center in the Library of Congress. (page 394)

III. There are many approaches to getting an expert's help. A basic requirement for getting answers from experts is to make it easy for them to reply.

    A. The telephone is one way to contact an expert. If you need information fast, you may have to call, regardless of the cost. (page 396)

        1. Telephoning first can save time even if you end up putting your request in writing.

        2. If your phone call isn't returned, try again. Some people don't return calls if they don't think they can help you.

    B. If you decide to write, put your request in a carefully composed letter (even if you call first). Make the letter legible and your meaning clear. (page 397)

        1. Check spelling and grammar. Your letter may not be taken seriously if you don't pay attention to fundamentals. (page 398)

        2. Limit the number of questions you ask in one letter, especially if they must be researched. (page 398)

        3. Give the person the option of responding by phone.

        4. Mention a deadline if you have one. The person will likely appreciate knowing that, so as to avoid spending time providing information that won't be used. (page 399)

        5. To help guide your letter to the appropriate person in a large organization, use the person's name and/or department or title on the envelope. (Check a directory or call the organization itself for this information.) Consider marking the envelope with the purpose or contents of the letter. (page 399)

        6. Double-check the address from old sources against something more recent such as a telephone book. (page 400)

IV. There are certain procedures to follow in querying any expert.

    A. Know what you want. Know something about your subject before you write or call for more information. You may be asking questions that have no answers. (page 400)

B. Do your homework. Gather background information before contacting an expert. This will avoid wasting his time and yours. (page 400)

C. Start close to home. Much information is available right in the library, or local branches of companies, or other local information centers. (page 401)

D. Learn how to ask for information. If your question is too vague or broad, you'll probably not get a response because people don't have time to write back for clarification. (page 402)

E. Be aware of the tone of your request. A little psychology goes a long way. Books on letter writing and conversational skills can help improve your communications skills. (page 402)

F. Ask about costs involved in filling your information request. When in doubt, enclose a self-addressed, stamped envelope, asking in advance what possible costs your request might incur. (page 403)

G. If you follow up on an unanswered mail or phone request, mention the date and subject of the original query. The person may not have received the letter at all; it could have been forwarded to someone else. Information about an original request will help an expert recall it and in turn give you the answer. (page 403)

PART FOUR

TOOLS
+
TECHNIQUES
=
RESEARCH SUCCESS

23

Putting It All Together:
SAMPLE SEARCHES

Everything should be made as simple as possible. . . .
—Albert Einstein,
quoted in *Newsweek*, April 16, 1979

All the research tools discussed in this book are nice to know about. But unless you can apply them to your own research projects, they are as useful to you as a $5,000 computer system is to someone who can't use it. This chapter, therefore, focuses on putting reference tools into practice. And before I set you loose on your local libraries, I'll show you how the reference tools come together to identify resources for solving five real-life research problems.

Throughout this book, I've said that much research, regardless of subject, follows a pattern. It's a series of steps that becomes apparent after you've researched a few hundred reference questions or projects. Unfortunately, that's something most of us haven't done. But the strategy for solving research problems exists, nevertheless.

As I discussed in Chapter 3, some questions are answered quickly by consulting just one reference directory. Examples of such "quick" research are included throughout the book. Other questions, however, demand that you apply a combination of resources to get the in-depth information you need.

The approach to the complex research tasks proposed in this chapter will show you how to begin and follow through any in-depth research project. The "sample searches" I've selected are based on the enormous popularity of those topics:
- Researching your family tree;
- Finding the history, authenticity, and value of an old Navajo rug (or any antique or collectible);
- Researching a job or career;
- Finding information on starting a business;
- Gathering background material for a historical novel.

To tackle these projects, you need a plan—in this case, the nine-point plan introduced in Chapter 3. For each search you will consult the following: periodical articles; books on the subject; encyclopedias;

reference books (directories, bibliographies, etc.); government documents; on-line data bases; microform; original sources (public records, private papers); and experts. The particular order in which you check these resources is not critical. But there are practical reasons why I've listed them the way I did. For example, I've listed periodical articles before books as most people prefer to begin with short, summary-type material before delving into book-length research tools; you may also find it easier to use print resources before nonprint ones.

In the interest of space, I will list only *some* of the things I found when I checked each of the nine types of resources. You will likely find additional material at each step. Don't expect to find pertinent information at every step. The material may or may not be relevant; and, as you will see, some steps are not appropriate for certain research tasks.

Realize, too, that your own in-depth research projects may not always "fit" the nine steps outlined above. You may be researching a biography, for example. In that case, you might find it better to follow the procedure for biographical research described in Chapter 15. Or, you may find that consulting newspapers (which are not itemized in the nine-point plan) is important in your research. If that's a logical supposition, then follow the steps for newspaper research outlined in Chapter 11.

Add or subtract steps to suit your project. Don't feel locked into this set procedure; adapt it to suit your information needs.

If your research project requires only two of the nine steps, fine; use those two and forget the others. Whatever steps you ultimately need to take, they've already been covered in this book.

My intention with the sample searches is to provide you with a framework for identifying a bulk of material in these or other fields, whether you need the information to answer a simple question or to pursue an entire course of study. Once you know the components of the research pattern, the plan is adaptable to any information search. And, as always, the resources you identify during the search are available through interlibrary loan if your own library does not have them.

What you do with the resources you find is another aspect of the research process—one that involves study, analysis, and judgment. To get to that point, however, you must first locate the appropriate materials.

Let the sample searches whet your appetite for sleuthing in search of your own resources—and ultimately, the information you need.

———————— SAMPLE SEARCH ONE ————————

RESEARCHING YOUR FAMILY TREE

Looking for genealogy material can be more confusing than enlightening, especially to the novice who needs instruction in genealogical research before he knows how and where to begin. Even basic genealogical how-to manuals are overwhelming because of the sheer bulk of information they contain.

Each of us must take a slightly different path to find material relevant to our unique lineage. One reason general genealogical how-to books seem complicated is that they try to be all things to all people. In the process, they force you to read everything in them and expect you to weed out what doesn't pertain to you.

Many of the books and articles you'll find listed will be inappropriate for your particular family history. Look for the ones that seem most pertinent, such as books on German genealogy if you want to trace German ancestors; books listing Revolutionary War soldiers if you suspect a link to the American Revolution.

Our sample search will only *identify* the material through which you must sort. Selecting which individual items are appropriate, and incorporating the relevant data into *your* family history, are separate steps of the research process.

1. Periodical Articles

Two guides that name periodical indexes are those compiled by Harzfeld and Owen/Hanchey (see page 157). Bill Katz's *Magazines for Libraries* is another reference book that does this. It mentions a periodical index called *Genealogical Periodical Annual Index* (*GPAI*) that started publication in 1962. *GPAI* now indexes over 145 genealogy magazines, many of them issued by city, county, or state genealogical societies. Most of the articles in the index are arranged by surname and geographical location. They may cover individual family histories: "Glinn Family of Kentucky (miscellaneous marriage records)"; "Names from the autograph book of Anna Lageman, 1888-1899." Or they may discuss or reproduce the contents of many local records files: "Crawford County [Indiana]: Marriage records, 1821-25." They also cover practical issues: "Using the LDS Computer File Index"; "The advantages of joining a state genealogical society."

It's quite possible that checking periodicals will yield nothing for your particular lineage. But like all articles, these tend to focus on a specific issue, and you may find something useful, such as the article teaching you how to use the LDS computer files, or perhaps a review of a genealogy book that looks pertinent to your needs. A sample entry from *GPAI*:

ALLEN, Sarah Sylvine b1867 to D A Reardon, Bible rec *CTN* 12:3:415.

[b = born, rec = record, *CTN* = *The Connecticut Nutmegger*, 12:3:415 = volume 12, no. 3, page 415.]

Any genealogy magazines also have their own indexes. Check various genealogy how-to books, such as Timothy Beard's *How to Find Your Family Roots*, for a list of the several other indexes that were published prior to 1962, with tips on how to use them.

2. Books

The *Subject Guide to Books in Print* mentions many books under a variety of headings like the ones below. Check for bibliographies first. These will lead to many additional genealogical books and directories which may no longer be in print but which are still used in genealogical research.

GENEALOGY
> Helmbold, F. Wilbur. *Tracing Your Ancestry: Step-by-Step Guide to Researching Your Family History.* Oxmoor House. 1978
>> (This is but one of the countless how-to books on the subject.)

GENEALOGY—BIBLIOGRAPHY
> Filby, P. William, ed. *Passenger & Immigration Lists Index: A Reference Guide to Published Lists of About 500,000 Passengers Who Arrived in America in the Seventeenth, Eighteenth & Nineteenth Centuries.* 3 vols. Gale Research Co. 1981.
>> (Don't get too excited about this set. Half a million passengers in 300 years is not much.)

> Schreiner-Yantis, Netti, ed. *Genealogical and Local History Books in Print.* 2 vols. 4th ed. Genealogical Books in Print. 1984.
>> (This excellent bibliography names regionally published books not in the mainstream of publishing, and therefore difficult to identify through many conventional reference sources like *Books in Print*.)

INDIANA—GENEALOGY
> Jackson, Ronald V., and Teeples Gary K. *Indiana Census Index, 1820.* Accelerated Indexing Systems, Inc. 1977.
>> (A list of names that appears in the Indiana census for 1820. This book is part of a series that covers up to five censuses for almost every state. They're listed in *SGBIP* under the name of the state, or you can check the title volume of *BIP* under one of the authors' names.)

UNITED STATES—GENEALOGY—BIBLIOGRAPHY
> Newberry Library, Chicago. *Genealogical Index of the Newberry Library, Chicago.* 4 vols. G. K. Hall. 1960.
>> (This is an index to names mentioned in several hundred family and regional histories in the Midwest.)

3. Encyclopedias

To get a sense of the history and perhaps some anecdotes about the town, city, state, region, or country your ancestors came from, check old encyclopedias. If you checked the 12-volume *Jewish Encyclopedia* published in 1901-1906, for example, you might get specific information on an ancestor's town or village in Europe, revealing facts about its Jewish history that might be hard to find in general history books. (You may still want to check *SGBIP* or the Schreiner-Yantis bibliography for lengthy histories in case there *are* some that are relevant.)

4. Reference Books (Directories, Bibliographies, Etc.)

Directory of Directories mentions a selection of publications to check. One of them is the *American Library Directory*. It will tell you which libraries have extensive genealogy collections. This could be significant if you want to write to a library in a part of the country in which your ancestors once lived. *DOD* also mentions the *Directory of Historical Societies and Agen-*

cies in the United States and Canada. This directory gives the addresses of historical societies nationwide.

DOD includes a variety of directories, some of which may not be as helpful as they seem. (This is one of the cautions I mentioned earlier.) Several guides listed give no page counts, so it's difficult to tell if they're books or pamphlets. (Remember, price is no indication.) Once you examine some of the guides closely, you may discover they're pamphlets that merely reprint addresses of agencies which are listed also in larger, more comprehensive directories.

If one of your ancestors was well known or prominent in some field, check biographical directories that might have included him or her: directories of artists, politicians, educators, etc. (See Chapter 15.) Some older directories are mentioned in the bibliographies of genealogy books you'll find through *SGBIP.*

5. Government Documents

Many old records needed in genealogical research (military records, census records, pension records, etc.) are in the National Archives. Many references to them, plus instructions on getting them, appear in genealogical how-to books. An excellent one to check is Val Greenwood's *The Researcher's Guide to American Genealogy.* The *Publications Reference File* (*PRF*) described in Chapter 12 also identifies the *Guide to Genealogical Records in the National Archives* as a useful tool for identifying specific government files such as the military records of Spanish American War veterans, with tips on how to get information from them.

6. On-Line Data Bases

This resource is not relevant in genealogical research at present. Genealogical searchers generally need historical records (newspapers, for example) that go back past the last decade, something which on-line data bases do not currently do. Private government computer files with names of possible relatives are also not old enough to be of much value, nor are they accessible to the public.

7. Microform

Useful tools in microform may be *Phonefiche,* various newspapers on microfilm, and the collection called *Genealogy and Local History* published by Microfilming Corp. of America. The latter consists of thousands of family histories, directories, and genealogical magazines. Many individual titles and articles in the set will already have been identified through the previous steps of this search but the set gives you easy access to them in one place.

8. Original Material (Private Papers, Public Records, Etc.)

If a prominent ancestor donated his personal papers to some archive or historical society, it might be listed in the *National Union Catalog of Manuscript Collections.* (See Chapter 18.)

Much of your research at this step will require sending away for certificates of birth, death, divorce, land holdings, military enlistment, etc. Many agency addresses appear in how-to books (such as Greenwood's) on genealogy, or they'll indicate the publications to check, such as *Where to Write for Birth and Death Records.*

9. Experts and Organizations

The *Encyclopedia of Associations* identifies over two and a half dozen genealogical organizations, including the Irish Genealogical Society based in Newton, Massachusetts, and the Polish Genealogical Society based in Chicago. These organizations are useful to someone needing help in tracing specific national lines.

Other organizations offer different services. The Association of Professional Genealogists in Salt Lake City, for example, issues a pamphlet called *How to Hire a Genealogist.* It tells you how to hire experienced genealogists in other states to extensively search records in their region that you can't (or don't want to) travel to search for yourself.

Also check your area for local genealogical groups. Sometimes experienced genealogists teach classes through their societies or through adult education programs. The society may also have its own library. One of the largest, of course, is the Mormon genealogy library (listed in the telephone book as Church of Jesus Christ of Latter Day Saints), which has branches in many large cities. You can borrow many materials (census rolls on microfilm, for example) from the main library in Salt Lake City through its various branches.

Most people dive into genealogical research with the notion that tracing their ancestors is a snap. It usually is not. One of the biggest roadblocks in reconstructing a family tree is not the lack of books, periodicals, and public records, but their sheer numbers. Prospective researchers don't usually know what exists or how to find it. This kind of structured nine-step approach will help you get started in the right direction.

——————————— SAMPLE SEARCH TWO ———————————

FINDING THE HISTORY, AUTHENTICITY, AND VALUE OF AN OLD NAVAJO RUG

In this search, you'll find publications that help you distinguish an original Navajo rug from a Navajo-style rug; give you its history; and suggest possible value. Some books offer tips for the collector even though this feature won't necessarily be obvious from their titles. By the time you've finished this sample search, you'll have identified just about everything written on the subject in the past two decades.

This search can be applied to any collectible, whether it's railroad memorabilia or old restaurant menus, jazz records or decorative match safes. The steps to follow are the same.

1. Periodical Articles

Since *Art Index* specifically covers art and antique magazines, I started searching here though *Magazine Index*, and *Reader's Guide to Periodical Literature* can also be used.

The following articles from *Art Index* are two of only a handful published on the subject between 1970 and 1983:

NAVAHO INDIANS[1]
Navajo chief blanket: a trade item among non-Navajo groups.
K.W. Bennett. bibl il(pt col) *Am Indian Art Mag* 7 no. 1: 6209 Wint '81
[bibl = bibliography. il(pt col) = illustrations, part color. *Am Indian Art Mag* = *American Indian Art Magazine.* 7 no.1:62-9 Wint '81 = volume 7, number 1:pages 62-69, Winter 1981.]

This short article repeats the information found elsewhere, but it does have a large bibliography of pertinent readings.

INDIANS OF NORTH AMERICA—TEXTILE INDUSTRY AND FABRICS
Navajo chief blankets—woven images of the American past.
J. Caan. col il *Archit Dig* 38:100-5 Mr'81.
[col il = color illustrations. *Archit Dig* = *Architectural Digest.* 38:100-5 Mr '81 = Volume 38: pages 100-105, March 1981.]

This article is a celebration of Navajo rugs by actor James Caan. It offers nothing pertinent to determining the value or history of your rug.

2. Books

Several useful books are listed in *SGBIP:*
INDIANS OF NORTH AMERICA—TEXTILE INDUSTRY AND FABRICS.
Berlant, Anthony, & Kahlenberg, Mary H. *Walk in Beauty: The Navajo & Their Blankets.* 1977. New York Graphic Society.

Berlant's name pops up in other sources as a prolific collector of and expert on Navajo rugs. The book he coauthored is a thorough history of the rugs, and the last chapter is called "For the Collector."

Rodee, Marian E. *Old Navajo Rugs: Their Development* From 1900-1940. 1981. University of New Mexico Press.

This is an interesting history profuse with photographs, but there is no collector information.

In looking for books on this or any subject, you might want to consult your own library's catalog first to determine whether any book resources are available close at hand.

[1]You'll find variant spellings of the word Navajo, depending on the source you use. Take this into consideration as you search, since other terms may separate the two forms of the word.

3. Encyclopedias

When you check your library's reference or circulating shelves in the antiques subject area, you'll easily find Time-Life's *Encyclopedia of Collectibles*. (Its subject heading is AMERICANA and since it has no subheading indicating that it's an encyclopedia, it's easy to miss through a catalog or *SGBIP*.)

The encyclopedia includes a 13-page article (with photographs) called "Navajo Blankets: Native American Works of Art."

Each article in the encyclopedia contains a bibliography and other sources of information on the collectible discussed: buttons, turn-of-the-century magazines, oak furniture, inkwells, lace, Lalique glass, comics, and over 100 more. The article on Navajo rugs mentions six museums specializing in American Indian art, two American Indian art periodicals, and six books on Navajo rugs. One book, evidently out of print since it's not in the current *SGBIP*, is Don Dedera's *Navajo Rugs: How to Find, Evaluate, Buy and Care for Them*. (Northland Press, 1975). This book is still helpful even though it's no longer in print.

4. Reference Books (Directories, Bibliographies, Etc.)

The *Directory of Directories* lists some potentially useful directories under INDIANS, NORTH AMERICA—ARTS AND CULTURE. One directory, the *American Indian Reference Book*, turns out to give little relevant information for this search; but it does list museums in the United States with outstanding Indian collections. One of them, the Museum of Navajo Ceremonial Art in Santa Fe, New Mexico, is not mentioned in Time-Life's *Encyclopedia of Collectibles*.[2]

5. Government documents

Not relevant. There are no references I could find on collectibles or their history through the *Publications Reference File* or *Index to United States Government Periodicals*.

6. On-Line Data Bases

Art Index, *Magazine Index*, business indexes, and large newspapers where articles on Navajo rugs may have run, are on-line, and you can search for them by computer if you choose to take this route.

7. Microfilm

Not relevant for recent books. These are still protected by copyright and therefore not available in microform. In any event, we've found enough information in the printed materials already checked.

8. Original Material (Private Papers, Public Records, Etc.)

Not needed for researching this topic.

---

[2]This is one reason why checking apparently overlapping steps and reference books is useful. Remember, no book is totally comprehensive.

9. Experts and Organizations

Check local museums and art galleries in the Yellow Pages of your phone book, or in the Yellow Pages of cities most likely to have Indian art experts. For example, in the Yellow Pages of Phoenix, Arizona, not only are there dealers in Indian arts (see ART GALLERIES—DEALERS AND CONSULTANTS), there is also a special heading called INDIAN GOODS—RETAIL with far more listings than my hometown phone book (even though San Diego is a larger city). Two Navajo rug dealers are given for Scottsdale and Sedona.

The *American Indian Art Magazine,* covered in *Art Index* above, also lists Navajo goods dealers throughout the Southwest in their advertisements.

Suppose you want to contact Anthony Berlant, the author/expert of one of the books mentioned above. Check the author biography in his book. These brief biographies usually mention an author's credentials as well as his employer or an organization with whom he's associated. You might also check phone books, biographical directories, and perhaps the publisher for his address.

If your information search isn't working well (depending on the antique or collectible you're researching), you may have to take a general approach. For example, a book on paper collectibles might give you the information you couldn't find elsewhere on your 17th-century land deed or your 18th-century almanac.

Perhaps the only thing you'll be able to find is a price guide. Although specific price guides are available on certain popular collectibles like Avon bottles and jars, the mention of other collectibles is buried in a general antiques price guide such as *Kovel's Complete Antiques Price List*, published annually.

You might have to rely solely on antiques dealers and experts. Indeed, the amount of information you find on different collectibles will vary, but one of the nine steps should produce something.

――――――――― SAMPLE SEARCH THREE ―――――――――

RESEARCHING A JOB OR CAREER

You can approach this kind of search through a general topic (e.g., EMPLOYMENT) or through a specific line of work (e.g., food service careers, accounting careers, health careers, fashion modeling, etc.). You'll save time and energy by starting with the specific approach, if you have a particular career in mind. For this example, let's search museum careers.

1. Periodical Articles

Most fields have at least one magazine (often more) devoted to their specialty. Some of them focus strictly on reporting research findings; others are the newsy type, such as *Broadcasting* and *Editor & Publisher.* Newsy magazines address professional issues, and they report on what's new and who's doing it. They may also include help-wanted/job-wanted advertising.

Ulrich's International Periodicals Directory can help you identify many of these magazines. If you have no specific titles in mind, check the category covering that field. (You can tell American periodicals from foreign ones in *Ulrich's* by the abbreviation for the country of origin—UK, US, FR— above the title.) The annotations tell you whether they accept advertising, one giveaway clue to whether they have a "classifed" section. Circulation figures are another clue. If these figures are low—about 5,000 or less—the magazine might be just a membership tabloid or newsletter available only to members of the parent organization. The issues may not be in libraries or available to nonmembers.

American museum magazines are easy to find through *Ulrich's.* The subject index in the *front* of the volume says that museum publications are listed under the heading MUSEUMS AND ART GALLERIES. One magazine I found is called *Museum News* issued by the American Association of Museums (AAM). It turns out to be interesting reading, and while it reports on the many activities of a museum, something that may help you understand how such an institution works, it doesn't include classifed ads. (Since the AAM's listing in the *Encyclopedia of Associations* says that it has a job placement service, you might want to write them for more information. In that way, you'd discover that its *Aviso Newsletter,* listed in *Ulrich's,* does have ads but it's for members only.)

Most of the other magazines listed in *Ulrich's* are guides to or newsletters for members of specific museums. But you can find out more about a group's publications through the *Encyclopedia of Associations.*

2. Books
SGBIP lists the following books that look at different kinds of museums and the jobs in them:
> MUSEUM WORK AS A PROFESSION
>> Burcaw, G. Ellis. *Introduction to Museum Work.* 1975. American Association for State and Local History.
>> Williams, Patrica M. *Museums of Natural History & the People Who Work in Them.* 1973. St. Martin's Press.

3. Encyclopedias
For overviews of a subject and a bibliography of books and magazines, it's often helpful to check the encyclopedia. A subject encyclopedia also works in this case. The *International Encyclopedia of Higher Education* has an article called MUSEUM STUDIES (FIELD OF STUDY). The article includes a bibliography of readings in international museum magazines, some of which pertain to employment. Even though they're not recent or American, they may offer useful background.

4. Reference Books (Directories, Bibliographies, Etc.)

Directory of Directories includes directories that identify general as well as special museums in sports, science, art, dolls, etc. The heading MUSE-UMS—ADMINISTRATION is particularly relevant. Two books listed under it are *Museum Studies in the U.S. and Abroad,* published by the Office of Museum Programs of the Smithsonian Institution (listing 350 museums and universities that offer museum administration and curatorship training programs); and *Survey of Arts Administration Training in the U.S. and Canada,* published by the American Council for the Arts (listing about 30 institutions with graduate programs, internships, and other training opportunities in performing arts companies, museums, and similar organizations).

5. Government Documents

There are several guides to and manuals for museums under the term MUSEUM in the *Publications Reference File (PRF).* One useful publication is called *Career Opportunities in Art Museums, Zoos, and Other Interesting Places,* a booklet giving broad background on several careers including museology. It's aimed at high school students.

6. On-Line Data Bases

This is not a relevant step in this in-depth investigation except to search for articles using the combined terms of MUSEUM(S) and CAREER (or JOBS or EMPLOYMENT). If my manual search was any clue, there won't be much on-line for this particular subject; but on that basis, an on-line search would also be inexpensive.

7. Microform

Not a relevant step in this search, as the information you need must be current and not of a historical nature.

8. Original Material (Private Papers, Public Records, Etc.)

Not relevant for a search on current jobs or training opportunities.

9. Experts and Organizations

As mentioned in the section on periodicals and articles, the *Encyclopedia of Associations* lists many museum associations: American Association of Youth Museums, International Association of Museums of Arms and Military History, etc.

Read the *EA* listing for information on employment and educational opportunities. For example, the Association of Science-Technology Centers mentions an internship program and a placement and referral service. And it publishes a newsletter. (Since many association newsletters are available only to member museums, not to individuals, call a local museum. They often receive a selection of museum newsletters, especially those listing employment and education opportunities, and they may let you check their copies.)

Local museum employees also, of course, are a potential information resource. One of them may be willing to offer you some tips and advice about opportunities, job leads, how to break in if you have a degree in another field, best museum programs in colleges, internships available in the field, etc.

As in most searches, the general approach may contribute information, too, and you should consider using some general sources in addition to the specific museum-related references. Don't forget to think in broad or related categories. Your subject may fall into a subdivision of one of these general topics. An annual directory called *Internships* (Writer's Digest Books) covers opportunities in a variety of fields including museum work. The multivolume *College Blue Book* (Macmillan) includes a volume that lists majors in alphabetical order (in this case, museum studies) and colleges and universities that offer programs in it.

——————— SAMPLE SEARCH FOUR ———————

FINDING INFORMATION ON STARTING A BUSINESS

As in the search above, you may take a general approach (e.g., using the term SMALL BUSINESS), or a specific approach (e.g., using the phrase TELEVISION REPAIRING). Or, you might use a little of both.

Particularly in doing a business search, there's an abundance of both print and on-line material. One of your biggest tasks will be to screen and weed out what's available so you can zero in on the information most appropriate to your needs. Therefore, be sure you know exactly what you want. If you have only a vague idea, you might find it useful to start with the general books on business. They cover the basics for setting up any kind of business. As soon as you identify the precise areas you want more information about, you can search those.

1. Periodical Articles
Ulrich's International Periodicals Directory mentions that *Electronic Technician Dealer Magazine,* the only relevant trade journal in this field, started publication in 1953 and suspended publication in 1982. Unless it resumes publication or another comes out to take its place, there isn't a relevant trade journal currently in print.

Business Periodicals Index or *Business Index* on microfilm are the most appropriate indexes to check for articles. There are literally hundreds of articles on small business published every year. The indexes are most useful for identifying those that address specific rather than general questions. For example (from *Business Periodicals Index*, 1983):
SMALL BUSINESS—INSURANCE
Tax relief for small business? J. Freer. *Nation's Bus* 71:52-3 Ap'83

Be sure you consult the most recent issues of business indexes so you don't use outdated material. This is especially important in certain aspects of starting up a business, such as insurance and legal matters.

2. Books

SGBIP lists many books under numerous headings related to your subject: NEW BUSINESS ENTERPRISES, SMALL BUSINESS, FRANCHISES (RETAIL TRADE), and of course TELEVISION—REPAIRING. The following books are just three of the hundreds listed.

> Toncre, Emery. *The Action Step Plan to Owning and Operating a Small Business.* 1983. Prentice-Hall.

A general book that gives you an overview of owning your own business. Not all of these "general" books are equally good, so you should check several.

> Schuler, Charles. *Introduction to Television Servicing.* 1979. McGraw-Hill.
> Goldberg, Joel. *Fundamentals of Television Servicing.* 1982. Prentice-Hall

These two books give you the fundamentals of repairing television sets. You might find some of them in the bookstore of a trade school or community college where TV repair is taught.

3. Encyclopedias

Unless you need some explanation of basic or overall concepts (What are the Dow-Jones Averages?; How does the Federal Reserve function?), encyclopedias will not be relevant for this kind of information search.

4. Reference Books (Directories, Bibliographies, Etc.)

The *Directory of Directories* lists many publications that cover everything from venture capital sources to trade show schedules. Certain ones may direct you to an aspect of setting up a business that is not specifically mentioned in the books and articles you're checking.

5. Government Documents

The Small Business Administration and the Internal Revenue Service issue countless publications for small-business people. Many of their guidebooks duplicate information found in commercial publications, but they're usually cheaper. Finding specific publications through the *Publications Reference File*, however, is difficult because most of the subject headings used are too broad (BUSINESS, TELEVISION, etc.). You may find it easier to check a bibliography covering Small Business Administration or IRS publications. You can find these in *Subject Bibliographies* (Chapter 12).

6. On-Line Data Bases

Search by computer for articles in business magazines and newspapers. There are also numerous economic and financial data bases such as the *Dow Jones News* (the full text of *The Wall Street Journal*, the *Dow Jones News Service*, and *Barron's* since 1979) or the *Electronic Yellow Pages* (there are six subsets, two of which might be appropriate here: *Manufacturers* and *Wholesale Directory*).

7. Microform

This step is not relevant unless you're checking historical information. However, many complete runs of business directories are in microform (*Thomas Register of American Manufacturers*, 1905-77, for example), as well as a complete set of corporate annual reports.

8. Original Material (Private Papers, Public Records, Etc.)

You might need public records for such things as tracing the owner of a piece of property or checking city plans for zoning or construction in a particular part of the city. Since most of the records you might need would be local, you can find out what's available and how you can use them by calling local agencies.

9. Experts and Organizations

There are general small business associations listed in the *Encyclopedia of Associations*, but there is one organization in particular for people interested in a TV repair business. (Use *EA*'s key-word index to find any organization by subject or its specific name.) It's the National Association of Television and Electronic Servicers of America. One of its publications, according to *EA*, is called *So You Want to be an Electronics Technician*.

Also check regional branches of federal agencies such as the Small Business Administration, organizations of retired businessmen, or other groups that offer free or low-cost consulting or advice.

People in the trade may or may not be helpful. Many business people see others as potential competitors. They may guard trade secrets and offer little information that will be of real use. On the other hand, you may find an expert technician willing to share his experiences in the business.

This sample search shows that in hunting for business information, you can take several directions. Even though it appears that you'll be deluged with information, much of it will not apply to your specific question. You will have to sort through a variety of data.

―――――――――――― SAMPLE SEARCH FIVE ――――――――――――

GATHERING BACKGROUND INFORMATION FOR A HISTORICAL NOVEL

Let's say you're researching a novel set in New Jersey between 1800 and 1850. You need information about life at the time—everything from typical salaries, customs, and attitudes of the day to the political setting.

1. Periodicals and Articles

Poole's Index to Periodical Literature (1802-1906) identifies articles from popular magazines. *Writings on American History* refers you to articles in history magazines. Let's try *WAH* for this search. The following examples come from *WAH*'s cumulative index for 1902-1940.

The entry we're checking is COOKING, with various subdivisions of that topic:

COOKING, Early, 14:2490 [14 = 1914, 2490 = item no.2490];
      Open Fire, 17:2256; Pennsylvania German, 35:2014, 35:3415,
      40:3844; New England Kitchen (1825), 23:1051,2529; Pilgrim,
      35:720 etc.

"See also" references follow this entry if still another aspect of COOKING is more pertinent to your search. Some of these "see also" references direct you to FIREPLACE, FOOD, KITCHEN, OVENS, and STOVES.

If you pursue one of the subdivisions under cooking, in this case PILGRIM, 35:720, it leads to this article (item no. 720) in the 1935 volume:

Biggs, Helen T. Pilgrim Cookery and Food Supplies of the 17th
      Century. *American Cookery*, XL, 214-27. (1935). (A close look at a
      17th-century kitchen that covers utensils used, the way women
      cooked, and the food the people ate.)

Another way to manipulate *WAH* for additional information is to check the subject index by city names. For example, under NEW BRUNSWICK, N.J., there are many subheadings such as CHARITY AND RELIEF, CIVIL WAR, FIRST FOOTBALL GAME, FIRST MAYOR, MARKETS, RELIGION, ROADS, SETTLEMENT, and TAVERNS. These will give you specific information—and possibly anecdotes—concerning an aspect of life in the city where your story is set.

Also check the table of contents to *WAH*. The chapters are arranged by topic. One section (in early volumes) is called U.S. REGIONAL (LOCAL) HISTORIES, with individual chapters on the various states. They identify historical articles written about particular states. Therefore, if you check under the state in which your novel is set, you can find even more articles giving background information and possibly anecdotes. For example, these articles from *WAH* (1935 volume under U.S. REGIONAL (LOCAL) HISTORIES: NEW JERSEY) discuss general transportation by water and stagecoach, give insight into a man's personality through his will, and offer details of a routine slave sale:

Lane, Wheaton J. Water Transportation in Colonial New Jersey. *New Jersey Historical Society Proceedings*. LIII, 77-89.

Boyer, Charles S. Stage Routes in West Jersey. A political reminiscence of 1870. *Camden County Historical Society. Camden History*. v.1, nos.10-12.

Gnichtel, Frederick W. Jasper Smith's Peculiar Will [1813]. *New Jersey Historical Society Proceedings*. LIII, 89-95.

Honeyman, A. Van Doren. A Slave Sale of 1827. *New Jersey Historical Society Proceedings*. LIII, 250-251.

2. Books

Subject Guide to Books in Print has countless history books, many in reprint editions. The following would be useful in this search if you wanted to portray the typical diet (barbecued squirrel, cabbage pudding, and jumbles); refer to some home remedies and the folk medicine practiced (mustard poultice); or describe the clothing they wore (breeches).

COOKERY

Webster, Mrs. A. L. *The Improved Housewife, or Book of Receipts by a Married Lady*. 6th ed. 1973. Reprint of the 1845 ed.

COOKERY, AMERICAN

Svenson, Jon-Erik. *Compendium of Early American Folk Remedies, Recipes and Advice*. 1977.

COSTUME—HISTORY

Young, Agatha. *Recurring Cycles of Fashion: 1760-1937*. 1966. Reprint of the 1937 ed.

COSTUME—UNITED STATES

Earle, Alice. *Two Centuries of Costume in America, 1620-1820*. 1968. Reprint of the 1903 ed.

You may also want to check the "see also" references in *SGBIP* that lead you to other, perhaps more pertinent headings such as CHILDREN—COSTUME, COSMETICS, INDIANS OF NORTH AMERICA—COSTUME AND ADORNMENT, HOSIERY, GLOVES, etc. Instead of a general book on costume you may find one specifically on rural Pennsylvania dress or early California dress.

Other topics (with their subsequent resources listed) are these:

EDUCATION—UNITED STATES—HISTORY

Butler, Vera. *Education as Revealed by New England Newspapers Prior to 1850*. 1969. Reprint of the 1935 ed.

Leslie, Eliza. *Miss Leslie's Behaviour Book: A Guide and Manual for Ladies*. 1972. Reprint of the 1859 ed.

FURNITURE—HISTORY

Tracy, Berry, et al. *Nineteenth Century America: Furniture and Other Decorative Arts*. 1973.

NEW JERSEY—HISTORY

Stockton, Frank R. *Stories of New Jersey*. 1961.

TRANSPORTATION—HISTORY

Boulton, W. H. *The Pageant of Tranportation Through the Ages*. 1976.

UNITED STATES-SOCIAL LIFE AND CUSTOMS

Bowne, Eliza S. *A Girl's Life Eighty Years Ago: Selections From the Letters of Eliza Southgate*. 1974. Reprint of the 1888 ed.

Historical novelists are often interested in using published diaries, because they record the intimate details of people's lives: the specific language they used, their personal thoughts, and often their verbatim comments that give authenticity to fiction. Check related subject headings from *SGBIP* that are given below. Many diaries have been reprinted as books or published in history magazines.

DIARIES

    Schaw, Janet. *Journal of a Lady of Quality: Being the Narrative of a Journey From Scotland to the West Indies, North Carolina and Portugal in the Years 1774 to 1776.* 1971. Reprint of the 1939 ed.

AMERICAN DIARIES

    Sloane, Eric. *Diary of an Early American Boy: Noah Blake, 1805.* 1974.

Also check PERSONAL NARRATIVES as a subtopic of certain subjects. These terms also lead to diaries. One such example is UNITED STATES—HISTORY—REVOLUTION, 1775-1783—PERSONAL NARRATIVES. Two books under this heading:

    Theatrum Majorum, the Cambridge of 1776: Diary of Dorothy Dudley. 1970. Reprint of the 1876 ed.
    Letters of Joseph Jones of Virginia, 1777-1787. 1970. Reprint of the 1889 ed.

Many books include the name of a series of which they are a part. The two books above listed in *SGBIP* indicate that they are part of a series called *Eyewitness Accounts of the American Revolution.* According to the reference work *Books in Series*, there are 101 books in this particular series and *BIS* names all of them.

These are only a fraction of the subject headings you might conceivably check. Other books can be found in subject bibliographies, *Cumulative Book Index (CBI)*, and earlier volumes of *SGBIP.*

3. Encyclopedias

I checked a 16-volume set of encyclopedias called *New American Cyclopaedia*, published in 1861, which focuses heavily on places and names. The entry for NEWARK, NEW JERSEY, for example, is fascinating, at least from the perspective of more than a century later. It describes the city's main street vividly ("shaded with majestic elms, adorned with numerous tasteful edifices"); gives the immigrant population for each of five decades between 1810 and 1860; names and describes noteworthy structures; details the city's water and gas supplies; gives the number and denomination of its churches; offers the size and expenditures of the public school system; reports on the "current" condition of the roads; and even reveals salaries of the day. (The police chief earned $900 annually, and his lowest private earned $550 a year. The average annual pay of teachers was $358.)

The NEW JERSEY article adds that the governor earned $1,800 a year. Other government employee salaries are mentioned along with the structure of the state government at the time. The article touches on chief ports, products of the region, distribution of immigrant groups in the state, and much more.

Other volumes of the *New American Cyclopaedia* contain potentially useful articles. Some topics to pursue are EDUCATION, MUSIC, ORGAN, SLAVERY, EMPHYSEMA, and even DUEL.

4. Reference Books (Directories, Bibliographies, Etc.)

There are hundreds of reference books to verify dates, names, historical events, etc. And now you know that if you need the dates or general description of a battle or a list of early American first names, you can assume (until convinced otherwise) that a book or directory covering such things exists. A checklist of reference books like those mentioned in Chapter 3 (*Where to Find What, Finding the Source*, etc.) are good places to start.

If you're hunting for bibliographies, check your topic followed by BIBLIOGRAPHY in *SGBIP* or *CBI*. (e.g., DIARIES—BIBLIOGRAPHY.) The following title alone leads you to the many diaries published as books or in history magazines.

DIARIES—BIBLIOGRAPHY
> Matthews, William. *American Diaries: An Annotated Bibliography of American Diaries Written Prior to the Year 1861.* 1974. Reprint of the 1945 ed.

Identifies largely military, travel, and personal diaries of more than a century ago.

5. Government Documents

Government documents may be useful to help establish certain facts and to research topics from a perspective different from one you would find in commercially published books. The *CIS Serial Set* (1789-1969) and the CIS index/microform collections to prints and hearings (from the early 1800s to 1969) may help, depending on the kind of information you need.

For example, the 1789-1857 volume of the *CIS Serial Set* Index uses NEW JERSEY as a subject heading, but it's too broad to be helpful. The documents listed are quite varied, running the gamut from "Citizens of New Jersey, for annulment of treaty made with Cherokees at New Echota, 1835" to "Information on stages and provisions made in cases of shipwreck on coast of New Jersey."

Other broad headings such as SCHOOL and RAILROAD will be of little help. However, if the headings are specific such as PRESIDENTIAL MESSAGE [and year] or an individual's name in a claim for a Civil War pension (listed under his name), your search will be more successful.

6. On-Line Data Bases

On-line data bases focus on current information, not retrospective history articles. Many data bases of article citations, of course, include articles on historical periods if they were written recently. You can use an on-line search to find these. The appropriate data base to search would be *America: history and life.* (The entire index, since its first issue in 1964, is on-line.)

If you need articles on a specific topic that you can't or don't have the time to search manually, and you're willing to pay at least $10, the on-line search is the appropriate path to take. For general background information, however, you should be able to gather enough through the printed indexes.

7. Microform

For this search, you should investigate both newspapers and books/articles in microform. If a local library owns *Early American Newspapers, 1704-1820* in microform, you should be able to get a sense of atmosphere about the period. Though most newspaper indexes are not sold commercially (notable exceptions are *The London Times,* 1790-date, and *The New York Times,* 1851-date), you won't have a problem as you generally won't need to refer to specific articles. Checking early newspapers by date and region is enough to get a sense of the times.

The directory *Newspapers in Microform, 1948-1972* lists New Jersey newspapers on film—for example, *The New Jersey Eagle* (Newark, N.J., which ran from 1820 to 1847, and *The Trenton Federalist* which was published between 1802 and 1829. These may be available through your library's interlibrary loan service.

As for books and articles on the history of the era, one good microform collection to use is the *Library of American Civilization.* It has a good subject index to the books and articles contained (see Chapter 7). Try a number of subjects. For example, under EDUCATION OF WOMEN, there are several books mentioned covering the time period of our hypothetical novel. They are *The Duty of American Women to Their Country,* by Catharine Beecher (1845); *A Lecture on the Education of Females,* by George Emerson (1831); and *Strictures on the Modern System of Female Education,* by Hannah More (1813).

Under NEW JERSEY—DESCRIPTION AND TRAVEL there's a tempting book entitled *Historical Collections of the State of New Jersey; Containing a General Collection of the Most Interesting Facts, Traditions, Biographical Sketches, Anecdotes, etc. Relating to Its History and Antiquities, with Geographical Descriptions of Every Township in the State* (1844).

Since *Poole's Index to Periodical Literature* covers many of the 19th-century magazines that have been filmed in the microform collection *American Periodicals, 1741-1900,* check that index for articles you can read (and photocopy) from the microform collection. (Or you can borrow them through interlibrary loan whether they're in microform or in hard copy.)

Some subjects under which articles appear in *Poole's Index* include the following:

LABORER'S DAILY LIFE
LABORER'S HOME

LABORER'S LEISURE
LABORING CLASSES
  —causes for complaint of
  —condition of
  —elevation of
  —legislation for
WOMAN CONVICTS
WOMAN NOVELISTS
WOMAN QUESTIONS
WOMAN REFORMERS
WOMANKIND ABROAD
WOMEN AND THEIR DOMESTIC CONDITIONS

8. Original Material (Private Papers, Public Records, Etc.)

If you live in New Jersey or plan to visit there, you may want to locate special collections of correspondence or diaries in the state's historical societies and libraries. The directories of special collections mentioned in Chapter 18 will help you find them. If your novel takes place in your home state, you may want to check these directories for collections near you. Some diary may just be waiting for you to discover its voice and transpose it into a novel.

9. Experts and Organizations

Research from printed sources would be more than adequate for your needs in this kind of search.

This search outline should suggest to novelists that their finished product needn't be a product of chance. Though serendipity and luck do play a significant role in research, they shouldn't be in control. *You* should be. With a plan of attack, you *can* be.

Whether or not your latest information search resembles any of these sample searches, you now have an inkling about how to use the various information-finding tools I have discussed. Sometimes your research is easily handled in one or two steps; sometimes an in-depth search is not finished until you check the last available resource.

The most important thing to remember is that you can do your own looking, your own research. And having a plan is the key, because there's a mountain of material waiting to be used on just about any subject; there's certainly more information than you or I will ever need.

With the tools and know-how that you've found in these pages, there's no longer any reason to say, "I can't find anything" or "I don't know where to look" for the answer to a research question or a barroom bet. If you truly can't find a place to look for the information you need, it's quite possible you've got the makings of a new book.

INDEX